CONQUEST AND UNION

Fashioning a British State, 1485–1725

Edited by

Steven G. Ellis and Sarah Barber

Longman
London and New York

Longman Group Limited,
Longman House, Burnt Mill,
Harlow, Essex CM20 2JE, England
and Associated Companies throughout the world.

Published in the United States of America
by Longman Publishing, New York

First published 1995

ISBN 0 582 209641 CSD
ISBN 0 582 209633 PPR

British Library Cataloguing-in-Publication Data

A catalogue record for this book is
available from the British Library

Library of Congress Cataloging-in-Publication Data

Conquest and union : fashioning a British state, 1485–1725 / edited by
Steven G. Ellis and Sarah Barber.
p. cm.
Includes bibliographical references and index.
ISBN 0–582–20964–1. – ISBN 0–582–20963–3 (pbk.)
1. Great Britain–Politics and government–1485–1603. 2. Great Britain–Politics and government–1603–1714. 3. Great Britain––Politics and government–1714–1727. I. Ellis, Steven G., 1950– . II. Barber, Sarah.
DA300.C72 1995
942.05–dc20 94–32380
CIP

Set by 7 in 10/12 New Baskerville
Produced by Longman Singapore Publishers (Pte) Ltd.
Printed in Singapore

Contents

List of maps

List of Abbreviations

AMH	*American Historical Review*
BBCS	*Bulletin of the Board of Celtic Studies*
BIHR	*Bulletin of the Institute of Historical Research*
BL	British Library, London
Bodl	Bodleian Library, Oxford
CRO	County Record Office
CSP Dom	*Calendar of State Papers, Domestic*
CSP For	*Calendar of State Papers, Foreign*
CSP Ire	*Calendar of State Papers, Ireland*
CSP Scot	*Calendar of State Papers, Scotland*
DNB	*Dictionary of National Biography*
EcHR	*Economic History Review*
EHR	*English Historical Review*
GD	Gift and Deposit
HJ	*Historical Journal*
HLQ	*Huntingdon Library Quarterly*
HMC	Historical Manuscripts Commission
HS	*Historical Studies*
ICA	Inveraray Castle Archives
IESH	*Irish Economic and Social History*
IHR	*International Historical Review*
IHS	*Irish Historical Studies*
IR	*Irish Review*
ITS	Irish Texts Society
JBS	*Journal of British Studies*
JEH	*Journal of Ecclesiastical History*
JMH	*Journal of Modern History*
JWEH	*Journal of Welsh Ecclesiastical History*

LP	Letters and Papers
NAI	National Archives of Ireland
NH	*Northern History*
NLI	National Library of Ireland
NLS	National Library of Scotland
NLW	National Library of Wales
NRA	National Register of Archives
P&P	*Past and Present*
PH	*Parliamentary History*
PRIA	*Proceedings of the Royal Irish Academy*
PRO	Public Record Office, London
PRONI	Public Record Office of Northern Ireland
SGS	*Scottish Gaelic Studies*
SGTS	Scottish Gaelic Texts Society
SH	*Studia Hibernica*
SHR	*Scottish Historical Review*
SHS	*Scottish Historical Studies*
SP	State Papers
SRO	Scottish Record Office
TCD	Trinity College, Dublin
TGSI	*Transactions of the Gaelic Society of Inverness*
THSC	*Transactions of the Honourable Society of the Cymmrodorion*
TRHS	*Transactions of the Royal Historical Society*
WHR	*Welsh History Review*

Glossary

Readers should note that where possible the linguistic origin of the word has been supplied. Thus: Ir – Irish Gaelic, G – common Gaelic, Sc – Scots Gaelic, Scots language, Fr – French, L – Latin.

attainder: the act of depriving a felon of rights to inherit or transmit an estate and the forfeiture of an estate as the consequence of outlawry.

banneret: title of rank, beneath baron, originally referring to one who could command a company of vassals under his own banner.

buannacht (Ir)/*buannachan* (Sc): tax or tribute levied by a Gaelic chief for the maintenance of soldiers.

cateran (Sc)/kerne (Ir): an individual or a band of Gaelic footsoldiers.

céilidh (G): literally an evening visit, but more usually an evening musical entertainment.

cess: originally any local tax, but especially in Ireland the levy of soldiers and provisions to the Lord Deputy or to billet soldiers within a community.

custos rotulorum (L): principal justice of the peace and keeper of the records within a county.

dúthchas (G): hereditary right or claim, patrimony, leading to a sense of native place or belonging.

escheat: reversion of an estate to the lord when a tenant died without an heir, used in the wider sense in Scotland to mean confiscation of property.

feu: tract of land held in return for money or produce as opposed to military service – hence feu-farm or fee-farm.

fine (G)/'clan elite': family elite within the Gaelic community.

Gael (G): collective noun for the Gaelic speaking inhabitants of Ireland and Scotland (Q-Celts). Usually used in contradistinction to Gall, used to describe the pre-Tudor, non-celtic settlers in Ireland and the Scots-speaking lowlanders of Scotland.

gens, gentes (L): a number of families united by a sense of common identity, perhaps of kin, religion or geography.

marches: pl. boundary or frontier territory, often of disputed jurisdiction, especially applied to the borders between England and Scotland or Wales and the area around the English Pale in Ireland.

mulct: to punish by levying a fine.

oighreachd (Sc) / *oidhreacht* (Ir): heritage, inheritance, property.

reiver: or reever/reaver. Robber, plunderer, one who takes something by force. 'Cateran' in the Scottish Highlands.

rentier (Fr): one whose income is derived from property or investment.

seneschal: one who administered justice on the lord's estate, now largely obsolete term for a governor or judicial officer.

sheriff: (Eng, Ire and W) representative of royal authority within a shire or county. In Scotland, sheriffs had slightly wider civil and criminal jurisdiction. Hence, 'shire', an administrative district used especially in the 16th and 17th centuries for the process of extending English jurisdiction in Ireland and Wales and 'shrievalties', the office or jurisdiction of a sheriff.

wadset (Sc): in Scottish law, the conveyance of land to satisfy a debt which can be redeemed. More colloquially, to pawn or mortgage.

Preface

In preparing this volume we have incurred a number of debts. In particular, we should like to acknowledge the support of Ken Churchill and of the British Council in Dublin which paid for a succession of visiting speakers to Galway and made a substantial grant towards the costs of holding the conference at which the concept of British history and preliminary drafts of the papers published here were debated. The Research and Development Committee of University College, Galway (UCG) also made a large contribution towards the project, and we are grateful to the president of UCG, Dr Colm Ó hEocha, and the college for their support and the use of their facilities. The Royal Historical Society gave financial assistance towards the costs of the keynote address at the conference, by Dr John Morrill, vice-president of the society. The publishers have also worked hard to ensure that they became a coherent volume of essays on a specific theme. Finally, we should like to thank our fellow contributors who agreed to write to an overall scheme and an ambitious schedule, and very often outside their own areas of expertise. In the interests of uniformity, we have standardized some of the terminology, but it should not be assumed that the contributors necessarily agree with these usages and with the overall perspective.

S.G.E. and S.B.

INTRODUCTION

The concept of British history

Steven G. Ellis
University College Galway

For about a dozen years or so now, historians have been exploring a new concept of British history, in the sense of developments throughout, and interaction between, the various peoples inhabiting the British Isles. This kind of British history did indeed have antecedents among nineteenth-century writers. British history focused on the role of the United Kingdom in the administration of a large and successful empire. It also investigated the origins and growth of those institutions and values which distinguished the United Kingdom from continental Europe and which, allegedly, were later to establish Britain's pre-eminence on the world stage – freedom, civilization, and democracy. And it treated of the dissemination from early modern times of this British heritage among what were seen as the less fortunate people of the Empire. Thus traditional British history stressed the common traditions and civilization of the peoples of the United Kingdom *vis-à-vis* Europe and the wider world. Even so, those institutions that were singled out by historians as epitomizing British culture – parliament, the common law, and the English language – were usually ones which were more closely identified with England. This in turn helps to explain the pronounced anglocentricity of traditional British history. What was then called 'British history' often amounted to little more than the history of England and of English interventions in Wales, Scotland, and Ireland.

With the professionalization of history as an academic discipline around the turn of the century came a renewed stress on the emergence and growth of the nation as the proper focus and organizing principle of historical study. To some extent, this development prompted a search for the supposed characteristics of a British national identity, especially in relation to continental Europe and the wider world. More often it led to a shift of focus, from the rise of the modern state, to the emergence of the modern nations which inhabit the British Isles. In particular, the focus narrowed to the study of England as the dominant nation within the archipelago. At the time, there was much to be said for the study of national history, since the wider British perspective tended to deflect historical attention from vital differences between the separate nations and kingdoms of these islands. Indeed the value of a nation-based approach to the history of Ireland, Scotland and Wales was explicitly endorsed in many of the new universities by the practice of studying the home nation apart from other branches of history in a separate department of national history.[1] This was particularly necessary for Ireland, where the creation of a second state in 1922 imposed on historians the duty of investigating the origins of its separate existence. The Irish Free State (now the Republic of Ireland) retained much in common with the United Kingdom, but at the time differences of national identity and religion were more important.

Yet nation-centred approaches also had considerable shortcomings, and for a number of reasons. Focus on the nation naturally tended to point up what was unique to each nation. But this tendency was artificially accentuated by the way in which the archipelago was divided up, for the purposes of teaching history at the universities, into separate sections or departments, each charged with courses in a particular national history. For the most part, these divisions reflected modern ideas of nationhood and modern national (as opposed to state) boundaries. Thus English history dealt with that part of Britain which had been settled by the Anglo-Saxons before 1066, disregarding the Englishries which were established in Ireland and Wales under the Norman kings. Irish history dealt with all those peoples who had inhabited the island of Ireland at different times and who collectively helped to shape the modern Irish nation; but it excluded the indigenous Gaelic peoples who happened to live across the North Channel in what is now Scotland.

Similarly, the research training of historians was geared to the source material relating to a particular national territory, as

1 A study of this process is much to be desired. Perhaps also relevant here is the date at which some of the academic journals that underpinned this development of national history first appeared – *English Historical Review* (1885), *Irish Historical Studies* (1938), *Scottish Historical Review* (1903) and *Welsh History Review* (1962).

presently defined, rather than to the archipelago as a whole. Thus the evidence concerning the broad pattern of interaction between Germanic and Celtic peoples and cultures, which is the essence of the British experience, was divided up between four groups of historians, each familiar with that relating to the home territory, but seldom equipped – in terms of linguistic competence, for instance – to develop comparisons based on the primary sources relating to another national territory. Finally, the concepts of the nation and of national territory developed by nation-centred approaches were of little help in assessing either the origins of the modern state or the present relationship between nation and state in each territory.

Thus there is clearly a need for a history of the British Isles which examines the relations between the different peoples of the archipelago and the process of state formation which created the two modern states there. But this is much easier said than done: even the terminology is problematic. The very concept of 'the British Isles' is rejected by some Irish historians. In part this reflects the different nuances of the term within the two islands: in nationalist Ireland, 'British' is the antithesis of 'Irish', is frequently synonymous with 'English', and it refers to the modern British state; whereas in Britain it is also frequently used as an 'umbrella' term to describe the peoples of the British Isles collectively without respect to their nationality. There is, however, clearly a need for a term to denote the modern mix of Celtic, Germanic and Romance cultures and peoples and the Anglo-Norman administrative structures which are common to Britain and Ireland. Thus in default of a convenient, neutral, and readily recognizable alternative, the traditional usage must be allowed to stand. Yet the very fact that no single word, analogous to Japan or Indonesia, exists to describe the group of islands dominated by Britain and Ireland is itself significant: the very phrase 'the British Isles' also draws attention to an arrested process of state formation.

Particularly since the collapse of the Union of Soviet Socialist Republics, the United Kingdom of Great Britain and Northern Ireland has enjoyed the unusual distinction of being one of the very few modern states which actually refuses nationality in its official title.[2] Like many modern states, however, it is a multinational one. For much of its history, successive governments of what was to become the United Kingdom have attempted, with only partial

2 B. Anderson, *Imagined Communities: Reflections on the Origin and Spread of Nationalism* (2nd edn, London, 1991), p.2.

success, to integrate its constituent nations and territories into a collective British nation, 'the Britons', inhabiting a British archipelago called 'Britain'.[3] The high points in this process were the various 'unions' and 'united kingdoms' which attempted to regulate relations between the different peoples of these islands. Among the more successful were the so-called Act of Union with Wales (1536), the Kingdom of Ireland (1541), and the Anglo-Scottish Act of Union (1707), all of which were important stages in the building of the modern states. By contrast, the respective terms of the Union of the Crowns of 1603, the Cromwellian Union of 1654, and the 1801 Act of Union with Ireland generated deep-seated hostility from powerful elite groups within the countries affected, and eventually had to be modified or abandoned.

British history thus ought properly to refer to the whole process of state-building in the archipelago. This wider perspective is important, if a more balanced assessment of the British pattern of state formation, its strengths and weaknesses, is to be constructed. Admittedly, nation-centred approaches treat of aspects of this process, in particular the role of the state as an external force in the shaping of the nation. Yet since so many of its categories are present-centred, it is hardly surprising that much nationalist history reads like triumphant progress towards the present. In this respect, traditional anglocentric presentations of British history are particularly misleading: concentration on the dominant nation in the archipelago skews the perceived pattern of development in favour of the area in which the process was most successful, since the eventual terms of the Union reflected English sensibilities more than any other. The real pattern of state formation, however, was more of a continuum of success and failure, ranging from southern England, through northern England and Wales, to Scotland, Northern Ireland, and at the opposite extreme the present Republic of Ireland.

The apparent exception to this pattern, Ireland, does indeed prove the rule. Uniquely in the case of Ireland, the terms of all of the successive strategies to integrate the island into a wider British

3 I take it that 'Britain', rather than 'the British Isles' would have been the preferred geographical term for the archipelago as the national territory, if this political process had enjoyed wider success. It is of course implied by the development of subcategories (which have had a chequered history) like 'Great Britain', 'North Britain' (for Scotland), 'the British mainland' (with reference to Northern Ireland), and 'West Briton' (now a term of abuse for an Irish person who apes British customs), as also by the earliest (Greek) usage which styled as British both the island of Albion and of Ierna.

state and to regulate relations between the different peoples of the archipelago proved so unacceptable to powerful interest groups there as to lead eventually to the establishment of a separate state. This pattern of rejection is very well described in traditional accounts of the making of modern Ireland. Yet nationalist approaches are much less useful in explaining why Northern Ireland remained part of the United Kingdom. And for all its political independence, is the Irish Republic any less British in terms of its cultural, administrative and legal traditions? The British perspective neatly accounts for this paradox of modern Irish history. The Irish Republic is in many ways no less a product of the British process of state formation than is Wales: the actual instruments of British integration were broadly acceptable in Ireland, but the terms of Union were not.

These remarks may help to clarify the differences between British history as a process of state formation and nationalist history as the making of the nation. They do not, however, explain the recent popularity of the concept. The last few years have seen an upsurge of interest in what one recent Irish prime minister has described as 'the totality of the relationships between the peoples of these islands'.[4] To some extent this may be a response to contemporary problems of European integration, exemplified by the difficulties over the Single European Act, 1986. Historiographically, it is manifested in such programmes as the European Science Foundation's collaborative project on 'The Origins of the Modern State in Europe, 13th–18th Centuries'.[5] More important, however, is surely a growing popular awareness of political tensions within the modern British state. This reflects a new political agenda as, following the retreat from Empire, public attention has shifted from the United Kingdom's role as a world power to a much more internalized perspective on relations between its constituent parts. The revival of separatist sentiments in the 1970s, exemplified by the growth of the Scottish National Party and of Plaid Cymru, indicate at the least a more critical attitude in some quarters to England's traditional dominance within the Union. Even more clearly, the instability of the Union in its present form is highlighted by the recent troubles in Northern Ireland,

4 *The Spirit of the Nation: The Speeches and Statements of Charles J. Haughey (1957–1986)*, ed. Martin Mansergh (Cork, 1986), p.476, echoing the phraseology of an intergovernmental communiqué (cf. ibid, p.406).

5 The proceedings of this programme will appear in seven volumes. The English version is being published by Oxford University Press.

which have also drawn attention to the ambiguity of the United Kingdom's relationship with the Republic of Ireland.

The present collection of essays is an attempt to address some of the major questions which surround the new British history. To what extent did a British monarchy, aristocracy, institutions or culture develop in the sixteenth and seventeenth centuries? How far was the British experience of state formation a response to a perceived need to integrate the three kingdoms of England, Ireland and Scotland into an United Kingdom, and with what results? The questions were suggested largely by experiences of teaching and research for new undergraduate courses in British history. Students complained, for instance, that the existing nation-centred historiography had comparatively little to say in regard to some aspects of the process of state formation in the Atlantic archipelago.

Nevertheless, in view of the underdeveloped nature of the subject, it was felt that the commissioning of the volume required a rather more collaborative approach than simply issuing invitations to eminent scholars to contribute chapters on relevant topics. The historiographical gaps which had been identified provided an agenda for research, which a panel of scholars with appropriate expertise was then asked to address. Eleven specialists of early modern England, Ireland, Scotland, and Wales were assembled for a three-day conference on early modern British history held at University College, Galway, in mid-September 1993. The speakers were asked to address a range of topics which had been identified as of central importance to the British perspective – in particular, strategies of state formation, religion and ideology, and the interaction between English and Celtic cultures. The panel included sceptics as well as converts to the new British history, but all the speakers agreed to present papers comparing their own area of interest with other parts of the British Isles. Each speaker then faced a searching 'interview' from the forty conference delegates – not least from Mr David Blatherwick, the British ambassador to Ireland, who opened the proceedings. Thus this is not simply a volume of conference proceedings: the chapters reflect both an overall plan and the often lively discussions (both formal and informal) which ensued, and also new problems and perspectives which were identified at the conference. Moreover, the overall aim was to commission a collection of essays which could be used by undergraduates in conjunction with the existing nationalist historiography and which would open up comparative themes and problems.

For all this, the new British perspective remains controversial. The welcome among English historians for the removal of the Home Counties from centre stage and their repositioning in the south-eastern periphery of the British Isles has been less than wholehearted, and some Scottish historians remain suspicious that the 'new British' will quickly degenerate into 'old anglocentric' history![6] Ideally, however, British history should complement nationalist history: the former focusing on common traditions and experiences and the process of state-building, the latter on the individual characteristics of the four nations of the British Isles.

6 K.M. Brown, 'British history: a sceptical comment', in R.G. Asch (ed.) *Three Nations: A Common History? England, Scotland, Ireland and British History c. 1600–1920* (Bochum, 1993), pp.117–27.

CHAPTER ONE

The fashioning of Britain

John Morrill,
Selwyn College, Cambridge

Anthem no. 51 in a collection published in 1662 to be sung in Christchurch Cathedral, Dublin, opens as follows:

> O God that are the well-spring of all peace
> Make all thy gifts in Charles his reign increase
> England preserve, Scotland protect,
> Make Ireland in thy service perfect.
> That all these kingdoms under Great Britains king
> may be watered by the Gospel Spring.
> Oh never let unhallowed breath have space
> to blight these blossoming buds of union
> But let us all with mutual love embrace
> ***One Name***, One king and one Religion.[1]

This is one swallow that did not make a summer. There never has been a single geopolitical term for 'the British Isles'. This must be the first and salutary lesson for anyone seeking to develop a holistic approach to the history of these islands. This book confronts a thicket of paradoxes. We are asked to tell a tale of two islands, to tell a story of what were emerging as three kingdoms, one of which had been fabricated by the will of another, and to seek to make sense of the relations of four emerging nations, each of which had an identity shaped or at least deeply stained by its contact with – mingling with – the others.

It is a story of dynastic ambition and dynastic chance. In the sixteenth century the family which provided the five monarchs who ruled three of the nations came from king-less Wales. They in turn

1 *Anthems to be sung at the celebration of divine service in the Cathedral of the Holy and Undivided Trinity in Dublin.* I wish to thank John McCafferty for drawing my attention to this anthem.

were supplanted by a family from Scotland. In due course, a new constitutional balance and a new multicultural dynamic was made possible by an agreement of the representatives of three of the nations sitting in two of the parliaments to admit an undistinguished continental European family to govern all three kingdoms and all four nations. It was an appropriately incoherent outcome.

This chapter must seek to unravel some of these competing ambiguities. The first part will seek to unravel the skeins of argument, especially by distinguishing two processes: it will distinguish the dynamics of state formation from the formation of national consciousness; the middle section of the chapter will suggest a model for exploring the dynamics of state formation within a European context; the final part will offer some tentative applications of this model during the first half of the seventeenth century.

NATIONS AND STATES

Our starting-point must be the work of John Pocock whose plea for 'British History: a new subject' has been the rather delayed-action inspiration behind most recent developments in the field.[2] In 1975 he called us to a holistic approach to what he has termed 'the Atlantic archipelago', insisting that we must adopt a pluralistic approach which recognizes but does not exaggerate the extent to which such a history must contain 'the increasing dominance of England as a political and cultural entity'.[3] He went on to say that British history must show how the component parts of these islands 'interacted so as to modify the conditions of one another's existence',[4] and that 'British history denotes the historiography of no single nation but of a problematic and uncompleted experiment in the creation and interaction of several nations'.[5]

2 See esp. J.G.A. Pocock, 'British History: a plea for a new subject', *JMH* 47 (1975), pp.601–28; J.G.A. Pocock, 'The limits and divisions of British History', *AHR* 87.2 (1982), pp.311–36; J.G.A. Pocock, 'History and sovereignty: the historiographical response to Europeanization in two British cultures', *JBS* 31 (1992), pp.352–89; J.G.A. Pocock, 'Two kingdoms and three histories: political thought in British contexts', in R.A. Mason, (ed.) *Scots and Britons: Scottish Political Thought and the Union of 1603* (Cambridge, 1994).

3 Pocock, 'Plea', p.619.

4 Pocock, 'Limits and divisions', p.317.

5 ibid, p.318.

His theme has been taken up mainly by medievalists, and finds perhaps its fullest expression in the work of Robin Frame, who summed it up:

> The whole of the British Isles form a historical context that deserves more attention than it has so far received. . . . There is value in trying to assemble their history in ways that make it more than the sum of 'Welsh History', 'Scottish History', 'Irish History' and 'English History'. Of course there is endless work to be done within these hallowed categories. Comparative studies are another desideratum. But comparisons by their very nature assume, and even reinforce, the solidity and separateness of whatever is compared. As well as looking over partition walls, we need to do some thinking about the design of the building itself.[6]

There is no reason why this should be less true of the sixteenth and seventeenth centuries than of the twelfth or thirteenth centuries.

Our second – and less widely recognized – starting-point should be Hugh Seton-Watson's *Nations and States*. Seton-Watson traces the development of what he terms 'the continuous nations' (the English, Scottish, French, Iberians and Russians), the modern nations (Germans, Italians and Greeks), the artificial nations created by European settlement outside Europe (Mexicans, Australians and Americans), diasporic nations (Jews and Chinese) and so on.[7] His magisterial study, largely ignored by historians of the Atlantic archipelago, reminds us of the complexity of the relations between ethnicity, nationality and polity. He has pointed out the confusions that abound in the concept of the nation-state ('at most a half truth,' he tells us, 'what is arguably true is that we live in the age of the sovereign state').[8] International relations are the relations between states not between nations; the United Nations, like the League of Nations before it, exists to keep the peace between states, not nations. It is rare and not common for a nation to be co-terminous with a state, and it is not necessarily a source of stability when it is so; states can exist without a nation, or with several nations among their peoples. Most states have had national minorities within them.[9] It is a logical consequence of Seton-Watson's work to say that historians of most 'states' need to

6 R. Frame, 'Aristocracies and the political configuration of the British Isles', in R.R. Davies (ed.) *The British Isles, 1100–1500* (Edinburgh, 1988), p.154.

7 H. Seton-Watson, *Nations and States: An Enquiry into the Origins of Nations and the Politics of Nationalism* (London, 1977).

8 ibid, p.2.

9 ibid, pp.1–9.

consider the presence of several nations within and straddling the frontiers of their 'state'.[10]

It is clear, then, that if 'British' history is to have any meaning it is both a history of state-building, of the development of political, administrative, social, cultural institutions appropriate to a state developed by dynastic accident and short-term political expediency, and it is a study of the development of a multinational or multicultural state such as has been the norm rather than the exception in European, indeed, world history. Historians of these islands need to realize that the existence of several nations within a loosely structured polity is the norm in European history and not the exception.

The work of others sits comfortably with Seton-Watson's. It is important to remember the slow development of the term 'nation', and how recently it spawned the terms 'nationalism' and 'nationhood'. The work of Benedict Anderson on the nation as an 'imagined' community is important here: imagined both because of its elastic, finite boundaries and because the sense of nationhood prioritizes a deep, horizontal comradeship in the face of so many actual inequalities and exploitations. Anderson shows how it takes strong external threats to create such bonding. His picture of the nation as the heir to the collapse of religious and of dynastic realms reminds us how risky it is to assume too early an emergence of such horizontal bonding.[11] Even more important though is the work of Rees Davies whose recent survey of the 'Peoples' of the British Isles in the high middle ages argues that the key medieval concept is that of the '*gens*', a people descended from a founding patriarch – the Latin root retained in such terms as 'generations' and, most tellingly, in 'de*gen*eration', the term used by the English in Ireland to dismiss those of English birth and blood who intermarried with the Gaels and 'went native'. Davies's account of the evolution of the various *gentes* on the British Isles is compelling at all kinds of levels, demonstrating how late and how contingent is the emergence of the four peoples (proto-nations) who were to interact in the early modern period.[12]

10 That the interaction of nations within a state does indeed modify the conditions of the existence of each is especially well shown by Peter Sahlins's *Boundaries* from the divergent histories of the territories artificially separated by the treaty of the Pyrenees of 1659: P. Sahlins, *Boundaries: The Making of France and Spain in the Pyrenees* (Berkeley, Calif., 1989), see esp. pp.1–9.

11 B. Anderson, *Imagined Communities: Reflections on the Origin and Spread of Nationalism* (2nd edn, London, 1991), ch.1.

12 R.R. Davies, 'The peoples of the British Isles and Ireland, 1100–1400: I, identities', *TRHS* 6th ser. 4(1994).

Seton-Watson's splendid book too reminds us how slow and how late was the emergence of Englishness and Scottishness.[13] The English language – a kind of linguistic mayonnaise, where Anglo-Saxon oil blended with Norman yolks to become the common language of the inhabitants of England – quickened only in the fourteenth century; only when this was reinforced by a vernacular print culture and specifically by a vernacular bible and liturgy, and above all by the ubiquity and daily visibility of royal writs, can English national consciousness be said to have fully emerged. Yet the emergence of such consciousnesses elsewhere in the archipelago was slower. In polyglot Scotland, where four (perhaps five) regionally specific languages remained entrenched into the fifteenth century, Geoffrey Barrow can speak of Scottishness as possessing a 'homogeneity that was not racial or linguistic but feudal and governmental';[14] those feudal and governmental elements were, of course, imported from England.

Is 'Irishness' any more evident in 1540 than the sense of 'Spanishness' or 'Welshness' by that time? The lack of a single political authority exercising any kind of authority over the whole of the island, the linguistic diversities that made for poor or non-existent communications among the inhabitants, the difficult terrain and manifest and manifold problems of communication, all of which inhibited internal trade, were common factors in the medieval experience of both Ireland and Iberia. All these factors and more – the existence of the English Pale and of the Lordship of the Isles which linked north-east Ulster to the Scottish Islands only fifteen miles away at the narrowest point – add to the parallels between Ireland and Wales, where regional differences in the Brythonic or Welsh (P-Celtic) language, geographical separateness, the inexorable economic contacts with urban centres across the Bristol Channel and Severn/Dee basins in England (that is with Bristol, Shrewsbury and Chester) are widely held to have militated against a single Welsh national self-consciousness at this time. Is it the case that Welshness and Irishness were the product of over-exposure to the English and of being treated as a single unit of government by the English?

Simply being an inhabitant of Ireland, then, does not create an Irish identity any more than being an inhabitant of Britain creates a

13 Seton-Watson, *Nations and States*, esp. pp.21–35.

14 G.W.S. Barrow, *Feudal Britain: The Completion of the Medieval Kingdoms 1066–1314* (London, 1956) p.410. Cited by Seton-Watson, *Nations and States*, p.26.

British identity. Is Welshness, Irishness and even (to an extent) Scottishness a product of having Britishness thrust upon them – a product of accommodation with writ-culture and print-culture? This would explain the irony that while every Scot and every Welshman (and more arguably) every Irishman knew and perhaps knows the difference between being British and being Scottish, Welsh or Irish, and knows which if either to be and when, so many English – including notoriously Alan Taylor in his debate with John Pocock – will not see that there is a difference or cannot see that it matters.[15] That nasty English habit of using the terms English and British interchangeably can in fact readily be found in the historical works published around the turn of the sixteenth century and readers of both Camden's *Britannia* and Milton's *History of Britain* would be forgiven for wondering what the significance of the distinction is.[16] Even a late-seventeenth-century writer like Aylett Sammes who in his *Britannia Antiqua Illustrata* denied the Brutus-Trojan myth (that is the myth of a founding conqueror who gave England to his eldest son and Wales and Scotland to his younger sons), and whose etymology of 'Britain' invoked the memory of Phoenician traders coming over in search of tin and dubbing these the Britannic Isles, incorporated the Scilly Isles and the Isle of Man but not Ireland into his Britain.[17]

This leads on to a similar and more controversial paradox. For while the early modern period does represent a fairly inexorable advance of lowland *English* social, political, religious and cultural institutions throughout the archipelago, it can be argued that the *English* are the least interested parties in thinking through, articulating, above all redefining the relationship of the component parts of what had become the multiple or composite kingdom of the house of Stewart.[18]

15 Pocock, 'Limits and divisions', pp.622–3; see also the stories in H. Kearney, 'Four nations or one', and B. Crick, 'The English and the British', both in B. Crick (ed.) *National Identities: The Constitution of the United Kingdom* (Edinburgh, 1991).

16 D. Woolf, *The Idea of History in Early Stuart England* (Toronto, 1990), esp. pp.55–72, 110–25.

17 A. Sammes, *Britannia Antiqua Illustrata* (vol.I [only vol. published], 1676), pp.1–4, 50–1.

18 See Ellis, Chapter 2 in this volume.

MULTIPLE KINGDOMS

To test out and move forward in discovering the limits of this approach, it is important to recognize another tension in the existing literature. John Pocock's concern has been to come to an understanding of the anglophone diaspora around the Atlantic rim in these centuries.[19] His work leads naturally on to that of the school, headed by Nicholas Canny, who wish to understand the period in terms of a process of internal and external migration from Britain via Ireland to the New World.[20] Canny's work – combined with that of Michael Hechter on internal colonization[21] – has proved immensely fruitful in developing our understanding of the cultural and institutional dialectic of the period;[22] this chapter does not challenge the conclusions of such an approach, but draws us away to a complementary way of examining the same process. The Canny and Hechter models, after all, seek to make sense of Anglo-Irish relations; they cannot help us with Anglo-Scottish relations, one of the most bewildering aspects of which is the complete absence of any pattern of internal migration.[23]

There is a second model to draw on in seeking to understand that pattern of interaction; the model that looks not across the Atlantic but across La Manche to continental Europe and that seeks to locate the history of these islands during the sixteenth and seventeenth centuries in the context of European state formation. Is there not a story to tell within the archipelago of the limited and resisted development of a hegemonic metropolitan language, political culture and social, fiscal and legal institutions which parallels what was happening in the congeries of territories brought together by little more than dynastic accident that became during this period the federated, composite kingdoms of France and Spain?[24] Thus for England, Ireland, Scotland read France,

19 This is most explicit in Pocock, 'Response to Europeanization', pp.358–89.

20 N. Canny, *Kingdom or Colony: Ireland and the Atlantic World, 1560–1800* (Baltimore, Md, 1988).

21 M. Hechter, *Internal Colonization: The Celtic Fringe in British National Development, 1536–1966* (Berkeley, Calif., 1975).

22 The limits to its usefulness are best expressed by Hiram Morgan in his two lengthy reviews of Nicholas Canny's *Kingdom or Colony: IHR* 13.4 (1991), pp.810–16, and 'Mid-Atlantic Blues', *IR* 11 (1991/92), pp.50–5.

23 See the comments of Jenny Wormald, 'The creation of Britain: multiple kingdoms or core and colonies?' *TRHS 6th ser.* 2 (1992), pp.183–94.

24 J.H. Elliott, 'A world of composite monarchies', *P&P* 137 (1992), pp.48–72, and the works cited there.

Burgundy, Brittany or Castile, Valencia, Catalonia or even Castile, Aragón, Portugal. Is it not a profound kind of whiggishness that denies that this period saw the creation of a Pocockian Britain as a parallel to the creation of France and Spain? If the culmination of that 'problematic and uncompleted interaction' was the creation 250 years later of an autonomous Irish Republic, is that enough to deny the significance of the process in the period before 1700 or to deny that the unit of study for the early modern period should be the archipelago?

TRIPLE MONARCHY

Yet we must acknowledge that troublesome problem of nomenclature, and the troublesome historical myths that lie behind it. The English fitfully exploited the Brutus myth in asserting authority over the whole of Britain in the sixteenth century, but it is the myth of a founding conqueror who divided up the three British kingdoms and which had nothing to say about Ireland.[25] Little of this myth survived the ultraviolet light of Renaissance humanist scholarship, let alone the acid of Scottish scepticism and counter-myth, and English claims on Scotland came increasingly to rely on feudal suzerainty until such time as dynastic chance brought the Scottish royal house to the English throne.

The relationship of the crowns of England and Ireland was odder still, the latter being a sixteenth-century creation. The deeply ambiguous status of the Irish crown was one for which there was no continental parallel. No ruling British monarch visited Ireland in the early modern period until two did so in 1689–90.[26] Tudor and Stewart monarchs had no Irish coronation (that is they were not acclaimed, anointed, or crowned in the face of their Irish subjects); they took no coronation oath to uphold the liberties of the Irish people; in 1649, 1660 and again in 1689 the kings of Ireland were removed and the crown abolished, restored or transferred without any consultation with or confirmation by the Irish people. The problem for the Irish political nation in this period was thus not

25 Woolf, *Idea of History*, p.55 and index, *sub* Trojans; F. Levy, *Tudor Historical Theory* (Chicago, 1967), pp. 130–6 and *passim*.

26 The only previous royal visits had been in the 1180s and 1390s; there was no further royal visit until 1849.

that they had a king with two bodies;[27] it was that they had a king with no body at all. Or to change the metaphor, the problem for the Old English was not that they had an emperor with no clothes, but no emperor to put in the clothes of royalty that they had so lovingly manufactured on their constitutional looms. Dublin-based (though often English-trained) lawyers and the long-established nobles who patronized them proclaimed the particular liberties of the Irish crown: they are enshrined in the Graces, a veritable Irish Magna Carta *après la lettre* and they never gave up trying.[28] Their finest exponent was only to come with William Molyneux – philosopher, mathematician, engineer, Dublin Member of Parliament (MP) and author of *The Case of Ireland's being Bound by Acts of parliament in England stated* – at the very end of the seventeenth century.[29] He and they stressed the independence and autonomy of the Irish parliament, the case for an Irish-born executive and for religious liberties unique to the Irish context. As a result, the native Irish and the Old English seem to have believed (both in times of peace and in the course of war and rebellion) that their liberties were less at risk from a strengthened Irish constitution than from full incorporation into a Greater England. Here being a catholic majority in the kingdom of Ireland may well have seemed more attractive than being among the catholic minority of an enhanced English state.

Perhaps more surprisingly, the idea of incorporating Ireland into a greater English state seems to have appealed no more across the

27 The theory of the king's Two Bodies – his 'natural' body as a person and his 'political' body as king – mattered in several ways. Much Renaissance political thought argued that subjects could resist the person of the king in order to protect the royal office, that loyalty was due to kingship, not to a particular individual, and such a distinction was certainly important in the resistance in all three kingdoms to Charles I in the 1640s. But the distinction was also at the centre of Calvin's case in 1608, in which the English judges were asked to decide whether or not the allegiance of Scots to James VI made them automatically naturalized Englishmen by virtue of his accession to the English throne. Was allegiance due to James's office (King of Scotland) or person (James Stewart)? For these issues, see B. Galloway, *The Union of England and Scotland, 1603–1608* (Edinburgh, 1984), pp. 148–57.

28 R. Dudley Edwards, '*Magna Carta Hiberniae*', in J. Ryan (ed.) *Essays and Studies Presented to Professor Eoin MacNeill* (Dublin, 1940), pp.307–18. This established that a version of Magna Carta tailored to Irish conditions (the Liffey *vice* the Thames etc.) was promulgated and registered in Ireland shortly after the death of King John, but that subsequent – and increasingly infrequent – references were to the English recensions.

29 The best starting-point is J.G. Simms, *William Molyneux and Dublin* (Dublin, 1952). But see W.J. Smyth, *Men of No Property* (London, 1992), pp.81–4. By the time he wrote, it is inappropriate to refer to him as Old English; perhaps John Pocock's term 'creole nationalist' is more appropriate.

Irish Sea. No monarch or royal official wanted the native Irish or even the descendants of the Anglo-Norman settlers to claim *cives Britannici sunt.* Equally, it suited the New English colonists to believe the native populations to be conquered and subject to dispossession and plantation.

Thus we must be careful not to exaggerate the truth in Steve Ellis's claim that the reforms culminating in the Act of 1541 'provided a mechanism for incorporating Gaelic Ireland into the Tudor state, broadly along the lines of the Welsh Union'.[30] The Irish monarchy, for all its wraith-like quality, was never threatened with dissolution; the dependent relationship of the Irish on the English crown did not spawn new geopolitical expressions to match 'Iberia'. Maps of Britain continued to omit it;[31] historians and antiquarians spurned the opportunity to invent a past that incorporated it.

ANGLO-SCOTTISH UNION

The confusion that had existed and that continued to exist in the relationship between England and Ireland contributed to the problems inherent in the union of the crowns of England and Scotland. This created not just a dual monarchy, but a more shadowy triple monarchy and the movements of peoples quickly gave each a stake in the others. Thus the Irish crown was unquestionably a dependency of the English crown and therefore the interference of the Scottish Council, nobility and Kirk in Ireland in solidarity with Scottish settlers created acute political problems. If understanding the relations of the three kingdoms creates a Trinitarian problem of Nicene complexity,[32] then the constitutional role of the Scots in Ireland must represent the *filioque* clause.

30 See pp.56–7 in this volume.

31 R. Helgeron, 'The land speaks: cartography, chorography and subversion in Renaissance England', in S. Greenblatt (ed.) *Representing the English Renaissance* (Berkeley, Calif., 1988); D.J. Baker, 'Off the map: charting uncertainty in Renaissance Ireland', in B. Bradshaw and A. Hadfield (eds) *Representing Ireland: Literature and the Origins of Conflict, 1534–1660* (Cambridge, 1993), pp.76–92.

32 J.S. Morrill, 'A British patriarchy? Ecclesiastical imperialism under the early Stuarts' in A. Fletcher and P. Roberts (eds) *Religion, Culture and Society in Early Modern Britain* (Cambridge, 1994), pp.209–37.

Historians, led by Conrad Russell, have recently made us reconsider how the union of 1603 contributed to the instability of English, Scottish and British history in the seventeenth century. Now it is a commonplace about James VI and I that he sought to use the Union of the Crowns as a stepping-stone towards a union of the kingdoms. In a remarkable metaphor which Jenny Wormald has recently brought to our attention, James in May 1607 defended his union proposals thus:

> It is merely idle and frivolous, to conceive that any unperfect union is desired or can be granted: it is no more unperfect, as now is projected, than a child that is born without a Beard. . . . It is now perfect in my title and descent, though it is not accomplisht and full union; for that Time hath all the lineaments and parts of a Body, yet it is but an Embrio and no child; and shall be born, though it then be a perfect child yet it is no man; it must gather strength and perfection by Time.[33]

James then aimed for perfect union, a new-modelled kingdom of Britain, brought about slowly, organically, via a union of hearts and minds. No one else (except perhaps Lord Keeper Ellesmere) shared his vision or his enthusiasm. But as Bruce Galloway and Brian Levack have shown,[34] there were alternative models that were available to James's unenthusiastic subjects, such as the incorporative model which had worked so well with respect to Wales that, as Philip Jenkins put it, by 1600 'it is difficult to discern a "Welsh political tradition" more distinctive from the English norm than conditions in (say) Norfolk or Lancashire'.[35] The very success of the Welsh union in integrating the Welsh and English economies, in spreading writ culture and English protestantism throughout Wales, in integrating Welsh elites into the societies of the west of England, and in making Wales perhaps the least rebellious region in the whole archipelago, made unreflective Englishmen assume that it was just the kind of union England should have with Scotland. Seventeenth-century Wales provided the Stewarts with a lord chamberlain, a lord keeper, a secretary of state, an archbishop of York, and provided Stewart parliaments with at least two speakers. In each case 'the distinctively Welsh component of their career would be hard to discern'.

33 *Journal of the House of Commons* I, 367; Wormald, 'Creation of Britain', pp.175–6.

34 B. Galloway, *The Union of England and Scotland, 1603–1608* (Edinburgh, 1984), *passim*; B.P. Levack, *The Formation of Britain* (Oxford, 1987), pp.29–34, 40–3, 48–51.

35 All quotations are from a paper by Philip Jenkins on 'Identities in seventeenth-century Wales' at a Trevelyan Fund Colloquium on *The British Problem 1534–1707* at Queen's College, Cambridge, 3–4 July 1993.

It was a success story that flattered to deceive. The English might humour the Welsh by publicizing the Celtic origins of the British churches and the specifically Welsh origins of the Tudors – as late as the Restoration an English genealogist could publish a pedigree of Charles II tracing it back to the tenth-century law-giver Hywel Dda, progenitor of the royal line of medieval Wales[36] – but such sweet-talking was never going to reassure the Scots or the Irish. For the English, any redefinition of relations with the Scots began with their well-attested vassal status in previous centuries. It was feudal overlordship and a willingness to engage in dynastic roulette, not a hankering after union – least of all incorporative union – that underlay Tudor policy in Scotland, and even then such ambition was largely concentrated in the period 1542–60.[37] The English, for reasons of national security, wanted to regulate the marriages and regencies of Scottish monarchs, not add the Scottish title to their English, French and Irish ones. This trajectory is still sometimes overlooked by historians of seventeenth-century Britain. As this chapter will show in the relations of the churches, there was marked reluctance on the English part to plan for, let alone precipitate, a union of the kingdoms in the later sixteenth century.

It was, however, a Scots preoccupation. Twice – in 1513 and 1541 – they had attempted opportunistic invasions of England only to see the cream of their nobility slain and their kings die. One should not overlook the consequent psychic numbing, the sense of military (though not, of course, cultural) inferiority that produced a recognition that Scotland's long-term future lay in either accepting a feudal dependency upon England or opting for being a colonial outreach of France. Hence the drastic polarizations and oscillations of the 1540s, 1550s and 1560s. If the English lost friends by their Rough Wooing in the 1540s, they regained them by their apparent magnanimity in victory in 1560;[38] hence that fascinating combination of self-effacement and assurance in the development

36 Percy Enderbie, *Cambria Triumphans* (1661), unpaginated genealogy placed after the dedication, shows the Stewarts as descended from the Welsh royal house through the marriage of Fleance, son of Banquo, and Nest, daughter of Griffith ap Llywelyn, King of Wales.

37 P. Hotle, 'Tradition, reform and diplomacy: Anglo-Scottish relations 1528–42' (Cambridge University, PhD thesis, 1992); A. Williamson, 'Scotland, Antichrist and the invention of Great Britain', in J. Dwyer, R.A. Mason and A. Murdoch (eds) *New Perspectives in the Politics and Culture of Early Modern Scotland* (Edinburgh, 1982), pp.34–58; M.L. Bush, *The Government Policy of Protector Somerset* (London, 1975) esp. ch.2. See Dawson, Chapter 4 in this volume.

38 See J. Dawson, 'William Cecil and the British dimension of early Elizabethan foreign policy', *History* 74 (1989), pp.196–216.

of a pan-British millenarianism in post-Marian Scotland described by Jane Dawson and Arthur Williamson.[39] The Scots devoted much thought and effort in the decades before 1603 to the necessity and hazards of the Stewart inheritance of the southern crowns. Apprehensive, unenthusiastic, but realistic, it was the Scots who would spend the seventeenth century embracing the unavoidability of the union and seeking to find a way of giving it an institutional coherence. In the 1640s, 1670 and 1689–90, it was the Scots who tried to force the pace and the English who buried their heads in the sand. If they could not have an incorporative union which they knew could be achieved only by conquest, the English were happy enough to leave Scotland unassimilated and uncolonized. No Englishman-born was to sit on the royal council in Edinburgh, hold a Scottish bishopric, or own Scottish manors in the seventeenth century. It was a story of benign neglect.

HERITAGES

None of this creates any problem for the Pocockian agenda; indeed in the Atlantic rim context it stirs the pot nicely, but it represents an important variable when state formation in these islands is examined in a wider western European context. For what is shared with the western European experience more than makes up for it.

This chapter suggests that the characteristics of French and Spanish state formation in the early modern period include the following: the maximization of royal authority within each of the constituent territories of a composite monarchy; the centralization and standardization within but not across the boundaries of each constituent territory; a single, increasingly homogeneous royal court and household; moves towards a greater linguistic, legal, social and economic integration everywhere imperfectly realized by 1700; moves towards a coordinated defence and foreign policy, controlled by a central council. But it did *not* include the development of a single law-making parliament or states general or Cortes general for the whole polity; the development of an integrated judicial system or courts with a supreme jurisdiction across the whole of each

39 ibid. English policy rested mostly on Elizabeth's parsimony rather than great statesmanship. For the Scottish side, see esp. A. Williamson, *Scottish National Consciousness in the Age of James VI* (Edinburgh, 1979) esp. pp.10–12, 42–3.

composite kingdom (that is, there may have been congruity of judicature between parallel hierarchies of courts, but there was no more a *parlement général* than an evolving states general).

Looked at in this way, what happens in the British archipelago does look sufficiently similar to be worth exploring. It is necessary to recognize that the early modern period saw not innovation but rather an intensification of forms of interaction that had been going on for centuries. Here the work of Rees Davies is especially instructive.[40]

Many historians have argued for an approach to Norman and Angevin history that straddles the English Channel and recognizes that the term 'Anglo-Norman' applies in physical as well as cultural terms to the *héritages* of many leading and secondary families throughout the twelfth to the fifteenth centuries. There is an *imperium* that straddles the English Channel. But Rees Davies has brought home as never before the reality of both royal and noble *héritages* across the boundaries *within* the archipelago.

> Feudal honours such as Brecon or Strigoil, Glamorgan or Colwyn straddled the Ango-Welsh border, while feudal tenants in Berkshire might find military service in Kidwelly in west Wales part of their tenurial obligations. . . . The lands of . . . the Marshal family ranged from the lordship of Longueville to the great liberty of Leinster, encompassing lands in England, the honours of Strigoul and Usk, the earldom of Pembroke and even the lordship of Haddington in Scotland. . . . The aristocratic families treated them as a single *héritage* . . . they encompassed them all within the arc of their visits . . . and within the ambit of their territorial strategies and financial extortions . . . Elizabeth de Burgh was partial in her household at Clare in East Anglia to salmon brought from her estates in Wales and stocked her stables from her Irish lands, while Roger Mortimer constructed a new bridge at Coleraine with timber from his estates in Usk.[41]

He also argued that

> By almost any measuring rod we can use – language, customs, law, culture, agriculture, political affiliation and so forth – the societies of much of lowland Gwent, Glamorgan, Gower and Pembroke and of the East coast of Southern Ireland, the inland counties of Leinster, South Tipperary, Waterford and even parts of Cork and Limerick in the late

40 R.R. Davies, *Dominion and Conquest: The Experience of Ireland, Scotland and Wales, 1100–1300* (Cambridge, 1990); Davies (ed.) *British Isles*, esp. introduction and ch.8.

41 Davies, (ed.) *British Isles*, pp.15–16; and cf. the discussion of the webs of marriage in the twelfth and thirteenth centuries in ibid, pp.142–59, esp. the chart on p.154.

> 13th century had more in common with the English county society than with native Welsh or Irish Society.[42]

This chapter suggests that a helpful way forward towards an archipelagic history might be to work with the concept of four medieval cores in lowland England, Lowland Scotland, the Englishries of Wales and the English Pale in Ireland. In each, English was established as the language of politics and Latin as the language of law and government; in each, the characteristic features of Anglo-Norman social and legal institutions were fully settled; each was a writ-governed culture; and in choosing marriage partners, social leaders looked to other cores before they looked to their hinterlands.

Each core had its own history: the English core of inexplorable expansion into its hinterland; the Welsh core of piecemeal expansion; the Scottish core waxed and waned with the fortunes – and regular infancy – of the monarchs; the Irish core (the Pale) experienced a gradual shrinkage back on itself after the initial Angevin irruption and settlement.

It is also suggested that what we witness in the sixteenth and seventeenth centuries is a twofold process of development: the incomplete expansion of each core within England, Ireland, Scotland and Wales; and the assertion of greater supervisory power by the English core over the other cores. Thus Thomas Cromwell's work in the 1530s created the 'unitary realm' of England, with the incorporation of the Palatinates, the extinction of liberties, the establishment of the ubiquitous royal writs, the establishment both of a veritable conciliar argus at the centre of government and of the characteristic institutions that replaced the noble household by the county courts and administrative offices where government business was effected. The reforms of 1536–43 both systematized and standardized the legal and social institutions of Cambrian Englishries and Welshries alike and also made Wales part of England for all purposes of government. As a prelude to the Union of the Crowns, James VI had begun an irreversible change in royal responsibility for and incorporation of the Scottish Highlands under the Scottish crown. The Act of 1541, the policy first of surrender and regrant and then of plantation underwrote the determination of the Tudors as kings of Ireland to make their authority effective throughout the island of Ireland. Thus as each crown extended its authority into its hinterlands, the attempt began

42 ibid, pp.13–14.

to bring effective control of the whole to a nerve centre in southern England. The question is what underlay this attempt.

COURTS AND COUNCILS

The royal councils, the royal court and the churches are three aspects of this process in the early modern period. The councils of sixteenth-century monarchs in England, Scotland and Ireland were highly unusual in that they combined deliberative and executive functions. In Geoffrey Elton's phrase, they 'did things'.[43] It can be argued that over time *deliberative* functions tended to be concentrated at the centre and *enforcement* left to 'regional councils' in Ludlow, Dublin and Edinburgh. This was an accelerating trend once the Stewarts arrived in Whitehall and not the least interesting aspect of Wentworth's time in Ireland was his unavailing attempt to buck the trend.[44] Is this not exactly the story of the Scottish privy council as told by Maurice Lee, Peter Donald and others?[45] The question is, which had the greater policy-making freedom in 1636 – the Scottish privy council or the council of the north? Indeed it could be suggested that the working model for Edinburgh by the 1630s was the regional council developed in sixteenth-century England. Meanwhile the king's council at Whitehall was becoming rather more than an English council. With permanent Scottish members (who regularly withdrew as a committee to discuss Scottish business as in 1607 when the Scottish members alone interrogated those responsible for the 'illegal' general assembly at Aberdeen),[46] and with a committee for Irish affairs, this was in the

43 G.R. Elton, 'Tudor government, the points of contact: II – The Council', in G.R. Elton, *Studies in Tudor and Stuart Politics and Government* (4 vols; Cambridge, 1974–92), III, p.23. The exact quote is 'the Tudor Privy Council reverberated with activity. Unlike the Councils of France or Spain, (only able to advise action which itself could never occur except on the signified authority of the king), that of England did things, had full executive authority, and by its own instruments . . . produced administrative results throughout the realm.' For important demonstrations of this point in regard to the Irish council, see S.G. Ellis, *Reform and Revival: English Government in Ireland 1470–1534* (London, 1986), ch.1.

44 My understanding of Anglo-Irish relations in the 1630s has been transformed by reading Patrick Little, 'Family and faction: the Irish nobility and the English court 1632–1642' (Trinity College, Dublin, MLitt thesis, 1992).

45 M. Lee, *The Road to Revolution: Scotland under Charles I, 1625–37* (Urbana, Ill., 1985), pp.29–39 and *passim*; P. Donald, *An Uncounselled King: Charles I and the Scottish Troubles, 1637–1641* (Cambridge, 1989), pp.16–25.

46 Morrill, 'British patriarchy?', pp.218–19.

process of becoming an imperial council determining the foreign policy of the whole archipelago and the regional policies of each constituent kingdom. The logical culmination of this policy was the Cromwellian council of state from 1654 to 1659; it prefigures the arrangements that were in place from 1707.[47]

None the less, the search for an archipelagic history should begin not by looking at royal councils but at the royal court. Neil Cuddy and Keith Brown have done much to make us aware of the way that James VI and I opened up his Household and Bedchamber to the Scots.[48] As we learn more about the politics of access as the key to politics in the early modern period, so the lack of royal interest in integrating privy councils seems unimportant in comparison with the growth of an integrated royal household, with the Bedchamber as a kind of embryonic *conseil d'en haut.*

James VI and I's policy towards the Scottish nobility – to encourage them to establish themselves as cultural amphibians, living partly in England and partly in Scotland, combining an economic centre-of-gravity north of the border and a political centre-of-gravity south of it, acquiring English titles as well as Scottish ones and English wives instead of Scottish ones – was a policy extended by Charles I to include the Irish nobility.[49]

The Irish protestant nobility were largely recent settlers who maintained strong links with the English gentry (the earl of Cork being the supreme example of this).[50] But it is vital not to forget how far wardship and intermarriage were integrating the Old English (and even the Irish) nobilities into English political culture: by the 1630s Clanrickard was after all a half-brother of the third earl of Essex, Inchiquin a son-in-law of St Leger, Ormond had been a royal ward brought up largely at Hatfield and Lambeth,[51] while

47 For some cautionary remarks, especially for pressing this point in the second half of the century, see Barnard, Chapter 10, and Hayton, Chapter 11 in this volume.

48 N. Cuddy, 'The revolution of the entourage: the bedchamber under James I', in D. Starkey (ed.) *The English Court 1450–1640* (London, 1985), pp.173–225; K. Brown, 'Courtiers and cavaliers: service, anglicization and loyalty among the royalist nobility', in J.S. Morrill (ed.) *The Scottish National Covenant in its British Perspective* (Edinburgh, 1990), pp.155–92; K. Brown, 'The Scottish aristocracy, anglicization and the court', *HJ* 36 (1993), pp.543–76.

49 K. Sharpe, 'The court of Charles I', in Starkey (ed.) *English Court*, pp.226–60; J. Scally, 'The political career of James, third marquis and first duke of Hamilton (1606–1647) to 1643', (Cambridge University, PhD thesis, 1993), esp. chs 4 and 5.

50 N. Canny, *The Upstart Earl: A Study of the Social and Mental World of Richard Boyle, 1st Earl of Cork* (Cambridge, 1982), pp.124–38; J.A. Murphy, 'The politics of the Munster protestants', *Journal of the Cork Archaeological Society* 76 (1971), pp.4–7; J.R. MacCormack, 'Irish adventurers and the English Civil War', *IHS* 10 (1956), pp.21–58.

51 *DNB*; J.C. Beckett, *The Cavalier Duke* (Dublin, 1990), chs 1–2.

Antrim married the widow of the great duke of Buckingham.[52] There were six Fitzgerald earls of Kildare between the 1580s and the 1630s. All had English wives and/or English mothers and three were born or brought up in England. The sixteenth earl was the grandson of Sir Thomas Randolph, Elizabeth's veteran ambassador in Scotland; he was the ward at the English court of the Scottish earl of Lennox and he married the daughter of the earl of Cork, the greatest of the New English protestant settlers in Ireland.[53] Not for nothing did James VI and I see a union of hearts and minds (and of bodies too, he might have added) as the key to a union of the Kingdoms. The stories told by Vincent Carey, Tom Connors and Jane Ohlmeyer of the Fitzgeralds, Burkes and MacDonnells respectively over the century from 1547 to 1641 is of an ever-greater assimilation of the Irish nobility to a dual identity.[54] These noble families were not so much amphibians as chameleons. But whereas Tom Connors can speak of the Burkes in the 1560s and 1570s literally changing from English to Gaelic garb as they crossed the Shannon, by the 1630s Jane Ohlmeyer can describe Randal MacDonnell, second earl of Antrim, reflecting the latest Whitehall taste in traditional Irish garb. These men were increasingly caught between their Gaelic past and an anglified future, and even their catholic religion was increasingly something, like their Gaelic tongue, that they left firmly behind as they crossed the Irish Sea. As Tom Connors put it:

> The fourth earl of Clanricarde drew clear lines between being a catholic in England and being an Irish catholic. He might protect the friars in Galway, but an Irish Franciscan expecting hospitality at his mansion in Kent was shown off the grounds with enough despatch to inspire an angry poem in retaliation. . . . Likewise he prevented the distribution of a life of St Patrick dedicated to him without his consent.[55]

There are two major lessons to be learned from all this. First, it is important in this talk of amphibious Scots and chameleon Irish not

52 J. Ohlmeyer, *Civil War and Restoration in Three Stuart Kingdoms: The Career of Randal MacDonnell, Marquis of Antrim* (Cambridge, 1993), p.29 and *passim.*

53 I am grateful to Vincent Carey for his discussion of the Fitzgeralds in this period. See *The Complete Peerage* ed. G.E. Cockayne (13 vols; London, 1910–59), VII, pp.239–43.

54 The stories were told at a joint session at the American Historical Association meeting in Washington, DC, in December 1992 at which I had the good fortune to be the commentator.

55 T. Connors, conference paper entitled 'Survival and anglicization in the West of Ireland, 1570–1640' (AHA meeting, Washington DC, December 1992).

to speak loosely about the anglicization of the nobility.[56] Englishmen might be acquiring land and titles in Ireland and a few titles without land in Scotland; Scots and some (Old English) Irish might be acquiring land, wives and titles in England but it may well be better to speak of the *briticization* of the nobility rather than *anglicization.* This is the conclusion of John Scally in his splendidly careful analysis of the mental world of the first duke of Hamilton;[57] it is certainly the implication of David Stevenson's work on Patrick Gordon's lament for the corruption of the Scottish nobility.[58] Second, the English are far less pro-active than might be expected in relation to the opportunities provided for the spoils made available by the Union of the Crowns. They might give up their daughters to Irish and Scottish earls but they were not scouring Scotland in search of wealthy heiresses for their sons or Scottish titles for themselves. No English peer became a major landowner in Scotland in the seventeenth century. This is the paradox that dominates the remainder of this chapter: that the expansion of English institutions and English cultural forms took place for almost all of the early modern period in the context of relative English indifference to any systematic absorption or integration of the outlying kingdoms into an enlarged English state.

THE BRITISH CHURCHES

The key to understanding the ecclesiastical policies of James and Charles lies not in a policy of ecclesiastical imperialism but in the naked authoritarianism of Charles I.[59] There was certainly no ecclesiastical imperialism under James VI and I. James had many reasons for restoring diocesan episcopacy in Scotland. To have his own appointees as constant moderators of the presbyteries and synods gave him eyes, ears and a voice in provincial Scotland; it gave him the means to control the Scottish parliament; and it helped him to beat down the authority of those who had drunk deeply from the vat of Buchanan and Melville and who, unlike

56 See Brown, Chapter 9 in this volume.

57 Scally, 'Political career', pp.342–6.

58 D. Stevenson, 'The English devil of keeping state: elite manners and the downfall of Charles I', in R. Mason and N. Macdougall (eds) *People and Power in Scotland* (Edinburgh, 1992), pp.126–44.

59 For what follows see Morrill, 'British patriarchy?', pp.222–35.

James himself, had not spewed it up but had swallowed it down. Furthermore James had a policy which aimed to build up the mutual respect of the churches of each of his kingdoms for the churches of the others: this is the real lesson of James's words at and his faltering actions after the Hampton Court Conference, and of his concern to raise preaching standards in England. In the case of the church of Scotland this meant restoring apostolic orders without jeopardizing the jurisdictional independence of the Kirk, and reforms to bring about a form of worship, but not by a slavish following of the English model. Similarly James pursued policies of ecclesiastical renovation in Ireland, which have been well described by Alan Ford.[60] Nor did he challenge any of the ways in which the Irish Church had developed separately from the English Church.[61] Interference by, let alone subordination to, the English Church was not part of that agenda.

Charles I's ecclesiastical policies in Scotland and Ireland were far more straightforwardly authoritarian, as, of course, they were in England. There were common elements in each kingdom such as the desire to restore to each church much of the wealth and jurisdiction wrenched from it during the Reformation. It is possible to see a detestation of sacrilege behind these policies. Charles had a far clearer and more *dirigiste* sense of how God should be worshipped, and he set out to change religious observance in each kingdom. But there seems to be no evidence that he strove for a narrow uniformity of practice, let alone the subordination of the Irish and Scottish churches to the English. Continental scholars might write learned treatises on the patriarchies of the early Church, including a Patriarchy of Britain encompassing the archipelago, and their work was enthusiastically taken up by lay antiquarian enthusiasts like Spelman; but neither Charles nor Laud showed a flicker of interest. Charles and Laud were shocked by the *laissez-faire* liturgical atmosphere in Scotland when they visited the northern Kingdom in 1633, but it was a distinctive Scottish prayer book designed by Scottish bishops (albeit with fraternal 'advice' from their English friends) and not just the English Prayer Book which Charles sought to impose in 1637. It was a prayer book which the Scots immediately saw as worse, more popish, than the English

60 A. Ford, *The Protestant Reformation in Ireland 1590–1641* (Frankfurt am Main, 1985).

61 A. Clarke, 'Varieties of uniformity: the first century of the Church of Ireland', in W. Sheils and D. Wood (eds) *The Churches, Ireland and the Irish* (Oxford, 1975), p.107.

Prayer Book and their first instinct was to claim not that they were being anglicized but being treated as guinea pigs for experiments which would be visited upon the English in due course. Only in 1639 did the charge of anglicization become the dominant one. In Ireland, although Laud was more careless in acting *ultra vires*, the key to understanding royal policy was the growth of royal power and the elimination of dissident forms of protestant practice, not the anglicanization of practice or jurisdiction.

THE WAR OF THE THREE KINGDOMS

This chapter concludes with a discussion of the 'War of the Three Kingdoms'.[62] A properly archipelagic study of the war(s) offers solutions to some of the problems which previous lines of approach have left unanswered, and does more than contribute to our understanding of the history of each. A long review of Conrad Russell's recent books not only expressed admiration for his achievement but also warned that his approach was ultimately not an archipelagic one but a kind of enriched English history.[63] He is concerned with the origins of the war(s), but he uses the collapse of royal power in Scotland and Ireland to explain the collapse of a demilitarized England into war. He should have been more concerned at explaining how a common civil and more particularly religious authoritarianism throughout the archipelago caused a sequence of events which led on to a struggle which many, though not all, saw as a single struggle.

Most obviously this is true of King Charles I. From the moment that the Scots resisted his authoritarian policies, Charles saw the implications for the archipelago. And he strove to mobilize the resources of Britain to deal with Scottish rebels as easily and unselfconsciously as the Tudors raised the resources of England to deal with rebels in the western, the eastern and the northern counties.[64]

62 This section and the following one draw heavily on J.S. Morrill, 'The Britishness of the English Revolution', in R. Asch (ed.) *Three Nations: A Common History? England, Scotland, Ireland and British History c.1600–1920* (Bochum, 1993).

63 J.S. Morrill, 'The causes of Britain's Civil Wars', which appeared first in abbreviated form in *JEH* 43 (1992), pp.624–33, and in full in J.S. Morrill, *The Nature of the English Revolution* (London, 1993), pp.252–72.

64 P. Donald, 'The Scottish National Covenant and British politics', in Morrill (ed.) *Scottish National Covenant*, pp.91–117.

From the very beginning of the Scottish crisis, Charles was convinced that the rebels intended to overthrow the Scottish bishops and he was convinced that this would undermine their standing in England and in Ireland. This would be fatal to royal authority in matters of religion and in the parliaments, where the bishops represented a powerful bloc vote. The defeat of the covenanters was seen as essential for the maintenance of royal authority throughout these islands. None of his obsessions was to prove so self-fulfilling. From the beginning, therefore, Charles determined to bring the military resources of all three kingdoms to bear on the Scots. It just did not occur to him that this was inappropriate. It was a policy he was vigorously to pursue in 1639, 1640, 1641(?),[65] 1643, 1645 and 1647–8. From the moment at which his authority was challenged in England he worked tirelessly to bring in Scottish troops and Irish troops – and he did not care whether they were Old English protestant or Irish Confederacy troops – into the English arena. His strategic planning always involved having troops from each of his kingdoms in the others.[66] This culminated in another three-kingdom rebellion against the Long parliament and its army in 1648.

Two of Charles's closest advisers further represent this unitary approach to the wars. Randal MacDonnell, second earl of Antrim, was a catholic, a courtier married to the widow of Charles's beloved and assassinated privado, the duke of Buckingham, the greatest landowner in the north of Ireland (with an estate of 15,000 hectares), and the heir to the ancient but suppressed lordship of the Isles, that is leadership of all the clans of the western Highlands and Islands, a suzerainty straddling the Irish Sea. Antrim's ambitions involved the restoration of his lands and titles in Scotland and therefore the destruction of his supplanters, the Clan Campbell, whose leader, the marquis of Argyll, was the dominant figure in the Covenanting movement from 1638 on. It is easy to dismiss him as a man consumed with an unreasoning desire to reclaim his patrimony. In fact as Jane Ohlmeyer has shown, he was an ambitious and sophisticated statesman trapped between a Gaelic past and an anglified future. His Ulster home, Dunluce Castle, was

65 See the debate between Jane Ohlmeyer and Michael Perceval-Maxwell under the title 'The Antrim Plot of 1641 – a myth?', *HJ* 35 (1992), pp.905–19; and *HJ* 37 (1994) pp.421–30 (Perceval-Maxwell), 431–7 (Ohlmeyer).

66 This is a subject well dealt with by C. Russell, *The Fall of the Stuart Monarchies 1637–1642* (Oxford, 1991); by Donald, *An Uncounselled King;* and by M. Mendle, *Dangerous Positions* (Tuscaloosa, Ala, 1985), pp.114–70.

lavishly furnished with the latest tapestries characteristic of southern English taste, while he and his household sat around on silken upholstered chairs as Gaelic bards and harpists entertained him, and while he was served at table by a retinue wearing traditional Irish garb. On no fewer than eight occasions between 1638 and 1648 Antrim put forward proposals for a pan-archipelagic military effort to restore the king's fortunes. On every occasion the dispatch of his Ulster kinsmen to recapture the forfeited MacDonald lands in Kintyre and Jura were a central feature, and the only part of any of the plans effectively realized was just such an expeditionary force. But before and after he joined the Irish Confederacy in the autumn of 1643 his plans always involved schemes for the liberation of Ireland and Scotland as the prelude to a pan-Gaelic assault on southern England. Antrim's travels between Ireland and the royal court, and between Britain and the continent had, as their dominant purpose, the realization of a royal victory not in three distinct wars but in the various theatres of a single war.[67]

A final example must be James, third marquis of Hamilton and second earl of Cambridge. An example *par excellence* of a Scots nobleman whose lands lay in Scotland and offices in England, a man whose base of operations was as gentleman of the bedchamber and master of horse to Charles I and who would have shared the sentiment of those Whitehall-based Scots who (caught between the covenanters who controlled their estates and the king who controlled their offices) petitioned Charles as his *British* subjects.[68] The Covenanting minister Robert Baillie described him as 'a great lover both of the king and country'; Keith Brown has written that it was his misfortune to lose the trust of both.[69] But the point is that, after early indiscretions in seeking to unleash Antrim's catholic Irish on Scotland in 1639, he worked tirelessly for a constitutional-royalist settlement throughout the archipelago, losing the trust of the king for his secret negotiations with the more moderate covenanters and of the covenanters for his secret negotiations with restraining voices around the court. It is symbolic that Hamilton, an architect of the Engagement of 1648, a truly pan-archipelagic document (by which the Scots agreed to send an army to join English and Irish troops to restore Charles to his authority in

67 Ohlmeyer, *Career of Randal MacDonnell, passim.*

68 E.J. Cowan, 'The Union of the Crowns and the crisis of the constitution in seventeenth century Scotland', in S. Dyrvik, K. Myklund and S. Oldervoll (eds) *The Satellite State in the Seventeenth and Eighteenth Centuries* (Oslo, 1980), p.131.

69 K. Brown, 'Courtiers and cavaliers', p.160.

England and Ireland), and the general of the army crushed by Cromwell at the battle of Preston, should be executed in England under his English title as earl of Cambridge.[70]

For all these men there was but one conflict and they always thought about it in three-dimensional terms. Whatever problem they had to solve, or whatever setback they experienced, they naturally and unselfconsciously thought about the implications for all three kingdoms. They did not envisage a postwar world in which there would be unitary institutions, but they assumed that no settlement was possible in one kingdom without there being a settlement in all three.

In many ways the leaders of the Covenanting movement in Scotland went further than this. From not later than the winter of 1639–40 they were fighting not simply or principally to nurture Scottish liberties under a Scottish king, but for a federal union of the three kingdoms and three churches. They had recognized that there would be no protection for Scotland against a king willing to mobilize the resources of the three kingdoms unless he was equally constrained in all kingdoms. Having in 1639–40 inflicted the first important Scots' defeat on an English army for over 300 years, they made a common form of church government and confession of faith, along with political structures designed to coordinate policy-making and legislation in the two kingdoms, a prime objective of the subsequent peace negotiations. They also assumed that the Irish Church would be reformed along identical lines and that the Scots would be accorded an active role in the affairs of Ireland. They were continually rebuffed by the English parliament, but they were ever more determined that there could be no settlement other than an archipelagic one. It was this that brought the covenanters into the war in Ireland in 1642 and in England in 1643. The Solemn League and Covenant is an agreement covering all three kingdoms and requiring changes in the government and religion of all three. The outcome the Scots sought was a federal union with separate political, legal and ecclesiastical institutions in each but a high degree of congruity and cooperation between them. This is most dramatically illustrated by the Westminster assembly, the meeting of English and Scots ministers and lay assessors which met to design a system of church government and discipline, confession of faith, catechism and service book which would be introduced into the

70 Hamilton's career down to 1641 is in Scally, 'The political career'. I have profited greatly from reading John Scally's work and discussing Anglo-Scottish relations in this period with him.

independent churches of England, Scotland and Ireland. The Scots were massively outnumbered at that assembly, but bound themselves to accept its decisions, although it would involve changes in the Kirk. Hence their rage when the English parliament chopped and changed what had been agreed in the assembly without any reference to them.[71]

The disillusionment of the Covenanting leadership with the English was concerned with a whole range of archipelagic (and not just British) issues: the dishonouring of agreements to provide for the Scottish army in Ireland;[72] the establishing of a new lord lieutenant to undertake an English reconquest of Ireland in defiance of promises that it would be a British undertaking;[73] the standing down of the Committee of Both Kingdoms, the only coordinating body created in the war years;[74] and the continuing indifference of the English to Scots demands for the appointment of *conservatores pacis* or other joint bodies of parliamentary commissioners and councillors from the two kingdoms.[75] No wonder many lukewarm supporters of the Solemn League transferred their hopes for a federal unionist future from an alliance with the Long parliament to an alliance with a hopefully chastened and wiser king.[76]

Nothing illustrates more dramatically the unswerving commitment of the Covenanting leadership to federal unionism, to a single historical destiny, than their response to the trial and execution of Charles I. On the very day that news of the regicide reached Scotland, Charles II was proclaimed king of Great Britain and Ireland in Edinburgh, and less than two years later he swore, again as king of Great Britain and Ireland, to introduce the

71 This paragraph is based on a great deal of reading in primary and secondary sources. Among the most accessible of the latter are D. Stevenson, *The Scottish Revolution 1637–1644* (Newton Abbot, 1973); D. Stevenson, *Scottish Covenanters and Irish Confederates* (Belfast, 1980); and the essays by D. Stevenson ('The early Covenanters and the Federal Union of Britain') and by E. Cowan ('The Solemn League and Covenant') in R. Mason (ed.) *Scotland and England 1286–1815* (Edinburgh, 1986).

72 D. Stevenson, *Revolution and Counter-Revolution in Scotland 1644–1651* (London, 1977), chs 1–3; D. Stevenson, 'Financing the cause of the covenant, 1637–1651', *SHR* 51 (1952), pp.89–123.

73 *Journal of the House of Lords* VIII, 127.

74 M.A. Kishlansky, *The Rise of the New Model Army* (Cambridge, 1979), pp.164–7.

75 Donald, *An Uncounselled King*, pp.273–306.

76 Anglo-Scottish relations in the later 1640s need a complete new study. In the mean time the relevant chapters in S.R. Gardiner, *History of the Great Civil War* (4 vols; London, 1893), III and IV, and Stevenson, *Revolution and Counter-Revolution*, remain valuable.

covenants into all his kingdoms.[77] If the Scots had proclaimed Charles as king of Scotland but not of England and Ireland, the chances are they would have been left alone by the English parliament and army. It was because they saw no historical security or destiny for themselves outside a union that the Scots proclaimed Charles king of Britain and mobilized themselves once more for a third and fateful archipelagic civil war.

THE BRITISHNESS OF THE IRISH

The situation in Ireland is more complex, both in the sense that political fragmentation was more complete, with deep divisions within as well as between the various political cultures, and in the sense that the aspirations of all groups are less elemental than those of the covenanters in Scotland.[78] What can be said is that even in the extremities of 1648–50, Irish separatism fails to emerge.[79] In the 1680s one finds in Ireland those catholic nationalists willing to contemplate a severance of the links with the crown of England and the development of an independent Irish Commonwealth, perhaps under the protectorship of the king of France (in the 1640s it would have been the king of Spain).[80] The model would have been

77 *The Forme and Coronation of Charles II*, Aberdeen 1651: most accessible in a generally reliable transcript in J. Kerr, *Covenants and Covenanters* (Edinburgh, 1895), pp.386–9.

78 What follows is based largely on T.W. Moody, F.X. Martin and F.J. Byrne (eds) *New History of Ireland, III, 1534–1691* (Oxford, 1976) chs X–XIV and works cited there; and Stevenson, *Scottish Covenanters and Irish Confederates.*

79 I base this on my own reading of the two principal collections of papers relating to the Confederacy of Kilkenny: Sir John Gilbert, *History of the Irish Confederation and the War in Ireland 1641—1649* (7 vols; Dublin, 1882–91) – see e.g. II, pp.80, 210–12; III, pp.190–4, 263–4, 336–9 – and *Commentarius Rinuccinianus de sedis apostolicae legatione ad foederatos Hiberniae catholicos* (6 vols; Dublin, 1932–49) – see e.g. I, pp.314–191; II, pp.510–18. I am also grateful to Tadhg Ó hAnnracháin of University College, Dublin for his knowledgeable confirmation of this view. Tomás Ó Fiaich, 'Republicanism and separatism in the seventeenth century', in *Léachtaí Cholm Cille* (Maynooth, 1971), pp.74–91, argues for a republican tradition among Irish exiles in Spain, but his best efforts fail to establish that these stray writings took root in Ireland. The only evidence I know to the contrary is the example of a Limerick confederate who is alleged to have stated that the Irish aimed 'to have a free state to themselves as they had in Holland, and not to be tied to any prince whatsoever'. The source – from one of the Depositions taken down in the course of the investigations into the Massacres – is not a good one and this is one single example (cited in M. Perceval-Maxwell, 'Ireland and Scotland, 1638–1648', in Morrill (ed.) *Scottish National Covenant*, p.207).

80 J. Miller, 'The earl of Tyrconnel and James II's Irish policy 1685–1688', *HJ* 20 (1977), pp.821–3.

the fledgling Dutch Republic under the Pacification of Ghent of 1576, where the seventeen provinces threw over Spanish sovereignty and sought the protection of England or Austria. But in fact Irish separatism was almost as rare as Cornish or Yorkshire separatism.[81]

The failure of any group to promote such a solution in the 1640s is a deafening silence indeed. Instead all groups sought to redefine their relationship to the crown. Most confederates wished to emphasize the autonomy and sovereignty of the Irish crown, to end the dependency upon the English council, to exclude the claims of the English parliament to legislate for, let alone exercise jurisdiction over, the affairs of Ireland, and to guarantee that autonomy by constitutional changes which echoed those measures which had – by the reforms enshrined in the 1641 treaty of London – secured effective autonomy for the Scottish elite and Scottish indigenous institutions. Confederate leaders were *not* divided over the sort of Irish constitutional settlement they wanted; they had little interest in the sort of federal union schemes that the Scots saw as essential to a new stability.[82] None was so sanguine as to see the establishment of catholicism in all three kingdoms as a precondition for its survival in one. But confederate leaders were divided about how far they could and should join Charles I in a three-kingdom war to secure his outright military victory which to one group – made up mainly but not exclusively of Old English catholics – was seen as the key to a new stability in Ireland.

The main divisions among the Irish confederates concerned some purely Irish issues, the most important of which (dividing the Old English from the Gaelic Irish) was the issue of the restoration of church lands.[83] But the other issue was the archipelagic one. The clerical party around Rinuccini saw no reason to help Charles win

81 J.C. Beckett, 'The Confederation of Kilkenny reviewed', *HS* 2 (1959), pp.29–41, remains a marvellously clear and decisive assessment of the agreement on ends and disagreements on means among the confederates. It is best supplemented by J. Lowe, 'Charles I and the confederation of Kilkenny', *IHS* 14 (1964), pp.1–19; J.I. Casway, *Owen Roe O'Neill and the Struggle for Catholic Ireland* (Philadelphia, Pa, 1984), esp. pp.84–101; Ohlmeyer, *Randal MacDonnell*, chs 3–5.

82 For the details of the deal struck between the earl of Glamorgan and a majority of the confederates that guaranteed an Ireland run by and for the catholic Irish in the same way as the treaty of London guaranteed a Scotland run by and for the protestant Scots, see J. Lowe, 'The Glamorgan mission to Ireland 1645–6', *SH* (1964), pp.155–94. The difference was precisely that the confederates did not believe that the security of such a deal required a federal union of the English and Irish crowns.

83 Well rehearsed by Beckett, *Confederation*, pp.36–8. Beckett is at pains to show how the confederates sought to prevent divisions along the lines of Old English/Irish but he shows how these proved to be in vain.

his war in England. Their task was to use his weakness in England to secure maximum concessions in Ireland. Others saw this as short-sighted: reaching a winning compromise on Irish issues and helping him win in England were seen as the best guarantees of Irish liberties. Rinuccini's policy risked demanding more than he would ever honour and risked costing him the English war with the very consequences that were to ensure. Both sides remained committed to the confederate oath to uphold the crown. At most the Old English were (in the words of the confederate motto) *pro deo, pro rege, pro patria* and the clerical party *pro deo, pro patria, pro rege.*[84]

The Old English protestants and the rainbow coalitions of groups that Ormond gathered together were perhaps closest to the Scots in seeing a postwar settlement in terms of a new harmony of interests between the kingdoms, though it is not yet possible to assess precisely what Ormond had in mind. For example, Lord Inchiquin, who appeared to change sides at least four times in the 1640s, is best seen rather as a man whose preoccupations were with the defeat of catholicism and with the rights of self-determination of those already settled in Munster. This made him relatively indifferent as to which English protestants he could enlist as the agents of that victory; but also as someone determined to keep out an interloping lord lieutenant (Lord Lisle, 1646–7) who sought to take over in the name of families like the Boyles, Percivals and Jephsons whose landed interests straddled the Irish Sea.[85] However, Ormond appears to have developed a more straightforwardly pan-archipelagic stance: the Engagement of January 1648 was a strategy involving Hamilton and a group of repentant Scottish nobles, Ormond and his allies in Ireland and key members of the former Essex group in England. The document lays out a pan-archipelagic strategy for re-establishing royal authority in all three kingdoms, and a federated structure in Great Britain once the war was over. But no provision was made for the constitutional arrangements that would define Irish relations with England.[86]

The New English were divided too. There were certainly those who had welcomed (and had indeed commanded) the direct

84 For some key documents on this theme, see *CSP Ire 1633–47*, p.336; Gilbert, *Confederation and War*, II, pp.24–8, 34–41, 71–84, 210–12; *Commentarius Rinuccinianus*, pp.728–32.

85 Murphy, 'Munster protestants', pp.7–19.

86 Moody, Martin and Byrne (eds) *New History of Ireland, III*, chs XII–XIV and works cited there; Beckett, *Cavalier Duke*, chs 2–3. This paragraph is more than usually tentative and awaits the elucidation of Billy Kelly and others who are working on the subject.

intervention of the Long Parliament in the internal affairs of Ireland back in 1641 (most obviously in having Strafford impeached in an English parliament for treasons against the crown of Ireland). By the later 1640s they were the group who welcomed Viscount Lisle as parliament's lord lieutenant in Ireland, with a brief to crush the confederates and reward the English Adventurers. The implications of this for the separate or coordinate constitutional development of Ireland were sufficiently disturbing for many leading members of the protestant communities in Ireland (headed by those around the Irish protestant Lord Inchiquin in Munster), to cause fighting to break out between rival groups within the former pro-parliamentary groups. With the Inchiquin faction, perhaps more than with any other in Ireland in the 1640s, we find a group that tries to hold the Britishness of the crisis at bay; to talk about the distinctness of the Irish monarchy and a longing to solve Ireland's problems without reference to events across the water.[87]

None the less there were those at the time who were single-minded in seeing the affairs of Scotland and Ireland as at best a noisome intrusion into English affairs, to be pushed out of sight and as far as possible out of mind: these were the very army grandees and Long Parliament leaders whose little-Englander attitudes drove the covenanters to distraction. The hallmarks of men like Viscount Saye and the earl of Northumberland in the Lords and Pym and later Marten and Rigby (and perhaps even St John and Cromwell) in the Commons was a desire to use Scots military muscle to defeat the king of England, but not to honour any political (let alone religious) agreements with them that created any kind of federal union; and a refusal to find out about the complexities of Irish political culture. Ireland was to be conquered and raped, and a policy of religious apartheid developed to justify the mass expropriation of the native peoples.[88] To complete the picture they were determined to deny the rights of the Scots to any involvement in the government of post-conquest Ireland.

87 Murphy, 'Munster protestants', pp.9–20.

88 The spokesman for this party was very much Sir John Temple, whose *The Irish Rebellion* (London, 1646) needs much more attention than it has hitherto received. Other spokesmen for the view that the barbarism of the Irish permitted a wholesale expropriation include Henry Parker, *The Irish Massacre* (London, 1649) and John Milton, *Observations upon the Articles of Peace with the Irish Rebels* (London, 1649) reprinted in *Complete Prose Works of John Milton* (8 vols; New Haven, Conn., 1954–82), III, pp.259–334. For an interpretation of protestant attitudes that puts more stress on religious factors, T.C. Barnard, 'Crises of identity amongst Irish protestants', *P & P* 127 (1990), pp.39–83.

Their view was certainly not a holistic one. In 1640 these men were willing to barter with Charles: he could have the funds to raise a major royal army against the covenanters if they could have grievances settled. In 1641 they were grateful to the Scots for ensuring a long parliament but they stalled every attempt to negotiate clause eight of the treaty of London which would have redefined the relationship of the kingdoms.[89] It set the pattern for the years that followed. The terms of the Solemn League and Covenant were taken seriously by the English only so far as they advanced military victory and as soon as that was accomplished the parliament did two things which showed its true feelings: it stood down the Committee of Both Kingdoms and it appointed a new lord lieutenant for Ireland with a remit that excluded the Scots.

Perhaps even more telling, however, was what happened when such actions and the emasculation of the accords of the Westminster assembly and the proclamation of a measure of religious liberty drove the Scots into an alliance with Charles I. Once Cromwell and the New Model Army had defeated the Scots, they showed little interest in conquering Scotland or in incorporating it into a British state. They delightedly withdrew as soon as Argyll and his faction staged a coup in Edinburgh. Although 'our brothers in Scotland', he reported, 'were our greatest enemies, God has justified us in their sight; caused us to requite good for evil, causing them to acknowledge it publicly by acts of state, and privately'. Conquest, he continued, 'was not unfeasible, but I think not Christian'.[90] As David Stevenson put it, 'By requiting evil with good, Cromwell hoped he had put the Scots under an unbreakable moral obligation to live in friendship with England'.[91] The English had no interest in Scotland so long as it posed no threat to England. When they executed Charles I (Charles I of Scotland) they abolished monarchy in England and Ireland but were silent about Scotland. As far as they were concerned the Union of the Crowns had been severed and Scotland was free to go along its own line as a free independent state. As Portugal had been united to Spain in 1580 and resumed its own separate historical path in 1640, so Scotland was now free to go its own way.

89 The fullest account of these proceedings is in Donald, *An Uncounselled King*, pp.273–306. The analysis by Scally in 'Political career' is also important.

90 W.C. Abbott, *The Writings and Speeches of Oliver Cromwell* (4 vols; Cambridge, Mass., 1937–47), I, pp. 677–8.

91 D. Stevenson, 'Cromwell, Scotland and Ireland', in J. Morrill (ed.) *Oliver Cromwell and the English Revolution* (Harlow, 1990), p.154.

The Little Englander politicians and generals who executed Charles were thus stunned and disoriented when the Scottish executive (on 5 February 1649, the very day that news reached Edinburgh) proclaimed Charles II as 'king of Great Britain, France and Ireland', and when the Scots went on in due course to crown Charles at Scone with a solemn oath to give his assent to acts to be passed 'enjoining [the covenants] in my other dominions'. Only this forced the English into reluctant conquest and incorporative union with its northern protestant neighbour.[92] What is amazing is the lack of intellectual fervour, enthusiasm, curiosity about the process of absorption, and the indifference in England to sustaining it beyond 1660. The unions of the 1650s involved the English in a sort of shotgun bigamy.[93]

CONCLUSION

The civil war thus became far more than three conflicts abutting one another and intersecting with one another, but less than a single conflict with English, Irish and Scottish theatres. It is a paradigm of the paradoxes we face. Who in 1630, 1660, 1690 or 1720 saw a historical identity for England, Ireland, Scotland and Wales outside a linked polity? Just as members of all traditions within the Church of England have been resigned for centuries to the expectation that their destiny was to share their present and future in irritated coexistence with contrary traditions, so early modern inhabitants of these islands were resigned to an irritated coexistence with those whom dynastic roulette and assertions of power had brought together under one sovereign lord.

This chapter has not suggested that there is no such thing as English, Irish, Scottish and Welsh history; only that in addition to those histories there is a British history which is concerned with how the component parts of these islands 'interacted so as to modify the conditions of one another's existence'.[94] This chapter also suggests two rather different things. First, that some of the

92 Morrill, *Nature of the English Revolution,* pp.116–17. Note that he was proclaimed and crowned as king of Great Britain not as king of Scotland and England (and cf. how, even after the incorporating union of 1652–4, the official title of the new state is the 'Commonwealth of England, Scotland and Ireland'.)

93 D. Hirst, 'The English republic and the meaning of Britain', *JMH* 66, 3 (1994), pp. 451–86.

94 Pocock, 'Limits and divisions', p.317.

most stubborn and insoluble problems in the history of each kingdom require a British dimension to be fully understood; and second, that when we move from the history of state formation to the history of political, religious and social culture we need to remember that 'British history denotes the historiography of no single nation but of a problematic and uncompleted experiment in the creation and interaction of several nations'.[95] My contention would be that historians of England need to learn more of the former, and historians of Scotland, Ireland and (perhaps) Wales more of the latter. The English have to overcome their indifference to what is happening elsewhere in the archipelago. This is not a problem for the historians of the northern and western kingdoms and principalities. Coping with, devising strategies to deal with, the reality of the superior might of the English is part of the warp and woof of Irish, Scottish and Welsh historiography. But there remains a tendency in Irish, Scottish and Welsh historiography to play down the effects on the Irish, Scottish, Welsh and English peoples of the dialectical process involved, the degree to which native cultures did not heroically resist acculturation and integration but interacted so as to experience profound change without disintegrating. Englishness is self-evidently the product of complex interactions of peoples and cultures; but Scottishness, Irishness and Welshness too are the product of complex interactions of peoples, one of them the English. Let us then seek to build a 'British history' that sets the whole of the British Isles into a single historical context and which teaches us – to adapt Robin Frame's aphorism[96] – not only to busy ourselves in our rooms and not only to look over partition walls but also to do some thinking about the design of the building itself.

95 ibid, p.318.
96 Frame, 'Aristocracies', p.154.

CHAPTER TWO

Tudor state formation and the shaping of the British Isles

Steven G. Ellis
University College Galway

Implicit in much writing on British history is the assumption that lowland England was the core region of an embryonic English state. From Anglo-Saxon times, it was the political centre of an imperium whose frontiers were constantly shifting, the one permanent feature in a changing political landscape. Under the Tudors, it is argued, this imperium finally achieved modernity and maturity as a centralized English nation-state. In so far as the focus of this narrative shifts from lowland England, it is to consider the strategy by which the different peripheries were gradually incorporated one by one into the centre by the successful imposition there of lowland norms and values. Thus lowland England was, as it were, the sun around which revolved a constantly changing number of satellites, attracted by the benefits of English civility radiating from the centre. Closely linked to this assumption about core and peripheries is a second supposition about state formation which also requires more careful consideration than it usually receives, the notion of progress by centralization and uniformity. Allegedly the Tudors created a more peaceful civil society by breaking down feudal particularism, taming over-mighty subjects, and extending uniform English structures of government throughout the Tudor state.[1]

This chapter offers a reappraisal of Tudor responses to the problem of state formation. It surveys inherited assumptions about the problem, together with Tudor developments, but it also reverses

1 See esp. G.R. Elton, *Reform and Reformation: England, 1509–1558* (London, 1977); A.G.R. Smith, *The Emergence of a Nation-State: The Commonwealth of England 1529–1660* (London, 1984).

the perspective from which events are normally viewed, looking at developments from the outside in. This perspective permits a more balanced discussion of the collective 'pull' exerted by the planets on the sun, as it were, particularly those like Ireland or the far north of England, which for long resisted the attractions of the centre. At the heart of this re-evaluation is the thesis that the outlying territories were central, rather than peripheral, to the problems of Tudor government. Lowland England, it is argued, was a wholly exceptional region of the Tudor state, and much more easily governed than the borderlands. It would be surprising indeed if Tudor government were not effective and successful in that region. Thus traditional analyses of Tudor developments are quite misleading.[2] Concentration on the south-east appears to vindicate the strategies pursued, to minimize the problems encountered or created, and generally to exaggerate the regime's successes. In addition, the Tudor experience of state formation also left English politicians blind or insensitive to the rather different problems of multiple monarchy presented by the dynastic union of 1603. By shifting the focus to the peripheries, however, a different picture emerges – one that identifies the failings and limitations of Tudor government as well as its achievements. Broadly, the Tudor approach may be characterized as state-building by integration and assimilation. It can be divided into two phases. The early-Tudor phase, lasting until 1534, witnessed piecemeal and conservative tinkering with the inherited structures and problems. It was followed by a much more radical, interventionist strategy which placed great strains on relations between the crown and the political communities of the borderlands.

THE PROBLEMS OF THE EARLY TUDORS

In 1485 Henry Tudor assumed control of a disparate group of territories which had been annexed piecemeal to the crown of England over the previous four centuries. These lands may be divided into two groups. To the south there were the Channel Isles

2 cf. M.A.R. Graves, *The Tudor Parliaments: Crown, Lords and Commons, 1485–1603* (London, 1985); J. Loach, *Parliament under the Tudors* (Oxford, 1991); A. Fletcher, *Tudor Rebellions* (3rd edn, London, 1983), which ignore parliaments and rebellions in Ireland.

and Calais, which were all that remained of the erstwhile Lancastrian empire. Under the early Tudors, the defence and recovery of the French territories remained a high priority. Henry VIII in particular spent millions of pounds in the pursuit of empire, attempting to recover Normandy and Gascony and so to add substance to traditional English claims to the crown of France; in the event his efforts produced only two short-lived occupations of continental towns – Tournai and Boulogne.[3] To the north and west lay another group of territories, of far greater extent, but traditionally a much lower priority for the government. This second group of territories was the product of intermittent attempts by medieval English kings to extend their dominion throughout the British Isles. Yet here the English military effort had been much more sporadic and small scale, reflecting the region's relative unimportance strategically, the poor quality of much of the land, and the fragmentation of power there. There were three borderlands. Wales was divided between approximately 130 marcher lordships in the east, and the principality established by Edward I. This division reflected an earlier military frontier between the original areas of English settlement and that part still controlled by native Welsh princes before the Edwardian conquest; but under the early Tudors its significance was chiefly administrative.[4] By contrast, the *raison d'être* of the other two borderlands was still primarily military. The far north of England formed a buffer zone between lowland England and the independent kingdom of the Scots. In Ireland, the Tudors shared a frontier with the Gaelic peoples, a politically fragmented tribal society which spanned the North Channel. The most powerful Gaelic chief, MacDonald Lord of the Isles, threatened both English power in Ulster and even the Scottish monarchy; but the English lordship of Ireland gave the crown control over the more fertile and strategically more important eastern and southern parts opposite England and Wales, thus denying the island's use to any foreign prince.

Although traditionally marginalized in Tudor surveys, these borderlands actually comprised over half the geographical area of the Tudor state. The justification for this treatment is apparently that each particular borderland presented an unique range of

3 J.J. Scarisbrick, *Henry VIII* (London, 1968), esp. chs 2, 13; C.G. Cruickshank, *Army Royal: Henry VIII's Invasion of France, 1513* (Oxford, 1969); C.G. Cruickshank, *The English Occupation of Tournai, 1513–1519* (Oxford, 1971).

4 R.R. Davies, *The Age of Conquest: Wales, 1063–1415* (Oxford, 1991); G. Williams, *Recovery, Reorientation and Reformation: Wales c.1415–1642* (Oxford, 1987).

problems for royal government. For instance, Celtic languages and culture distinguished Ireland and Wales not only from the English north, but also from each other. Problems of defence were most acute in the far north, but Ireland was geographically separate, and the Welsh marches were politically highly fragmented. Superficially too, the institutions of government in the three regions were also different: Ireland had a separate central administration based in Dublin, the far north of England had wardens of the marches, and Wales had marcher lordships.[5]

Yet these three regions had much in common, in terms of geography, politics and society, and therefore in the kinds of problems which their rule presented to the Tudor regime. Geographically, they were predominantly pastoral regions of mountain, forest, and bog, all remote from London, with a harsher climate and poorer soils than the rich arable land of lowland England. Thus, the settlement patterns and social structures of the borderlands were also different: the numerous towns and prosperous nucleated villages of the heavily manorialized lowlands gave place to a more desolate, sparsely populated landscape of isolated farmsteads, large parishes and manors, and few substantial gentry or major towns. The more turbulent conditions and fragmented power structures of the borderlands encouraged the maintenance of extended kinship bonds, consolidated patterns of noble landholding, and strong landlord–tenant ties. In short, these were more militarized communities than the English lowlands. The Tudors depended heavily on the borderlands in wartime for troops and military service, so enhancing their political influence, but they also feared that the great accumulations of power and authority in the hands of over-mighty subjects might constitute a challenge to royal authority, as occurred in the Wars of the Roses.[6]

5 Ibid; A.J. Pollard, *North-Eastern England during the Wars of the Roses* (Oxford, 1990); S.G. Ellis, *Tudor Ireland: Crown, Community and the Conflict of Cultures, 1470–1603* (London, 1985).

6 The points in this and the following two paragraphs are developed in S.G. Ellis, *Tudor Frontiers and Noble Power: The Making of the British State* (Oxford, 1995). See also S.G. Ellis, *The Pale and the Far North: Government and Society in Two Early Tudor Borderlands* (Galway, 1988). To divide the Tudor state into an English lowland zone surrounded by borderlands is of course a gross oversimplification of a much more complex pattern. The English lowlands also included regions like the Fens with different patterns of land utilization and social structures which were unlike those of mixed farming regions. The borderlands also had some fertile plains, notably the four shires of the English Pale in Ireland, but none was large enough to allow the lowlanders there to exercise the same political dominance as the English lowlands did over the borderlands. In some respects too, a division between 'feudal' and kin-based structures of society is useful, but this too has its limitations.

In governmental terms too, they were areas in which the traditional English system of administration was only partially in force. Each region had its own system of march law and other regional customs. They were only marginally represented in the English parliament; mostly there were no justices of the peace (JPs) or quarter sessions, but many feudal lordships where judicial and military power rested with the local lord. The purpose of this dual system of administration was primarily military: it was much less effective in maintaining law and order. Problems arose, for instance, over the extradition of offenders from one jurisdiction to another and over neglect by absentee lords. The last phase of medieval English expansion had seen a more consistent preference for English shire government, which had been established in the principality of Wales, parts of Ireland, and Cumbria, but this created problems of a different sort. Many basic tasks of law and order were reserved for itinerant justices at their assizes, held once or twice yearly, and they depended on an elaborate system of writs issued from distant administrative capitals. The system reflected the early development in lowland England of a comparatively centralized kingdom, in which a culturally homogeneous people was governed through an uniform system of administration. Yet centralized control worked much less effectively in the different conditions elsewhere. Frequently, assizes were cancelled because of war and disorders, sheriffs required a posse to serve writs, and quarter sessions were not kept because there were too few gentry to serve on the peace commissions. Overall, the basic problem was that the administrative structures devised for lowland England were unsuited to the rest of the Tudor state. Local conditions demanded a devolution of power, but political experience, ideology, and administrative practice all suggested increased centralization. The early Tudor response was a sporadic and only partially successful search for a solution which would balance these conflicting pressures.

THE DIVERGENT ENGLISHRIES

Tudor officials were accustomed to think of England as an island, rather than simply that part of Britain colonized by the English before 1066.[7] Accordingly, for England's dealings with the rest of

7 R.A. Griffiths, '*This Royal Throne of Kings, This Scept'red Isle': The English Realm and Nation in the Later Middle Ages* (Swansea, 1983); H. Kearney, *The British Isles: A History of Four Nations* (Cambridge, 1989), pp.1–9.

the British Isles, there seemed no need to maintain a standing army or even the normal international frontier arrangements between states in continental Europe. In Wales, the consequences of this misconception were not too serious. The native population had been only partially assimilated or displaced by English settlers. Thus in the Welsh marches there existed side-by-side separate communities – Englishries and Welshries – with different cultures, languages and laws. Yet since there was no longer a military frontier, the chief result was a perpetuation of the existing disorders and marcher forms of society.[8]

In the far north of England and Ireland, however, the consequences were more serious. The piecemeal and partial nature of English settlement in Ireland and the failure to conquer Scotland meant that the English state's northern and western boundaries were marked by two long landed frontiers. The Anglo-Scottish border was over 110 miles long from Berwick-on-Tweed to the Solway Firth; the Anglo-Gaelic marches in Ireland were still more remote, extended and discontinuous. International frontiers were commonplace throughout Europe, but these were not normal frontiers, nor were England's relations with Scotland and Gaelic Ireland normal. Traditional English claims to empire throughout the British Isles meant that instead of cooperation and mutual recognition, England's relations with these polities were usually poor. Specifically, English kings claimed an overlordship over Scotland and tended to treat their Scottish counterparts as disobedient vassals: between 1333 and 1502 there was no formal peace between England and Scotland, only periodic truces and temporary abstinences from warfare. Gaelic chiefs were treated even more contemptuously, and their titles to land and property were not recognized. Power in Gaelic Ireland was so fragmented that there was no one figure with whom the king's deputy could negotiate: Ireland was indeed 'a land of many marches', in each of which the balance of power was constantly shifting. Even the comparatively stable Scottish monarchy, however, was frequently too weak to control its border subjects. Thus in both regions the English government was encouraged to secure its own ends by mischief and interference.[9]

8 R.R. Davies, *Lordship and Society in the March of Wales 1282–1400* (Oxford, 1978); R.R. Davies, 'Frontier arrangements in fragmented societies: Ireland and Wales', in R. Bartlett and A. MacKay (eds) *Medieval Frontier Societies* (Oxford, 1989), pp.77–100.

9 Ellis, *Pale and the Far North*; Bartlett and MacKay (eds) *Medieval Frontier Societies*; R. Frame, 'Power and society in the lordship of Ireland, 1272–1377', *P&P* 76 (1977), pp.3–33 (quotation on p.32).

The result was that large parts of these northern and western borderlands were war zones, where endemic insecurity led to the emergence of highly militarized forms of society like the border surnames.[10] The crown's limited financial resources and the sheer length of the frontiers precluded the construction of an elaborate system of defences manned by a permanent garrison, as at Calais. Certainly, garrisons guarded the main routes of entry, but frontier defence relied chiefly on the march itself – the territory protected by castles and fortified towers and extending many miles inland – and its local population, who were obliged, like other Englishmen, to do military service in defence of their country. This defensive system was sufficient to exclude petty raiders and to delay major invasions for long enough for the authorities to concentrate a superior force. Yet the traditional arrangements for border rule relied on deploying in the crown's interest the political influence of the great provincial magnates which rested on their consolidated holdings, strong castles and numerous tenantry in the region. Their cooperation was secured by the creation of special offices and institutions which were financially and politically attractive to the nobles. These included the great feudal franchises such as Durham or Tipperary, the lieutenancies and the wardenships of the marches. Thus, although the borderers had the same rights and privileges as Englishmen elsewhere, in practice they were partly excluded from English law and government as it 'normally' operated, so accentuating still further the socio-political differences between the English lowlands and the borderlands. The tensions between the claims of English subjects and the constraints imposed by marcher conditions lay at the heart of the problem of the borderlands.[11]

For its part, the government was increasingly disposed to view the border problem as one of cultural degeneracy by the inhabitants there; this in turn shaped its response. Tudor officials shared the assumption of magistrates all over Europe that

10 The border surnames were a clan-based society living in the marches on both sides of the Anglo-Scottish frontier. For a comparison with the English marcher lineages in Ireland, see Ellis, *Pale and the Far North.*

11 A. Goodman (ed.) *War and Border Societies in the Middle Ages* (Gloucester, 1992); A. Goodman, 'The Anglo-Scottish marches in the fifteenth century: a frontier society?', in R.A. Mason (ed.) *Scotland and England, 1286–1815* (Edinburgh, 1987), pp.18–33; R. Frame, 'Military service in the lordship of Ireland 1290–1360: institutions and society on the Anglo-Gaelic frontier', in Bartlett and MacKay (eds) *Medieval Frontier Societies,* pp.101–26; J.F. Lydon, 'The problem of the frontier in medieval Ireland', *Topic 13* (Washington, DC, 1967), pp.5–22.

civilization resided chiefly in towns – reflected, for instance, in their separate representation in parliament – or at least in the peaceful tenant villages of the arable lowlands. Experience seemed to confirm this: public order and central control in the borderlands were invariably less secure than in the south-east. Official reports attributed the disorders, not to failings in crown policy, but to the borderers' wildness and lawlessness. In all three regions, moreover, the king's loyal English lieges were surrounded by enemies and rebels. Giraldus Cambrensis had regarded the Welsh as an untamed and undisciplined people, living like animals. Though now partially anglicized, they remained light-headed and liable to rebel. Likewise the Irish were consigned to the lower links of the great chain of being: Polydore Vergil described them as 'wild men of the woods', 'savage, rude and uncouth'. So too the Scots who infiltrated the English marches in large numbers were seen as beggarly rogues, reivers and thieves, who undermined border defence. The Scots were aliens, but the mere Welsh and mere Irish were also disabled at law from holding land or office within the Englishries. And despite selfless efforts by successive kings to bring the natives to a knowledge of their allegiance and the benefits of English civility, they persisted in their evil ways and beastly habits and also corrupted the king's true English subjects living near them. In these circumstances, the king's officers felt, the proper course was to strengthen the common law and to execute sharp justice among them, both to civilize the natives and to recover the king's subjects to their allegiance.[12]

Unfortunately, 'good governance' and 'indifferent justice' cost time and money, and early Tudor priorities lay elsewhere. Henry VII was primarily concerned to secure the new dynasty against internal and external enemies. His border policies were essentially conservative, though he enjoyed some success in Wales where his Welsh birth and descent were an advantage. Traditionally, only freeborn Englishmen were allowed access to the king's courts, and the mere Welsh and mere Irish were treated like serfs and prevented from holding many royal offices. In some respects, Henry VII's belated sale of charters (1504–7), granting whole communities

12 Felipe Fernández-Armesto, *Before Columbus: Exploration and Colonisation from the Mediterranean to the Atlantic* (London, 1987), pp.224–6, 240–1; J. Th. Leerssen, *Mere Irish & fíor-Ghael: Studies in the Idea of Irish Nationality* (Amsterdam, 1986); Davies, *Age of Conquest*, pp. 112–13, 139–41, 150–2, 161–2; A. Cosgrove (ed.) *A New History of Ireland, II, Medieval Ireland 1169–1534* (Oxford, 1987), pp.60–1, 242; Polydore Vergil, *Anglica Historia*, ed. D. Hay (London, 1950), p.79; Ellis, *Pale and the Far North.*

in north Wales the status of freeborn Englishmen, anticipated the more general emancipation of the Welsh in 1536. Yet charters had long been sold to individuals: 'wild Irish' living among the English of Ireland, for instance, could also purchase their freedom. Henry VII also restored Edward IV's device of regional councils supervising government, but the decisive factor in the rule of the early Tudor borderlands was the king's handling of the great territorial magnates there. In Wales, starting in 1490, the king exacted from marcher lords an 'indenture for the marches', requiring each lord to exact surety from his men for good behaviour, due appearance in court, and to surrender suspects on request for trial elsewhere. No doubt Henry VII's personal application to the details of government had some impact in curbing the country's lawlessness, but Henry VIII had little interest in this work. Thus a more important development was that many of the larger lordships came into crown hands by inheritance or forfeiture. With the attainder and execution of the third duke of Buckingham in 1521 the last of the great marcher lords disappeared. This addressed the underlying causes of the region's lawlessness, the fragmentation of authority there. Wales was increasingly bereft of great territorial magnates capable of challenging royal power, and these changes allowed the council greater scope in supervising lordships in the king's hands. After Prince Arthur's death, it continued to operate (1502–4) under a president, Bishop Smyth of Lincoln, as it did after 1509, albeit ineffectually, when it became the king's council.[13]

By contrast, the north of England and Ireland had to be defended as well as governed. In the north of England, for instance, large tracts of marchland lay waste in 1485 following the recent Scottish war.[14] Henry VII's main priority, however, was to stifle any internal challenge to his position from Yorkist sympathizers in these regions. Accordingly, power was deliberately diffused in the north, financial subventions were reduced, and reliance on the regional magnates was curtailed. The chief royal castles of Berwick-on-Tweed and Carlisle, with their garrisons, were placed under separate royal constables.[15] As lieutenant, Henry appointed a rank outsider, Thomas Howard, earl of Surrey, after

13 Williams, *Recovery, Reorientation and Reformation*, chs 8–11.

14 For example, *Calendar of inquisitions post mortem, Henry VII*, I, no.157; III, nos 7–28.

15 R.L. Storey, 'The wardens of the marches of England towards Scotland, 1377–1489', *EHR* 72 (1957), pp.608–9, PRO, SP 1/12 f49 (*LP Hen. VIII*, II, no.1365); A. Conway, *Henry VII's Relations with Scotland and Ireland, 1485–98* (Cambridge, 1932).

the murder in 1489 of Henry Percy, earl of Northumberland. His salary in wartime was only £1,000 a year. Essentially this appointment was an extension of Richard III's policy for the west march, where a minor peer, Thomas, Lord Dacre, was appointed lieutenant, also with a greatly reduced salary. Until 1525, the two most powerful northern families, the Nevilles and the Percies, were excluded from the wardenships that were traditionally theirs.[16]

These changes resulted in a significant weakening, not only of noble influence there, but also of the entire marches. As the Yorkist threat collapsed, so too did law and order. In the west, Dacre held the strategically vital baronies of Burgh and Gilsland, but (until Henry VII restored his wife's Greystoke inheritance) he lacked the resources even to defend his own estates properly, let alone maintain good rule.[17] Only five commissions of the peace were issued for Cumberland and Westmorland throughout the reign, and there were so few JPs that quarter sessions were rarely held. Instead murders were followed by feuds or financial compositions.[18] Across the Pennines, extensive liberty jurisdictions hindered the work of government, rather like the Welsh marches. Surrey found that the king's commission was no substitute for a territorial power base in the region. The king resorted to the ancient practice of farming the shrievalties, and from 1506 Nicholas Ridley of Willimoteswick, a lawless borderer, paid 100 marks a year to be sheriff of Northumberland. Between 1461 and 1515 no sheriff or escheator of Northumberland accounted at the exchequer, and by 1526 quarter sessions had not been kept for a long time.[19]

Only a firm truce (1500) and then peace (1502) with Scotland obviated worse disorders, but then Surrey was replaced by Archbishop Savage of York, appointed president of a restored northern council in 1501. The council prevented disorders from spreading into Yorkshire, to which its authority was restricted, but it

16 Storey, 'Wardens of the marches', pp.604–9; M. Condon, 'Ruling élites in the reign of Henry VII', in C. Ross (ed.) *Patronage, Pedigree and Power in Later Medieval England* (Gloucester, 1979), pp.116–20; PRO, E403/2558, ff51, 58, 69, 75v.

17 Ellis, *Tudor Frontiers and Noble Power*, ch.3.

18 PRO, SP 1/37, ff250–1 (*LP Hen. VIII*, IV(i), no.2052); R.L. Storey, *The Reign of Henry VII* (London, 1968), p.149; J.F. Curwen, 'Isel Hall', *Transactions of the Cumberland and Westmorland Antiquarian and Archaeological Society*, ns 11 (1911), p.123; Cumbria CRO Carlisle, MS D/Lons/L LO 117; Castle Howard MS A1/182.

19 *LP Hen. VIII* IV(i), no.2435; *Calendar of Close Rolls, 1500–09*, no.657; PRO, E36/214, pp.397, 403; SP 1/11, ff4–6 (*LP Hen. VIII*, II, no.596); Storey, *Reign of Henry VII*, pp.149–50; John Hodgson, *A History of Northumberland* (3 pts in 7 vols; Newcastle, 1820–5), I, i pp.363–6; Condon, 'Ruling élites', p.117.

lapsed again with Henry VII's death.[20] In the west, Dacre was promoted warden, and allowed to farm the shrievalty of Cumberland and the captaincy of Carlisle, so reducing the king's charges and concentrating power in his hands.[21] Indeed, from 1511 until his death in 1525, Lord Thomas usually acted as warden-general of all three marches. This would have been an impossible task if Henry VIII had expected Dacre to discharge effectively all aspects of the warden's duties. In fact, the young king was primarily interested in military matters, and his belligerent foreign policy soon breathed new life into the 'auld alliance' between France and Scotland. Although superseded for major campaigns, Dacre otherwise defended the English marches with minimal assistance from the king, he intrigued against the French party, and made the Scottish marches ungovernable. In the process, he built up his own position, exploiting his public authority and private resources. A programme of castle-building and military reorganization on the Dacre estates transformed Dacre into a powerful regional magnate, able to raise 5,000 men to invade Scotland from his battle-hardened tenantry. Yet he was hard put to control Northumberland from his modest territorial base around Morpeth. In consequence, the marches remained lawless and disturbed, and after Dacre's dismissal in 1525, allegedly for misconduct, bands of up to 400 thieves pillaged the countryside around Durham and Newcastle. It took a military campaign to subdue them.[22] Thus the first forty years of Tudor rule saw a disastrous collapse of 'good governance' in the far north of England.

In English Ireland a similar crisis of lordship had occurred rather earlier, following the Gaelic revival, the ending of the traditional financial and military subventions from England, and the lordship's important role in the Wars of the Roses. Edward IV's eventual solution had been to entrust the governorship to the Fitzgeralds of Kildare. Of the three Irish-based earls, Kildare was best placed, from his estates in the English Pale, to defend the lordship on the reduced terms now offered. Short of restoring the old subventions, Henry VII had little option but to reappoint the eighth earl as deputy. He even overlooked Kildare's leading role in the Yorkist

20 Condon, 'Ruling élites', pp.117–18; Storey, *Reign of Henry VII*, pp.87, 149.

21 PRO, E101/413/2/3, pp.63, 133, 221; E101/414/16, f120v; E101/415/3, ff243v, 292; E404/80, no.267; *Calendar of Close Rolls, 1500–09*, no.602.

22 S.G. Ellis, 'A border baron and the Tudor state: the rise and fall of Lord Dacre of the North', *HJ* 35 (1992), pp.253–77.

invasion of 1487, after Lambert Simnel had been crowned King Edward VI of England in Dublin. When, however, Kildare reacted equivocally to another Yorkist pretender, Perkin Warbeck, he was dismissed from office (1492). In Ireland, it proved easier to develop good relations with Kildare than to find an effective replacement for him. Sir Edward Poynings's little army of 650 men cost Henry about £7,000 (sterling) per year (1494–5), and after he had lifted Warbeck's siege of Waterford, he was recalled. Kildare was married to Henry's kinswoman, given a generous grant of crown lands, and following guarantees for his good conduct, he was reappointed deputy.[23]

Thereafter the king exhibited only a sporadic interest in Irish affairs, as did Henry VIII until 1519. Despite the absence of subventions from England, the concentration of power in local hands, and the political stability that ensued from a good working relationship between king and magnate, ensured that the lordship was actually more effectively governed than under the traditional indenture system. Successive earls exploited their position as governor to recover from the Gaelic Irish and rebuild ancestral estates and castles, to strengthen the Pale marches, and to expand into Gaelic Leinster, the midlands, and east Ulster. Although Henry VII's Irish policies were characterized by the same overriding concern for dynastic security as in the north of England, the results were less disastrous in Ireland. In part this was because the fluidity of the Anglo-Gaelic marches and the relative weakness of individual Gaelic chieftaincies gave Kildare more leverage in Gaelic Ireland. The earl built up a Gaelic clientage network, sometimes cemented by marriage alliances, to strengthen border defence in a way which was only partially possible in the Scottish borders. And the ninth earl, with an income exceeding 2,000 marks sterling per year, stood head and shoulders above any other noble in Ireland.[24] Thus, as with Lord Dacre, long tenure of office helped to transform a local noble into a great regional magnate; but the personal system of defences and alliances which each magnate built up to offset the shortcomings of royal government made their eventual replacement extremely difficult, as Henry VIII discovered in the 1520s.

23 Ellis, *Tudor Ireland*, ch.3.
24 ibid, ch.4; Ellis, *Tudor Frontiers and Noble Power*, ch.4.

HENRY VIII

If Henry VII did little to tackle underlying border problems, at least he expected little more than loyalty from his officers there. By contrast, Henry VIII could be much more demanding, and the 1530s saw fundamental changes. The new king showed little real interest in the borderlands until 1525. Then, with the ending of the French and Scottish wars, attention switched to problems of internal order and, increasingly with the divorce crisis and the Reformation, of internal security. The initial response was to revive the Yorkist conciliar initiative and to replace the established ruling family with another noble. These quasi-bureaucratic initiatives were weakly supported, and in each borderland the principal result was to antagonize established local interests. In Wales, a remodelled council was established at Ludlow, with Princess Mary as figurehead, resulting in a feud between Lord Ferrers and Sir Rhys ap Thomas's disappointed grandson, Rhys ap Gruffydd.[25]

In the north of England the king's son, created duke of Richmond, was dispatched to Sheriff Hutton to head a new council, which in turn supervised the marches. The appointment as deputy-wardens of the earls of Westmorland and Cumberland antagonized the Percies and Dacres, however, and the resultant disorders soon forced the king to back down. In late 1527 the council's jurisdiction over the marches was curtailed; William, Lord Dacre, was appointed warden of the west marches and, after renewed feuding with Clifford, earl of Cumberland, also captain of Carlisle (1529). In the east, the earl of Northumberland received the wardenship on greatly improved terms to help him restore order. These changes strengthened the marches at a time when deteriorating relations with Scotland were leading to renewed war (1532–4), this time over disputed territory known as the Debateable Land.[26]

Affairs were no better in Ireland, where the king's insensitive handling of Kildare (charged, like Dacre, with maladministration) frustrated successive experiments with the Butler earl as governor (1522–4, 1528–9), and with Richmond as absentee head of an

25 Williams, *Recovery, Reorientation and Reformation*, ch.10; G. Williams, *Wales and the Act of Union* (Bangor, 1992), pp.5–8.

26 R.R. Reid, *The King's Council in the North* (London, 1921), ch.5; Ellis, 'Border baron', pp.269–73; M. James, *Society, Politics and Culture: Studies in Early Modern England* (Cambridge, 1986), pp.80–2, 95, 98–9, *LP Hen. VIII*, IV(iii), nos 5906(6), 5952.

executive 'secret council' (1529–30) – a weak imitation of the northern conciliar experiment. Kildare's obstructive attitude earned him lengthy periods of detention in England (1519–23, 1526–30), interspersed with a short spell as deputy (1524–6); but as the lordship's precarious peace degenerated into feuds, disorder and Gaelic raids, the king was obliged to send back Kildare with the master of the ordnance and 300 men to restore order. Very soon, the cost of this experiment led to Kildare's reappointment as governor (1532–4).[27]

Overall, therefore, Henry VIII's handling of the borderlands was inept. The Reformation crisis rapidly led to a breakdown in all three regions, forcing the king into administrative reform and a more interventionist strategy. In each case the new structures strengthened central control and reduced aristocratic influence, but they also increased political tensions, cost more and did not necessarily result in stronger government.

In Ireland and the north of England, the charges of treason levelled simultaneously (May 1534) against Kildare and Dacre look like a pre-emptive strike by the king against potentially the most dangerous of the nobles suspected of plotting against him. Dacre was arrested immediately after the conclusion of peace with Scotland. Although dismissed from office and fined £10,000 sterling, his unexpected acquittal on the main charge of making private treaties with Scots enemies in wartime left the king still dependent on his cooperation to govern the west marches but unable to use him as warden. Sir Thomas Wharton eventually urged that Dacre's Cumberland estates should be 'exchanged' by the crown so that the warden could rule the marches effectively.[28]

By contrast, Kildare's resistance to his impending dismissal led to a major rebellion which took fourteen months and cost the king £40,000 sterling to suppress. The earl's destruction undermined the system of defences and alliances by which English rule had been consolidated during his ascendancy. Government through an outside deputy and a remodelled council was no substitute for a local magnate with royal support, and the dissolution of the monasteries further disrupted traditional power structures. Gaelic chiefs exploited the resultant crisis of lordship to encroach on the English marches. Thus the government was forced to maintain a

27 Ellis, *Tudor Ireland*, ch.5.

28 Ellis, 'Border baron', pp.253, 270–5; LP *Hen. VIII*, XVIII (i), no.799; SP *Hen. VIII*, V, 309.

permanent garrison there, usually around 500 men before 1547. As the wasted marchlands confiscated from Kildare and the church yielded far less than the additional costs of an outside governor and garrison, Ireland now became an increasing drain on English finances. The crown, however, remained generally unwilling to accept this financial deficit as the price of increased control: hence the general neglect of Ireland, interspersed with frenzied bursts of activity and unexpected reversals of policy, which characterized Tudor rule there after 1534.[29]

In many ways northern developments followed a similar pattern, but there were significant differences. By 1536 the government had moved much further in strengthening royal control in response to the Reformation crisis. The suppression of the liberties and lesser monasteries, the Statute of Uses, and taxation in peacetime had followed the royal divorce and supremacy and the curbing of noble power. Thus rebel demands in the Pilgrimage reflected a similar combination of noble, regional and religious grievances, but were more specific and broadly based than in Ireland. They demanded a parliament at York or Nottingham, for instance, to redress grievances and repeal unpopular legislation. Throughout the revolt the great regional magnates lay low, and in Cumbria socio-economic grievances were prominent among the peasantry; but without active noble support the northern council proved powerless to contain rebellion.[30] This pattern of noble-inspired rebellion in defence of provincial autonomy was to be a recurring feature of the border response to Tudor centralization, and presented a most serious challenge to the regime. In the ensuing reorganization of northern government, the king was likewise prepared initially to pay for increased control. A remodelled council and gentlemen deputy-wardens replaced the ineffectual Cumberland and the recently deceased Northumberland, but the changes again undermined traditional structures of lordship in the marches, creating a power vacuum which the government attempted to fill by feeing the local gentry. While peace held with Scotland, the effects were not too disastrous, but renewed war after 1541 forced the king to abandon conciliar supervision of the wardenries and to entrust defence to a southern noble with a substantial garrison. Thus the overall impact of these changes was

29 Ellis, *Tudor Ireland*, ch.5.

30 Fletcher, *Tudor Rebellions*, pp.17–37, 108–14; Reid, *King's Council in the North*, pp.113–44.

mixed. The council performed effectively around Yorkshire, containing simmering discontent there, but the crown's acquisition of the Percy and monastic estates left the marches weak and the border surnames uncontrollable. The Somerset regime soon moved to strengthen border defences by reappointing Dacre as warden, and rehabilitating the Percies.[31]

Far more successful were the arrangements for Wales, where there was no frontier to defend. Continuing feuding there had led to ap Gruffydd's execution for treason (1531), but disorders continued. In May 1534 Bishop Rowland Lee was appointed president, and parliament passed five statutes to tighten the administration of justice. Lee toured the marches, pursuing thieves and murderers, hanging even gentlemen, but more important in pacifying Wales were the statutes enacted and gradually enforced between 1536 and 1543, the so-called Act of Union. Effectively, they abolished the distinction between the principality and the marches, shired the marches, and imposed English law and administrative structures throughout Wales. Sheriffs, JPs and other officers of English local government were introduced, Welsh shires and ancient boroughs received representation in parliament (but only one member each, not the normal two), Welsh law and custom were abolished, and the English language was made compulsory for administrative and judicial business. Thus Wales was now united to England and the Welsh enjoyed the same rights and privileges as Englishmen. Lee opposed the changes, arguing that the natives were not ready for English-style self-government and that few Welsh gentry had sufficient land or discretion to serve as JPs. His presidency was long remembered for his draconian rule – reputedly 5,000 executions in six years. The imposition of English civility was a traumatic experience and certainly not the unqualified blessing which Elizabethan apologists implied. Yet the Union did lead to a gradual strengthening of law and order.[32] More problematical was the impact of this success on English political ideas about the incorporation and assimilation of other borderlands. It strengthened official convictions that peace and civility could be established only by imposing the same administrative structures that operated so effectively in lowland England. Thus it was no accident

31 M.L. Bush, 'The problem of the far north: a study of the crisis of 1537 and its consequences', *NH* 6 (1971), pp.40–63 (which revises James); James, *Society, Politics and Culture*, ch.3; Fletcher, *Tudor Rebellions*, pp.37–9; M.L. Bush, *The Government Policy of Protector Somerset* (London, 1975), pp.129, 141–2.

32 Williams, *Wales and the Act of Union*.

that when affairs in Ireland deteriorated under Elizabeth, leading officials with experience of both countries, such as Sir Henry Sidney and William Gerard, urged the same treatment for Ireland.[33]

In the short term too, experience in Wales was seen as offering lessons for Ireland. The lordship's military weakness had been underlined by the unprecedented joint invasion of the Pale by O'Neill and O'Donnell in 1539. The government rushed in reinforcements and then tried a new political initiative. By erecting Ireland into a kingdom (1541) and offering the Gaelic peoples the status of freeborn Englishmen, the government hoped to abolish the island's medieval partition between Englishry and Irishry and to extend English rule and administrative structures thoughout Ireland. Lord Deputy St Leger's 'surrender and regrant' strategy involved Gaelic chiefs recognizing English sovereignty in return for feudal charters confirming the lands they occupied. Thus they would become English subjects instead of Irish enemies, with common-law titles to their land and property, and the Gaelic lordships would become English shires. 'Surrender and regrant' was ambitious, but of all the Tudor initiatives for Ireland, it most nearly matched ultimate aims with available resources, providing for a gradual extension of English rule with Gaelic cooperation. A promising start was made, reducing racial tensions and enabling the deployment of Irish troops in France and Scotland (1544–5).[34] Yet progress was slow. Ireland was four times the size of Wales, which had taken seven years to assimilate administratively to England; Gaelic Ireland had yet to accept Tudor sovereignty; its peoples had no natural ties with the king, unlike the Welsh; and the extension of royal government in Ireland was not accompanied, as in Wales, by a corresponding increase in the size of the bureaucracy there.

Ireland's new status had also seemed to mark a significant departure from Tudor policies of centralization. In practice, this change had little impact on constitutional relations between the two kingdoms, but it had important implications for the Union of the Crowns in 1603. Ireland was now styled a kingdom, not a lordship,

33 N. Canny, *The Elizabethan Conquest of Ireland: A Pattern Established 1565–1576* (Hassocks, 1976), ch.3; Ellis, *Tudor Ireland*, pp.248–53, 273–4. See also Brady, Chapter 3 in this volume.

34 B. Bradshaw, *The Irish Constitutional Revolution of the Sixteenth Century* (Cambridge, 1979), pp.174–257; D.G. White, 'Henry VIII's Irish kerne in France and Scotland, 1544–5', *Irish Sword* 3, (1957–8), pp.213–25. An important critique of Bradshaw is C. Brady, 'The decline of the Irish kingdom', in M. Greengrass (ed.) *Conquest and Coalescence: The Shaping of the State in Early Modern Europe* (London, 1991), ch.6.

but it remained an English dependency, not a sovereign kingdom. Policy for Ireland, and much other administrative or quasi-judicial business was determined by king and council in England; king's bench in London still tried Irish lawsuits on appeal; appointments of Irish ministers were made under the great seal of England, and without a licence so warranted, the Irish parliament could not meet or pass legislation. Moreover, the English parliament retained the right (rarely exercised) to legislate for Ireland, even though Ireland was not now given representation there: in effect, the local community was excluded from an increasingly important means of influencing policy-making.[35] Thus in practice, this alleged 'constitutional revolution' provided a mechanism for incorporating Gaelic Ireland into the Tudor state, broadly along the lines of the Welsh Union, while consolidating control in the hands of king and council in London. In the longer term, the device of a dependent kingdom provided an attractive but misleading model for English politicians wrestling with the problems of a multiple monarchy after 1603.

After Henry VIII's death, the Edwardian government quadrupled the army in a bid to force the pace. After a rising by the midland Irish, it confiscated their territories to enlarge the Pale by colonization. Forts Governor and Protector were established to defend the colonists, and the lordships of Leix and Offaly were later shired. The natives were transplanted into Gaelic reservations nearer the Shannon; and with the renewed emphasis on coercion and colonization, Anglo-Gaelic relations again broke down. Moreover hopes that colonial rents would offset additional defence costs, so that conquest would be self-financing, proved disastrously wrong. As the Irish deficit snowballed from £4,700 to £35,000 sterling per year, Queen Mary reappointed St Leger as deputy to restore order and reduce costs.[36]

The Leix-Offaly plantation was apparently inspired by Protector Somerset's Scottish policy, which attempted to coerce the Scots into fulfilling the treaty of Greenwich by garrisoning southern Scotland. The eventual aim was a puppet kingdom controlled from London: meanwhile a revived English Pale would protect the 'assured Scots' and, as in Ireland, facilitate defence by advancing the frontier into

35 C. Brady, 'Court, castle and country: the framework of government in Tudor Ireland', in C. Brady and R. Gillespie (eds) *Natives and Newcomers: Essays on the Making of Irish Colonial Society 1534–1641* (Dublin, 1986), pp.27–9; Ellis, *Tudor Ireland*, p.166. For a contrary view, see Bradshaw, *Irish Consitutional Revolution*, pt 2.

36 D.G. White 'The reign of Edward VI in Ireland: some political, social and economic aspects', *IHS* 14 (1964–5) pp.197–211; Ellis, *Tudor Ireland*, pp.228–32.

enemy territory. Yet military costs, exceeding £140,000 sterling a year, far outweighed these advantages, which were increasingly negated by the arrival of French troops: the garrisons were withdrawn in 1550. By contrast in Ireland, where there was no agreed frontier, it proved more difficult to extricate the army: 1,500 troops were now viewed as an effective minimum to maintain royal authority there.[37]

THE REFORMATION

Of more fundamental importance to the shaping of the British Isles at this time was the advance of protestantism. In effect, the Tudor Reformation marked the extension to the religious sphere of the existing policies of centralization and cultural imperialism. Most obviously, this development was reflected in the interventions and injunctions of the royal supremacy and the parallel upsurge in ecclesiastical legislation by a parliament in which the borderlands remained seriously under-represented. Behind these changes was a shift from a visual presentation of Christianity to a bibliocentric one: its enforcement created major problems in the 'dark corners of the land' where parishes were larger and poorer, and levels of literacy much lower. In parts of Wales, Ireland and Cornwall, moreover, the introduction of English prayer books and bibles amounted to a major challenge to indigenous Celtic cultures rather than simply an intensification of existing pressures for linguistic and cultural uniformity. The Prayer Book and Bible were translated into the local vernacular, quite quickly in Wales, much more tardily in Ireland; even so, the need to operate through two languages dissipated reforming energies. Thus the Reformation process exacerbated the border problem at a time when, in Wales at least, the government had seemed to be making progress. Moreover, the individualism of the Elizabethan settlement was also an obstacle to a future religious union with Scotland: it was in many ways *sui generis*, a bizarre combination of a reformed theology with a catholic liturgy and polity which reflected state power as much as continental protestantism.[38]

37 Bush, *Government Policy of Protector Somerset*, esp. ch.2.

38 See Jenkins, Chapter 5 in this volume, and Mag Craith, Chapter 6 in this volume; S.G. Ellis, 'Economic problems of the church: why the Reformation failed in Ireland', *JEH* 41 (1990), pp.239–65.

Initially, however, the protestant advance eased the government's difficulties in defending its northern frontier. The Scottish revolution of 1559–60, the English invasion and the treaty of Edinburgh (1560) established a second protestant regime in Scotland. Ideological affinities greatly improved Anglo-Scottish relations, at the expense of the 'auld alliance' between Scotland and France. Thus, although the far north of England remained troublesome and costly to rule, the military threat was much reduced.[39] Better relations with Scotland also reduced the government's dependence on the great territorial magnates for border defence. Northumberland and Dacre were soon eased out of the wardenships, and gradually key northern offices were transferred to lesser nobles or southerners. The circumstances surrounding Mary Queen of Scots' deposition and flight into England led to a court conspiracy, centring on the duke of Norfolk, with whom the earls of Northumberland and Westmorland were allied. The northern earls sensed the opportunity to rescue Queen Mary, restore catholicism and, with it, their traditional influence in northern government. Their rising (November 1569), following Norfolk's arrest, was poorly coordinated and quickly collapsed, however. It was followed immediately by a clash between the queen's forces and Leonard Dacre who, ironically, had been alienated by Norfolk's claims to the Dacre inheritance. Following the attainder of the earls and Dacre, northern patronage was reorganized to build up a court party: a southern noble was appointed president of the council.[40]

THE PROBLEM OF IRELAND

The British political system was now increasingly self-contained. With the collapse of the MacDonald lordship (1475–1545), and the advance of protestantism in Scottish Gaeldom (among the Campbell earls of Argyll, for instance), the Gaelic world looked increasingly marginalized and divided in the face of centralization

39 See Dawson, Chapter 4 in this volume; M. Lynch, *Scotland: A New History* (London, 1991), chs 13–14; J. Wormald, *Mary Queen of Scots: A Study in Failure* (London, 1991), chs 4–7.

40 Fletcher, *Tudor Rebellions*, ch.8; Wormald, *Mary Queen of Scots*, chs 6–7; James, *Society, Politics and Culture*, ch.7; Reid, *King's Council in the North*, pp.191–239.

and expansion from London and Edinburgh.[41] Thus, as dynastic union looked increasingly likely to resolve the problem of the north, the Tudor reduction of Irish Gaeldom seemed the one outstanding question relating to British unification.

For most of Elizabeth's reign, Ireland remained a festering sore in the body politic. Unlike the north, where rivalry between the local elite and southerners was kept in check, the gradual polarization of political opinion between the local Englishry and the post-1534 English settlers was a serious complication, with Old English and New English officials proposing different strategies and the queen concerned above all to reduce her expenses. At different times the government's Irish policies drew on the whole range of medieval English political ideas and administrative strategies developed for the conquest and assimilation of outlying territories. Gaelic chiefs were made responsible for the conduct of their own clansmen and dependants through the system of booking and pledges, as with the northern surnames. 'Surrender and regrant' transformed Gaelic warlords into English nobles, lordships into shires, and tribal holdings into feudal tenures, although the terms offered to Gaelic chiefs were increasingly disadvantageous. English colonists were introduced to control strategically important districts: in east Ulster against the Scots (1570–3); and in Munster after the Desmond rebellion (1584–9). Regional councils were established in Connaught (1569) and Munster (1570) to oversee the rule of outlying parts, but the decision to furnish Irish presidents with a military retinue and power of martial law reflected the increasing militarization of Irish society. Successive compositions in the Pale and Connaught turned the obligation to military service and the royal right of purveyance into an alternative system of military taxation which further undermined the already attenuated role of the local parliament. By 1590 English rule had been gradually extended until only Ulster lay outside the system of shire government.[42]

41 J. Dawson, 'Two kingdoms or three? Ireland in Anglo-Scottish relations in the middle of the sixteenth century', in Mason (ed.) *Scotland and England*, pp.113–38; J. Dawson, 'The fifth earl of Argyle, Gaelic lordship and political power in sixteenth-century Scotland', *SHS* 67 (1988), pp.1–27; Alexander Grant, 'Scotland's "Celtic fringe" in the late middle ages: the MacDonald lords of the isles and the kingdom of Scotland', in R.R. Davies (ed.) *The British Isles 1100–1500: Comparisons, Contrasts and Connections* (Edinburgh, 1988), pp.118–41; J. Kirk, *Patterns of Reform: Continuity and Change in the Reformation Kirk* (Edinburgh, 1989), chs 7–8.

42 Ellis, *Tudor Ireland*, for this and the following paragraph. On the Nine Years War, H. Morgan, *Tyrone's Rebellion: The Outbreak of the Nine Years War in Tudor Ireland* (Woodbridge, 1993).

These measures were as much a reaction to successive crises as the result of forward planning. Ambitious but weakly supported initiatives were by turn authorized by a divided Dublin administration and countermanded by the queen when they raised expenditure or encountered opposition. Moreover, this opposition was not confined to Gaelic Ireland because these strategies had also aimed to strengthen control over the outlying English districts. The upshot was mounting unrest and a wave of rebellions: the Butler rising and the earl of Thomond's rebellion were Irish echoes of the intrigues surrounding Norfolk, but there were other revolts in the south and west (1568–73), in Leinster and Munster (1579–83), and in Ulster from 1593, spreading into Connaught and Munster. Insurrections in English Ireland generally followed the mainland pattern of political demonstrations within a context of overall obedience – by contrast with the localized Gaelic 'wars of independence' – but political discontent increasingly coalesced with an originally distinct tradition of opposition to protestantism, so that resistance became increasingly widespread, bitter and ideological. Politics thus degenerated into a ruthless kind of warfare, with widespread atrocities on both sides. Yet only by attracting substantial military assistance from Spain had the most formidable of these resistance movements, the Ulster confederacy led by Hugh O'Neill, earl of Tyrone, any real hope of matching the superior resources of the Tudor state. The confederates won occasional victories, and Elizabeth was very stretched to find money and men for the Nine Years War (1594–1603) besides her commitments in France and the Netherlands. Yet the 3,500 Spanish troops who eventually landed at Kinsale in 1601 proved insufficient to tip the scales, and Lord Mountjoy's ruthless but professional campaign gradually crushed the rebellion. The war cost Elizabeth £1 million sterling, but with Tyrone's surrender at Mellifont, the political unification of the British Isles was finally completed.

THE TRIUMPH OF TUDOR POLICY?

From London's perspective, therefore, 1603 appeared to mark the successful conclusion of a long-term goal of Tudor policy: to break down local autonomy and extend royal authority and English civility throughout the Tudor state. The Tudors had tackled the problems of Wales, Ireland, and the north of England by a policy of political centralization, administrative uniformity, and cultural imperialism. The great provincial magnates, with their compact landholdings, warlike tenantry, and control of local offices had been tamed, and the values of lowland England imposed on the borderlands. The year 1603 removed the final obstacles to centralized control, with the dismantling of the traditional military frontiers.

A more considered assessment of Tudor policy discloses serious shortcomings, however. The Tudors had inherited a balanced polity, in which the political influence of the lowlands was offset by the military and strategic value of semi-autonomous borderlands. The imposition of the highly centralized administrative structures of lowland England on the borderlands led to serious and continuing tensions between the court and local political communities and destroyed this balance. After their incorporation, Wales and the far north of England presented fewer problems, since they were smaller, and more easily dominated from London: but their effective marginalization within the English nation-state was reflected, for instance, in their representation in parliament, where Wales had only 29 MPs and the far north of England only 16 in a House of Commons which had expanded to 462 Members by 1601.[43] Then, however, Tudor politicians faced the problem of how to deal with two new borderlands – Scotland and Gaelic Ireland – which were even larger, more remote and 'uncivilized', a problem which previous experiences now left the English state singularly ill equipped to tackle. The military conquest of Ireland left a bitter legacy of racial and religious animosity. The Dublin administration was controlled by an unrepresentative clique of New English adventurers, with little indigenous support, and dependent on an army to maintain its authority.[44] Moreover, the strategy of hiving Ireland off into a dependent kingdom, controlled from London but without a substantial input into the political process there, was an unfortunate precedent and a major and continuing source of political instability in the developing British state. Beguiled by this precedent, English politicians saw Ireland as a model for the integration of Scotland into the English state, even though the circumstances of the dynastic union precluded its application there

43 Calculated from F.A. Youngs, jr (ed.) *Guide to Local Administrative Units of England, II, Northern England* (London, 1991), pt 3; Loach, *Parliament and the Tudors*, p.35.

44 N. Canny, *From Reformation to Restoration: Ireland 1534–1660* (Dublin, 1987), chs 5–6.

– at least in the short term. Thus, it is hard not to see in this Tudor legacy of state formation the origins of the pan-British crisis of 1638–60 once described as the English Civil War.[45] In the longer term, the Tudor consolidation of that south-eastern supremacy which remains a characteristic of the British state also helps to explain the persistence of separatist movements in the modern state. Perhaps the failing of the Tudors was that their eagerness to centralize their authority was not matched by a willingness to extend an effective mechanism for political dialogue and redress of grievances beyond the original boundaries of Anglo-Saxon England. But until Tudor specialists agree to address the Tudor state as a whole, the untidy pattern of success and failure which constituted the Tudor experience of state formation will continue to be obscured by the nationalist illusion of triumphant progress towards the present.

45 C. Russell, *The Fall of the British Monarchies, 1637–1642* (Oxford, 1991); B. Levack, *The Formation of the British State: England, Scotland and the Union 1603–1707* (Oxford, 1987); B. Galloway, *The Union of England and Scotland, 1603–1608* (Edinburgh, 1986).

CHAPTER THREE

Comparable histories?: Tudor reform in Wales and Ireland

Ciarán Brady
Trinity College Dublin

In some respects the ostensible subject matter of this chapter – an examination of the interrelation of reform policies in Tudor Ireland and Wales – may seem to be little more than a futile exercise in the comparison of apples and pears. For while medieval scholars like Rees Davies, Robin Frame and Robert Bartlett have derived significant results from a sustained comparison of Wales's history of conquest and settlement and Ireland's near contemporaneous experience of a similar process, and while modern historians of politics and administration have fruitfully examined the relative impact of Westminster's rule upon the two provinces of British government, early modernists in the main have perceived little benefit in essaying a systematic comparison of Wales and Ireland in the critical period in which the former completed its assimilation into English political culture, and the latter commenced its seemingly endless history of political, social and religious division.[1]

1 See e.g. R.R. Davies, *Lordship and Society in the March of Wales, 1282–1400* (Oxford, 1982); R.R. Davies, *Conquest, Coexistence and Change: Wales 1063–1415* (Oxford, 1987); R.R. Davies, *Domination and Conquest: The Experience of Ireland, Scotland and Wales, 1000–1300* (Cambridge, 1990); R.R. Davies 'Lordship and colony', in J. Lydon (ed.) *The English in Medieval Ireland* (Dublin, 1984), pp.142–60; R. Frame, *Colonial Ireland 1169–1369* (Dublin, 1981); R. Frame, *English Lordship in Ireland 1318–1361* (Oxford, 1982); R.J. Bartlett, *The Making of Europe: Conquest, Colonization and Cultural Change, 950–1350* (London, 1993); among the large body of literature dealing with the modern period in which fruitful comparisons are made between Wales and Ireland, see esp. K. Robbins, *Nineteenth-Century Britain: Integration and Diversity* (Oxford, 1988); K.O. Morgan, *Wales in British Politics, 1868–1922* (3rd edn, Cardiff, 1988).

In the light of such obvious differences historians have for the most part been content simply to note the occasional cross-currents and casual connections between the two regions, some remarking on the number of Tudor administrators who held office in both, others on the substantial Welsh contingent in the English garrison in Ireland, and on the high degree of migration from Wales to plantations in Ireland, and others again on the far less frequent instances of Irish migration to Wales and the persistent, though usually unjustified, fear in Wales of imminent invasion from Ireland.[2] Any attempt at a more sustained comparison of the two areas has been left to the political sociologists, like Immanuel Wallerstein and Michael Hechter, and they have not much enjoyed the attention of the historians.[3]

Wallerstein's identification of the two countries' histories is really not systematic at all, but arises implicitly from his argument that both represent typical peripheral zones ripe for dominance and exploitation by a centre of imperial expansion. Regardless of the different paths they took, Ireland and Wales were both integrated into the dominant British system of empire condemned to supply merely the raw materials of land, natural resources and labour on which the empire prospered.[4] Hechter's case is more explicitly stated. By different methods, by connivance with and co-optation of ruling elites in one case, and by their outright destruction in another, Tudor England asserted its dominance over Wales and Ireland, depriving both of their potential for independent sovereignty for centuries. Again, while the strategies adopted in both cases differed, the aims of domination, territorial security, economic exploitation and political hegemony were the same – as were the consequences, the social, economic and cultural inequities of a classic colonial situation.[5] Historians of Wales and Ireland have

2 See e.g. A.H. Dodd, 'Wales and Ireland from Reformation to Revolution', in *Studies in Stuart Wales* (Cardiff, 1952) pp.76–109; P. Williams, *The Council in the Marches of Wales under Elizabeth I* (Cardiff, 1958); E.G. Jones, 'Anglesey and invasion, 1539–1603', *Transactions of the Anglesey Antiquarian Society* (1947), pp.26–37; J.J.N. McGurk 'A survey of the demands made on the Welsh shires to supply soldiers for the Irish war, 1594–1603', *THSC* (1983), pp.56–68; M. MacCarthy-Morrogh, *The Munster Plantation* (Oxford, 1986) pp.47–8, 162–3, 191–2; A.L. Beier, *Masterless Men: The Vagrancy Problem in England, 1560–1640* (London, 1985) pp. 32–5, 72–3.

3 I. Wallerstein *The Modern World System, I, Capitalist Agriculture and the Origin of the World Economy in the Sixteenth Century* (London, 1974); M. Hechter, *Internal Colonialism: The Celtic fringe in British National Development* (London, 1975)

4 Wallerstein, *Modern World System*, pp.38, 228, 233, 250, 261.

5 Hechter, *Internal Colonialism*, pp.57–78.

in their various ways cavilled with the details of Hechter's argument, objecting to his frequent misrepresentations and oversimplifications and highlighting the many lacunae in his account.[6] But their principal concern has been at once more modest and more profound. For whatever the larger significance of his thesis, it is clear that for historians Hechter has done little to explicate the reasons behind those differences in strategies, timings and reactions which he notes, but passes them over as of little consequence to his primary concerns. It is to these very differences that the historians attend and in attending to them the Welsh and Irish scholars have independently discovered such contrasting and opposed developments in both regions in the period of Tudor expansion as to make any comparative approach, other than the recording of occasional overlaps in personnel and other casual interconnections, seem redundant.

CONTRASTS AND SIMILARITIES

The contrasts were multiple. In Wales political and social discontent gradually became diffused over the course of the sixteenth century into riot, crime, family feuding and the occasional fracas at a parliamentary election.[7] In Ireland rebellion became endemic.[8] In Wales the principal aristocratic families led the way in encouraging the acceptance of English law and government: in Ireland, with few exceptions, they led the resistance.[9] In Wales the gentry supplied the basic element of the intricate tissue of regional and local administration by which the Tudors consolidated and extended

6 For representative reviews from both Irish and Welsh historians, see J.C. Beckett, *History* 62 (1977), pp.85–6; P.J. Madgwick, *WHR* 8 (1976–7), pp.241–4.

7 For a general overview, G. Williams, *Recovery, Reorientation and Reformation: Wales, c.1415–1642* (Oxford, 1987), esp. chs 11, 14.

8 For a general overview S.G. Ellis, *Tudor Ireland: Crown, Community and the Conflict of Cultures, 1470–1603* (London, 1985).

9 Compare W.R.B. Robinson, 'The marcher lords of Wales, 1523–31', *BBCS* 26 (1972–3) and his three-part article 'Early Tudor policy toward Wales', *BBCS* 20–1 (1962–6), with S.G. Ellis, 'Tudor policy and the Kildare ascendancy in the lordship of Ireland, 1496–1534', *IHS* 20 (1976–7), pp.235–71; B. Bradshaw, 'Cromwellian reform and the origins of the Kildare rebellion, 1533–4', *TRHS* 5th ser. 27 (1977), pp.69–94. N. Canny, *The Elizabethan Conquest of Ireland: A Pattern Established 1565–76* (Hassocks, 1975) ch.7; C. Brady, 'Faction and the origins of the Desmond rebellion of 1579', *IHS* 22 (1980–1), pp.289–312.

English law in the region.[10] In Ireland by the close of the century, gentlemen had either been excluded or excluded themselves from administrative offices whose authority they were then working, often effectively, to subvert.[11] In Wales the constitutional and doctrinal changes of the Reformation were adopted with relatively little overt dissent, and an outward conformity was enforced by the generally supportive ruling elite.[12] In Ireland the Reformation failed and the Counter-Reformation prospered.[13] In Ireland the written and oral expressions of Gaelic culture provided the ideological basis of radical resistance to English rule.[14] In Wales native culture declined or survived only by accommodating itself to a distinctly subordinate place in the new world view of the reformed Tudor state.[15]

The factors underlying these strikingly different experiences seem easy enough to identify. The accession of the Tudors as England's ruling dynasty provided a powerful cement binding Welsh loyalties to the English crown. It is true, of course, that few of

10 The importance of the role of the gentry is a central tenet of early modern Welsh history: see e.g. H.A. Lloyd, *The Gentry of South-West Wales, 1540–1640* (Cardiff, 1968); for a general survey, G. Jones, *The Gentry and the Elizabethan State* (Swansea, 1977).

11 In early modern Irish history the concept of the gentry has not been regarded as a useful interpretative instrument at all, so no studies comparable to the several monographs available in relation to Wales exist; for accounts of the community of the English Pale whose leadership comes closest to resembling a recognizable gentry group see N. Canny, *The Formation of the Old English Elite* (O'Donnell Lecture, Dublin, 1975), and C. Brady, 'Conservative subversives: the community of the Pale and the Dublin administration, 1556–1586', in P.J. Corish (ed.) *Radicals, Rebels and Establishments: Historical Studies XV* (Belfast, 1985), pp.11–32.

12 See Williams, *Recovery, Reorientation and Reformation,* chs 12 and 13, and the more detailed studies collected in G. Williams, *Welsh Reformation Essays* (Cardiff, 1967).

13 See the chapters by A. Ford and C. Lennon on the Reformation and Counter-Reformation respectively in C. Brady and R. Gillespie (eds) *Natives and Newcomers: Essays on the Making of Irish Colonial Society* (Dublin, 1986). For a summary of recent controversies see K.S. Bottigheimener, 'Why the reformation failed in Ireland: une question bien posée', *JEH* 36 (1985), pp.196–207.

14 For a good introductory survey see B. Cunningham, 'Native culture and political change in Ireland, 1580–1640', in Brady and Gillespie (eds) *Natives and Newcomers,* pp.148–70; some important studies are B. Bradshaw, 'Native reaction to the westward enterprise: a case study in Gaelic ideology', in K.R. Andrews, N.P. Canny & P.E.H. Hair, (eds) *The Westward Enterprise: English Activities in Ireland, the Atlantic and America 1480–1650* (Liverpool, 1978) pp.66–80, and N. Canny, 'The formation of the Irish mind: religion, politics and Gaelic Irish literature 1580–1750', *P&P* 95 (1982), pp.91–116.

15 Williams, *Recovery, Reorientation and Reformation,* ch.18; G. Williams, *Religion, Language and Nationality in Wales* (Cardiff, 1979); W.O. Williams, 'The Survival of the Welsh language after the Union of England and Wales: the first phase 1536–1642', *WHR* 2 (1964–5), pp.67–93; see the perceptive comments in P. Jenkins, *A History of Modern Wales, 1536–1990* (London, 1992) pp.57–70 and in Jenkins, ch. 5 in this vol.

the Tudors displayed any great affection toward their place of origin; but the idea that Wales enjoyed a special place in the hearts of the monarchs which ensured that the interests of its people would be protected and nurtured was a persistent and highly persuasive theme carefully elaborated by Welsh political and cultural propagandists throughout the sixteenth century.[16] The Tudors, however, enjoyed no such status in Ireland; nor did they evince much interest in cultivating in Ireland the common British origin-myth which had worked so effectively in Wales, even though the (admittedly specious) materials for such an ideological history were relatively plentiful.[17] Similarly, the suggestion frequently and plaintively raised that one member of the royal family should visit their Irish kingdom was never taken seriously.

There were more concrete bonds between Wales and the English crown. Through the inheritance of the principality and a variety of historical accidents – attainder, purchase and escheat – the Tudor monarchs had become the largest landed proprietors in Wales, enjoying a supremacy which no individual magnate could dream of challenging.[18] In Ireland, however, the extent of land directly inherited by the Tudors was small – it was valued at a mere IR£500 in the early 1530s – and though crown holdings were in a nominal way substantially increased by attainder, plantation and religious confiscations, the real benefit to the monarchy was considerably diluted by generous grants, long-term leases and reversions and restorations.[19] The Tudor monarchs never came to enjoy the status of powerful individual landlords that they had automatically inherited in Wales.

Moreover while the old feudal aristocracy had by no means disappeared in Wales, its numbers had been considerably reduced by the convulsions of the later fifteenth century and its conduct tamed. By the 1530s, major families like the Herbert earls of Pembroke, or the Devereux Lords Ferrers or the Somerset earls of Worcester continued to enjoy great authority and to exercise

16 T.D. Kendrick, *British Antiquity* (London, 1950); B.G. Charles, *George Owen of Henllys: A Welsh Elizabethan* (Aberystwyth, 1977).

17 A. Hadfield, 'Briton and Scythian: Tudor representations of Irish origins', *IHS* 28 (1992–3), pp.390–408.

18 B.P. Wolffe, *The Royal Demesne in English History: The Crown Estate in the Governance of the Realm from the Conquest to 1509* (London, 1974), ch.7; F. Jones, *The Princes and the Principality of Wales* (Cardiff, 1969), chs 2 and 4.

19 S.G. Ellis, *Reform and Revival: English Government in Ireland, 1470–1534* (Woodbridge, 1985), pp.74–8; A. Sheehan, 'Irish revenues and English subventions 1559–1622', *PRIA* 90C (1990), pp.35–65.

substantial influence in their respective areas. But with the decline in the military and strategic importance of marcher lordship in Wales, their continuing status was due less to their own autonomous strength than to their loyalty towards and dependence on the English crown, while the intrinsic weakness of those aristocrats who rejected or undervalued the importance of obedience to the monarch had been painfully revealed in the recent past by the exemplary fate of such figures as Rhys ap Gruffydd and Edward Stafford, the third duke of Buckingham.[20]

The Irish aristocracy, by contrast, remained deeply divided in its attitude toward the Tudors. The Geraldines, suspect of course as active Yorkists in the fifteenth and early sixteenth centuries, responded to the reformist initiatives of the 1530s with defiance and rebellion. And over the remainder of the Tudor era, through successive trials, pardons and restorations, the Fitzgerald houses of Kildare and Desmond and their allies continued to be at the head of repeated conspiracies and open rebellions against the crown in Ireland.[21] It is true, conversely, that the Geraldines' greatest rival, the Butler house of Ormond, came to enjoy a place of especial trust with the monarchs, particularly through the remarkable influence exercised at the court of Elizabeth by Thomas, the tenth earl. But Ormond's place was exceptional, and the failure to allow compensating representation for his rivals or subordinates did nothing to improve the Tudor court's capacity as a means of resolving Irish political argument.[22] Most serious of all perhaps, the late Tudor monarchs failed to honour the promise of Henry VIII to use the court as an instrument for the political re-education and assimilation of the great Gaelic lords. The great ceremonial surrenders of the 1540s were never repeated, and no Gaelic Irishman was to succeed to the close personal relationship with the monarch once, briefly, held by Sir Barnaby Fitzpatrick.[23]

20 Williams, *Recovery, Reorientation and Reformation*, pp.248–50; Robinson, 'Early Tudor policy toward Wales'; Robinson, 'Marcher lords of Wales'.

21 C.W. Fitzgerald, *The Earls of Kildare and their Ancestors from 1057 to 1773* (Dublin, 1862), esp. pp.59–270; B. Fitzgerald, *The Geraldines* (New York, 1951); S. Hayman (ed.) 'Unpublished Geraldine documents', *Journal of the Royal Society of Antiquaries of Ireland*, 3rd ser. 1 (1868), pp.356–416.

22 C. Brady, 'Thomas Butler, 10th earl of Ormond', in C. Brady (ed.) *Worsted in the Game: Losers in Irish History* (Dublin, 1989) pp.49–59.

23 Shane O'Neill, the lord of Tír Eoghain, was one of the few major Gaelic lords to be received at Elizabeth's court, but his visit there was regarded as rather an exotic episode: J. Hogan, 'Shane O'Neill comes to the court of Elizabeth', in S. Pender (ed.) *Féil-scríbhinn Torna* (Cork, 1947), pp.154–72; on Fitzpatrick see DNB s.v.

A more profound precondition underlying the success of Tudor reform in Wales was the steady process of de-feudalization which had been taking place on both royal and noble estates for about a century before the so-called union. The gradual transformation of the great marcher landowners into *rentiers* and their willingness to convert a significant portion of their rights of lordship into transferable leaseholds encouraged the development of a mobile land market in the marches. This tendency was paralleled in ethnically Welsh regions by the steady, if by no means complete decline in the importance of the ancient clans' territorial rights, and the gradual abandonment of traditional modes of inheritance, in particular that of equal partition.[24] Together these developments were steadily giving rise to the appearance of freeholding elements at various levels of society. Most importantly they encouraged the emergence of a substantial gentry group which, though it continued to acknowledge political and social allegiance to the aristocracy, was becoming increasingly independent economically and willing to defend their independence by exploiting the opportunities made available by Tudor innovations in regional and local administration.[25]

In Ireland, however, the development of such important structural changes in society was halting and slow, and in many areas was being retarded by counterveiling forces. Irish historians have in recent years uncovered evidence of social and tenurial changes within the Irish lordships in the later middle ages which do indeed seem to parallel those underway in Wales. The gradual diminution of the political authority of the Gaelic chieftains, the emergence of distinct groups from within the ruling families which eschewed competition for the chieftancy in favour of independence or quasi-autonomy, the establishment of increasingly precise and closely regulated mechanisms of land distribution and inheritance all suggest a gradual decline in the importance of the ruling clan, or dynasty, as the primary unit of political and social life.[26] Similarly

24 F. Emery, 'The farming regions of Wales', and T. Jones Pierce, 'Landlords in Wales', both in J. Thirsk (ed.) *The Agrarian History of England and Wales, IV, 1500–1640* (Cambridge, 1967) pp.124–60, 357–81.

25 Jones Pierce, 'Landlords', esp. pp.372–81; T. Jones Pierce, *Medieval Welsh Society* (Cardiff, 1972), esp. pp.195–227; Williams, *Recovery, Reorientation and Reformation* pp.78–89, 95–110.

26 K.W. Nicholls, 'Gaelic society and economy in the high middle ages', in A. Cosgrove (ed.) *A New History of Ireland, II, Medieval Ireland 1169–1534* (Oxford, 1987), pp.397–438; K.W. Nicholls, *Land, Law and Society in Sixteenth Century Ireland* (O'Donnell Lecture, Dublin 1976); K. Simms, *From Kings to Warlords: the Changing Political Structure of Gaelic Ireland in the Later Middle Ages* (Woodbridge, 1987).

the considerable improvement in the currency and efficiency of the instruments of English law and administration in the Pale and in Munster, which has been ably reconstructed by Steven Ellis as a hitherto neglected feature of the late fifteenth and early sixteenth centuries, may also be seen to follow the increasing recourse to law and appeals to English justice that Welsh historians have noted as a distinctive development in the marches, even before the reconstruction of the Welsh council.[27]

Yet such similarities should not be exaggerated. The appearance of a freeholding interest amid the ruling families of Gaelic and gaelicized Ireland in the first half of the sixteenth century was not a uniform process but an intermittent, uncertain phenomenon, the continuance of which depended upon a whole series of local and temporal accidents: it was in no way so well founded nor so advanced as to be compared with the emergence of the gentry as a force in Wales.[28] In the same way, the revival of English law and administration was itself a highly unstable process. Fuelled primarily by successive, and short-lived initiatives from England, it was constantly threatened both by the overt challenge made to it by the great lords' conduct of arbitration through intimidation and by the subversion of its offices and procedures regularly practised by Kildare and the other lords of English descent granted royal authority in Ireland.[29]

The continuing power of these great lords – of the Geraldines, Kildare and Desmond, and of their major rivals among the Butlers and the Burkes – indeed their marked increase in strength in the late fifteenth and early sixteenth centuries remains, of course, the principal point of contrast with Welsh political history. Its origins can be easily traced in the most general terms: the great English campaigns of conquest had never succeeded in Ireland to the same degree as they had done in Wales. Edward II had not attempted in Ireland what he had achieved in Wales, Richard II had hardly dealt with the Irish as Henry IV treated the Welsh less than two decades later. Thereafter the chronic weakness of the English crown in the fifteenth century confirmed the status of the surviving magnates of

27 Ellis, *Reform and Revival*, esp. pp.110–35 and ch.7.

28 Nicholls, 'Gaelic society and economy', esp. pp.423–5, 430–1.

29 For a general overview, D.B. Quinn, 'The hegemony of the earls of Kildare, 1494–1520', in Cosgrove (ed.) *A New History of Ireland*, II, pp.638–61; among a large contemporary literature of complaint the anonymous tract on the 'State of Ireland', *c.*1515 in SP *Hen. VIII*, II, 1–31, and Sir William Darcy's 'Articles on the decay of Ireland' *c.*1515, printed in *Calendar of Carew MSS 1515–74*, pp.3–5, are most relevant.

English descent as the primary representatives of English rule in Ireland who were left to defend the lordship by whatever expedients, compromises and strategems they chose.[30]

THE IMPACT OF TUDOR REFORMS

Such is the well-known account: but the practical consequences of the quasi-autonomy which had evolved in the English lordship in Ireland are of more relevance here. For much of the later middle ages Ireland and Wales, as Rees Davies and others have noted, shared several distinctive features in common.[31] Both were deeply unstable societies, lands of chronic war, feuding and labyrinthine alliance-making, short-term diplomacy and political duplicity. Neither was a simple frontier society, where the lines of demarcation between friends and enemies could be neatly delimited by a clear geographical border. Both rather were highly fragmented polities, *congeries* of large numbers of almost entirely autonomous lordships, each with their own legal, fiscal and political structures and processes. With the completion of the conquest and the establishment of a general peace in Wales, however, the effects of such formal similarities began to diverge significantly. In Wales, relative peace allowed for the stabilization of relations between the lordships through agreed procedures of negotiation and arbitration, and for the development within the lordships of institutions – such as the day of the march – which offered a regular and formal mechanism for the settlement of civil and criminal cases.[32]

In Ireland, however, where war persisted, and the pretence that the crown could maintain any real control over its own subjects steadily dissolved, an opposite momentum began to apply. Intense local fragmentation provided the basis for the construction of

30 Compare Williams, *Recovery, Reorientation and Reformation*, ch.1, with the chronological surveys by J.A. Watt and A. Cosgrove in Cosgrove (ed.) *A New History of Ireland*, II, chs 13, 17–19.

31 R.R. Davies, 'Frontier arrangements in fragmented societies: Ireland and Wales', in R.J. Bartlett and A. McKay (eds) *Medieval Frontier Societies* (Oxford, 1989), pp.77–100; R.R. Davies, 'Lordship or colony', in Lydon (ed.) *English in medieval Ireland*, pp.142–60; see also the chapters by R.J. Bartlett and R. Frame in *Medieval Frontier Societies*, pp.23–48, 101–26.

32 Davies, 'Frontier arrangements', esp. pp.89–100; R. Frame, 'Military service in the lordship of Ireland 1290–1360: institutions and society on the Anglo-Gaelic frontier', in Bartlett and McKay (eds) *Medieval Frontier Societies*, pp.101–26, K. Simms, 'Warfare in the medieval Gaelic lordships', *Irish Sword* 12 (1975–6), pp.98–108.

elaborate, if unstable, political alliances at provincial and regional level which transcended the old ethnic distinctions between English and Gaelic Irish and served to consolidate the interests of the strong and well-connected among both groups.[33] Again this process of faction-building through alliances, arbitrations, compromises and marriage settlement has been noted by Welsh scholars, but in Ireland it evolved in a distinctive manner through the operation of two factors.

The first was the ability of the major Gaelic and English lords to establish a more or less permanent hegemony over several groups of nominally independent septs in their area by means of a permanent military presence, the great private armies, often numbering upwards of 1,500 professional soldiers, whose extortions ensured the obedience of lesser groups around them.[34] Thus, despite their unsteadiness and their internal frictions, power groups in Ireland tended to be large enough to sustain or repel a force of conquest. The second distinguishing feature was the steady appropriation of control over the institutions of royal government by one or other of the great families, usually the Geraldines, which enabled them to exercise an influence in the island's affairs beyond the concern of regional politics. By means of such claims to governmental authority, local issues could easily be transformed into national ones, and conversely, resistance to the claims of a particular local English figure in office could lead to local disturbances in parts of the island untouched by any of his direct actions.[35]

An underlying paradox may thus be discerned in the contrasting patterns of Welsh and Irish history in the decades leading up to the Tudor interventions in both areas in the 1530s. In Wales fragmentation both in the marches and in the principality had progressed so far as to create a whole variety of constituents, each of which showed a common receptiveness to the local and

33 A. Cosgrove, 'Ireland beyond the Pale', and D.B. Quinn 'Irish Ireland and English Ireland', both in Cosgrove (ed.) *A New History of Ireland*, II, pp.569–90, 619–37.

34 'State of Ireland *c.*1515, SP *Hen. VIII*, II, 1'31; 'An estimate of the forces in Ireland in the reign of King Henry VIII', NLI MS 669.

35 D.B. Quinn, 'Aristocratic autonomy, 1460–1494' and 'The hegemony of the earls of Kildare 1494–1520', both in Cosgrove (ed.) *A New History of Ireland*, II, pp.591–618, 638–61; a clear picture of the extent to which public and private interests were mixed under the Geraldines is provided by the Kildare rental now re-edited with much additional material by Gearóid Mac Niocaill in *Crown Surveys of Lands 1540–41* (Dublin, 1992), pp.232–358.

particularist opportunities proffered by Tudor legal and administrative reforms. Thus though they were certainly prompted by circumstances outside of Wales, the Henrician reforms of the 1530s and 1540s were admirably suited to internal developments. The major statutes of 1536 and 1543 effected a radical transformation of Wales both constitutionally and administratively, ending the centuries old distinction between the principality and the marches and, so far as parliamentary representation was concerned, between Wales and the shires of England, and introduced a new coherent administrative infrastructure at regional and local levels. Yet this rapid reconstruction of the Welsh polity was accomplished with remarkable ease. Thus the provision of representation for Wales at Westminster, the extension of English shire administration and the destruction of the autonomy of the marches, the enforcement of primogeniture and proscription of Welsh customs of land tenure, the reconstruction of the council in the marches, the establishment of the Welsh general sessions, and the introduction of the office of justice of the peace throughout the region were all smoothly effected; because each was generally congruent with the concerns and interests that were already emerging within Welsh political and social life. For the same reason, each proved to be remarkably successful as instruments of integration within a relatively short period.[36]

In Ireland, however, a different scenario had been shaped from circumstances that were once quite comparable with conditions in Wales. Through a combination of localism, lawlessness and the central government's weakness, a small set of large, powerful and opposing interests had emerged for whom the Henrician initiatives seemed to offer only the prospect of total defeat for one, or total victory for the other. Thus while in Wales the reforms were relatively well received as simply accelerating processes that were already under way and went on to provide a basis for the evolution of a familiar kind of provincial politics in the later sixteenth century, in Ireland these same efforts immediately provoked suspicion, instability and rebellion.[37]

36 W. Rees, 'The union of England and Wales', *THSC* (1938), pp.27–100; P.R. Roberts, 'The Act of Union in Welsh history', *THSC* (1972–3), pp.49–72; P.R. Roberts (ed.) 'A breviat of the effects devised for Wales', *Camden Miscellany*, 4th ser. 26 (1975), pp.31–47; W.R.B. Robinson, 'The Tudor revolution in Welsh government 1536–1543: its effects on gentry participation', *EHR* 103(1988), pp.1–20.

37 Compare the accounts of Wales in the 1530s and 1540s given in the works cited in note 35 with accounts of contemporary Ireland offered by L. Corristine, *The Revolt of Silken Thomas* (Dublin, 1989), and P. Wilson, *The Beginnings of Modern Ireland* (Dublin, 1912).

In view of the sharply contrasting reactions which their first efforts at reform provoked in both countries – cautious approbation in one, outright rebellion in the other – it seems hardly necessary to stress that by the later 1530s Henry VIII and his advisers had themselves come to recognize that fundamental differences had emerged between the two regions. Thus they attempted in Ireland no Act of Union, abandoned any effort to govern by direct rule, and accepted that, if the costly and uncertain business of a full conquest were not to be undertaken, their Irish *outre-mer* would have to be recognized as a separate constitutional entity with a distinct recent history whose reconstruction as a model English polity would have to be carried out by a parliament, legal system and administrative structure of its own: to be treated, in short, as a kingdom. Thus through the Act for the Kingly Title (1541) and the political initiatives that followed from it, the Tudors appeared to have conceded that the reform of Ireland represented a specific problem quite independent of the government of Wales; it seems only proper that subsequent historians should have followed them in maintaining that distinction.[38]

All of this would seem clear were it not for the curious fact that, notwithstanding their recognition of the obvious historical and political differences that had developed between Ireland and Wales and their constitutional endorsement of such differences, Tudor commentators continued to declare that there were after all important similarities between the two regions which justified continuing comparison, and to argue that policies applied with such success in Wales would succeed also in Ireland if properly implemented. The reason why the advocates of reform in Ireland should have chosen to ignore their own constitutional distinctions and to have insisted that the Tudor success in Wales remained a central guide, a model for the development of an effective reform strategy in Ireland, lies in part outside either region and may be found in an area where, on the face of it, conditions seemed to have more in common with those prevailing in early-sixteenth-century Ireland: the Tudor north of England.

Under the early Tudors, the north of England – unlike Wales after 1283 – remained a frontier zone in the military sense too. The rule and defence of a turbulent frontier against the Scots and the border surnames necessitated a greater devolution of authority by

38 B. Bradshaw, *The Irish Constitutional Revolution of the Sixteenth Century* (Cambridge, 1979).

the Tudor government and a concentration of power in local hands.[39] Thus at a time when the balance of power was gradually shifting in Wales, as in lowland England, towards the crown and an independently minded gentry, the exigencies of war in the far north, as in English Ireland, exerted strong countervailing pressures, placing a premium on resident marcher lordship by the great magnates there.[40]

At one level, Tudor officials seemed to be aware of these parallels in conditions between the Anglo-Scottish and Anglo-Irish marches and of the north of England's potential as a model for the reduction of Ireland. Trusted councillors like Sir Henry Wyatt under Henry VII and the duke of Norfolk under Henry VIII drew on their personal experience of both marches in advising on major policy decisions for Ireland; northern troops served in Ireland in 1520–2, 1530–2 and 1534–6, as did Irish troops in the north of England in 1544–6; and northern practices and personnel were considered when arrangements for the defence of Ireland were under review. In practice, however, the Tudors found the north of England almost as intractable a problem as Ireland. Henry VII orchestrated a diffusion of power among his officials in the region, but weakened its administrative and military base. Henry VIII mounted a more direct attack on established noble power there, restoring the council in the north and attempting to build up a royal affinity among the northern gentry. But when relations with Scotland again deteriorated, he was forced into the costly expedient of recruiting a standing garrison under a southern noble to defend the borders. Thus the north of England supplied not so much a model as a timely warning concerning the reduction of Ireland.[41]

The unhappy experience of Tudor reformers in the north of England accounts in part, therefore, for their unwillingness to draw many close parallels with Ireland, but it hardly explains why many should have actively continued to promote the Welsh alternative and, despite its many obvious incongruities, to have pressed it with increasing urgency as the century progressed as a model for the

39 For border surnames, see Ellis, Chapter 2 in this volume.

40 M. James, *Society, Politics and Culture* (Cambridge, 1986); M.L. Bush, 'The problem of the far north: a study of the crisis of 1537 and its consequences', *NH* 6 (1971), pp.40–63; S.G. Ellis, 'A border baron and the Tudor state: the rise and fall of Lord Dacre of the North', *HJ* 35 (1992), pp.253–77.

41 A. Conway, *Henry VII's Relations with 'Scotland and Ireland, 1485–98* (Cambridge, 1932); S.G. Ellis, *The Pale and the Far North: Government and Society in Two Early Tudor Borderlands* (Galway, 1988); SP *Hen. VIII* II, 329; LP *Hen. VIII* X 1112; see also the works cited in note 40.

formulation of English policy towards Ireland. In their concern to suppress the similarities with the north of England and to emphasize the relevance of Wales, there existed a hidden set of assumptions in the reformers' language which they themselves were unwilling to elaborate, and few historians since have attempted to address.

THE BIRTH OF A WELSH POLICY

Though historians have frequently noted the considerable number of Tudor officials who in passing had offered comparisons between the problems of government in Ireland and in Wales, the suggestion that a distinctive 'Welsh policy' could be discerned in Irish political treaties was first raised, with characteristic acuity, by D.B. Quinn.[42] According to Quinn, this was a conservative and moderate position. Discounting the problems that it raised in relation to the aspirations inherent in the act for the kingly title, he stressed that confidence in the gradual assimilation of Gaelic Ireland by means of legal and cultural reforms similar to those applied in Wales was being proposed in conscious opposition to alternative arguments from outright dispossession and colonization which were gaining ground in some circles in Elizabethan England. It was, he noted, the dominant school in Elizabethan thinking on Ireland, being preferred well above any radical alternatives by the most influential figures in Irish government until almost the close of the century. Until then, to make reference to the continuing relevance of Wales was to give a clear signal of political orthodoxy.[43]

The gap between the apparent recognitions of 1541 and the implications of this 'moderate' Elizabethan position remains unexplained in this account, yet it seems oversimplistic to attempt to extract a distinctive 'Welsh policy' from the several treatises composed between the 1560s and the 1590s alluding to the Welsh experience to which Quinn made reference as a model for future action in Ireland. For within this large body of material serious differences both in attitude and in strategy are to be found, while

42 D.B. Quinn, 'Ireland and sixteenth century European expansions', in T.D. Williams (ed.) *Historical studies I* (London, 1958), pp.20–32.

43 ibid, esp. pp.29–32.

many of them contain *inter alia* proposals for policy in Ireland that were never seriously contemplated for Wales.

Sir William Gerrard, the writer whose work displays the most sustained attempt to make use of the record of recent Welsh history, was for instance sharply critical of the conduct in office of his former superior in the council in Wales, Lord Deputy Sir Henry Sidney.[44] Sidney's own version of a Welsh policy had attempted to erect a new legal and administrative system throughout the whole island by a mixture of coercion, favouritism and diplomacy in much the same manner as Bishop Rowland Lee had established respect for English law, often initially by arbitrary measures in Wales in the 1530s.[45] Instead, Gerrard used his Welsh experience to argue for a narrow and intense reconstruction of the English Pale as the chief priority of reform. Only thereafter, when the Pale had been thoroughly reclaimed, Gerrard believed, could a gradual expansion of English laws and institutions through the rest of the island be seriously considered.[46] Yet, Sir John Perrot, whose several papers on government also sought support from the Welsh success, rejected Gerrard's contained strategy in favour of a broad, nationwide approach to reform that even exceeded Sidney's schemes in its ambition and comprehensiveness.[47] Sir William Herbert in *Croftus* and in his tracts of the 1580s also made several allusions to the success of Tudor policy in Wales.[48] He shared Perrot's broad view and so implicitly rejected Gerrard's. Yet his own recommendations concerning the means by which English laws and institutions should be established – which included the extensive use of colonies and native transplantation – were far more forceful than those attempted by Sidney and Perrot and far more radical even than the conventional legal mechanisms supported by Gerrard. Finally, Sir

44 Sir William Gerrard, 'Observations on the government of Ireland', 29 March 1578, PRO SP 63/60/29; see also his 'Remembrances for Ireland', 11 April 1578, PRO SP 63/60/33.

45 For a discussion of Sir Henry Sidney's strategy for the reform of Ireland, C. Brady, *The Chief Governors: The Rise and Fall of Reform Government in Tudor Ireland* (Cambridge, 1994) ch.4. the underlying assumptions of Sidney's reform policy are made explicit in the treaties composed during his campaign for reappointment by his sometime secretary, Edmund Tremayne: see esp. Tremayne's memoranda in PRO SP 63/32/14–16; BL Add MSS 48015 ff274–9.

46 'Lord Chancellor Gerrard's Notes of his report on Ireland', ed. C. McNeill, *Analecta Hibernica* 2 (1931), pp.93–291 esp. pp.93–8.

47 Perrot's 'Plat for Ireland' *c*.1581, B.L. Stowe MSS 159; see also his several memoranda in PRO SP 63/112/22–3, 41, 45; BL Add MSS 48015 ff291–5, 313–18.

48 Sir William Herbert, *Croftus sive de Hibernia liber*, ed. A. Keaveney and J.A. Madden (Dublin, 1992); *CSP Ire 1586–8*, pp.

James Croft, ostensibly Herbert's inspiration, was himself the proposer of strategies referring to the Tudor success in Wales which outdistanced everyone in their confidence that conciliation, persuasion and patient education would finally establish English rule peacefully in Ireland with even less force than had been necessary in Wales.[49]

These differences concerning the scope and character of the enterprise were paralleled by important variations in the tactics of reform. Gerrard deplored the over-use of martial law and was highly critical of the use of military men.[50] Croft, exceptionally, insisted that the only captains allowed to remain in Ireland should be of Irish birth or at least those who retained the confidence of the country-people.[51] Yet for Sidney and Perrot, the use of a select cadre of military men as presidents of regional councils, seneschals and constables was essential to the success of their programme.[52] The establishment of regional councils was of central importance to Sidney, Perrot, Croft and Herbert, but not to Gerrard, who viewed them as important but secondary instruments which should not hold precedence over the establishment of more local institutions of justice, assize circuits and quarter sessions.[53] Gerrard indeed wished to see a court of general sessions established along Welsh lines before the councils were introduced, and he argued strongly for the expansion of his own court of chancery as a place of final appeal, but none of the other Welsh strategists pursued such ideas.[54] Gerrard and Herbert were both vehemently opposed to any toleration of Gaelic or localist means of arbitration but Sidney and Perrot were both entirely flexible in this regard. Perrot envisaged the continuing operation of courts baron and manor courts where they presently existed, but Gerrard wished to see them superseded by sessions.[55] The extension of the royal prerogative to include the cessing and billeting of the soldiers on the country was condemned by Croft and (more mildly) by Herbert.[56] Gerrard demonstrated to

49 Sir James Croft, 'Discourse for the reformation of Ireland', *c.*1583, Northumberland CRO Fitzwilliam MSS (Irish) 68.

50 See esp. Gerrard, 'Observations on the government of Ireland' (note 44 above).

51 Croft, 'Discourse for the reformation of Ireland' (note 49 above).

52 Brady, *Chief Governors*, ch.4 and epilogue.

53 Gerrard, 'Notes', pp.96, 183–7; Gerrard, 'Observations'.

54 Gerrard, 'Notes', pp.183–7; Gerrard, 'Treatise on Ireland, *c.* 1576', BL, Cotton MSS Titus B XIII, ff229–30.

55 Gerrard, 'Treatise'.

56 Croft, 'Discourse' (note 49 above).

his own satisfaction that the cess was constitutionally justified, but viewed it none the less as a dangerous expedient to be employed only when absolutely necessary.[57] But for both Sidney and Perrot the employment of cess as a means of sustaining a large army and as a means of persuading the great lords to abandon their own extensive military exactions was a crucial element of their strategy.[58] Finally, underneath the general approbation of regional councils, there lay very profound differences as to how they were to be constituted. For Croft, Herbert and Gerrard they were to follow closely upon the Welsh model, primarily as legal and administrative instruments that were to be staffed, in addition to the president and a small bodyguard, primarily by lawyers, drawn from England and from the localities, while the place of the local lords at the council board was assured. For Sidney (in the later 1570s) and for Perrot, the presidencies were primarily heavily armed military instruments enforcing crown authority and dismounting the extra-legal structures of power in the localities, in the first instance at least, by coercion and intimidation.

These significant differences among those who hailed the Welsh model are evidence, of course, of the rhetorical use to which the story of a Tudor success might be put to support policies which were quite different in scope and in their underlying ideological assumptions. The fate of Wales, that is to say, could be cited by supporters of policies that aimed toward a general peaceful reconciliation in Ireland, a coercive but integrationist approach toward reform or a narrow, gradualist approach, in which the question of reconciling the bulk of the native population was left open because its valency as an unalloyed Tudor achievement remained strong.

RESTRUCTURING IRELAND FROM WITHIN

Yet beneath all of these differences there are some basic similarities, other than mere rhetoric, which help to explain both the continuing attraction of the appeal to Wales and a subtle alteration

57 Gerrard, 'Notes', pp.104–9.

58 See esp. Tremayne's memoranda, PRO SP 63/32/66; BL Add MSS 48015, esp. ff276–7; Perrot's schemes in Northumberland CRO, Fitzwilliam MSS (Irish) 66; BL Add MSS 48015, ff309–11.

that had occurred in Tudor thinking on Ireland since the early 1540s. Though they differed greatly in their strategies, the advocates of 'a Welsh approach' were moderate, as Quinn noted, only because, in contrast to contemporary proponents of a new conquest and genocide, they believed, to quote Gerrard, 'that the disease of the country was not yet so taken as to be beyond cure'.[59] They agreed further that such a cure could be found short of total war and in measures which, for all their differences, were primarily institutional. They shared the belief that the political, geographical, cultural and historical obstacles which confronted Tudor rule in Ireland could be gradually dissolved by the repeated ministration of procedures and rules and structures which on their own possessed the capacity to effect social transformation.

The underlying assumptions of this instrumentalist approach were to a large extent unstated. But they were explicitly discussed by Gerrard in one of his lengthier position papers.[60] Gerrard's point of departure in this argument was apparently historical and quite conventional: the country's decay had begun to occur in the late fourteenth century through the adoption by the great English lords of Irish modes of extortion and intimidation which had flourished ever since. And his solution was apparently just as simplistic: bring back the laws that were in place before the decline and all would be well. But how could he be so sure? His answer was economic and sociological. In the years before the decay, he argued, the lordship had enjoyed unparalleled prosperity; self-sufficient both agriculturally and financially, it required no significant support from England, and on occasion made good the wants of the crown in England and Wales. Underlying this order of prosperity was a rigorous adherence to laws which ensured that the property rights and constitutional liberties of all groups in the community were protected regardless of their place in society or the extent of their political influence. The institutions of law thus underwrote prosperity and prosperity in turn increased respect for the authority of the law. The system was almost but not quite self-sustaining. It depended crucially on the condition that the independence of these offices of law be maintained by a regular turnover of personnel and by a rule ensuring the appointment of Englishmen to the most senior positions. When the interest of the crown over these offices waned, however, and they came under the

59 Gerrard, 'Treatise', f229; for a similar formulation see Gerrard, 'Notes', p.118.
60 Gerrard, 'Notes', pp.118–23, 210–65.

influence of powerful local interests, the decline of the Irish lordship began; the decay had set in, Gerrard argued, long before the political crises of the fifteenth century confirmed the process.[61]

The precision of Gerrard's explanation of decline allowed for his simple administrative solution; reform the courts and the offices of law, ensure their impartiality and indifference through the appointment of English judges and attorneys, and the desire for order and potential for prosperity which lay inherent in the surviving remnants of the old lordship would soon re-emerge. In urging this administrative initiative, Gerrard spoke strictly of the Pale and denied that anything could be done beyond until the Pale had been thoroughly revived. His attitude toward the reform of the outerparts and of the Gaelic Irish was ambivalent or cautious. He sometimes expressed his view, like many old colonial hands, that the natives were congenitally unfit for reform, but in his more reflective moments he suggested that some of the Gaelic Irish, like some of the degenerate English, would prove responsive to the appeal of law while others would not depending upon such factors as their location, the available political opportunities and their experience.[62] But whatever its success throughout Ireland, Gerrard knew that the reformed law would work in the Pale because manifestly it had done so before.

It was here that Sidney and Perrot parted company with Gerrard. Like him they recognized that the key to the country's malaise lay in the bastard feudal rackets practised by Gaelic and English lords alike. Like him they perceived that the rackets were wasteful of the country's natural resources and that their unrestrained escalation was gradually consuming the wealth even of those who seemed to profit most from them. They recognized also that there existed a growing interest at all levels of society for the revival of the system and the establishment of an order under which the right and obligations of all parties would be recognized and upheld by law alone. But unlike Gerrard they denied that such a reconstruction of a law-based society could be undertaken piecemeal. Extortion and intimidation were so pervasive and infectious that the isolation of any one region for special reform treatment would merely leave it vulnerable to attack and require such a constant military protection as to be self-defeating. The disease had to be tackled directly throughout the country, and because the existing social structures in the provincial lordships differed considerably from those existing

61 Gerrard, 'Notes', pp.122–3, 266–7.
62 Gerrard, 'Observations', PRO SP 63/60/20.

in the Pale or in contemporary Wales, different institutions would be required to fulfil the same objectives of instrumental reform. Thus they developed the so-called composition presidency for Munster and Connaught, military agencies which were designed to enforce the commutation of bastard-feudal exactions among lords, vassals and tenants into fixed sums to be collected by the agents of the crown. Compared to Wales these were presidents in name only and the policy of composition was considerably more coercive and arbitrary than anything enforced in Wales, including even the operation of the Welsh council in the heyday of Bishop Lee. But in so far as they were instruments designed to restructure Irish society from within by exploiting its own internal tendencies, the policy of composition and its means of enforcement were seen by their advocates to imitate the strategies pursued in the reform of Wales, all necessary changes being made to account for the inevitable variations that occurred in a different country at a different stage of development.[63]

It was of course this national composition version of the 'Welsh policy' that prevailed in the government of Ireland over the limited schemes of Gerrard and even the alternative broad approaches advocated by Herbert and Croft. And it was the failure and collapse of this same strategy that most modern scholars agree precipated the major political crises of the later sixteenth century, the outbreak of the Munster rebellion following Sidney's recall, and the rapid destabilization of Ulster following the dismissal of Perrot.[64] Yet these defeats, could have afforded little satisfaction to the advocates of Gerrard's modest alternative, for in each case the most deadly challenge to reform arose not in the most lawless areas where it was meant to apply, but in the English Pale itself. And it had arisen, moreover, in response to the very policies which Gerrard once believed would rapidly encourage general approval.

In relation to the Pale, both Gerrard and those who moved beyond him shared a basic set of desiderata. All believed, that is, that the central offices of law should be subjected to severe overhaul, and that (with the exception of a few dependable

63 P. Williams, 'The council in Munster in the late sixteenth century', *Bulletin of the Irish Committee of Historical Sciences* 123 (1959–61) no pagination; D.J. Kennedy, 'The presidency of Munster' (University College, Cork, MA thesis, 1973); B. Cunningham. 'The composition of Connacht in the lordships of Clanrickard and Thomond', *IHS* 24 (1984–5), pp.1–14; Brady, *Chief Governors,* chs 4–5.

64 C. Brady, 'Faction and the origins of the Desmond rebellion of 1579', *IHS* 22 (1980–1), pp.289–312; H. Morgan, *Tyrone's Rebellion: The Outbreak of the Nine Years War in Tudor Ireland* (Woodbridge, 1993), chs 3–4, 7.

favourites) the current personnel should be replaced. All believed also that assize circuits, not unknown, but irregular and infrequent, should be reformed and regularized; all were agreed further that the appointment of sheriffs should be more carefully scrutinized and that the conduct of those included on the Pale shires' commissions of peace be subject to assessment. More importantly all believed that the principles of the reform programmes both particular and general should be presented for ratification and financial subvention to an Irish parliament. Finally, though with varying degrees of regret, all conceded that the country's acquiescence in the use of the royal prerogative to supply and lodge an onerous English garrison was a necessary, if short-term, precondition of reform.

Yet it was against these basic requirements, common to all the promoters of any Welsh policy, that the English Irish, the surviving representatives of the old lordship, gibbed. From the 1570s attempts to reform even the small number of central law offices gave rise to such resentment and subversion in the Pale that the new appointments almost immediately became isolated from and hostile towards the community that they came to serve.[65] Likewise, such efforts as were made to reform local government ended in failure: Sidney's attempts to choose military men as sheriffs provoked widespread discontent, and Perrot's brave effort, as late as 1586, to require the oath of supremacy from anyone seeking appointment to a commission of the peace failed utterly.[66] More seriously, a parliament dominated by Palesmen successfully undermined the statutory and financial basis of Perrot's version of a Welsh solution, based on the idea of national composition.[67] Most seriously of all, the Palesmen from the beginning refused to acknowledge any obligation to any programme of reform, narrow or grand, by their resolute resistance to any encroachment on their English constitutional liberties by the use of the royal prerogative of purveyance applied on the grounds of the temporary exigencies of reform policy.[68]

65 For a representative example see the correspondence of Attorney-General Thomas Snagge and his allegations of corruption, throughout 1577–9, SP 63/59/42, 61; 63/64/8; 63/66/46–8.

66 'Order for the oath of supremacy', June 1585, SP 63/119/32, enclosure (i); Bishop Lyon to Lord Hunsdon, 6 July 1596, SP 63/191/12.

67 Victor Treadwell, 'Sir John Perrot and the Irish parliament of 1585–6', *PRIA* 95C (1985), pp.259–308.

68 C. Brady, 'Conservative subversives: the community of the Pale and the Dublin administration, 1556–1586', in P.J. Corish (ed.) *Radicals, Rebels and Establishments: Historical Studies XV* (Belfast, 1985) pp.11–32.

THE FAILURE OF THE WELSH POLICY

Whether it was conducted by passive resistance or subversion, by supplication, intrigue and the overt assertion of their rights as Englishmen, the Palesmen's denial of an obligation to lend support to a policy over which they had no influence constituted the clearest possible rejection of the several roles which each of the advocates of a Welsh model had either consciously or inadvertently reserved for them. What was at stake in their defiance of their English governors' reform policies was something more than a grievance concerning the burdens of military taxation, more even than an acute sensitivity to their constitutional liberties: they rejected the implicit unhistorical assumption that lay at the centre of every argument affirming that the benefits of the Welsh experience could be applied to Ireland. This was the unstated belief that recent Irish history could be wound back, and that the preconditions of the success of reform which had matured in Wales over the previous two centuries could be replicated in Ireland instantly, simply by means of instrumentalist intervention. For them it was no longer possible to return to the days of Edward III, by sacrificing the securities, customs and rights which they had preserved since those days. Nor was it practicable to expect them to risk the tenuous sense of identity they had nurtured since that time by surrendering their liberties to a government that aimed eventually to envelop their interests with those of the old Irish enemies under the aegis of a single sovereignty. For the Palesmen, that is, the idea that a larger Wales could be artificially constructed in Ireland was both unrealistic and unacceptable: too much had happened since the time when the paths of both regions had begun to diverge to make it otherwise.

The Palesmen's rejection of the 'moderate' Welsh policy was, as is well known to Irish historians, to summon its own nemesis.[69] In the wake of the crisis of the sixteenth century it was they rather than the native Irish who came to be seen as the true enemies of English government in the island, whose power was to be destroyed by any means. But the inherent irony of their fate bears reiteration. By their refusal to be treated as historical anachronisms – subjects

69 A. Clarke, 'Colonial identity in early seventeenth century Ireland', in T.W. Moody (ed.) *Nationality and the Pursuit of National Independence: Historical Studies XI* (Belfast, 1978), pp.57–71; A. Clarke, 'Colonial constitutional attitudes in Ireland, 1640–1660's, *PRIA* 90C (1990), pp.357–75.

only in embryo as the Welsh had once been – and by their insistence that they were modern English gentlemen with a status equal to any in any other part of the Tudor realms, they ensured that they should never be received as such.

CHAPTER FOUR

Anglo-Scottish protestant culture and integration in sixteenth-century Britain

Jane Dawson
University of Edinburgh

In the second half of the sixteenth century an Anglo-Scottish protestant culture developed within the island of Britain. It rested on the twin foundations of a mutually comprehensible language, English, and a common religion, protestantism, and took shape against the background of a hostile catholic Europe. This Anglo-Scottish culture formed part of the broader linguistic world comprising the English-speaking peoples throughout the British Isles and the North American colonies. Its wider culture reflected the same dual emphases as the Anglo-Scottish version. It also gradually came to rest upon protestantism as much as upon the shared English language. This ensured the eventual exclusion of those groups of English speakers who retained their catholic religion, such as the Old English within Ireland. Protestantism emerged as one of the defining characteristics of the dominant culture of the English-speaking people during the early modern period. The Anglo-Scottish culture which developed in the sixteenth century was the first to turn the vital connection between the English language and protestantism into a vehicle for integration.[1]

The dynamic combination of religion and language created a basis for integration between the separate kingdoms within the

1 J.G.A. Pocock, 'British History: a plea for a new subject', *JMH* 47 (1975), pp.601–28; J.G.A. Pocock, 'The limits and divisions of British History', *AHR* 87 (1982), pp.311–36; J.G.A. Pocock, 'England', in O. Ranum (ed.) *National Consciousness, History and Political Culture in Early-Modern Europe* (Baltimore, Md, 1975), pp.98–117; N. Canny, 'Identity formation in Ireland: the emergence of the Anglo-Irish', in N. Canny and A. Pagden (eds) *Colonial Identity in the Atlantic World, 1500–1800* (Princeton, NJ, 1981); J. Wormald, 'The creation of Britain: multiple kingdoms or core and colonies?', *TRHS* 6th ser. 2 (1992), pp.175–94.

island of Britain. By 1603 the two peoples of England and Scotland shared a set of key concepts and this had achieved a measure of cultural integration. However, although it was essential in the slow and painful progress of integration, Anglo-Scottish protestant culture could never provide the political foundations for a new state of Greater Britain. This was by no means clear at the time. From the accession of James VI to the English throne in 1603 until the Union of 1707, the very existence and success of the new protestant culture produced a dangerous illusion for supporters of greater Anglo-Scottish union. They could see that a partial unity of hearts and minds had been formed on the bedrock of a common religious culture. They assumed that this culture could unify the two peoples completely and make a full constitutional and ecclesiastical union possible. This was a reasonable deduction in the early modern period when religion provided the fundamental framework within which most people in England and Scotland conducted their lives. Religious vocabulary and concepts permeated their view of politics and, more obviously, determined attitudes towards the two national churches.

The common religious outlook which united Scottish and English protestants seemed to those intent on greater union to promise far more than cultural integration. But, these enthusiasts did not appreciate that the Anglo-Scottish culture was itself incapable of transcending the strong identities already present within the island of Britain. Scotland and England had previously developed two very distinct and mutually antagonistic national and ecclesiastical identities. By the end of the sixteenth century, these identities were also rooted in different interpretations of protestantism. England and Scotland might share some aspects of a religious culture but, crucially, they did not share a common political and religious identity. The complete failure of James VI and I's plans for union between the two realms demonstrated the severe limitations of the common religious culture. It might be able to advance the integration of Britain, but it could never bring about a formal political unification.[2]

2 B.P. Levack, *The Formation of the British State: England, Scotland and the Union 1603–1707* (Oxford, 1987); C. Russell, *The Causes of the English Civil War* (Oxford, 1990), chs 2 and 3; J.H. Burns, 'Scotland and England: culture and nationality, 1500–1800', in J.S. Bromley and E.H. Kossmann (eds) *Metropolis, Dominion and Province*, Britain and the Netherlands IV (The Hague, 1971), pp.17–41; R. Mason, 'The Scottish Reformation and the origins of Anglo-British imperialism', in R. Mason (ed.) *Scots and Britons: Scottish Political Thought and the Union of 1603* (Cambridge, 1994), pp.161–86. I am most grateful to Dr Mason for allowing me to read this chapter before publication.

TOWARDS A UNIFIED BRITIAN

The reign of Elizabeth I witnessed a crucial phase in the process of integration within the island of Britain. During the forty years of her rule, Anglo-Scottish relations were transformed. At Elizabeth's accession in 1558, Scotland and England were at war. When she died in 1603, there was a quiet transition of power when James VI, king of Scotland, succeeded her to become James I of England. In the intervening years the English and the Scots had been at peace, joined by a diplomatic alliance between the two kingdoms. They also shared a common religion. Protestantism had been reintroduced to England in 1559 and was first established in Scotland in the following year. By the turn of the century the protestant character of both kingdoms had come to be regarded by contemporaries as an essential and predestined feature of the island of Britain. The separate protestant status of Britain was highlighted by the struggle against resurgent catholicism inspired by the council of Trent and led by Philip II of Spain.

Ideas about the unity of the island of Britain were not new. In his celebrated history of Greater Britain published in 1521, John Mair had argued persuasively for a full dynastic alliance to end the long hostility between the kingdoms of Scotland and England. Arguments for union rested on a number of common factors. The two countries were contained in the one large island and the languages of Scots and English were mutually comprehensible. Many of their administrative, social and legal traditions were similar and at the start of the sixteenth century there were no complications about a religious division as both nations were part of the Catholic Church which spread throughout Christendom. The marriage in 1503 of 'the thistle and the rose', between James IV of Scotland and Margaret Tudor, daughter of Henry VII, opened the possibility of long-term peace and dynastic unity between the two realms. This hope was shattered on the field of Flodden in 1513 when James and many of the Scottish nobility died fighting in yet another episode in the wars which had existed between England and Scotland for a couple of centuries.[3]

From the days of the Wars of Independence, the Scots had been linked to the French in the 'auld alliance'. With less continuity and

3 R. Mason, 'Kingship, nobility and Anglo-Scottish union: John Mair's *History of Greater Britain* (1521)', *Innes Review* 41 (1990), pp.182–222.

consistency, the English had been allied to the kings of Spain or the rulers of the Low Countries, both of which areas had, by the sixteenth century, come under the control of the Habsburg family. Anglo-Scottish relations had been, and throughout the sixteenth century remained, part of the wider European diplomatic scene. Both the Scots and the English were used by their more powerful European partners as pawns in the major power struggle between the Habsburgs and the Valois kings of France which dominated European politics in the first half of the sixteenth century.

Such factors made the change that occurred in 1559–60 within the British Isles all the more dramatic. They were part of a major shift in European politics which followed the peace of Câteau Cambrésis of April 1559 and the subsequent collapse of France into civil war. This encouraged new alignments along confessional rather than dynastic lines, which by the end of the sixteenth century had divided Europe into two hostile camps. The years 1559–60 witnessed a revolution in Scotland which brought about a reversal of the country's political, diplomatic and religious position. In February 1560 the English signed the treaty of Berwick with the Scottish Lords of the Congregation who had rebelled against Mary of Guise, the queen regent of Scotland. With the aid of English troops and ships, the Lords of the Congregation seized power in Scotland and were then able to bring about a protestant reformation of the church. This change in both the diplomatic and ecclesiastical stance of Scotland ushered in a new era of Anglo-Scottish friendship and one destined to grow into the Union of the Crowns in 1603 and the 1707 incorporating union which were major landmarks in the creation of the British state.

The new Anglo-Scottish friendship begun in 1560 provoked euphoric outpourings on the subject of the unity of the island of Britain, particularly from north of the border. The 'auld alliance' with France had become fatally associated with catholicism and was now regarded as a threat to Scottish sovereignty. The English, who had been the 'auld enemies' bent on an imperial conquest of Scotland, became instead firm friends and brothers in the protestant faith. This new amity had been cemented on the battlefield when the Scots and the English had fought together – not very successfully – against the queen regent and her French soldiers.

The hope that their brief military cooperation would be the beginning of a complete transformation in Anglo-Scottish relations was strengthened by the novel attitude displayed by the English in the negotiations of 1559–60. Masterminded by William Cecil, Elizabeth I's secretary, English policy had shown an unprecedented awareness of Scottish sensibilities in the negotiations and in the assistance which had been provided for the Scots. Even more remarkable in Scottish eyes, the English army and navy could not leave Scotland quickly enough after the hostilities were over. Although this probably owed more to Queen Elizabeth's parsimony than to her tact, it did allay residual Scottish fears concerning English imperialist ambitions.

The Scottish confidence that this new English sensitivity was more than a temporary ploy, rested upon what they regarded as the most solid of foundations, the bond of a common religion. Three hundred years of warfare and hostile propaganda could not easily be set aside. However strong the mutual interest of the two kingdoms within the island of Britain and the arguments for union which had been gaining ground since the beginning of the century, they were incapable of overcoming those accumulated depths of feeling. To contemporaries, religion was the only force capable of providing the emotional power to eradicate the long-standing enmity which existed between the two peoples and so transform their deep-rooted hatred into an enduring amity.[4]

As Elizabeth's reign progressed, both the friendship and the religious unity which had characterized the early years of the Anglo-Scottish alliance were supplanted by England's succession problems. The claim to the English throne, first that of Mary Queen of Scots and subsequently of her son, James VI, came to dominate Anglo-Scottish relations. It slowly became apparent that Elizabeth would not marry and would thus be the last of the Tudor rulers of England. Although Queen Elizabeth flatly refused to name her successor, the absence of serious alternative candidates by the last two decades of the century made the Scottish king the most likely heir. However, the lack of certainty on the matter ensured that relations between Scotland and England remained focused upon the succession question right up to Elizabeth's death. The prospect of a dynastic link between Scotland and England had pushed the ideals of amity based on the common religious bond into second place. At the highest diplomatic and political levels, hard-headed calculation of mutual advantage seemed to replace the belief in the transforming power of a shared protestantism. But if

4 J. Dawson, 'William Cecil and the British dimension of early Elizabethan foreign policy', *History* 74 (1989), pp.196–216.

they had been shunted to one side by the politicians, such ideals did not simply fade away. Instead they became part of the new joint religious culture which developed independently of political or ecclesiastical policy-making.

PRINT AND PROTESTANTISM

Anglo-Scottish protestant culture could develop on its own because England and Lowland Scotland shared a mutually comprehensible language. Most protestants in Scotland and England read the same key religious texts and, crucially, the same Bible. There was also considerable overlap in the personnel who spread religious ideas which helped to produce a common outlook. In addition, two Anglo-Scottish ecclesiastical parties emerged in the final part of the sixteenth century. The two mutually antagonistic parties sought allies in the other kingdom. The English puritans looked to the Scottish presbyterians for support and the Scottish bishops sought aid from the English clerical hierarchy. Each party saw its struggles against the other within a 'British' context and regarded their own cause as one that transcended the national churches. Both groups tried to use the common religious culture on behalf of their own ecclesiastical programmes. Their activities did increase the general awareness of events and attitudes in the other country and forged many close personal links. The two parties indirectly encouraged the spread of Anglo-Scottish protestant culture, but they did not change its essentially lay and non-partisan nature. It remained firmly outside ecclesiastical politics because it was never a specific ecclesiastical programme but a set of shared religious ideas which were spread in the sixteenth century primarily through the media of books and people.

The dominance of English as the main language of print within the British Isles was the essential ingredient in the formation of an Anglo-Scottish protestant culture.[5] British protestants read their religious literature in English or in the international language of Latin. The Welsh provided the major exception to this British pattern, producing a small, though significant, protestant literature

5 V. Durkacz, *The Decline of the Celtic Languages* (Edinburgh, 1983), ch.1; R. Wardhaugh, *Languages in Competition* (London, 1987), ch.4; J.N. Wall, 'The Reformation in England and the typographical revolution', in G.P. Tyson and S.S. Wagonheim (eds) *Print and Culture in the Renaissance* (Newark, NJ, 1986), pp.208–21.

in their own language.[6] All levels of religious writing, from chap-books to the Bible itself, were printed in an English which was becoming more standardized as the century progressed. This created a linguistic area, an English-reading world, where the English language could be read and understood, even where it was not spoken, as in Scotland. Here the increasingly strong anglicizing influence upon the Scots language, particularly in its written form, was most noticeable in the area of religion.[7] The two key religious texts, the Bible and the liturgy, were both written and printed in English. The Geneva Bible was the translation used in Scotland from 1560 until the end of the century and well beyond. It had been produced by the English exile community who had settled in Geneva during the reign of Mary Tudor. The first edition, published in 1560, might be dedicated to the young Queen Elizabeth but its 'Epistle to the Reader' made it clear that it was explicitly directed to all the 'Brethren of England, Scotland, Ireland etc'.[8] It assumed without question that protestants within the British Isles could read the same language, the English of the translation. There was an optimistic willingness to include all the kingdoms, Ireland and Scotland as well as England and Wales, in this comprehensive British view.

The same English exile community who had produced the Geneva Bible provided the Scottish Church with the basis for its liturgy. The *Form of Prayers* was written for the English Church in Geneva of which the Scot, John Knox, and the Englishman, Christopher Goodman, were ministers. After the adoption of protestantism in Scotland in 1560, it became the Scottish *Book of Common Order.* As with the Geneva Bible, the *Book of Common Order* was written and printed in English and was not altered linguistically for use in Lowland Scotland. However, it was translated into Gaelic to be comprehensible both in the Highlands and Islands of Scotland and also in Ireland, as the introduction by its translator, John Carswell, makes clear.[9]

6 G. Williams, 'Religion and Welsh literature in the age of the Reformation', *Proceedings of the British Academy* 69 (1983), pp.371–408. See also Jenkins, Chapter 5 in this volume.

7 M. Robinson, 'Language choice in the Reformation: the Scots Confession of 1560', in J.D. Maclure (ed.) *Scotland and the Lowland Tongue* (Aberdeen, 1983), pp.59–78; D. Wright (ed.) *The Bible in Scottish Life and Literature* (Edinburgh, 1988).

8 Geneva Bible (facsimile of 1560 edn, Milwaukee, Wis., 1969) ed. Lloyd Berry, sig. iii.

9 *John Carswell's Foirm na n-Urrnuidheadh,* ed. R.L. Thomson, SGTS 11 (Edinburgh, 1970), pp.173–82.

To have these key religious texts circulating and being reproduced in English was a fatal blow to Scots as a language of print. The spoken tongue remained quite clearly different from spoken English. This created the unusual situation that the standard texts were read and pronounced in Scots.[10] In the second half of the sixteenth century a whole variety of spoken and written forms had coexisted within Lowland Scotland. The range and diversity of language which was produced can be seen in the painted ceilings at Crathes Castle, which were decorated between 1599 and 1602. The biblical quotations found in the Green Lady's Room were all taken from the Geneva version and appeared in standard English whilst the other quotations and inscriptions range through the spectrum to broad Scots.[11] In the long run, however, it was the English language, spelling and orthography of the Bible which dominated the written word in Scotland.

Such a major split between the printed and the spoken language had a serious effect upon the subsequent development of Scotland's literary culture. The dominance of English as the standard printed form ensured that Scots lost ground as a language of literary composition, even though there had been a vigorous tradition of vernacular poetry. By the beginning of the seventeenth century most Scots wrote their works for publication in English. The vital area of erosion for Scots was the printed word itself. It was controlled by the economics of the printing industry within Britain. Although there were a few printers operating in Scotland, the great bulk of vernacular publishing was done in London. A number of the Edinburgh printers, such as Vautrollier and Waldegrave, had previously been in business in London and usually employed English spelling and orthography. Apart from the standard religious texts, the Bible, the *Book of Common Order*, and the catechisms, there was little specifically Scottish religious literature published within the country until the late 1580s. Many books clearly intended for the Scottish market continued to be published in London, such as John Knox's *History of the Reformation.* By the 1590s a small market for popular Scottish religious works had developed which allowed the publication within Scotland of collections of sermons from

10 M. Robinson, 'Language choice', p.62; J.D. Maclure, 'Scottis, Inglis, Suddroun: language labels and language attitudes', in R.J. Lyall and F. Riddy (eds) *Proceedings of the Third International Conference on Scottish Language and Literature* (Stirling/Glasgow, 1981), pp.52–69.

11 H. Hargreaves, 'The Crathes ceiling inscriptions', in J.D. Maclure and M. Spiller (eds.) *Bryght Lanternis* (Aberdeen, 1989), p.374.

leading Scottish ministers such as Robert Rollock. Few English books were reprinted in Scotland. This reinforces the impression gained from Edinburgh booksellers' lists that texts were imported directly from England. The lists show that popular English authors were all well represented. As Marjorie Bald concluded, 'the habit of sending to England for theological works had been established when the native printing press was in its first stages; and the habit was never broken'.[12]

With the dominance of the London printing industry, most of the protestant literature in the vernacular was aimed primarily at English protestants, especially in the capital and the southern counties. A considerable market developed for popular religious literature.[13] Some of these tracts and chap-books found their way to Scotland through booksellers such as John Norton, the Englishman who was operating in Edinburgh during the 1580s. Religious books accounted for about half of the stock recorded in Edinburgh booksellers' wills and the Scottish reading public turned its attention first to theological works before moving on to other forms of literature. In this sense, 'the Reformation may be said to have founded the book trade in Scotland'.[14] The Scottish reading public were drawn into the orbit of English popular religious literature by market forces rather than by a self-conscious cultural imperialism. Reading the same religious books brought a convergence in thinking among the literate lay protestant enthusiasts within each country.

Although the general diffusion of popular English religious literature was important, it could not have the impact of that central protestant text, the Bible. The use of the Geneva Bible throughout England and Scotland brought far more than the anglicization of the printed word in Scotland. In addition to a linguistic convergence, it provided the foundation for the cultural unity between Scottish and English protestants. In the sixteenth century, protestant culture in Britain was firmly rooted in the Bible. It supplied the main and sometimes the only reading for protestants and in this way shaped all their thinking. Their views and writings were saturated by biblical imagery and their whole lives

12 M.A. Bald, 'Vernacular books imported into Scotland: 1500 to 1625', *SHR* 23 (1926), p.266; M.A. Bald, 'The pioneers of anglicised speech in Scotland', *SHR* 24 (1926–7), pp.179–93; G. Donaldson, 'Foundations of Anglo-Scottish union', in *Scottish Church History* (Edinburgh, 1985), pp.137–63.

13 T. Watt, *Cheap Print and Popular Piety* (Cambridge, 1991); J.N. King, *English Reformation Literature* (London, 1982).

14 Bald, 'Vernacular books', p.266.

were lived and understood within a biblically conceived framework. To share the same Bible, especially the same version, was to share the same culture.[15]

The Geneva Bible was adopted by the Scottish Church after 1560, but south of the border it met with the official disapproval of the English Church hierarchy who produced their own version in the Bishops' Bible of 1568. This did not prevent the Geneva translation being the most popular version in Elizabethan England. The Geneva version was easy to read, being printed in italic and not black letter type. It was sold in cheap, relatively small and pocket-sized editions which were still equipped with a full set of biblical aids. Both the popularity and the disapproval arose from what James VI referred to as the 'bitter notes' attached to the biblical text. The Geneva version had sidenotes to the individual words or verses explaining particular points of interpretation or translation. It provided 'arguments', summaries at the start of every book of the Bible and for each chapter within it. There were also several types of index, a number of helpful lists and numerous fine diagrams and maps in the text. Together, these aids provided the reader with a comprehensive and controversial interpretation of the whole Bible all contained within its own covers. By using the Geneva Bible, Scottish and English protestants shared far more than the one translation of the text. They read that biblical message within the same clear interpretative framework and absorbed the covenant ideas and apocalyptic framework which had been stressed by the Marian exile translators. Anglo-Scottish protestant culture grew out of the Geneva Bible and its notes.[16]

To a lesser extent the English and Scottish liturgies were also common property between the realms. Before 1560 the English *Book of Common Prayer* had been used in some of the protestant households and privy kirks in Scotland. In Elizabeth's reign, English puritans certainly knew of, revered and sometimes employed (even though it was illegal) the *Form of Prayers* which they felt was far superior to the insufficiently reformed 1559 *Book of Common Prayer.* This ensured that there was at least a strong familiarity with the liturgies of the other protestant nation and for the Scots and most of the 'godly' in England an almost complete identity of outlook on the matter. The other book which achieved a semi-canonical status

15 C. Hill, *The English Bible and the Seventeenth-Century Revolution* (London, 1993), ch.1.

16 S. Greenslade (ed.) *The Cambridge History of the Bible* (Cambridge, 1965), chs 4 and 5.

in both realms was John Foxe's *Acts and Monuments.* Foxe had specifically included all the Scottish martyrs in his history when he chronicled the persecutions 'in this Realme of England and Scotland'.[17] It was through reading their copies of Foxe's *Book of Martyrs* that British protestants came to appreciate that the deaths of these faithful witnesses were part of the struggles of the True Church against the forces of Antichrist. Foxe had carefully set out the chronological pattern of that cosmic battle and brought the record right up to the present time. It was within this apocalyptic perspective that protestants viewed their world.

PERSONAL CONTACTS AND RIVAL PARTIES

The cultural unity brought by sharing a Bible, and having a martyrology and liturgical tradition in common, was reinforced by strong personal links. There was considerable interchange of personnel between England and Scotland throughout the sixteenth century. Before 1560 many Scottish protestants found refuge in England, especially during the congenial reign of Edward VI. The most famous, though by no means the most representative, was John Knox. During the decade after 1548 Knox pursued his career almost exclusively within an English context, married an English wife and acquired a noticeably English accent and a hybrid Anglo-Scottish literary style. Knox's close friend and colleague, the Englishman Christopher Goodman, came to Scotland in 1559 and ministered to the congregations in Ayr and St Andrews. Although he left Scotland in 1565, Goodman remained in touch with his Scottish friends until his death in 1603 and was an important point of contact between the protestant radicals in both England and Scotland. In the latter years of Elizabeth's reign, George Buchanan, the Scottish humanist, was a member of the circle who gathered around Sir Philip Sidney. This wide-ranging cultural and intellectual group kept in close contact with Scottish affairs.[18]

17 J. Dawson, 'The Scottish Reformation and the theatre of martyrdom', in D. Wood (ed.) *Martyrs and Martyrologies,* Studies in Church History, 30 (Oxford, 1993), pp.259–70.

18 Donaldson, 'Foundations', pp.154–8; J. Dawson, 'The two John Knoxes', *JEH* 42 (1991), pp.555–76; J.E. Phillipps, 'George Buchanan and the Sidney Circle', *HLQ* 12 (1948–9), pp.23–55; see also A.H. Williamson, 'A patriot nobility? Calvinism, kin-ties and civic humanism', *SHR* 72 (1993), pp.1–21. More research is needed on the personal contacts between Scotsmen and Englishmen in this period.

For both Knox and Goodman crossing the border was a 'natural' response to persecution at home. The similarity of the language made it possible for such exiles to be understood, though there were probably some difficulties with the full comprehension of the spoken tongue of the exile. It enabled them to operate as ministers in the other country, to 'travail in our vocation as it should please the Lord to give occasion', as the Scottish exiles expressed it in 1584.[19] The close links between the presbyterian groups of England and Scotland were demonstrated in the very warm welcome which those Scottish presbyterian exiles received from the English puritans. The Scots saw England as 'a receptacle for the troubled and persecuted saints of God', where they would be able to have 'consultation with learned men, zealous brethren and whoever has defended the Lord's cause'. The solidarity produced by this personal contact created a strong Anglo-Scottish party campaigning jointly for the presbyterian cause in both countries. There was an impressive shown of strength at the funeral of one of the Scots who died while he was in London. On 13 October 1584 James Lawson's funeral was attended by over 500 people, including most of the Scottish ministers and the leading English puritans. These connections worried Queen Elizabeth and some of the Anglican bishops. They prompted one of Elizabeth's more offensive pieces of gratuitous advice given in 1590 to James VI, who had long been aware of the activities of the presbyterians and their threat to his royal position: 'Let me warne you that ther is risen, bothe in your realme and myne, a secte of perilous consequence, such as wold have no kings but a presbytrye'.[20]

During these years another Anglo-Scottish ecclesiastical party of the opposite persuasion had also emerged. The Scottish bishops, especially Patrick Adamson, the archbishop of St Andrews, had sought help and advice from their English counterparts. Archbishop Whitgift had been careful to maintain a diplomatic distance from Adamson, during the Scot's visit to London in 1583–4. But Richard Bancroft was anxious to increase his Scottish contacts in order to gain more material for his attack upon the Scottish presbyterians. He first lambasted the Scots in his sermon at Paul's Cross on 9 February 1589 and followed this up in his books

19 G. Donaldson, 'Scottish Presbyterian exiles', in *Scottish Church History* (Edinburgh, 1985), pp.180–1.

20 G. Donaldson, 'Foundations', p.156; Russell, *Causes*, p.35.

Dangerous Positions and Proceedings and *A Survay of the pretended holy discipline*, both published in 1593.[21]

The many ties and friendships formed between Scottish and English protestants and the formation of these two mutually antagonistic ecclesiastical parties guaranteed that a steady stream of news passed from one realm to the other. It increased the general level of interest in the religious developments within the other country. Despite the divisive nature of the parties, they did encourage the assumption that the protestants of Scotland and England were engaged in the same enterprise. Through all these means Anglo-Scottish protestant culture took shape and was disseminated during the second half of the sixteenth century.

'THE STRAYTEST KNOT OF AMITYE'

At the heart of Anglo-Scottish protestant culture was the assumption that the two kingdoms shared a common bond of religion. For supporters of greater union between the realms, this basic presupposition had a beguiling attraction. The writings of Robert Pont, an influential Scottish minister who had been active since 1560, demonstrated the central place that the concept of a common religion had in unionist thinking. In his dialogue *Of the Union of Britayne*, written in his retirement and published in 1604, Robert Pont posed the rhetorical question

> after a peace made fiftie yeares since, what hath continued love and friendship inviolable betwixt these two kingdomes which seldome before hapned? Did not I pray you the conformity in religion worke a correspondency in theyr mindes, and knit them in an unseparable bande of interchanged and reciprocal amity?

In his flowery language, Pont was giving expression to a familiar theme found in pamphlets during the second half of the sixteenth century: that since 1560 England and Scotland had shared the same religion and that it had formed the basis for their friendly alliance. From this premise he deduced, incorrectly, that religion would also provide the strongest bond to link the two nations in a closer

21 G. Donaldson, 'Whitgift and Bancroft', in *Scottish Church History* (Edinburgh, 1985), pp.171–2. Replies to Bancroft by John Penry, *A Briefe Discovery of the Untruthes and Slanders* (1588); and John Davidson, *D. Bancrofts Rashenes in Rayling against the Church of Scotland* (1590); were published in Edinburgh.

political union in the future. Pont was well aware of the counter-argument that within Britain religion was an essentially divisive force. He placed in the mouth of Hospes, one of his disputants, the comment, 'I know well that unity of religion is a great motive to concord, but the adversaryes say that in many pointes of religion the English and Scottish agree not'. This received the sharp reply

> It is a wicked slaunder. They agree in doctrine, and their difference in some matters of discipline empeacheth not so their religion but that their may be a sweet harmony in their kingedomes and unity in their churches. For where the fundamentall doctrine is (as the worship of one God, a true invocation of Christe's name, an assurance of salvation by Him onely, the right administration of the sacrements, baptisme and the supper of the Lord) although in matters and discipline their be not found in all an equality and perfection, to such an assemblie the faithfull never douted to joyne themselves.[22]

Here was the heart of the problem, not simply for Pont but for all those sixteenth-century commentators who had been asserting that England and Scotland shared one religion. By 1603, and for some observers ever since 1560, it had been apparent that the Scottish and English church organizations – 'discipline' in its widest sense – were different. To many, the two ecclesiastical polities were actually diverging, rather than converging. Pont was able to emphasize the doctrinal agreement which would keep the two churches in communion with each other. He believed that this might provide a sufficient basis for future ecclesiastical harmony and even for eventual political union.

However, in his definition of 'fundamentall doctrine', Pont did not refer to the high tenets of reformed theology. He might have been expected to be alluding to the calvinist consensus that characterized the doctrinal orthodoxy of both the English and Scottish confessions, particularly in the Jacobean period. Instead, Pont spoke of the essential marks of a True Church which made it identifiably protestant and permitted full fellowship with all other protestants. Unfortunately, this minimalist definition did not appear sufficient to support his strong conviction that England and Scotland shared the same religion.

22 B. Galloway and B. Levack (eds) *The Jacobean Union* (Edinburgh, 1985), p.7; B. Galloway, *The Union of England and Scotland 1603–1608* (Edinburgh, 1986). Pont is discussed in A.H. Williamson, 'Number and national consciousness: the Edinburgh mathematicians and Scottish political culture at the union of the crowns', in Mason (ed.) *Scots and Britons*, pp.193f. I am most grateful to Professor Williamson for allowing me to read this chapter before publication.

Along with many of his contemporaries, Pont was struggling to find the correct vocabulary to express his awareness of a shared protestant culture which existed despite the fact that the English and Scottish churches were self-consciously separate and distinct. Early modern writers dealt with this problem of nomenclature by employing the straightforward assertion that the two countries were of the same religion. This phrase, which appeared so frequently throughout the sixteenth century, was their method of describing the Anglo-Scottish protestant culture which had developed by 1603. The belief in a shared religion was usually kept separate from any comment upon the two ecclesiastical organizations. It was nearly always linked to the amity and alliance between the realms of England and Scotland and regarded as the foundation of that friendship.

This was evident from the very beginning of that new relationship. In jubilant mood, William Maitland of Lethington wrote to his friend, William Cecil, about the Anglo-Scottish alliance which the two men had done so much to construct in 1559–60:

> When, in the days of zour princes off maist noble memory king Henry VIII and king Edward the VI meanes were opened off amytye betwixt baith realms; was not at all tymes the difference of religion the onley stay they were not embraced? But now has God off his mercy removed that block furth off the way . . . when we are comme to a conformity of doctrine, and profes the same religion with zow, quhilk I take to be the straytest knot of amitye can be devised.[23]

Maitland here separated doctrine and religion, implying that 'the same religion' meant something broader than agreement over doctrinal niceties. The link between religion and the diplomatic special relationship was again made explicit in 1565 by the fifth earl of Argyll. He was certain that a common faith made him the friend and ally of the protestants in England and Ireland. In his letter to the archbishop of Armagh, he declared, 'For our religion and union of fayth is ane sufficient knot of amite and acquentance betuix us'. On these grounds he sought diplomatic and military help from the Irish privy council and through them the English privy council, against the catholic threat which might emerge from the marriage of Mary Queen of Scots to Henry, Lord Darnley. Queen Elizabeth

23 20 January 1559/60, printed in W. Robertson, *History of Scotland* (Edinburgh, 1806 edn), III, Appendix II, p.276.

was unmoved by that kind of appeal and the rebellious Scottish lords were left to their fate.[24]

Many of Elizabeth's subjects, however, wanted to acknowledge the special bond which had been formed in 1559–60 between the two peoples of England and Scotland. This was evident in 1562 when the fate of continental protestants was being considered. Although upset by the persecution which the Huguenots were suffering, one of the tracts which described the massacre at Vassy seemed to suggest a distinction between England's French and Scottish co-religionists. It called on all nations of the gospel to unite against the Romish beast but spoke of the Scots as 'our own flesh and blood, knit to us afore by nature and linked now also by profession of the gospel . . . hold fast to the Word of God lately graffed unto thee'.[25]

The novelty of Scotland's adoption of protestantism had completely disappeared by 1585, when articles for a new treaty were being negotiated. The assumption that England and Scotland shared the same faith and that religion held the diplomatic alliance together was now securely established. The articles declared that one of the purposes of the treaty was 'the better maintenance of the true, ancient Christian religion which they now profess'. In this connection, Maitland of Thirlstane described 'this isle' of Britain as 'naturally joined by situation, language and most happily by religion'.[26] The same sentiment was expressed in his rather ingratiating manner by Patrick Adamson, archbishop of St Andrews. At the time of his visit to England in 1583–4, he wrote to Archbishop Whitgift, 'I shall endeavour myself to the preservation of ye true religion professit in the whole yle, and common quietnes and mutuall amitie of her majestie and our master'.[27]

Even Richard Bancroft, the arch-enemy of Scottish presbyterianism and its pernicious, 'scotticizing' influence in England, was prepared to concede that a basic religious unity existed between the two countries. In 1606 he spoke to Andrew Melville, the leader of the Scottish presbyterians, who was then in exile in London. To this most unlikely of confidants, the archbishop admitted, 'we differ onlye in the forme of government

24 18 November 1565, Argyll to Archbishop of Armagh, PRO SP 63/15 f172; J. Dawson, 'Mary Queen of Scots, Lord Darnley, and Anglo-Scottish relations in 1565', *IHR* 8 (1986), pp.1–24.

25 *A Dialogue against the Tyrannye of the Papistes*, trans. E.C. (1562) STC 19176, sig. C3.

26 Donaldson, 'Foundations', pp.141–2.

27 Russell, *Causes*, p.37.

of the church, and some ceremonies'. He could not resist adding maliciously, 'but as I understand, since yee came from Scotland, your church is brought to be almost one with ours in that also'.[28]

In the debates following 1603, it was clear that both the supporters and the opponents of greater union were as aware as Robert Pont had been that a common faith did not imply uniformity in church government and ceremonies. One of the main flash-points in the negotiations between 1604 and 1607 was the fear that a single organization or liturgical formula might be imposed upon the two churches. Such a proposal was regarded as an altogether different and much more contentious proposition than the celebration of a shared religious culture. It was this inflammable issue which aroused the deepest antagonism between the English and the Scots throughout the seventeenth century. In 1604 the commissioners of the Scottish synods summed up the fear of such a loss of national ecclesiastical identity: 'without unioun and conformitie of the kirks, government and worship: how could the kirks be united, unless one gave place to the other?'[29]

THE ISLAND BASTION

In the early modern period, Anglo-Scottish protestant culture failed to produce any 'conformity' in church government or worship. Although a religious culture, it flourished in a non-institutional form and was almost entirely divorced from both English and Scottish ecclesiastical structures and practices. It reflected non-clerical perspectives and concerns. Even though it embraced ministers as well as laymen, it was, in this sense, a lay culture. Its core was a set of concepts and beliefs which were held by the committed protestants of both realms.

They started from the basic assumption that they shared a common faith. They were convinced that this religious bond had been initiated and sustained by God. Through his special providence, the Almighty had created the island of Britain which accommodated the two different peoples within a single geographical area. Its island status and the surrounding seas protected Britain from its catholic enemies who, in the second half

28 ibid, p.48.
29 ibid, p.38.

of the sixteenth century, appeared especially menacing to the protestants. On the basis of this favoured geographical position, British protestants then proceeded to fit God's recent dealings with the island into a precise chronological pattern of callings. This prophetic and providential interpretation of the immediate past encouraged the belief in a common future destiny for the two realms. All of these ideas could be accommodated within the broader framework of apocalyptic thinking, much of which was common property for English and Scottish protestants. Similarly, they shared many aspects of the concepts of the people of God and its covenant relationship with the Almighty. This Anglo-Scottish protestant culture did not produce identical outlooks in the two countries and each preserved its own individual national emphases and interpretations. But it did provide sufficient common ground for protestants in Scotland and England to assume that they shared the same religious outlook and language and that they were joined together in a common effort to fulfil the joint destiny which God had planned for them.

One of the main arguments which had been employed since the start of the sixteenth century on behalf of greater unity between England, Wales and Scotland was that of geographical proximity. Both kingdoms were contained in the one island of Britain and, as Maitland of Lethington phrased it, the Scots were 'lyeng dry marche with zow' English in the borders.[30] This geographical and strategic argument was nearly always placed in a religious context. It was assumed that God had specifically created the island of Britain as a natural sign that He wanted the two realms of Scotland and England to join together. In His Providence, the Almighty had protected the island of Britain by surrounding it with the bastion of the seas. This was done for the special purpose of making Britain a safe haven for protestantism. Behind its sea defences, not only would the protestantism of the two realms be protected, but also they could provide a refuge for other protestants who might be harried in their own countries or across their land boundaries by catholic neighbours on the continent.

In his *Admonition to England and Scotland, to call them to repentance* of 1558,[31] Anthony Gilby addressed 'you twaine, (O England and Scotland, both makinge one Island, most happie if you could know

30 See note 22; Dawson, 'Cecil and the British dimension', pp. 208–10.

31 Attached to John Knox's *Appellation . . . addressed to the Nobility and Estates of Scotland*, in D. Laing (ed.) *Works of John Knox* (6 vols; Edinburgh, 1846–64), IV, pp. 553–71.

your own happines)'.[32] His message was simple: both realms were being punished by God for their sins. God had sent the same plague to Scotland and England, permitting foreign oppressors, the French and the Spanish respectively, to rule over the native inhabitants. The Scots and the English should repent of their sins and turn to God:

> Give eare therefore betymes, O Britanie, (for of that name both rejoyseth) whiles the Lord calleth, exhorteth, and admonisheth, that is the acceptable tyme when he will be founde. . . . Lo, the way in few wordes, O Britanie, to winne Goddes favour, and therefore to overcome thyne ennemies.[33]

Gilby set out the stages of God's pursuit of the peoples of the two realms of Britain. He used the gospel parable of the two sons who had been asked by their father to work in his vineyard. During Edward VI's reign, when England had enjoyed protestantism, Scotland had been like the son who had refused point blank to 'joyne handes with us in the Lorde's worke'. Gilby explained that this had been the work of Satan because

> His old fostered malice, and Antichrist his sonne, could not abyde that Christ should grow so strong by joynynge that Ile togither in perfect religion, whome God hath so many waies coupled and strengthened by his worke in nature: the Papistes practised all theyr fyne craftes in England, Scotland, and in France, that the Ghospellers should not with so strong walles be defensed, lest this one Iland should becomme a safe sanctuarie, as it began to be, to all the persecuted in all places.[34]

Gilby's greatest censure was reserved for England, which was like the second son who had promised his father that he would work in the vineyard and then had not done so. He underlined the contrasting reactions of the two countries to God's call.

> Somme hope is in Scotland . . . but lyke wanton children, have contemned the commaundement of theyr father, partilie of frailtie, partely of ignorance. But Englande, the servante that knew the will of his Lord and Maister, . . . which hath boasted to professe Christ with great boldnes before all the worlde, must be beaten with many stripes, it can not now be avoided.

The remedy was plain: 'this only remaineth for bothe these Nations, that they repent and returne into the vineyarde with the fyrst sonne

32 Knox, *Works*, IV, p.553; A.H. Williamson, *Scottish National Consciousness in the Age of James VI* (Edinburgh, 1979), pp.12–13.
33 ibid, p.554.
34 ibid, p.558.

(Christ)'.[35] If repentance did not come, then God's judgment would shortly follow.

Already in 1558, at a time when both England and Scotland were formally catholic countries, the full connection had been made between the island status of Britain, the unity brought by the protestant religion, the identification of the common external foe of catholicism and the idea of Britain as a sanctuary for persecuted protestants in Europe. Gilby was making explicit the extremely influential and pervasive concept that the island of Britain was a bulwark of protestantism. Encouraged by the French Religious Wars and the Dutch Revolt, this belief deepened during the 1560s and 1570s. It became part of the general analysis of European politics in confessional terms which dominated the thinking on foreign policy of most of Elizabeth's advisers. The perception of a catholic threat to the security of Britain was sharpened by the belief in an international catholic conspiracy, orchestrated by the papacy. This was regarded as the contemporary manifestation of the great apocalyptic struggle between the forces of Christ and Antichrist. It was the special destiny of the island of Britain, led by Queen Elizabeth, to protect protestantism.[36]

By the major crises of the 1580s, this view was nearly universally held (except by the queen herself), and seemed to be gloriously confirmed by the Armada victory of 1588. In a most effusive manner, Sir William Herbert (writing in the early 1590s) celebrated Queen Elizabeth who 'with stately sceptre guides the British realms'. Under her rule

> the happiness of Ireland . . . may be added to . . . the most admirable and virtuous government of England, the protection and defence of Scotland, the repression and curbing of the madness and frenzy of France, the protection of the life and liberty of the Netherlands, the containment and repulsion of the arrogance, the ambition and the cruelty of the Spaniards, the advancement and defence of Christian truth and teaching, the destruction and otherthrow of the tyranny and deceit of the Antichrist.[37]

Herbert was describing Queen Elizabeth's place within God's plan for the British Isles and protestant Europe in its widest possible terms. A fully conquered and reformed Ireland was seen as an

35 ibid, p.567.

36 P. Lake, 'The significance of the Elizabethan identification of the pope as Antichrist', *JEH* 31 (1980), pp.161–78.

37 Sir William Herbert, *Croftus sive de Hibernia Liber* (eds) A. Keaveney and J.A. Madden (Dublin, 1992), p.117.

integral part of that destiny. It presumed that the whole of the British Isles was under the control of the English monarch, who ensured the strategic security and protestant nature of the entire geographical area. From this bastion on the edge of Europe, the queen of England could act as the chief defender of the protestant cause on the continent against the great catholic conspiracy which sought to overthrow all true religion. In particular, the French Huguenots and the Dutch rebels could be assisted to fight against the papacy and Philip II of Spain. This battle was part of the cosmic conflict raging between the forces of Christ and Antichrist and in this analysis of contemporary international politics a protestant British Isles had a vital role to play.[38]

England was clearly the major British state and thus the dominant partner and main actor in the area of foreign policy. An awareness of its leadership created a tendency within England to relegate the British dimension of the concept to the background. At times, Englishmen gave the impression of believing that being the champion of protestantism was an exclusively English role. Sometimes, this was a reaction to the practical reality that, whatever the rhetoric, Elizabethan Ireland was obviously not under full political control nor was it, even nominally, protestant. If such a pessimistic assessment was made of the Irish situation, it was possible simply to exclude Ireland from this British destiny. The optimistic and broad inclusion of the whole of the British Isles could be reduced once more to the mainland. However, for the 'island' imagery to work at all the kingdom of Scotland could not be left out of consideration, despite the fact that it was a separate country ruled over by a different monarch.

The quintessentially British nature of the idea of the protestant bastion was always apparent in the basic assumption of Britain's geographical and political security. Internal safety was impossible without the peace which had been established between England and Scotland in 1560, two years after the loss of Calais to the French finally removed the toehold which the English crown had held on the continent of Europe. These two events emphasized the crucial importance of the island of Britain.[39] The existence of a secure and united British mainland provided the fundamental

38 This is not the same as the idea of England as *the* Elect Nation, W. Haller, *Foxe's Book of Martyrs and the Elect Nation* (London, 1963) which is challenged by V.N. Olsen, *John Foxe and the Elizabethan Church* (Berkeley, Calif., 1973); K. Firth, *The Apocalyptic Tradition in Reformation Britain* (Oxford, 1979); R. Bauckham, *Tudor Apocalypse* (Appleford, 1978).

39 Dawson, 'Cecil and the British dimension'.

presupposition behind the rhetoric of the catholic threat to the 'beleaguered isle'.[40] It also underlay such eloquent celebrations of 'English' national consciousness as the speech which Shakespeare in *Richard II* placed in the mouth of John of Gaunt:

> This royal throne of kings, this scepter'd isle,
> This earth of majesty, this seat of Mars,
> This other Eden, demi-paradise,
> This fortress built by Nature for herself
> Against infection and the hand of war,
> This happy breed of men, this little world,
> This precious stone set in the silver sea,
> Which serves it in the office of a wall,
> Or as a moat defensive to a house,
> Against the envy of less happier lands,
> This blessed plot, this earth, this realm, this England.[41]

The special destiny which the Almighty had planned for the two realms of England and Scotland could be recognized most clearly at certain key moments in their recent history. British protestants could discern a chronological pattern which justified and reinforced their consciousness of the providential hand of God and gave momentum to the whole process. They highlighted the various moments when God had specifically called the two kingdoms to follow His plan. These particular experiences could be fitted into the general apocalyptic and prophetic framework which dominated British protestantism. The opening events of the chronology, the 'Edwardian moment',[42] and the assumption that they demonstrated Divine Providence at work had already become established when Gilby wrote. Both English and Scottish protestants accepted the same explanation for the failure of union at the time of the Rough Wooing in the 1540s. They were convinced that Scotland at that point had refused to heed God's call to join England.

40 C. Wiener, 'The beleaguered isle: a study of Elizabethan and early Jacobean anti-catholicism', *P&P* 51 (1971), pp.27–62; P. Collinson, *The Birthpangs of Protestant England* (London, 1988), ch.1; D. Loades, 'The origins of English protestant nationalism', and A. Fletcher, 'The first century of English protestantism and the growth of national identity', both in S. Mews (ed.) *Religion and National Identity*, Studies in Church History 18 (Oxford, 1982), pp.297–307, 309–17.

41 Act II, 2, 11. 40–50.

42 The phrase is borrowed from A.H. Williamson, 'Scotland, antichrist and the invention of Great Britain', in J. Dwyer, R. Mason and A. Murdoch (eds) *New Perspectives on the Politics and Culture of Early Modern Scotland* (Edinburgh, 1982), p.39; Williamson, *Scottish National Consciousness*. Although there is a different emphasis in this chapter from the arguments developed by Professor Williamson, I have made extensive use of, and am heavily indebted to, his work.

This idea had even been adopted by some Scottish protestants at the time, as can be seen in James Henrisoun's impassioned plea in 1548 in his *An Exhortation to the Scottes to conforme themselfes to the honorable, Expedient and godly union between the two Realmes of Englande and Scotland*:

> But if God of his goodnesse, without our dessertes, hath in these latter daies, provided that blessed mean and remedy for the glorie of his name and for our wealth and commoditie: and wee for our parte, either of stubbornesse will not or of wilfulnesse liste not, thankfully to receive his synguler grace and benefit so freely offered, what then maie be thought in us?[43]

The dire consequences of that missed opportunity were spelled out by Gilby and by Maitland of Lethington. In their view it was imperative that when the next call came from the Almighty, neither Scotland nor England should be found wanting. The Lords of the Congregation were acutely conscious of the joint destiny of the two realms. In their formal proposal in 1560 of the marriage of the earl of Arran to Queen Elizabeth they sought to make good the earlier Scottish failure to join with England. In the 1540s Scotland had refused to accept God's 'appointment', but the country had now been offered another and better opportunity to follow His Will and to unite the realms:

> Experience hath taught us (to our payns) how foully we did erre when as we did not embrace the occasion when it was offered of the union. God did ones appoint fitt instrumentis for the purpose, the mean was propounded unto us, but we weare not so happy as to receive hit, . . . ones again it hath pleased God of his mercy to propound to us the lyke meanes, yff his appointment be followed.[44]

Queen Elizabeth had no desire to accept her part in this scheme for union. She refused the marriage but accepted the less demanding diplomatic alliance with relief. She was unconvinced by arguments about Divine Providence and throughout her reign appeared completely indifferent to any of the obligations of a joint Anglo-Scottish protestant destiny. Although many of the high hopes

43 Williamson, 'Antichrist', p.37; M. Merriman, 'James Henrisoun and "Great Britain": British Union and the Scottish Commonwealth', and R. Mason, 'Scotching the Brut: politics, history and national myth in 16th century Britain', both in R. Mason (ed.) *Scotland and England* (Edinburgh, 1987), pp.85–112; 60–84; Henrisoun's *Exhortation* reprinted in *The Complaynt of Scotland*, ed. J. Murray (Early English Text Society, London, 1872) pp.207–36.

44 Cited in Williamson, 'Antichrist' p.41; *CSP For Elizabeth* ed. J. Stevenson *et al.* (23 vols; London, 1863–1950), 1560–1, pp.433–6.

raised at this stage would later be dashed, it was still recognized that there had been a positive response from Scotland and England to God's call in 1560. Commentators, such as Pont, assumed that the friendship which had preserved the peace between the two former enemies was a direct blessing given by the Almighty in reward for the cooperation of the two nations in His cause.

Though it did not provide a precise chronological turning-point or direct call from God, the 'British' problem created by Mary Queen of Scots was viewed within that context. It was regarded as a test for the united resolve of the protestant regimes in London and Edinburgh. In her own person, Mary Queen of Scots and the intrigues that surrounded her during her long captivity in England fused together the political and religious threats to the two realms. She jeopardized the continuation of Britain's new and still fragile diplomatic unity. She also personalized and focused the catholic menace and helped bring together the deep reservoirs of anti-catholicism which were present in Scotland and England to create a united front against the common foe. After her execution, the Spanish Armada provoked a protestant frenzy in both realms. The year 1588 was regarded as a time of testing and ultimate triumph by English and Scottish protestants alike and itself became a major episode in the chronology of God's plan for the British Isles. For many, the whole pattern culminated in 1603 when James VI fulfilled one part of the joint destiny of the two kingdoms by uniting them under one monarch. Even though such expectations went unrealized, the idea of a common destiny remained alive and reappeared with renewed force at the time of the Solemn League and Covenant in 1643.

EXILE AND APOCALYPSE

These specific moments of common destiny could also be fitted into the national patterns which explained the separate roles of England and Scotland within a general apocalyptic framework. This was made possible by the shared experience of exile during the 1550s when English and some Scottish protestants had been forced to take refuge together on the continent by the seeming victory of catholicism throughout the British Isles. The personal contacts and the literary products of the exile, especially the Geneva Bible and the *Form of Prayers*, or *Book of Common Order* as it became known in Scotland, were to be of immense importance in the development of Anglo-Scottish protestant culture. The broad and flexible protestant tradition which emerged from the Marian exile subsequently shaped both English and Scottish apocalyptic thought. That tradition ranged over a wide spectrum. It was found in simple slogans, such as 'The Pope is Antichrist'; in sophisticated chronological patterns of ecclesiastical history; or in precise mathematical calculations concerning the number of the Beast. Because of their versatility, apocalyptic ideas appealed to all levels within British society. They provided a unifying force which could hold together without any apparent contradiction the many differing emphases found within all sections of Scottish and English apocalypticism.[45]

The basic structure of British apocalyptic thought had been created during the Marian exile. It then permeated Scotland and England by means of the Geneva Bible, the *Book of Common Order*, the other polemical writings of that period and the returned exiles themselves. During the exile two main strands of thought, the concepts of the True Church and the People of God, were woven together to produce the new broad tradition. These concepts were linked by the imagery of the fight against Antichrist. By combining these three basic themes, apocalyptic thinking moved effortlessly from one to the other. In the descriptions of the joint destiny of Scotland and England, the True Church strand contributed the concept of a chronological pattern of Divine Providence, with God's callings to the two kingdoms. It could then be placed alongside the biblical imagery of the People of God as a vineyard, as in Gilby's detailed analysis of the parable of working in the vineyard. The third theme was provided by the rhetoric of the cosmic battle against Antichrist, which for British protestants meant the papacy, the Catholic Church and the catholic monarchs of Europe. All three strands were woven into the belief that the peoples of God within Britain had been specially called by the Almighty to fight the catholic threat at home and abroad.

45 J. Dawson, 'The Apocalyptic thinking of the Marian exiles', in M. Wilks (ed.) *Prophecy and Eschatology*, Studies in Church History, Subsidia 10 (Oxford, 1994), which stresses the common ground between Scottish and English apocalypticism. The differences between the two countries are set out in Williamson, *Scottish National Consciousness*. These two approaches are complementary rather than mutually exclusive.

The incorporation of the language of the People of God into the broad apocalyptic tradition also enabled it to be linked to covenant ideas. The concept of the covenant was derived from the Old Testament where it had described the special relationship which God had entered into with His People, the Jews. The protestants within both realms saw themselves and their kingdoms as part of a new Israel in a covenant relationship with God. The use of covenant imagery became increasingly important in both English and Scottish protestant thought. It was employed in different contexts in the two kingdoms due to their different political and ecclesiological situations. Within England the political use of the covenant idea was gradually abandoned by puritan thinkers who tended to restrict its language to the sphere of individuals or of single congregations. In Scotland the national political and ecclesiastical aspects of the covenant concept were emphasized. The constant use of the language of the People of God and of the covenant relationship laid the foundations for the National Covenant of 1638 and the 1643 Solemn League and Covenant with England. Despite these varieties of emphasis, there remained the firm conviction among both English and Scottish protestants that they were all part of the People of God and were in a covenant relationship with Him.[46]

For British protestants both the apocalyptic tradition and covenant ideas were subsumed within the overarching doctrine of God's Providence. They believed that God was in control of, and worked in, every aspect of their lives from the commonplace of daily tasks to the complexities of international politics. Protestants searched for, and expected to find, the marks and patterns of God's Will in their personal, local, national and international affairs. The recognition of a common destiny for the two kingdoms of the island of Britain was simply one aspect of this general approach. It was this determination to follow the Will of God at every level of life which characterized the protestant consciousness that emerged in the early modern period throughout the English-reading world.[47]

46 S. Burrell, 'The Covenant Idea as a revolutionary symbol: Scotland, 1596–1637', *Church History* 27 (1958) pp.338–50; S. Burrell, 'The apocalyptic vision of the early Covenanters', *SHR* 43 (1964) pp.1–24; M. McGiffert, 'Covenant, crown and Commons in Elizabethan puritanism', *JBS* 20 (1980), pp.32–52; M. McGiffert, 'Grace and works: the rise and division of covenant divinity in Elizabethan Puritanism', *Harvard Theological Review* 75 (1982), pp.463–502; M. McGiffert, 'God's controversy with Jacobean England', *AHR* 88 (1983), pp.1,151–74; J. Morrill (ed.) *The Scottish National Covenant in its British Context* (Edinburgh, 1990).

47 J. Coolidge, *The Pauline Renaissance in England* (Oxford, 1970).

PROTESTANT CULTURE AND NATIONAL IDENTITY

By 1603 England and Scotland shared a sufficient number of religious ideas and assumptions for there to be a recognizably common protestant culture. This did not imply that the Scottish and English cultural worlds had been fused into one, either by aggressive English imperialism or by cultural assimilation. Much of the literature and art of the two countries remained separate and developed along quite distinct lines. What had emerged by the end of the sixteenth century was a matrix of common assumptions based on the twin pillars of protestant ideology and the English language. Such a 'lowest common denominator' was the main ingredient for the wider cultural unity which bound together the whole of the English-speaking or English-reading world in the early modern period. Each of the constituent parts of the world produced its own particular cultural emphases which made it distinctive. But their overall cultural and linguistic unity permitted the English-reading peoples of the British Isles and, later, the North American colonies to 'speak the same language' in the widest sense of that term.

Within the British Isles themselves there were, in addition, three entirely different cultures based on the other vernaculars. The Welsh and the Gaels of both Scotland and Ireland could boast their own languages, cultural traditions and values. Although these cultures managed to survive, they were not strong enough to challenge or modify the immense cultural dominance of the English language. The main threat to the broad cultural world of the English-speaking peoples was not the rivalry with Gaelic or Welsh cultures but the emergence of separate and mutually exclusive national identities. The strength of these identities, particularly those of the English and the Scots, was the main reason why James VI and I's dream of a true kingdom of Greater Britain failed to materialize after he became king of England.[48]

Religion provided a central and essential component in both the English and Scottish identities. Each identity was deeply and inextricably associated with the organization and ceremonies of its respective churches. There were a variety of unsuccessful attempts

48 J. Wormald, 'James VI and I: Two kings or one?', *History* 68 (1983), pp.187–209; R. Mason, 'Chivalry and citizenship: aspects of national identity in Renaissance Scotland', R. Mason and N. Macdougall (eds) *People and Power in Scotland: Essays in Honour of T.C. Smout* (Edinburgh, 1992), pp.50–73.

at some form of religious or ecclesiastical union throughout the seventeenth century. However, when an incorporating union came in 1707, the legislators were forced to recognize and preserve two totally separate and different churches, the Anglican Church of England and the Presbyterian Church of Scotland.[49]

The immense importance of the religious element within the English and Scottish identities and the failures of ecclesiastical union have sometimes obscured the common Anglo-Scottish protestant culture. When that religious culture was recognized, it was assumed that it could form the basis for a new 'British' identity which would be able to transcend the strong national identities. The great success of Anglo-Scottish protestant culture in promoting a measure of cultural integration between the two realms was deeply deceptive. Contemporaries, and some later historians, have misunderstood the nature of Anglo-Scottish culture. It was incapable of creating a comprehensive ecclesiastical organization. It was equally unable to provide the foundations for a set of common political institutions. It was, in other words, a cultural bond and not an identity. Anglo-Scottish protestant culture could help to integrate the English and the Scots but it could not forge a new multinational British state.

Acknowledgements

I am most grateful for the advice and encouragement on earlier drafts of this chapter which I received from Dr Roger Mason, Dr John Morrill and Professor Arthur H. Williamson and for the many points raised in the discussion of the original paper at the Galway conference.

49 Levack, *Formation*, ch.4; C. Russell, *The Fall of the British Monarchies 1637–1642* (Oxford, 1991), ch. 2.

CHAPTER FIVE

The Anglican Church and the unity of Britain: the Welsh experience, 1560–1714

Philip Jenkins
Pennsylvania State University

From the seventeenth century until the time of Victoria, the established Anglican Church was central to political culture in Wales.[1] Although its enemies grew steadily in numbers and power, the church remained for many an object of political and intellectual devotion, around which we can find a 'church party' that was one of the constant realities of Welsh politics until disestablishment in 1913.[2] In addition to defining partisan loyalties, the church also played a key role in integrating the politics of Wales into those of the wider kingdom, ensuring that religious debates would be located within a national British institution, and providing a national stage for recurrent, and usually bloodless, battles over promotion and patronage.[3]

Yet the success of the 'national' church in Wales should not be seen as an inevitable development. From the point of view of the later sixteenth century, the new ecclesiastical order in Wales suffered from many disadvantages, which cumulatively seemed so ominous as to threaten the hard-won political tranquility of the Tudor dynasty. Religious institutions in Wales had never been wealthy, but they had been hit very hard by the rapacity of the new secular landed elites.[4] The bishoprics were impoverished, many

1 Among the general histories of Wales used throughout this chapter are G.E. Jones, *Modern Wales: A Concise History 1485–1979* (Cambridge, 1984), and J. Davies, *Hanes Cymru* (London, 1990).

2 P. Jenkins, *A History of Modern Wales 1536–1990* (London, 1992).

3 For recent scholarship on the unification of the British state, see e.g. L. Colley, *Britons: Forging the Nation 1707–1837* (New Haven, Conn., 1992); H. Kearney, *The British Isles: A History of Four Nations* (Cambridge, 1989).

4 G. Williams, *Welsh Reformation Essays* (Cardiff, 1967).

parish livings plundered, and the success of reform usually tended to be proportionate to the number of wealthy benefices, which could attract able and educated men. By this criterion, Wales faced bleak prospects: in the 1530s the *Valor Ecclesiasticus* estimated that some 70 per cent of livings were worth less than £10, and one-quarter brought in only £5. At the end of the eighteenth century, almost one-sixth of livings were worth less than £75, at a time when even double that figure barely constituted a respectable income.[5]

Meanwhile, the new protestant order was slow to establish itself. There had been protestant rumblings in some Welsh regions, especially in southern towns such as Cardiff, Carmarthen and Haverfordwest; but given the tiny scale of Welsh urban life, this was a weak foundation on which to depend.[6] Moreover, the new church was initially an 'English Reformation' in a country still overwhelmingly Welsh-speaking, and frequently monoglot.[7] When in 1560 the new Elizabethan bishops took the protestant step of requiring the use of the new Prayer Book in their Welsh dioceses, they were commanding the use of an English work. The early years of the Reformation in Wales were characterized by a shift from incomprehensible Latin to barely understood English.

The new church was quite as intellectually inaccessible as the old, and lacked the familiar liturgical and customary frameworks which the pre-Reformation church offered for structuring everyday life.[8] While there were some convinced protestants among the new clergy, they were not numerous. Worse, some of the reformers among the Elizabethan bishops were also among the most serious abusers of church wealth, including men like George Barlow and Richard Davies in the diocese of St Davids, or William Hughes in St Asaph.[9]

Of course, there were some vested interests in the new church: wealthy families had benefited from the purchase of monastic lands, and both dynastic loyalism and self-interest ensured that many would not wish to see catholicism restored by Spanish forces. Even

5 S.G. Ellis 'Economic problems of the church: why the Reformation failed in Ireland', *JEH* 41 (1990), pp.239–65; Jenkins *History of Modern Wales*, pp.190–2.

6 G. Williams, *Recovery, Reorientation and Reformation: Wales c. 1415–1642* (Oxford, 1987).

7 G. Williams, *Religion, Language and Nationality in Wales* (Cardiff, 1979).

8 P. Jenkins, 'Times and seasons: the cycles of the year in eighteenth century Glamorgan', *Morgannwg* 30 (1986), pp.20–41.

9 Williams, *Recovery, Reorientation and Reformation*, pp.305–31; Jenkins, *History of Modern Wales*, pp. 102–23

so, catholic loyalties were widespread in Elizabethan Wales, even among those who had acquired church lands.[10] In 1580 Welsh anglicanism looked like an unloved pragmatic compromise, a largely political affirmation of dynastic adherence.

By the 1640s, however, there is abundant evidence of intense and widespread loyalty to the church, chiefly among Welsh political and cultural elites, but also spreading into lower social categories. The Anglican Church had quite literally become something worth dying for, while the liturgy was preserved (at considerable risk) through the Interregnum in a clandestine church movement. By the beginning of the eighteenth century, the passionate depths of church loyalty were amply illustrated by the nationwide response to the Sacheverell trial, and concern for the 'church in danger' became an enormous political force. Wales had become a bastion of church Toryism as definitively as the country would be central to the 'nonconformist interest' under Queen Victoria.[11]

Such a far-reaching change requires explanation, and it is possible to imagine a world where successive regimes failed to secure Welsh adherence to the new order. In this hypothetical situation, it is not difficult to suppose that catholic interests might have filled the spiritual vacuum, and established themselves even more strongly than they did in areas of Wales in the period 1603–42. The seminary priests were active from the 1580s, and the catholics were willing to carry out propaganda in Welsh, the tongue 'understanded of the people'. A catholic summary of doctrine was published in Welsh as early as 1568 (*Athravaeth Gristionogawl*, or *Christian Teaching*); in fact, the first book printed on Welsh soil is a catholic tract of 1585, *Y Drych Cristionogawl* (*The Christian Mirror*).[12]

If large parts of Wales had become as solidly catholic as much of Monmouthshire was in reality, then the country would have posed a public security threat comparable to that of Ireland or the Scottish Highlands, a magnet for domestic dissidents and foreign conspiracies, and in a land located across an indefensible land border with England. The religious integration of England and Wales can therefore be seen as a decisive victory in the process of national unification.

10 See e.g. H.A. Lloyd, *The Gentry of South-West Wales 1540–1640* (Cardiff, 1968); G. Dyfnallt Owen, *Wales in the Reign of James I* (London, 1988); J. Gwynfor Jones, *Wales and the Tudor State* (Cardiff, 1989); J. Gwynfor Jones (ed.) *Class, Community and Culture in Tudor Wales* (Cardiff, 1989).

11 Jenkins, *History of Modern Wales*, pp.109–10, 165–6, 291–7.

12 G. Bowen, *Y Drych Cristianogawl: Astudiaeth*, supplement to *JWEH* (1988); T. Parry, *A History of Welsh Literature*, trans. H. Idris Bell (Oxford, 1970), p.200.

TOWARDS A WELSH REFORMATION 1560–1620

At the end of the sixteenth century, Welsh was the normal means of communication for perhaps 90 per cent of the inhabitants of the thirteen traditional counties, and the usage spilled over the border into Shropshire and Herefordshire. Undoubtedly, the worst policy for the regime would have been to have attempted to impose linguistic uniformity at the same time as demanding religious innovation; this is perilously close to what actually occurred in the 1540s. Throughout the remainder of the century, Welsh clergy translating documents into the vernacular continued to pay lip-service to the ideal that one day the whole realm of England-and-Wales would be of one tongue; while the grammar schools that proliferated during these years explicitly attempted to suppress the speaking of Welsh among their pupils.[13]

Fortunately for the anglican establishment, the Welsh vernacular prevailed at an early date, and there now commenced a series of projects to translate liturgical services and other documents.[14] In 1547 there appeared *Yn Y Llyvyr Hwn . . . (In This Book . . .)*, the first book printed in Welsh. This contained Welsh versions of the Ten Commandments, the Lord's Prayer and the Creed. In 1551 William Salesbury published *Kynniver Llith a Ban O'r Ysgrythur Lân*, with the epistles and gospels used in services, and these entered regular use in the 1560s. By 1561 Bishop Richard Davies was requiring that the catechism be read in Welsh throughout his diocese of St Asaph, while 'after the epistle and gospel in English, the same should be read also in Welsh'.[15]

In 1563 Parliament ordered the publication of the Bible in Welsh, a work entrusted to the four Welsh bishops and their colleague at Hereford. The sanity of such a proposal may appear self-evident, but even so, the order required that an English Bible should also be made available, so that comparison might contribute to 'the knowledge of the English tongue'. It is still unclear who should be given credit for advocating this linguistic master-stroke, but likely candidates include William Salesbury and Bishop Richard

13 P.R. Roberts, 'The union with England and the identity of anglican Wales' *TRHS* 22 (1972) pp.61–5.

14 Williams, *Recovery, Reorientation and Reformation*; D. Walker (ed.) *History of the Church in Wales* (Penarth, 1976).

15 J. Gwynfor Jones, 'The reformation bishops of St Asaph', *JWEH* 7 (1990), p.27.

Davies. By 1567 the Welsh had access to both the Prayer Book and New Testament in their own language, creating the possibility for a wholly Welsh liturgy, while there were four new versions of the Prayer Book between 1586 and 1630.[16] Parish records show that these books were purchased and presumably used. In Swansea, for example, the Jacobean parish bought several Welsh books, including a Bible, Psalter and Book of Homilies.[17] By 1588 William Morgan sponsored the publication of a complete Bible in Welsh, an event commonly taken as one of the crucial moments in Welsh culture, though an accessible five-shilling edition had to wait until 1630.[18] The Morgan Bible is given credit for maintaining and disseminating high standards of literary Welsh, much like the service performed by the King James Authorized Version for English.

At the turn of the century, the Welsh episcopate included some dedicated and remarkably able men, including several of the scholars involved in the various translations. William Morgan himself was appointed to the see of Llandaff in 1595, and moved to become bishop of St Asaph in 1601. One of the Bangor incumbents was Lewis Bayly, bishop from 1616 to 1631, and author of a highly regarded *Practice of Piety* (though published in English, it appeared in Welsh translation by 1630, and this was reprinted several times). At St Asaph, the bishop was Richard Parry, who in 1620 published a new translation of the Bible and Prayer Book.[19]

Under such leadership, it is not surprising that much attention was devoted to continuing the work of translation and popularization. One prominent figure was John Davies, rector of Mallwyd in Merionethshire (*c.* 1604–44), a notable Welsh grammarian who may have been largely responsible for Parry's biblical project. Edmund Prys, archdeacon of Merioneth (1576–1623), was a Welsh poet who undertook a metrical rendering of the Psalms into Welsh. In 1606 the Glamorgan cleric, Edward

16 Parry, *History of Welsh Literature*, p.195.

17 O.W. Jones and D. Walker (eds) *Links with the Past: Swansea and Brecon Historial Essays* (Swansea, 1974), pp. 108–9.

18 J. Gwynfor Jones, *The Translation of the Scriptures into Welsh* (Cardiff, 1988); J. Gwynfor Jones, 'Bishop William Morgan', *JWEH* 5 (1988), pp.1–30.

19 For Bayly and the Bangor diocese, A.H. Dodd, *History of Caernarvonshire* (Caernarfon, 1968); Jones, 'Reformation bishops of St Asaph'. Research on the Reformation church in Wales is a thriving field. See e.g. J. Gwynfor Jones, 'The reformation bishops of Llandaff', *Morgannwg* 32 (1988), pp.38–69; M. Gray 'The diocese of Bangor in the late sixteenth century', *JWEH* 5 (1988), pp.31–72; M. Gray, 'The church in Gwent in 1603', *JWEH* 2 (1985), pp.7–26.

James, translated the Book of Homilies (*Pregethau*). There were also devout lay people who promoted the interests of the church in Wales. In 1595 Morris Kyffin published *Deffynniad Ffydd Eglwys Loegr*, a translation of Bishop Jewel's *Apology* for anglicanism, and the work would have great popularity in Wales for three centuries to come.[20]

However, it was in the south that there was the most celebrated work, with the activity of Rhys Prichard, vicar of Llandovery (1614–44). Prichard earned his fame from the lively and memorable Welsh verses he created to explain Christian and specifically protestant doctrine to the unlettered. His verses circulated for decades before eventually being compiled and published in the 1660s, in what became a Welsh classic, *Canwyll y Cymry* (*The Welshman's Candle*). This would be frequently reprinted into the nineteenth century, both in Welsh and English.[21]

The popularization of new doctrines in Welsh can be seen from the frequent republication of the Elizabethan *Llyfr Plygain* (*Book of Matins*), a bizarre synthesis of almanac information and lists of fairs, together with prayers, creeds and devotions. This was already in a sixth edition by 1633. From the 1590s onwards there appeared a steady stream of Welsh tracts from parish clergy like Robert Llwyd, vicar of Chirk, or Robert Holland of Llanddowror. These included works of popular devotions, books warning against swearing or resorting to conjurors and soothsayers, and especially translations of English divinity of all types.[22] By 1640, therefore, Welsh people had available to them a substantial and growing corpus of literature in the Welsh language.

In the churches, the Welsh language was used where appropriate and necessary. Some parishes were wholly Welsh in usage, some completely English, some bilingual, and practices changed according to changing linguistic realities. However, there was a firmly accepted principle that at least some familiarity with Welsh was an absolute prerequisite for clergy appointed to Welsh-speaking parishes. Any departure from this principle was 'unreasonable and arbitrary', and grounds for appeal to the bishop; the 1688 case from which this quotation comes occurred not in the pastoral uplands,

20 Parry, *History of Welsh Literature*, pp.192–217; G. Williams, 'Edward James a llyfr yr homiliau', *Morgannwg* 25 (1981), pp.79–99.

21 P. Jenkins, *The Making of a Ruling Class: The Glamorgan Gentry 1640–1790* (Cambridge, 1983), p.106, for Prichard's political milieu.

22 Parry, *History of Welsh Literature*, pp.238–42.

but within three miles of Cardiff.[23] At an absolute minimum, an anglophone rector who was 'an utter stranger' to Welsh was expected to employ a Welsh-speaking curate. The fact that Welsh was used for services in a particular parish was taken so much for granted that the records usually fail to state the point explicitly, and we have to depend on negative evidence. In 1758, for example, an Anglesey diarist felt it worthy of special note that one Sunday, 'the curate priest preached an English sermon'.[24]

IRELAND AND SCOTLAND: A CONTRAST

Wales spoke Welsh, and so did the church in Wales. This may seem an obvious and logical development, but it makes a striking contrast with the situation in Ireland and Scotland. At roughly the same time that one parliament in London was ordering the translation of the Prayer Book into Welsh, another in Dublin (1560) was demanding that English be used throughout the Irish Church (though with concessions for Latin usage where appropriate).

The Irish comparison is instructive, as the proportion of Gaelic speakers about 1700 was not wildly different from the state of affairs in Wales: perhaps 60 per cent of Irish people then spoke a Celtic tongue, compared to 90 per cent in Wales.[25] From the 1560s onwards, there were sporadic calls for evangelization of the Irish people in their native language, but progress was slow. Although an Irish catechism appeared in 1571, an Irish Prayer Book and New Testament had to wait until Jacobean times, while a complete translation of the Bible was made only in the time of Bishop Bedell. Bedell and Archbishop Ussher did persuade the convocation of the Irish Church to permit the use of Irish in the liturgy (1634), but few besides Bedell made use of the provision. Bedell was also unusual in the preference he gave to clergy with some knowledge of the language, in striking contrast to Welsh circumstances.[26]

23 Bodl MSS Tanner 146 ff147–9; Jones and Walker (eds) *Links with the Past*, pp.108–9.

24 NLW Church in Wales MSS SD/Misc. 1199; G. Nesta Evans, *Religion and Politics in Mid-Eighteenth Century Anglesey* (Cardiff, 1953), p.79.

25 T.W. Moody and W.E. Vaughan (eds) *A New History of Ireland*, IV (Oxford 1986), pp.375–6.

26 ibid, pp.84–104; V.E. Durkacz, *The Decline of the Celtic Languages* (Edinburgh, 1983), p.7; *DNB* for Bedell; Richard Parr, *Life of the Most Reverend Father in God James Ussher, Late Lord Archbishop of Armagh, Primate and Metropolitan of all Ireland* (London, 1686).

Between about 1680 and 1720 the established church in Ireland intensified its efforts to promote work in the Irish language.[27] It was at this point that divinity students at Trinity College, Dublin, were encouraged to acquire or maintain a knowledge of Gaelic. The first protestant works in Irish were printed in the 1680s and 1690s, and there was a movement to translate the entire liturgy into the language. In the 1680s Bedell's Irish Bible was published under the auspices of Robert Boyle and Narcissus Marsh, provost of Trinity. In 1710 the Irish House of Commons passed a resolution calling for the use of clergy skilled in that language.

However, sustained enthusiasm was lacking; in 1724 Archbishop King wrote that 'the methods that have been taken since the reformation and which are yet pursued by both the civil and ecclesiastical powers [are such as to suggest] that there never was nor is any design that all should be protestants'.[28] It might be recalled that by this point, the Welsh Church had about 150 years of experience of conducting protestant services in the vernacular, while the printed Welsh Bible predated its Irish counterpart by a century. Even in the early nineteenth century, Whitley Stokes would still feel the need to justify the translation of the scriptures into Irish. Of course, there had since Jacobean times been a growing body of religious texts published in Irish, including catechetical, devotional and controversial tracts, but this literature was produced on the continent, and it was invariably catholic.[29]

English was the normal language of choice for a much larger proportion of the population in Scotland than in Ireland, so the strong preference accorded to the language made more sense; but in Scotland too, the Celtic tongue received poor treatment. Measuring the progress of the Reformation in different cultures is complicated by the tendency of historians to emphasize concrete and easily datable records such as printed books, whereas Scots Gaelic culture was firmly rooted in oral tradition. Jane Dawson has shown convincingly that in the century after 1560, the personal and family influence of the calvinist lords resulted in protestant influences becoming quite widely disseminated in the Highlands and Islands, using oral rather than printed materials. The result was 'a rural Calvinism which worked'. Even so, the diffusion of printed materials was slow even by Irish standards, to say nothing of

27 Durkacz, *Decline of the Celtic Languages.*

28 Quoted in Moody and Vaughan (eds) *New History of Ireland,* IV, p.89.

29 N. Canny, 'The formation of the Irish mind: religion, politics and Gaelic Irish literature 1580–1750', *P & P* 95 (1982) pp.94–7.

Welsh.[30] The first printed book in Gaelic appeared in 1567, but the next effort was not produced until 1631. A Gaelic Psalter followed in 1684. A Gaelic New Testament was proposed by the synod of Argyll in 1657, but it was not available until the 1690s, and a complete New Testament in vernacular Scots Gaelic had to wait until 1767. A complete Bible appeared only after 1800. To put this in context, the pace of scriptural translations into Scots Gaelic lagged behind endeavours in such Asian languages as Tamil and Malay, and efforts in Ireland were not greatly superior.[31]

Moreover, such popular evangelism as was attempted in the Highlands and Islands usually made use of English. From its inception in 1709 until as late as 1766, the Scottish SPCK (Society for Promoting Christian Knowledge) prohibited the use of Gaelic in its endeavours. Hostility to the language was reflected in attempts to prohibit the culture associated with it, including aspects like the bardic order, a policy that found expression in laws like the Statutes of Iona (1609).[32] In contrast, the Welsh bards throughout the seventeenth century would be the chief standard-bearers of high royalist and anglican sentiment, and the bane of religious and political dissent.[33]

The woeful story of the treatment of Scots Gaelic resulted in what Durkacz has called 'that destructive alienation of language from literacy which pursued it into the nineteenth century' – again, a striking contrast to Welsh conditions.[34] One reason for the reluctance to use the vernacular in the Gaelic lands was that in both Ireland and the Scottish Highlands, the Celtic language had acquired connotations of religious and political sedition and open rebellion, so that it seemed self-evident that the old language would need to be suppressed as an essential precursor for reformation and 'improvement'. This tended to drive the Gaelic areas into the arms

30 J. Dawson, 'Calvinism and the Gaidhealtachd in Scotland', in A. Duke, G. Lewis and A. Pettegree (eds) *Calvinism in Europe 1560–1620* (Cambridge, 1994); Durkacz, *Decline of the Celtic Languages* p.15.

31 T.C. Smout, *A History of the Scottish People 1560–1830* (London, 1972), pp.432–5; D.F. Wright (ed.) *The Bible in Scottish Life and Literature* (Edinburgh, 1988). For Bible translations in Asian languages, S. Neill, *A History of Christian Missions* (London, 1964), pp.224–30.

32 Durkacz, *Decline of the Celtic Languages.* The 'Statutes of Iona' resulted from a conference into which James VI and I dragooned the Gaelic lords, in which they agreed to various measures intended to keep the peace and spread the protestant religion. The lords agreed among other things to send their children to be educated in the Lowlands.

33 Jenkins, *Making of a Ruling Class*, pp.205–7.

34 Durkacz, *Decline of the Celtic Languages*, p.25.

of the Catholic Church, which had its own reasons for rejecting the use of vernacular scriptures of the sort that had so spectacular an influence in Wales. In Wales, on the other hand, the stereotypical Welshman was as likely to be a fanatical loyalist like Judge Jenkins or Sir John Owen (see p.130), a simple but faithful Fluellen, and his odd language had no seditious implications.

The contrast between Wales and the Gaelic regions originated at a very early stage, with the parliamentary decision in the 1560s to create Welsh translations of the Bible and Prayer Book, a move which in itself did much to prevent the kind of stigmatization suffered by Gaelic. The reasons for this critical difference may have been largely a matter of chance, in that a handful of far-sighted Welsh ecclesiastics in the 1560s were sufficiently well placed to secure a reversal of the normal Tudor policy towards the minority languages. Alternatively, perhaps Wales differed from the other nations in that this Celtic language so obviously predominated even among the elite, and there were no English-speaking minorities who could optimistically be seen as the basis for systematic anglicization, nor any substantial anglophone towns or squires.

THE CHURCH AND WELSH CULTURE

The formal creation of an autonomous Welsh Church had to wait until 1920, and the after-effects of disestablishment. Prior to that date, the four Welsh dioceses lacked a metropolitan or any coordinating institution.[35] However, throughout the early modern period, the church was strongly national and even patriotic in character. The Welsh language was maintained and promoted, so it was only logical to staff livings with Welsh men, and regimes were usually careful to respect issues of national origin. Thirteen of sixteen Welsh bishops appointed by Elizabeth were of Welsh origin, a proportion far superior to anything observed in the later middle ages, and Stewart regimes maintained the tradition into the 1680s.[36] The lower clergy were usually linked to the local community they served, and to Welsh cultural and linguistic interests in general.

35 Jenkins, *History of Modern Wales*, pp.291–7, 339–41.
36 Williams, *Recovery, Reorientation and Reformation*, p. 307

This must be emphasized, as there is a long tradition of undervaluing the cultural contributions of 'the church of England in Wales'. Unfortunately, such charges have been reproduced by modern scholars like Durkacz, who in his otherwise fine book on *The Decline of the Celtic Languages* makes some questionable statements on the history of Welsh culture. In particular, he comments on the hostility of the established church towards the Welsh language,[37] affirming that

> a link was forged between language, literacy and religion in eighteenth-century Wales, but only through the activities of the Welsh methodists and nonconformists who had no vested interest in the anglicization of the principality. It is a commonplace remark in Welsh historiography that anglican cures were filled with English placemen who disparaged the Welsh language and actively sought to destroy it.

Commonplace it may be, but that does not make it true. The view owes much to methodist and nonconformist mythology, anxious to exaggerate the 'long sleep', the 'heathenish darkness' that prevailed in Wales before the evangelical revival. This perception of the Welsh clergy is wholly inaccurate for the seventeenth century; even in the eighteenth century, many of the evangelical reformers who preached and wrote so enthusiastically in Welsh were themselves ministers of the established church.[38]

Many of the criticisms of the pre-revival church themselves carry a loaded religious agenda, as the criterion of quality was whether the clergy preached in a language and manner understandable to the laity. Of course, this view accepts somewhat uncritically the reformed theory of the vast superiority of the sermon to the formal liturgy, a preference which not all would accept, then or now. Many clergy did preach in Welsh, but even when they did not, they still used Welsh texts and formulae; in many areas, the sermon was replaced by the use of *halsingod*, popular Welsh carols which aimed to instruct while entertaining.[39] It is difficult to agree that such a church was wholly failing to tend to the spiritual and cultural needs of its people.

But of course, the Stewart church was not lacking in clergy of outstanding ability, and passionate commitment to Welsh traditional culture and antiquities. Our knowledge of early Welsh poetry depends largely on the preservation of works like the *Red*

37 Durkacz, *Decline of the Celtic Languages*, pp. 8–9.

38 Jenkins, *History of Modern Wales*, pp.153–63.

39 G.H. Jenkins, *The Foundations of Modern Wales: Wales 1642–1780* (Oxford, 1987).

Book of Hergest by antiquarian clergy like the Wilkins family of Glamorgan. Clerical copyists like John Price, rector of Mechteyrn in Llŷn, preserved contemporary poetry and scholarship.[40] John Davies of Mallwyd was perhaps the greatest Welsh scholar of his time, who debated the Welsh bards, urging them to accept the new learning. Apart from the clergy, most of the key figures in the preservation of traditional learning were devout anglican laymen like Rowland Vaughan of Caergai.

It was no coincidence that historical and antiquarian work was at the forefront of cultural debate in this period. History provided an essential intellectual justification for the Reformation, which was seen not as an innovation but as the restoration of an authentic proto-protestantism which the British church had possessed before it was swamped by Roman and monastic pollution.[41] For scholars like Salesbury and John Davies, the 'anglican' church was a return to authentic Welsh traditions. Of course, we find similar trends in Ireland, most notably with Ussher's account of early Celtic 'protestantism' in his *Discourse of Religion Anciently Professed by the Irish and Scottish*; but in contrast to Wales, his theories lacked the patriotic glorification of the native language and culture. As Peter Roberts has written, the Welsh scholars and antiquaries ensured the reception of the new faith 'by assimilating it into the Welsh experience. They were the makers of anglican Wales, as we may characterize that period when protestantism became an inseparable part of Welsh culture'.[42]

The Welsh clergy played a critical role both in writing books and tracts in Welsh, and in providing a market for such works.[43] Between 1546 and 1660, about 108 separate titles were published in Welsh, while another 215 followed between 1660 and 1710, and 330 more between 1710 and 1730. Works of piety and religious controversy represented the largest part of this output, and the increase after 1660 can be linked to the work of movements like the Welsh Trust and the SPCK in promoting popular evangelism and asserting moderate protestant doctrine. The work of Geraint H. Jenkins has shown how consistently such works were patronized by Welsh clergy. Under George I, between forty and fifty clerical subscribers could be found for each of the pious Welsh books of

40 Parry, *History of Welsh Literature*, pp.218–59.

41 Williams, *Welsh Reformation Essays*; Jenkins, *History of Modern Wales*, pp.68–9.

42 Roberts, 'Union with England', pp.66–9.

43 This account is wholly drawn from G.H. Jenkins, *Literature, Religion and Society in Wales 1660–1730* (Cardiff, 1978).

Edward Samuel, while sixty Welsh parsons subscribed to the militantly anglican *Prydferthwch Sancteiddrwydd* (*The Beauty of Holiness*) of Theophilus Evans (1722). Of 140 authors of Welsh-language books between 1660 and 1730, 40 were anglican clergy, and 2 were bishops. Once again, the contrast with the established church in contemporary Ireland will be dramatically apparent.

At the end of the seventeenth century, the scale and quality of this clerical scholarship was illustrated by the work of Edward Lhuyd the antiquary, as he collected Welsh materials for the 1695 revision of the classic text *Britannia*, and sought subscribers for his own *Archaeologia Britannica* (1707).[44] In his collection of parochial surveys, the respondents were usually clerics who demonstrated a great interest in local history and Welsh culture. One of his best allies was John Williams, archdeacon of Cardigan, who urged Lhuyd to create a new Welsh history purged from the 'fabulous traditions of our own countrymen, or the dry partial accounts of the English writers'.[45]

Lhuyd's assistants included the Welsh clergyman, Moses Williams, a successor in Lhuyd's Welsh and pan-Celtic interests. Another key supporter was Humphrey Humphreys, bishop of Bangor (1689–1701), described by Lhuyd as 'incomparably the best skill'd in our antiquities of any person in Wales', and supposedly a linguist comparable to Lhuyd himself.[46] He received tributes from the bards, and patronized a circle of Welsh antiquaries among his local clergy, while he pioneered the use of Welsh as the medium of his episcopal visitation. Also in the 1690s the clerical scholar, William Wynne, wrote a *History of Wales* that, while of no great merit of itself, remained for two centuries a standard source for the study of medieval Wales.[47]

This cultural commitment declined somewhat in the next century, as the Hanoverian episcopate tended to be overwhelmingly English and non-resident. At Llandaff, Bishop William Lloyd (1675–9) was the last native Welsh incumbent for two centuries, though there would be attempts to install patriotic candidates for

44 F.V. Emery, *Edward Lhuyd 1660–1709* (Cardiff, 1971); B.F. Roberts, *Edward Lhuyd: The Making of a Scientist* (Cardiff, 1980); Edward Lhuyd, 'Parochalia', ed. R.H. Morris, *Archaeologia Cambrensis* supplements (1909–11).

45 F.V. Emery, 'Edward Lhuyd and some of his correspondents', *THSC* (1965).

46 *Dictionary of Welsh Biography* (Cardiff, 1959).

47 ibid.

years afterwards.[48] In St Asaph, John Wynne (1715–27) was the last Welsh native bishop until 1870. However, the parochial clergy maintained their critical role, copying and preserving manuscripts of poetry, writing Welsh books or subscribing to new publications, promoting Welsh antiquarianism.

In the generation after Lhuyd, other English antiquaries like Browne Willis found continuing networks of fine scholars among the local clergy, like the Llandaff prebend Francis Davies. Another was the Anglesey minister, Henry Rowlands, whose 1723 study of his county laid the foundations for the immensely influential 'druid' mythology that would flourish for two centuries.[49] In 1720 proposals to move the Welsh sees to more logical centres in thriving towns were greeted by vigorous patriotic objections based on the long history of the 'British devotion' of the clerical 'lovers of the prosperity of Wales'. Their rhetoric drew heavily on the notion of the primitive and apostolic foundation of the Welsh Church.[50]

It was also in this period that Welsh parsons produced some of the finest works of Welsh prose, including the *Gweledigaethau y Bardd Cwsc* (*The Dream of the Sleeping Bard*), published in 1703 by Ellis Wynne. In 1716 Theophilus Evans published the *Drych y Prif Oesoedd* (*Mirror of the Early Ages*), a wildly inaccurate but long popular survey of early Welsh history. In 1710 another vicar named Dafydd Lewys published the first attempt at collecting the best works of the Welsh poets throughout the ages, in his *Flores Poetarum Britannicorum.* For the next two centuries, the clergy of the established church would be central to every movement to promote learning and literature in the Welsh language.[51]

WALES AND THE HIGH CHURCH MOVEMENT 1620–70

The seventeenth-century church in Wales should therefore be seen as a bastion of Welsh culture. However, its political life was decisively oriented towards the national regime, towards religious and political trends emanating from the metropolis and the

48 In the 1690s one likely candidate for Llandaff was Lhuyd's associate John Williams: NLW Penrice and Margam MSS L228.

49 Jenkins, *History of Modern Wales*, pp.74–7.

50 P. Jenkins, 'From Edward Lhuyd to Iolo Morganwg', *Morgannwg* 23 (1979), pp.29–48; Bodl MSS Tanner 146 f142.

51 Jenkins, *History of Modern Wales*, pp.291–7.

universities. There was thus no serious conflict between the maintenance of national (Welsh) culture and the assertion of British unity and harmony. In part, loyalty in church and state was cemented by the judicious use of patronage, access to which depended on preserving contacts with the central regime, but we should not underestimate more ideological influences, especially the new High Church movement which would enhance the power of central authority and promote conformity to new standards of thought and liturgy throughout the three kingdoms.

When considering the progressive integration of the United Kingdom, one of the central differences between Wales and the other Celtic lands concerns higher education. Wales did not possess its own university until Victorian times, and only in the 1640s was there even discussion of creating such an institution. On the other hand, there was a Welsh university college of sorts, in the form of Jesus College, Oxford, founded in 1571 and revived in the 1660s.[52] Between 1571 and 1700 Welshmen wishing to attend university showed an overwhelming preference for Oxford over Cambridge, and for Jesus over other Oxford colleges. This meant that the great majority of Welsh clergy had been educated at one institution, and specifically one college located in an English university.

Between 1620 and 1640 Oxford was profoundly influenced by the new High Anglican traditions associated with figures like Archbishop Laud, a vision of a liturgically based church that was no mere erastian compromise between catholic and calvinist. These doctrines had a particular influence at Jesus College, where they created a generation of Welsh clergy and gentry who would be vigorous (if not fanatical) supporters of the church cause through the catastrophes of the mid-century.[53]

The origins of the 'High' circle can be located in several associations formed in Oxford about 1620. One crucial event was the elevation of Francis Mansell to the position of principal of Jesus. Mansell had extensive connections among the gentry of the counties of Glamorgan and Carmarthen; he was linked to All Souls College, where he had previously been a fellow.[54] Also about 1620 there developed a friendship at Oxford between Gilbert Sheldon

52 ibid, pp.105–10.

53 The High Church movement is the subject of a series of three articles by P. Jenkins, 'The sufferings of the clergy', *JWEH* 3 (1986), pp.1–17; *JWEH* 4 (1987), pp.9–41; *JWEH* 5 (1988) pp.73–80.

54 Bodl MSS Wood f30, 'Life of Francis Mansell'; William Wynne, *Life of Sir Leoline Jenkins* (London, 1724).

and the Glamorgan squire, Sir John Aubrey of Llantrithyd, a link which 'continued to their deaths'.[55] Sheldon became an influential ally, whom Laud would present to an Oxfordshire living. Sheldon would himself become archbishop of Canterbury from 1663 to 1677, and was a primary architect of the church settlement of the 1660s. These connections influenced the group of south Wales gentry who were related by marriage to the Aubreys, families like the Kemyses, Stradlings and Jenkinses of Hensol. Sheldon made All Souls a High Anglican centre, and fellows of this college included Dr William Bassett of Glamorgan, as well as figures of national celebrity like Brian Duppa and Jeremy Taylor. The new ideas inevitably spread to Mansell's college of Jesus.[56]

Though this was initially a south Wales movement focused in the shires of Glamorgan, Carmarthen and Brecon, the influence of High Church doctrines elsewhere is indicated by the construction of new churches or private chapels within a few miles of each other in the north, at Llanfair Dyffryn Clwyd, near Ruthin, at Gwydir, and at Rûg, Corwen, all between 1619 and 1637.[57] High Church doctrines influenced northern gentry families like the Mostyns, Salusburys, and Owens of Clenennau, all of whom controlled extensive ecclesiastical patronage.

To have attended Jesus College in Mansell's time was to have been exposed to the highest doctrines of church loyalism, and this generation would have included a large portion of the clergy of mid-century Wales. The gentry associated with Mansell and Sheldon also played a crucial role in the fate of the royalist cause in south Wales, maintaining a firm church loyalist tradition distinct from the powerful catholic royalism of the marquis of Worcester's family.[58] It was in these years that Wales earned a reputation as a haven of High Church sentiment, a tradition that owes much to the heroic picture of the royalist judge David Jenkins of Hensol offering to die with the Bible in one hand and a copy of Magna Carta in the other, as well as to other royalist 'sufferers' like Sir John Owen of Clenennau, or Francis Mansell himself.[59]

55 Jenkins, 'Sufferings of the clergy', *JWEH* 3 (1986) pp.1–17; *JWEH* 4 (1987), pp.9–41.

56 P. Jenkins, 'Welsh anglicans and the Interregnum', *Journal of the Historical Society of the Church in Wales* 27 (1990), pp.51–9.

57 Nigel Yates, 'The Welsh church and celtic nationalism', *JWEH* 1 (1984), pp.1–10.

58 Jenkins, *Making of a Ruling Class* pp.101–32.

59 Jenkins, 'Sufferings of the clergy', *JWEH* 4 (1987), pp.20–1.

Many gentry houses produced anglican martyrs or confessors, as members of these families suffered death, exile or imprisonment, or watched the ravaging of their mansions and the confiscation of their estates and tithe income. The group remained staunch, and provided refuge to some of the leading figures of the Anglican Church in crisis. There may have been as many as five bishops in residence at the Stradling castle of St Donat's in 1645, including Archbishop Ussher.[60] The High Church gentry created a whole network of alternative schools and other institutions which would prevent them being forced into contact with the puritan regime, whether in Wales or at Oxford. This 'separatist' tradition survived the Restoration, and it was two Kemys women who would maintain an innovative 'protestant nunnery' near Bristol, a project with nonjuror connections.[61]

The political ruin of the church cause was naturally enough seen in religious terms, as God's wrath against the blasphemy and impiety of the regicide regime. The flavour of these views is preserved by the meditations of one ejected Flintshire clergyman,[62] who recalled hearing of the appearance in 1641 of 'a man in black with a discomposed visage and an insolent walk and began a discourse of devils tied in chains in a valley of the land who were shortly to be set at liberty with a sudden charge to chastise the country'. At first, this seemed 'malapert and mad', but since then 'the jugglers have cosened many silly souls both of their revenues and religion; the powers of the air have turned our sunshine often into sulphurous mists; the fiends, the sowers of discords, the women's jars have produced men's wars, where steel hath killed its thousands but silver and gold their ten thousands'. The events of the 1650s were viewed in terms that were quite literally apocalyptic.

At the Restoration, the old 'sufferers' found themselves close to the centres of power in both church and state, with Sheldon determined to remember his friends.[63] George Stradling represented the Glamorgan clergy in convocation; Francis Davies became bishop of Llandaff in 1667. Stradling himself became chaplain to Sheldon, preached sermons before the king, and was

60 Jenkins, 'Welsh anglicans and the Interregnum'.

61 B. Hill, 'A refuge from men: the idea of a protestant nunnery', *P & P* 117 (1986), p.112.

62 NLW Add MSS 12463B, f70.

63 P. Jenkins, 'Wales and the order of the royal oak', *National Library of Wales Journal* 24 (1986), pp. 339–51. For the Welsh court circle of the 1680s, P. Jenkins, 'Francis Gwyn and the birth of the Tory party', *WHR* 11 (1983), pp.183–201.

generally following the precisely correct course to a bishopric.[64] Sir John Aubrey exercised great influence in ecclesiastical appointments, and his brother became chancellor of St David's.

The pattern described here was followed by many other gentry houses, such as the Glamorgan Bassetts. One royalist leader in that county was the Revd Thomas Bassett of Llantrisant who, while imprisoned after 1647, wrote a tract expounding high royalist political theory and vigorous Laudian churchmanship.[65] Thomas was a relative both of the Oxford Laudian scholar, William Bassett, and of the Llandaff diocesan chancellor, Richard Bassett. At the Restoration, Henry Bassett became the new chancellor of Llandaff.

George Stradling and Thomas Bassett were among the few members of this group who left sizeable bodies of writing, both published and otherwise, to suggest the depth of their commitment to High Church sentiment, and the ways in which their thought developed during the mid-century crisis. However, there are indications that the High Church views represented by Sheldon's Welsh circle were quite widely shared. In the whole of Wales, for example, some 240 clergy were ejected under the Propagation regime of the 1650s. It is quite possible that many of these were indeed as inadequate or immoral as puritan rhetoric suggested; but others were intellectual or spiritual followers of Laud or Sheldon, and in most cases we can trace personal links. Especially in the southern counties, we can trace the emergence of a radically new form of churchmanship among the parish clergy, and these ideas had become intimately connected with the force of family ties and traditions.

From many examples, we find Evan Price of St Athan (Glamorgan) who continued so outspoken in his church loyalty that he came close to being hanged by the Propagation authorities. In understanding his devotion, it is helpful to recall that he had attended Sheldon's college of All Souls during the 1630s.[66] In the same county, we find Rees Davies who, after ejection, 'by stealth [performed] the duty and office of priesthood according to the liturgy of the church of England' (it is not clear whether this was in English or Welsh).[67] At the Restoration, Rees's brother Francis

64 George Stradling, *Sermons and Discourses . . .* (London, 1692), biographical introduction.

65 Thomas Bassett, 'A caveat for subjects, or the danger of submitting themselves to the mock authority . . .', Cardiff Central Library MSS.

66 Quoted in Jenkins, 'Sufferings of the clergy', *JWEH* 4 (1987), p.35; A.H. Johnson, 'Wales during the Commonwealth and Protectorate', in D.H. Pennington and K. Thomas (eds) *Puritans and Revolutionaries* (Oxford, 1978), pp. 233–56.

67 Quoted in Jenkins, 'Sufferings of the clergy', *JWEH* 4 (1987), p.20.

Davies became first archdeacon of Llandaff, and later bishop (1667–75). In Carmarthenshire, the ejected cleric William Thomas 'sometimes read the common prayer' at Laugharne. He would also become a bishop under the restored order, holding the diocese of St Davids from 1667 to 1683.[68]

THE CIVIL WAR INHERITANCE

At the Restoration, the core of High Anglican gentry and clergy dominated the hierarchy of the church throughout south Wales. At parish level too, cases like the Bassett and Davies families indicate the degree to which the church had become 'established' in county society, in the sense that the same clerical 'dynasties' produced anglican ministers generation after generation, often to fill the same livings.[69] Glamorgan offers a classic example in the form of the Gamage family, nine of whom held livings in the county between 1608 and 1734.

Such families had so entrenched themselves in the local clerical establishment that church loyalism appeared a natural part of political culture, even if rarely justified in terms as intellectual as we might expect from a George Stradling or a Thomas Bassett. It was these houses above all which bore the brunt of the puritan persecutions, and which bore the bitterest memories when they came into their own after 1660. The best illustration of this emerges in the time of Anne when the anglican scholar John Walker collected evidence of the sufferings of the clergy during the Interregnum. In every Welsh region, Walker found contacts who vividly recalled the atrocities wrought upon their families, the 'barefaced and notorious impieties' committed by 'those topping rulers, preachers and encroachers upon the rights of the faithful members of the Church of England'.[70]

By the Restoration, anglicanism had not only matured, but also become inseparable from the family pride and tradition of some of

68 *Dictionary of Welsh Biography*.

69 P. Jenkins, 'Church patronage and clerical politics in eighteenth century Glamorgan', *Morgannwg* 28 (1984), pp.32–47; J.R. Guy, 'Plurality, patronage and non-residence in the old diocese of Llandaff 1660–1800', University of Wales, Lampeter, PhD dissertation, 1983; J.H. Pruett, *The Parish Clergy under the Later Stuarts* (Urbana, Ill., 1978).

70 Quoted in Jenkins, 'Sufferings of the clergy', *JWEH* 4 (1987), p.41.

the wealthiest houses in Wales. It also had political significance, as the High Anglicans were determined to avoid a return to the religious subversion that had almost destroyed their church. Such memories became a mainstay of the Tory cause in Wales in the century after 1660, and would be reflected in support for nonjuror and Jacobite movements.

THE CATHOLIC THREAT 1670–90

Oxford connections go far towards explaining how a High Church tradition was created in Wales, but not necessarily how that movement came to dominate political culture to the extent that it did under Anne. After all, the old Laudians were not strong outside the southern counties, while even there there were other trends within the church which were not wholly eclipsed at the Restoration. There were powerful gentry who were much more accommodating to the puritan regimes than were the Aubreys or Owens of Clenennau, and who favoured broad toleration in the 1660s. These views were reflected among the clergy whom they appointed and patronized. Throughout Wales, such moderate gentry and clergy maintained excellent relations with ejected puritan ministers during the worst years of persecution, refusing to enforce the laws closing dissenting schools and chapels.[71]

Puritan sentiments also remained strong in the towns, where civic elites often contained a strong dissenting element.[72] Between about 1660 and 1690, church authority was weak in the Welsh boroughs, in large part due to the perceived threat posed by catholic conspiracies. There were lasting fears of military threats from Irish invaders, and in particular regions, these concerns were compounded by charges that local catholic magnates would serve as a fifth column.[73] There would be major scares about catholic plots in 1641, 1679 and 1688, usually accompanied by widespread public disorder. In south-east Wales, in the middle borders, and in Flintshire, catholic strength appeared sufficient to incite anti-popery

71 Jenkins, *Making of a Ruling Class*, pp.121–31.

72 P. Jenkins, 'The old leaven', *HJ* 24 (1981), pp. 807–823; Bodl Tanner MSS 146, ff113, 138 for riots and dissent in towns.

73 A.H. Dodd, 'The pattern of politics in Stuart Wales', *THSC* (1948), pp.8–91; A.H. Dodd, *Studies in Stuart Wales* (Cardiff, 1952, revised edn 1971).

fears, and this encouraged many to emphasize the need for a protestant 'united front', including moderate nonconformists.

Between about 1660 and 1690 ecclesiastical history in Wales is dominated by the conflict between these two views, which ultimately depended on perceptions of whether resurgent puritanism or catholic aggression represented the greater threat to the church. Some families never wavered in their loyalties, and the Aubreys or Kemyses, for example, remained firmly anti-puritan throughout. However, the emphasis on anti-popery (and protestant toleration) had a growing attraction within the church during the 1670s, and this affected senior clergy in Wales and the borders. For some years, this threatened to create divisions between the metropolis and the Welsh periphery, as regional perceptions of political danger were fundamentally at odds with those prevailing in Charles II's regime.

During the 1670s anti-popery fears focused on peers like the marquis of Worcester in Monmouthshire and Lord Powis in Montgomeryshire, and it was rumoured that catholic conversions were increasing dramatically. One response was to promote popular evangelism and education, with extensive translation and popularization of protestant works like *The Whole Duty of Man* and *The Practice of Piety*, and new editions of Welsh authors like Rhys Prichard. This activity was coordinated by the Welsh Trust founded in 1674, the leadership of which involved most of the 'moderate' and anti-popish gentry in Wales and the borders.[74] In contrast to Ireland and Scotland, anti-popery campaigns in Wales resulted not in the penalization of the traditional language, but in a new incentive for the production of vernacular books and tracts.

There was also an important clerical element in the evangelization movement, including several bishops. The bishop of Bangor condemned the Welsh Trust as a Whiggish plot, but he was an exception. In St Davids, Bishop William Thomas was involved in the translation of edifying works into Welsh, and was friendly with Whiggish squires active in the anti-popery cause and the Trust. At Llandaff, similarly, William Lloyd came from a distinctly 'High' background, and he had been ejected during the Interregnum, but his career and associations in the 1670s were definitely Whiggish and anti-catholic.[75]

74 P. Jenkins, 'Anti-popery on the Welsh marches in the seventeenth century', *HJ* 23 (1980), pp.275–93.
75 ibid.

THE HIGH CHURCH TRIUMPH 1690–1714

At the height of popery fears under Charles and James, there were major divisions within the Welsh Church, but these passed with the Revolution, and the triumph of an impeccably protestant sovereign who definitively ended the perceived Irish and catholic threats to Wales. With this danger gone, the way was prepared for the triumph of the High Church tradition which saw the dissenters and nonconformists as its greatest rivals: this movement carried all before it under Queen Anne.[76] This victory had an economic basis, in that the Welsh elites had a vested interest in Tory 'blue-water' attitudes towards war and commerce. The ideal foreign policy involved largely self-financing naval warfare to seize colonies, while maintaining as far as possible the west European markets for Welsh goods such as coal.[77]

Toryism thus made excellent economic sense, for squires as much as for merchants or industrialists. In the early eighteenth century the Welsh *bourgeoisie* (such as it was) increasingly found common cause with the old High Church squires and peers, with whom they cooperated on industrial and commercial development. Inevitably, social and political connections followed, and there was a clear High Church and even nonjuror tone to the Welsh mercantile elites of this time.[78] Conversely, dissenters provided a local symbol for the misdeeds and exactions of the Whig regimes, and they were subject to frequent acts of persecution and violence. Not coincidentally, the worst excesses occurred in the Welsh trading towns, like Swansea, and all the towns now show evidence of Jacobite sympathies.

With much of its former support gone, the 'old dissent' of Wales began a half-century of stagnation and endemic internal controversy – a period of weakness one might not suspect when considering the disproportionate attention paid by Welsh historians to the nation's dissenting tradition.[79] Meanwhile, chances of protestant 'comprehension' were gravely damaged by the

76 Jenkins, *Foundations of Modern Wales*, pp.132–72.

77 P. Jenkins, 'Tory industrialism and town politics: Swansea in the eighteenth century', *HJ* 28 (1985), pp. 102–23; Jenkins, *History of Modern Wales*, pp. 215–19.

78 P. Jenkins, 'The Tory tradition in eighteenth century Cardiff', *WHR* 12 (1984), pp.180–96.

79 Jenkins, *History of Modern Wales*, pp.145–52.

well-publicized persecution of Scots episcopalians after 1689 by the 'plaguey hypocritical kirk'.[80]

In religious terms, the beneficiaries of these developments were the local High Church clergy, who achieved their greatest success in the last years of Queen Anne. In every part of Wales, surviving sermons demonstrate the influence of the highest Laudian doctrines, and vigorous support for the martyr, Dr Sacheverell, who undertook a near-royal progress to north Wales.[81] Under the Tory government of 1710, every Welsh county now acquired numbers of clerical justices of the peace, a radical departure from local precedent.[82] In cultural matters, the years between 1690 and 1720 marked a new peak in clerical involvement in scholarly research and literary patronage, the age of Edward Lhuyd, Ellis Wynne and Theophilus Evans. The anglican clergy had secured a virtual hegemony over the traditional culture of Wales.

Though the political successes were thwarted by the change of dynasty in 1714, the High Church tradition would survive to become the main political orthodoxy of eighteenth-century Wales. Old 'moderate' and even puritan gentry families increasingly drifted into high-flying opinions; while Whig squires appointed moderate clergy of Hanoverian sympathies, the ecclesiastical 'middle ground' was far to the right of what had seemed conceivable a generation earlier.[83] The national church had become the central fact of Welsh political life.

CONCLUSION

Ellis Wynne and Bishop Humphreys were no more representative of the Welsh Church under the Stewarts than Jonathan Swift was typical of the Irish Church, or John Donne of the English. The quality of the Welsh clergy varied enormously, as did their

80 NLW Brogyntyn MSS (Clenennau letters) 901 (1691); from a large anglican literature, see e.g. *Account of the Present Persecutions of the Church in Scotland in Several Letters* . . . (London, 1690).

81 Jenkins, *Making of a Ruling Class*, pp.139–57; Jenkins, 'Church patronage and clerical politics'.

82 Jenkins, *Making of a Ruling Class*, pp.89–91, 143–4; Jenkins, *History of Modern Wales*, pp. 164–74.

83 It can also be argued that a clear tradition links the evangelical revival in Wales with earlier High Church ideas, while calvinistic methodism did not formally break with the established church until the early nineteenth century.

commitment to Welsh language and culture, and it would be wrong to romanticize their goals or exaggerate their achievement. However, if we consider the cultural efforts of the Welsh Church alongside the situation of Czech, Breton, Catalan or other minority languages, then that achievement is very substantial, and even precocious.

To put it in context, is it possible to conceive that Swift might have been able to appeal simultaneously and naturally to the Irish people in both their languges, to present the *Drapier's Letters* or the *Modest Proposal* in both English and Gaelic? The fact that this image is so jarring is itself testimony to the apparent inevitability of the schism between official English and vernacular Celtic, with the church as a primary vehicle for the language of administration, and with all that implies for the success of religious dissidence. In Wales, however, such a perilous 'colonial' division was largely avoided, with the consequence that one of the most linguistically alien and distinctive components of any European state achieved political integration with astonishingly little difficulty or unrest. To say the least, this was a significant achievement of early modern statecraft and ecclesiastical policy.

Acknowledgements

In undertaking the research on which this chapter is based, I have been assisted by the generosity of the Institute for the Arts and Humanistic Studies and the Research and Graduate Office of the College of the Liberal Arts, at the Pennsylvania State University.

CHAPTER SIX

The Gaelic reaction to the Reformation

Mícheál Mac Craith
University College Galway

Links between the two parts of the Gaelic world, Ireland and the Scottish Highlands, became particularly close from the fourteenth to the sixteenth centuries. Large numbers of Clan Donald South had been settling in Antrim from about 1399 after the marriage of Eoin Mór, brother of Donald, Lord of the Isles, to Margaret Bisset, heiress of the Glens of Antrim. Despite the split of the clan into an Irish and a Scottish branch after Sorly Boy MacDonald's annexation of the Antrim lands in 1565, social and personal ties between the two groups remained strong. In the late sixteenth century many Highland clans intervened directly in the wars of Ulster, serving both Irish and English masters as mercenaries. Because of a shared common language, cultural ties between the two parts of Gaeldom were also close, with free movement of poets, musicians and harpists, and many Highland learned and professional families had Irish origins.[1] A number of Gaelic prose texts associated with the Reformation throw some further light on the relations between Ireland, Scotland and England during that turbulent period.

ARGYLL AND THE PROGRESS OF THE REFORMATION

When the Irish parliament passed the Act of Uniformity in 1560, it

1 D. S. Thomson, 'Gaelic learned orders and literati in medieval Scotland', in W.F.H. Nicolaisen (ed.) *Proceedings of the Third International Congress of Celtic Studies* (Edinburgh, 1968), pp.57–78.

added a rider permitting church functionaries who did not know English to conduct services in Latin:

> that in every church or place, where the common minisyter or priest hath not the vse or knowledge of the English tongue, it shall be lawfull for the same minister or priest to say and vse the mattens, evensong, celebration of the Lord's supper, amd administration of each of the Sacraments, and all their common and open prayer in the Latine tongue in such order and forme as they be mentioned and set forth in the said booke established by this act.[2]

The use of the vernacular for scripture and public worship was one of the most significant features of the Protestant Reformation. Yet this principle was easily discarded by royal officials in Dublin when faced with the problem of subduing Gaelic Ireland, the use and cultivation of the Gaelic language being seen as disloyalty to the crown. Spiritual renewal went hand in hand with anglicization and military conquest, and the guiding principles of the former were regulated by what were seen to be the exigencies of the latter.

The year 1560 was also significant for the progress of the Reformation in Scotland. In February 1560 a treaty of mutual assistance was signed at Berwick between England and the Lords of the Congregation. In July the 'auld alliance' between France and Scotland effectively came to an end when it was agreed by the treaty of Edinburgh that French and English armies would both leave Scotland, that Mary and Francis abandon the title and arms of the crown of England, and that Elizabeth be recognized as queen of England. The Reformation parliament of August 1560 repudiated the supremacy of the pope, forbade the celebration of the Latin mass, and drew up a Confession of Faith. One of the leading members of the Lords of the Congregation was Archibald Campbell, fifth earl of Argyll.[3] Argyll offered his services to the English queen in gratitude for English aid in expelling the French and establishing protestantism in Scotland. Since Campbell was both a Highland chief and a Lowland lord, his domination of western Scotland meant that he could intervene in Ulster with considerable ease. In 1555 he had personally led the expedition that had helped Calvagh O'Donnell to defeat his father Manus, lord

2 Richard Bolton (ed.) *The Statutes of Ireland Neatly Perused and Examined* (Dublin, 1621), p.273.

3 For an account of Argyll's involvement in Irish affairs see J. Dawson, 'Two kingdoms or three? Ireland in Anglo-Scottish relations in the middle of the sixteenth century' in R.A. Mason (ed.) *Scotland and England 1286–1815* (Edinburgh, 1987), pp.113–38.

of Tyrconnell. Tudor difficulties in Ulster were increased by the presence of Scottish mercenaries there and by the power of the MacDonalds. Tudor officials hoped that Argyll could take over and control the trade in mercenaries between Ireland and the Scottish Isles. In addition to this control of the mercenary trade, Argyll himself could put up to 5,000 trained soldiers in the field, men who cost little and who were much more accustomed to the Irish way of fighting than English troops.

Elizabeth hoped to secure Argyll's help in two distinct ways; direct military assistance against Shane O'Neill and peaceful persuasion of his own Campbell relatives in Ireland, especially the MacDonalds of Antrim and Calvagh O' Donnell. James MacDonald was married to Argyll's aunt, Lady Agnes Campbell, while Calvagh O'Donnell was the second husband of Catherine McLean, Argyll's stepmother. In return Argyll was offered harquebusiers and heavy cannon if needed against his own enemies in western Scotland. Despite Argyll's offer of aid, the English authorities were most reluctant to exploit his services and his mercenaries were not called into action. His good offices were used mainly in the supply of information about the situation in Ulster and the Isles to Randolph, the English ambassador in Edinburgh. The earl was often better informed about events in Ulster than the authorities in Dublin. The frequent communications between Shane O'Neill and Argyll were translated from Gaelic by the latter and then relayed to Randolph. Following the marriage of Mary Queen of Scots to Lord Darnley in 1565, fears of a catholic revival drove the earl of Moray into rebellion. Argyll, who supported his friend's rebellion discreetly, withdrew to the west while Moray and his followers were driven into exile across the Anglo-Scottish border. Moray was consequently rebuked by Elizabeth in front of the French ambassador, for going into rebellion. This public humiliation of his friend led Argyll to transform his attitude towards England from one of benevolence into open hostility, and as a consequence his offer of military aid in Ireland was withdrawn. This new suspicion of the English led him to become a fervent supporter of Mary Queen of Scots during the civil wars of 1567–73, despite his deep commitment to the protestant faith. After Mary's flight into England in 1568, Argyll demanded that Elizabeth should not merely release her but actually help her to regain her throne. If she refused he threatened to use his military power against the English in Ulster.

In 1569 Argyll persuaded his aunt, Lady Agnes Campbell, the widow of James MacDonald, to marry Turlough Luineach O' Neill, lord of Tyrone, and on the very same day Fionnuala Campbell, daughter of Agnes and James MacDonald, married Hugh O'Donnell, lord of Tyrconnell. The joint celebration of these marriages marked the beginning of an important reconciliation between these erstwhile Ulster rivals, the O'Neills and the O'Donnells. Both Agnes and Fionnuala were very forceful characters and between them were responsible for most of the Scottish mercenaries who were hired in Ulster at this time. By 1569 both Agnes and Fionnuala were so feared that they were accused of being

> trayners of all scotts into Ireland, as allso conveighers of all commodities oute of the relme, so that by these twoo woomen arriseth all mischief against thinglishe Pale for by these means onell and odonill are specyall frends. what countennaunce soever odonill showeth to be a subiecte.[4]

In addition to his arranging of these strategic marriages, Argyll lent his support to the MacDonalds of Antrim in their struggle against the Dublin government. As a result of this support the MacDonalds were able to recover from a crushing defeat inflicted on them by Shane O'Neill in 1565, and to re-emerge under the leadership of Sorley Boy MacDonald as a serious threat to the English.

In 1567 Argyll was patron of the first printed book to be published in Gaelic in either Ireland or Scotland. This was John Carswell's *Foirm na n-Urrnuidheadh*, a translation of the *Book of Common Order* (Edinburgh, 1564), which in turn was a revision of the *Geneva Book*, sometimes called John Knox's Liturgy, printed in Edinburgh in 1562.[5] In his epistle to the reader and introductory poem Carswell refers to the Gaels of Ireland and Scotland six times, and states that his work was intended for dissemination in Gaelic Ireland as well as in Scotland. The translator's choice of classical common Gaelic as his medium, with relatively few concessions to Scotticisms, is another indication that this work was not intended solely for usage in Scotland. Given that Elizabeth already faced demands for a more thorough reform of the Elizabethan church, and that the Scottish and English churches were both calvinist in theology, it was not wholly unreasonable to expect that further reformation might have succeeded in persuading the churches of England and Ireland to adopt the Genevan Order. Carswell's work

4 'John Smyths Advice for the realme of Ireland', Appendix no. One in G.A. Hayes-McCoy, *Scots Mercenary Forces in Ireland (1565–1603)* (Dublin, 1937), p.346.

5 *John Carswell's Foirm na n-Urrnuidheadh*, ed. R.L. Thomson, SGTS 11 (Edinburgh, 1970).

was prepared for this eventuality, and nobody could have surmised in 1567 that Elizabeth would resist all pressure against the Prayer Book and episcopacy during the remainder of her reign. Only three copies of what was apparently the only edition of *Foirm na n-Urrnuidheadh* have survived, and it is not known how many were printed nor what was the ultimate dissemination and effect of the book.

In the dedicatory epistle to the earl of Argyll, Carswell praises his patron for his zeal in promoting the reformation:

> You have succeeded, my Lord, . . . in every work and great enterprise you have begun, through the grace of the Holy spirit and by knowledge of the holy scripture, without considering any danger or peril or hazard in which you were, that is in destroying the false faith and false worship and in burning images and idols and in casting down and smashing altars and places where false sacrifices were offered of old, and in destroying thieves and immoral persons and plunderers and oppressors, and after that in fostering and protecting and honouring the Christian church to the full. For this triumph is more permanent for you in the sight of God, than every other worldly triumph, such as harrying and despoiling neighbours and strangers and killing and exterminating their men and burning and destroying their houses and their residences.[6]

In the same year that Argyll was the recipient of these fulsome praises he was offering to break off negotiations with Shane O'Neill in return for Elizabeth's help in promoting the Reformation in Scotland. Argyll's interventions in Irish affairs were largely determined by English policy towards Scotland on two specific occasions, Elizabeth's support for the Lords of the Congregation in 1559–60 and her failure to intervene on Moray's behalf in 1565. He had no difficulty in combining calvinistic fervour with a deep-felt hostility to England. Knox himself, who was on the opposite side of the political divide, had to concede Argyll's religious commitment, though he added, 'God be merciful to his other offences'.[7] The appearance of Carswell's book seems to have finally galvanized the authorities in Dublin into providing spiritual material for the native Irish.

In the 1560s Elizabeth had sent the not inconsiderable sum of £66 13s 4d to Adam Loftus, archbishop of Armagh, and Hugh Brady, bishop of Meath, 'for the making of character to print the New Testament in Irish'. When nothing had been achieved by the

6 Thomson (ed.), *Foirm na n-Urrnuidheadh,* pp.176–7.
7 Dawson, 'Two kingdoms or three?', p.127.

end of 1567, she threatened to demand that the money be returned 'unles they presently put the same in print'. The same year, 'she provided characters and other instruments for the Presse, in hope that God in mercy would raise up some to translate the New Testament into their mother tongue'.[8] The latent presbyterianism of Carswell's work was arguably a real challenge to the anglican settlement, a threat that was augmented by the presence of the powerful Argyll as Carswell's patron, and it is most probably this second factor that ultimately forced the hand of the Dublin authorities. In 1571 Seán Ó Cearnaigh, treasurer of St Patrick's Cathedral, published the first Gaelic book to be printed in Ireland, *Aibidil Gaoidheilge 7 Caiticiosma.*[9] One of the most interesting features of this work was Ó Cearnaigh's willingness to cull some liturgically neutral prayers from Carswell's book, prayers that would in no way prove offensive to loyal subjects. In addition to an epistle to the reader and a brief account of the Gaelic alphabet, this work contains a translation of the catechism of the *Book of Common Prayer* (1559), various prayers for private recitation, and a Gaelic version of Archbishop Matthew Parker's twelve articles of religion (1561). Two hundred copies of this work were printed but only two have survived, and we have no evidence as to how they were distributed. Ó Cearnaigh's reference to Elizabeth as 'our allpowerful divine high prince' must be one of the earliest acknowledgements in the Gaelic language of the English monarch's legitimacy in Ireland.

GAELIC RESISTANCE

The first stirrings of opposition to Elizabeth's imposition of protestantism in Ireland are to be seen in the rebellions of James Fitzmaurice Fitzgerald. In a Latin statement explaining the justice of his cause in 1579, he is careful to point out that this insurrection is not against the legitimate monarch of England but against a tyrant:

> Thus, then, we are not at war against the legitimate and honourable crown of England, but against that she-tyrant who, by refusing to hear Christ in the person of His vicar, and even by daring to subject the

8 Breandán Ó Madagáin, 'Bíobla: an Bíobla i nGaeilge', *Diagacht don phobal,* 1 (Maynooth, 1986), p.43.

9 N. Williams, *I bprionta i leabhair, na Protastúin agus prós na Gaeilge 1567–1724* (Dublin, 1986), pp.21–6.

> Church of Christ to a woman in matters of faith, on which she has no right to pronounce, has deservedly forfeited her royal authority.[10]

In three of his Gaelic letters seeking mercenary aid Fitzgerald explains the aims of his crusade, *sinne ag cosnamh ár gcreidimh 7 ár ndúthaighe,*[11] that is, we are defending our faith and our territory. Some commentators translate the final Gaelic word as native land. The word *dúthaig* is capable of a wide range of meanings from native district to native land. It seems that 1579 is too early to see a fully developed faith and fatherland ideology being promoted by Gaelic leaders and that it is more prudent to understand the word *dúthaig* in a more localized sense. For example, in a treaty between O'Donnell and Argyll in 1555, O'Donnell undertakes to maintain 500 of Argyll's mercenaries each year *'na dhúthaigh an Érinn'*, in his territory in Ireland.[12] On this basis the prime factors in Fitzgerald's struggle are defence of the catholic religion and defence of territory, with the added clarification that it is Elizabeth's heretical status that frees her Irish subjects from the obligation of offering her allegiance. The crown itself is not an issue, rather the perceived heretical status of the monarch. In his English letters and proclamations, however, Fitzgerald adopted a more overt faith and fatherland ideology, demanding of his cousin, the earl of Desmond, for instance, that he stand for 'God's honour, the health of our country and for the restoring of the Catholic again'.[13] On different occasions he refers to 'the common good and weal of this noble Ireland',[14] 'our dear country',[15] 'zeal for God's honour and their own country'.[16] It would appear that Fitzgerald is addressing two distinct constituencies in his Gaelic and English texts, and that his appeals to the Old English community contain a much more inclusive brand of patriotism than those addressed to the Gaelic leaders.

10 M. Ronan, *The Reformation in Ireland under Elizabeth 1558–1580* (London, 1930), p.620. Itaque non iam contra legitimum angliae sceptrum, et honorabile solium dimicamus, sed contra Tyrannnam, quae Christum in vicario suo loquentem recusans audire, imo Christi Ecclesiam suo foemineo sexui etiam in Fidei causis (de quibus cum aucthoritate nec loqui deberet) ausa subjicere, meritam regiam potestatem amisit. 'Correspondence of James Fitzmaurice Fitzgerald', *Journal of the Kilkenny Archaeological Society 1858–59*, p.369.

11 'Correspondence of James Fitzmaurice Fitzgerald', p.363.

12 John Mackenzie, 'Treaty between Argyll and O'Donnell', *SGS* 7 (1953), p.98.

13 Ronan, *Reformation in Ireland*, p.617.

14 ibid, p.615.

15 ibid, p.615.

16 ibid, p.615.

Hiram Morgan contends that this brand of patriotism, reflecting a love of one's native land rather than adherence to a racial identity, first gained prominence among Commonwealth supporters in the Old English community in the 1550s. Though this reform movement ultimately failed, Catholic exiles on the continent later combined the patriotic ideal with the religious ideals of the Counter-Reformation, which was then repatriated to Ireland by James Fitzmaurice Fitzgerald.[17] In the early part of the Nine Years War, Hugh O'Neill adopted the stance of a religious crusader, stunning the Dublin government in 1596 with his demand for liberty of conscience. By 1598 he went even further and made faith and fatherland an essential component of his ideology, a stance well exemplified by this letter to James Fitzpiers:

> And forasmuch as it is lawful to die in the quarrel and defence of the native soil, and that we Irishmen are exiled and made bond slaves and servitors to a strange and foreign prince, have neither joy nor felicity in anything, remaining still in captivity; to reform all things to the will of God and goodness of the commonwealth, we have thought it convenient to desire and admonish you, as our dear friend, to convert and establish our pretended action and enterprise. You may consider how your father ended his life, what torments he did suffer in this world; and such and greater is provided in hell for all sinners and offenders against God's commandments and the commonwealth.[18]

It was in his effort to win over the Old English that O'Neill exploited the ideology of faith and fatherland. Using their own Commonwealth rhetoric, he emphasized a common land and a common religion without reference to race or language, and began to use the terms 'Ireland' and 'Irishmen' with increasing frequency and with a deliberately unifying intent.[19]

Ironically enough this new ideology does not manifest itself in a Gaelic text until after the defeated O'Neill's death in exile in Rome in 1616. The text in question is a life of Red Hugh O'Donnell written by Lughaidh Ó Cléirigh between 1616 and 1630.[20] This exercise in Renaissance biography is not written in classical common Gaelic but in a deliberately inflated artificial style. The convoluted language may be partly responsible for its apparent lack

17 H. Morgan, 'Hugh O'Neill and the Nine Years War in Tudor Ireland', *HJ* 36. 1 (1993), p.27; B. Bradshaw, *The Irish Constitutional Revolution of the Sixteenth Century* (Cambridge, 1979), pp.276–82.

18 Morgan, 'Hugh O'Neill', p.24.

19 ibid, p.27.

20 *Beatha Aodha Ruaidh Uí Dhomhnaill*, pt I Text and translation, ITS 42 (Dublin, 1948); pt II Introduction, glossary, etc., ITS 45 (Dublin, 1957).

of popularity, surviving in only one manuscript, but it was possibly intended for translation into Latin on the continent as a work of propaganda to win more support for the Irish catholic cause. We know for example that there was a proposal in Louvain to produce a dictionary *de viris illustribus Hiberniae* in the early part of the seventeenth century.[21] The Ó Cléirigh family were historians to the O'Donnells, and modern commentators fault the *Life* in its effort to portray Red Hugh O'Donnell as the major partner in the course of the Nine Years War, relegating Hugh O'Neill to a minor role. Despite this partisan representation of O'Donnell's career, the life is by no means devoid of importance. Of particular interest is Ó Cléirigh's stress that O'Donnell was a most worthy catholic leader. His address to his troops before the battle of the Curlew mountains in 1599 is a construct of the author's based on a speech from the First Book of Maccabees (I Mac 3:16–22) in which Judas Maccabeus exorts his soldiers to defend Israel's laws, customs and religion from being swamped by Hellenization. Ó Cléirigh underlines the fact that this battle was fought on the Feast of the Assumption of the Blessed Virgin Mary, and in drawing attention to O'Donnell's religious observance of this feast in particular and to his normal religious demeanour prior to battle, the author underscores the specific Catholic dimension of both O'Donnell's leadership and his campaign.

In O'Donnell's request to the king of Spain for aid in 1596 he refers to the enemies of the Irish taking their fatherland (*athardha*) from them and perverting them from the Roman Catholic faith (*creidemh catholocda Romhanda*).[22] It is no accident that the *dúthaig* of James Fitzmaurice Fitzgerald has now become *athardha* in Ó Cléirigh's work. In the lament for the death of Hugh Maguire in 1600, Ó Cléirigh describes him as having fought to protect his faith and fatherland, *ag imdhiden a irse agus a atharda.*[23] When the Spaniards refused to surrender at Kinsale, they referred to the nobles they had come to support, defending their faith and their fatherland, *ag cosnamh a nirsi 7 a nathardha.*[24] In commenting on the defeat of Kinsale, Ó Cléirigh noted the failure of the Irish to defend their faith, their fatherland and their lives, *do chosnamh a nirsi a nathardha 7 a nanma.*[25]

21 *Analecta Hibernica* 6 (1934), p.214.
22 *Beatha Aodha Ruaidh Uí Dhomhnaill*, pt I, p.123.
23 ibid, p.240.
24 ibid, p.314.
25 ibid, p.336.

The Gaelic word *athardha* occurs frequently in this text and is given a wide range of meanings, the editor translating it variously as patrimony, country, inheritance, native land. An examination of its use in the *Life* indicates that it occasionally refers to O'Donnell's own lands, at other times the lands of both O'Donnell and O'Neill are indicated, and on other occasions the whole province of Ulster. But when used in conjunction with either *iress* or *creidemh*, each of which means faith, the word indicates fatherland, a meaning borne out by its derivation from *athair*, father.

This is the earliest known use of this particular ideology to have survived in a Gaelic source, but by the time the biography was written, the insurgents' version of the faith and fatherland ideal had been shattered by the defeat of the Irish at Kinsale; in the aftermath of defeat a new Gaelic Catholic ideology was already in the making. With the defeat of O'Neill and O'Donnell Gaelic Ireland was finally subdued and a new era in Anglo-Irish relations was ushered in with the accession of James VI and I to the crown. Both Spain and the papacy showed little interest in maintaining a military struggle against England. As far as the Vatican was concerned, the interests of English catholics would be best achieved by coming to an accommodation with the new monarch, and Irish requests for aid would only prejudice such a possibility.

THE INFLUENCE OF THE FRANCISCANS

In the meantime the Gaelic New Testament had finally appeared in 1602, followed by the *Book of Common Prayer* in 1608. Inspired by the principles of catholic Counter-Reformation, Irish clerical exiles on the continent devoted their best efforts to countering protestant religious material in Gaelic with works promoting catholic doctrine. The focus for this new educational religious campaign was the Irish Franciscan college of Louvain, founded by Florence Conry in 1606. Conry's own career is a paradigm for many of those involved in the Louvain enterprise. Born a member of a Gaelic professional literary family, Conry practised his profession until he entered the Franciscan order. On going to Spain he studied at the university of Salamanca and composed an unpublished catechism in Gaelic in 1593. He returned to Ireland in his official capacity as legate of Pope Clement VII with the Spanish forces that landed at Kinsale. After the Irish defeat he accompanied Red Hugh O'Donnell back to Spain to seek further aid. He was appointed provincial of the

Irish Franciscan province at a general chapter of the Franciscan order in Toledo in 1606, and due to the support of Hugh O'Neill was appointed archbishop of Tuam in 1609. It was at Conry's insistence that Philip III of Spain gave permission to the Irish Franciscans to found a college at Louvain. Conry's career, completely acted out on the continent of Europe from 1602 until his death in 1629, shows a close connection between Gaelic learned families, the Franciscan order, the Spanish crown, and support for O'Neill.

The first Catholic work written by a member of the Louvain community was a catechism composed by Bonabhentura Ó hEoghusa, a member of a famous bardic family who were poets to the Maguires of Fermanagh.[26] This work was first printed in Antwerp in 1611, and again in Louvain in 1615, on the friars' own printing press, the English authorities having previously tried in vain to persuade Archduke Albert to refuse his permission. A letter from Sir Ralph Winwood to William Turnbull referred to the failure of the archduke to prevent 'the unworthy proceedings of the Irish friars at Louvain in printing and publishing these seditious libels, and that in their own language'. The only hope, as far as Winwood was concerned, was 'that all copies of such books be called in and publicly burned'. Turnbull in turn, writing to King James, inveighed against 'the perfidious Machiavellian friars of Louvain', friars who

> seek by all means to reconcile their countrymen in their affections and to combine those that are descended of the English race and those that are mere Irish in a league of friendship and concurrence against your majesty and the true religion now professed in your kingdom.[27]

The next work to come from the press at Louvain was Conry's *Desiderius* in 1615, which was in the main a translation of a very popular Spanish religious text.[28] Conry took considerable liberties with his original, however, as regards both omissions and additions of his own. One particularly lengthy addition, which added nearly a quarter to the original work, was composed for the purpose of encouraging Irish catholics to remain steadfast in their faith. Of particular interest is a passage in which Conry declared that civil government derived its authority from the governed:

26 Fearghall Mac Raghnaill (ed.) *An Teagasg Críosdaidhe* (Dublin, 1976), pp.xiv, xv.

27 C.P. Meehan, *The Fate and Fortunes of the Earls of Tyrone and Tyrconnel* (Dublin, 1868), p.328.

28 T.F. O'Rahilly (ed.) *Desiderius* (Dublin, 1941).

> and it is certain that the spiritual powers and the temporal powers originated in a different and dissimilar way for the reason that it is the people or their ancestors who gave the kings whatever power they now possess; and it is Christ himself and not the people who gave the spiritual powers to Peter and to the other apostles; through whom the same powers were given to the bishops, without any permission being sought from the people, as can be proved from Paul's epistle to Titus and from his other epistle to Timothy.[29]

Conry's theological training on the continent put him in touch with the most up-to-date thinking of Counter-Reformation catholic Europe. Robert Bellarmine in the university of Louvain had articulated the clear distinction betwen spiritual and temporal powers, while Suarez, the Spanish theologian from the university of Salamanca, had advanced the revolutionary theory that power derived from the people, a theory that cut right across the doctrine of the divine right of kings, a doctrine enunciated by James VI of Scotland and future king of England in his *Trew Law of Free Monarchies* (1598). It follows from Bellarmine's views

> that secular government ought not to be able to exact an absolute obedience from its subjects, and also that spiritual authority, for spiritual purposes, has the right to direct and control secular. There are circumstances, then, in which the pope is justified in deposing an heretical ruler and absolving subjects from their allegiance.[30]

The insertion of a clause into the oath of allegiance in 1607, deliberately framed to counteract this claim, led to a protracted controversy between James and Bellarmine, and Conry's work is best situated within this debate. While the latter does not enter into the specific question of the oath of allegiance, his denial of the divine right of kings was not destined to win him any favours from James. Conry's espousal of power deriving from the people may not have been a total rejection of James, however, rather an indication that James would have to earn the allegiance of his catholic Irish subjects, an allegiance conditional on his granting freedom of religion.

FROM RESISTANCE TO ACCORD

Peter Lombard, titular archbishop of Armagh (1601–25) and resident in Rome for the duration of that period, had been one of

29 ibid, p.128.
30 G.H. Sabine, *A History of Political Thought* (3rd edn, London, 1966) p.387.

O'Neill's strongest supporters during the Nine Years War, but he gradually withdrew his support after Tyrone's submission. Reasoning that an accord with James was the best way to secure tolerance towards catholics under his jurisdiction, Lombard introduced the distinction between subjective and objective heresy. Objectively James was a heretic, but subjectively he was not, since he could not be held culpable for the way in which he was educated. This distinction provided an opening for catholics to acknowledge the king as their lawful sovereign in temporal matters. From 1612 onwards Lombard did his best to weaken O'Neill's influence on ecclesiastical affairs in Ireland, and ensured that men holding similar views to his own, and of similar Old English background, were promoted to the episcopacy. He complained to the pope of the elevation of two men of Gaelic stock, Conry as archbishop of Tuam and Owen McMahon as archbishop of Dublin; both were firm supporters of O'Neill and held intransigent political views.

Lombard's successor as archbishop of Armagh was Hugh McCaghwell. Born in 1571, he studied law in the Isle of Man. Engaged as tutor to the sons of Hugh O'Neill, McCaghwell accompanied Henry O'Neill to Spain when he was sent there by his father in 1600 as a hostage to ensure Spanish aid. He studied at the university of Salamanca and entered the Fransciscan order about 1603, becoming a teacher of theology in the university soon after his ordination. A co-founder with Conry of the Irish Franciscan College at Louvain, McCaghwell arrived there in June 1607. From 1609 to 1614 he was heavily involved in diplomatic activities, negotiating with England's agent in Brussels, William Trumbull, on behalf of O'Neill, and promoting Irish interests with Guido Bentivoglio, the papal nuncio in Flanders. In 1613 the English spy John Bathe reported that that he had advised the king of Spain to disregard any information supplied to him by either Conry or McCaghwell.

In addition to his diplomatic activities, McCaghwell was a reputed theologian, and he found time to publish a work in Gaelic on the sacrament of penance in 1618, *Scáthán Shacramuinte na hAithridhe*, based on the teaching of the fourteenth session of the council of Trent (15 October 1550 to 25 November 1551), with the incorporation of recent material from the *Rituale Romanum* of 1614.[31] Closer perusal, however, yields some very interesting

31 Cainneach Ó Maonaigh, OFM (ed.) *Scáthán Shacramuinte na hAithridhe* (Dublin, 1952).

evidence of shifts in Gaelic political ideology. In his introduction McCaghwell cited his reasons for writing. Every other catholic nation, *gach náision Chatoilic eili,* had printed religious books and they were more necessary in Ireland than elsewhere because of the dearth of priests and preachers. His description of Ireland as a catholic nation is most interesting, as is the frequency of the word 'nation' in the work as a whole, sixteen times in all. The earliest occurrence of the word *náision* known to me, incidentally, is also associated with the Franciscan College at Louvain. When Robert Chamberlain was making his will prior to entering the Franciscan order in 1610, he left whatever money he had *le h-aghaidh an Clódh-Gaoidheilge agus neithe do chur a ccló do rachas an onóir do Dhia, a cclú dár násion agus d'Órd San Froinsias* – for the Gaelic printing type, and for publishing of things that will give honour to God, fame to our nation and the order of St Francis.[32]

McCaghwell adopted a most polemical stance in his introduction, but the body of the text is remarkably free from controversy until the final section, which treats of indulgences. McCaghwell alerts the reader that he is writing in 1617, exactly one hundred years after the outbreak of the Reformation which is depicted originating from Luther's pique at being passed over in favour of Tetzel to preach the indulgence granted by Pope Leo X to those who would support the war against the Turks. The polemical note was reintroduced and both Luther and Calvin were accused of all sorts of gross indecencies, based for the greater part on Johannes Cochlaeus' *Commentaria de actis et scriptis Martini Lutheri* (1549). The real aim of this invective, however, was less to discredit Luther and Calvin, and more to highlight the contrast between them and James VI and I. Though brought up in the faith of Luther and Calvin he did not follow the paths of these two malicious masters in pride and arrogance. James, in fact, was our noble illustrious king, *ar rí uasal óirdheirc.*[33] McCaghwell seemed to have Lombard's distinction between subjective and objective heresy in mind here, but he referred to it only in passing, and followed a totally different line of argument. Through a highly selective use of James's own work, the *Praefatio monitoria,* and through studiously avoiding passages that would prove offensive to catholics, McCaghwell demonstrated to his own satisfaction that the content of James's faith was either explicitly or implicitly the same as that held by Roman Catholics.

32 Colm Ó Lochlainn, *Tobar fioghlan Gaedhilge* (Dublin, 1939), p.97.
33 ibid, l.5456, p.166.

The Irishman stressed the king's acceptance of the three symbols of faith, the first four general church councils, the unanimous teachings of the fathers of the church for the first five hundred years after Christ, and above all the role of scripture. On this final point, however, McCaghwell's mask slipped somewhat when he conceded in an aside that James did not mention which particular books of scripture he accepted, while conveniently ignoring the king's stated refusal to assign the Apocrypha canonical status despite his reverence for them. In thus manipulating the king's own words, McCaghwell concluded that James was a catholic in fact if not in name, and that catholics were therefore justified in granting him their allegiance as their lawful sovereign. If Lombard was preoccupied with defining the relations between catholics and a heretical sovereign, McCaghwell solved the problem by demonstrating that James was not a heretic at all. If Ireland was a unique country in so far as the principle of Augsburg could not apply to it, *cuius regio eius religio*, McCaghwell's solution simply changed the sovereign's *religio* and made it coincide with that of the *regio*. It was this aim of making James acceptable as a lawful monarch to catholics that caused McCaghwell earlier in the text to refrain from naming those who tried to force catholics into obeying laws that went against their conscience. It was the king's officials who were guilty in this regard, but not the king himself.

For McCaghwell, Ireland was a catholic nation, but this spiritual allegiance to Rome was in no way incompatible with temporal allegiance to the English crown, nor was this allegiance incompatible with Gaelic culture. In his ability to distinguish between spiritual, temporal and cultural realms, McCaghwell succeeded in creating a new version of the faith and fatherland ideology, replacing hostility to the Tudor crown with allegiance to the Stewart one. This description of Ireland as a catholic nation seems also to apply to Gaelic Scotland, since the author specifically referred to Ireland and her dear daughter Scotland, *Éri . . . agus a hinghean ionmhuin Alba*,[34] as the only countries to have received the privilege of being free from all taint of heresy.

Gráinne Henry has singled out two tendencies being manifested in the Irish military community in the Spanish Netherlands in the early years of the seventeenth century, one a militant movement to be identified mainly with those of Gaelic Irish stock, the other a conciliatory movement promoted mainly by those of Old English

34 ibid, l.6288, p.190.

origin.[35] Ultimately there seems to be very little difference between the two attitudes, at least in clerical circles. There is nothing to separate McCaghwell's views from those of Bishop John Roche, who, in a report in 1611 drawn up for Bentivoglio, described Ireland 'as a Catholic nation . . . always inclined to the Catholic faith and the see of Rome . . . even before the Norman invasion'.[36] In the final analysis the difference seems to consist in McCaghwell – and the Louvain writers in general – making special provision for the spiritual formation of the Gaelic-speaking world, both in Ireland and Scotland, as well as in the *émigré* community of the Spanish Netherlands.[37] If Peter Lombard gradually abandoned his support for the militant policy of Hugh O'Neill after the accession of James VI and I, he was soon to be followed by the Franciscans of Gaelic background. Lombard's initial support for O'Neill can only be described as reluctant, and only embarked on in the best interests of Irish Catholics; one can say that the Old Irish cleric's abandonment of O'Neill was equally reluctant, but equally dictated by what was perceived to be the best interests of Irish Catholics in general, and Gaelic Catholics in particular.

The publication of O'Neill's correspondence (written between 1602 and 1616) suggests that his desire for a reconciliation with James VI and I was merely strategic, and that his principal objective was always to return to Ireland at the the head of an army, with Spanish support.[38] His last letter to Spain (dated March 1615) declared that he would rather go to Ireland with a hundred soldiers and die there in 'defence of the catholic faith and of his fatherland' than remain in Rome.[39] Members of the Irish Franciscan community of Louvain, notably Florence Conry, Hugh McCaghwell and Robert Chamberlain, figure prominently in this correspondence; Lombard once remarked that Conry was 'more

35 G. Henry, *The Irish Military Community in Spanish Flanders 1586–1621* (Dublin, 1992), ch.6.

36 ibid, p.136.

37 It is worth noting the report of Richard Morrés in 1611 that: 'After his coming from Prague, he saw one of the books among the Irish soldiers, printed in Irish in Antwerp, and set forth by the friars of Louvaine confirming their own religion, and to the contrary infirming and refusing that of the Protestants'. (*CSP Ire 1611–14,* p.184.) The book in question has to be Bonabhentura Ó hEoghusa's *Teagasg Críosdaidhe,* the first work to be produced by the Irish Fransciscans of Louvain.

38 M. Kerney Walsh, '*Destruction by Peace*': *Hugh O'Neill after Kinsale* (Armagh, 1986), pp.5–6.

39 ibid, p.347.

eager to sustain the war than the very officers themselves'.[40] While international politics, especially relations between Spain and England, strongly influenced the policies of Irish *émigré* ecclesiastics on the continent, it would appear that those of Old Irish stock maintained their support for military intervention in Ireland until the death of O'Neill in 1616, notwithstanding the reluctance of Spain to break the treaty with England that had endured from 1604 to 1622. The contrast between the *Life* of Red Hugh O'Donnell and McCaghwell's treatise could hardly be more striking. While the former work displays an irredentist faith and fatherland ideology, the latter, published almost simultaneously in Louvain, marks a striking modification of that policy. The place of composition seems to have been the deciding factor in the changed perspectives. Residence in the Spanish Netherlands, with close and frequent contacts with Madrid, Brussels and Rome, gradually brought home to the Gaelic Irish exiles the fact that neither Spain nor the Vatican was prepared to engage in hostilities with James, something that became more obvious after the demise of O'Neill.

Even more striking is the contrast between Conry's hardline approach in stressing that kingly power derived from the people, and McCaghwell's most conciliatory stance in relation to James; and yet there was only a two-year gap between the appearance of these two views, both of which were Louvain publications.[41] During this interval O'Neill died, an event that sounded the death knell for whatever slender hopes remained for Spanish military aid, thus making an accommodation with James all the more imperative. It was this realization that led the Gaelic exiles to abandon their dearly held hopes, and finally come round to what had always been the preferred option of those of Old English stock. Yet despite McCaghwell's pragmatic decision to promote allegiance to James for the sake of his faith, his personal preference still came to the fore in a letter written to Propaganda Fidei on the last day of July 1626, less than eight weeks before his death: '[The] Spaniards are

40 F. O'Brien, 'Florence Conroy, archbishop of Tuam', *Irish Rosary* 31 (1928), p.454.

41 At present it is not known when precisely in 1616 Conry's work was published. If it appeared before O'Neill's death at the end of July, the author's insistence on sovereignty deriving from the people could be construed as a total rejection of James. If the book appeared after O'Neill's death, however, the author could be interpreted as allowing the people to accept James on their own terms. There was no way, however, that James could countenance such conditional loyalty.

so slow, that one can scarcely hope that they will do anything this year'.[42]

The acceptance of the Stewart monarchy became even more obvious in the hagiographical and historical work undertaken from Louvain. The annalist, Mícheál Ó Cléirigh, informs us that he concluded his *Genealogiae regum et sanctorum Hiberniae* on 4 November 1630, 'the fifth year of King Charles'. He finished re-editing the old chronicle *Leabhar Gabhála* in 1631, 'the sixth year of the kingship of King Charles over England, France, Scotland and Ireland'.[43] The editor's aims in accomplishing this task were as follows: *dochum go rachadh i nglóir do Dhia, in onóir do na naomhaibh, do ríoghacht Éirionn, & i leas anama dhamh féin* [for the glory of God, the honour of the saints, the kingdom of Ireland, and for the benefit of my own soul].[44] Ó Cléirigh's major work, *Annála Ríoghachta Éireann, Annals of the Kingdom of Ireland* compiled between 1632 and 1636, also referred to 'the eleventh year of the kingship of our king Charles over England, France, Scotland and Ireland'. Not only was Charles recognized as lawful sovereign, but also the Annals contained laudatory references to James as well. Also pertinent is the fact that the annalist thrice uses the phrase *creideamh agus athartha*, faith and fatherland – for the years 1601, 1608 and 1616, respectively. In striking contrast with its previous occurrence in the *Life* of Red Hugh O'Donnell, the phrase is now bereft of all hostility to the English crown, and now connotes an allegiance both to Roman Catholicism and to Ireland that is in no way incompatible with acceptance of the Stewart monarchy. Although Ó Cléirigh's projects were conceived in Louvain, his research and writing took place in Ireland under the patronage of Old Irish lords who had come to terms with the new regime and had obtained prominent positions under English jurisdiction as Members of Parliament and on county commissions. The ideology towards which they had been tentatively groping in the first quarter of the seventeenth century became an established fact in the historical writings of Ó Cléirigh and his Old English contemporary, Keating. Instead of seeing the work of Ó Cléirigh and his associates as a noble gesture to save the memory of a doomed civilization from oblivion, one can much more fruitfully consider them using

42 'Hispani sunt tam tardi, ut vix sperari possit aliquid hoc anno per eos effectum iri': B. Jennings, *Mícheál Ó Cléirigh and his Associates* (Dublin, 1936), p.192.

43 Breandán Ó Buachalla, '*Annála Ríoghachta Éireann is Foras Feasa ar Éirinn*: an comhthéacs comhaimseartha', *SH* 22–3 (1982–3), pp.94–6, for this and the following.

44 ibid, p.95.

the best resources of learning available at the time, native documents and Renaissance methodology, to compose for their fellow countrymen an authoritative history of the new catholic nation that had come into being under the general peace established by James VI and I and maintained by Charles, the kingdom of Ireland, a nation composed of both Old Irish and Old English, united under the common name of *Éireannach*, Irishman.[45] Unfortunately for the moulders of this new ideology, lack of funds prevented them putting the fruits of their research into print, and the outbreak of hostilities in Ireland in 1642 resulted in promised funds being diverted to the military campaign. Despite the attractiveness of the new ideology formed by a religious elite in the intellectual environment of the Counter-Reformation, the fortunes of the catholic confederate armies in Ireland during the 1640s demonstrate just how fragile the alliance of Gaelic Irish, Old English and the English crown was in reality.

THE SHARED PARADOX OF GAELIC POLITY

It is surely one of the great ironies of the history of these islands that it took a Scottish calvinist to bring about a reconciliation between the O'Neills and O'Donnells, leading them to join forces in defence of the catholic faith in the most serious rebellion that the Elizabethan government faced. Jane Dawson has noted many similarities between the fifth earl of Argyll and Hugh O'Neill, suggesting that just as Argyll's involvement in Anglo-Scottish diplomacy prevented Scottish Gaeldom from taking the lead, so his intervention in Ireland helped to prevent an Irish-led Gaelic state from coming into being. When Hugh O'Neill sought outside support, it was to catholic Spain that he turned rather than to the

45 Mícheál Mag Craith, 'Gaelic Ireland and the Renaissance', in G. Williams and R.O. Jones (eds) *The Celts and the Renaissance Tradition and Innovation*, (Cardiff,1990), pp.79–82; B. Bradshaw, 'Geoffrey Keating: apologist of Irish Ireland', in B. Bradshaw, A. Hadfield and W. Maley (eds) *Representing Ireland: Literature and the Origins of Conflict, 1534–1660* (Cambridge, 1993), pp.166–90. Breandán Ó Buachalla finds it significant that the first poem in Irish to incorporate the new thinking on the Old English was composed, not in Ireland, but on the continent, by Eoghan Ruadh Mac an Bhaird around the year 1627. ('James our true king: the ideology of Irish royalism in the seventeenth century', in D.G. Boyce (ed.) *Political Thought in Ireland since the Seventeenth Century* (London, 1993), pp.15–16.)

Gaelic Highlands, thus demonstrating that the split within the Gaelic world into distinct Irish and Scottish units was already under way, a fissure that was mainly due to the fifth earl of Argyll.[46] It could be argued that with the hardening of the confessional nature of the struggle in Ireland, the Argylls were never likely to be supporters of O'Neill's cause, but O'Neill was in regular communication with James VI of Scotland, who tended to adopt an attitude of benevolent neutrality if not one of active support for the Irish leader. That the Reformation was placing a strain on the cultural unity between Gaelic Ireland and Gaelic Scotland is shown by a poem composed by Fearghal Óg Mac an Bhaird during a visit to Scotland at the beginning of the seventeenth century. The poet, who in another poem refers to the three crowns in James's charter, felt uneasy precisely because the Gaelic Scots were alleged to no longer believe in the Eucharist, religious disunity being thus seen as undermining cultural unity.[47] Nevertheless the exiled O'Neill seems to have made much play of the catholic aspect of the Scottish Gaelic card in his requests for further aid from Spain. In a memorial from O'Neill and O'Donnell (forwarded to Philip III on 13 April 1608) the earls underlined the fact that Ulster was only four or five hours' navigation from Scotland:

> For this reason the Earls often marry Scottish women and thus it is they are related to the principal lords of all Scotland, particularly with those of the neighbouring parts, of whom the lord of Ile and Quintir (= Kintyre) is an uncle of Earl of Tyrconel and Earl of Erguil (= Argyll) and the lord of Ereton are his cousins; they are among the most powerful lords of that kingdom.[48]

46 Dawson, 'Two kingdoms or three?', pp.130–1.

47 Mícheál Ó Mainnín, 'An tuiscint Ghaelach in Albain c. 1200–1715' (University College, Galway, MA thesis, 1987), pp.34–5. A translation of two verses gives some idea of the poet's distress:

Tánag don tír nach adhair don abhluinn ghil ghrásamhail; mó do mheall an saoghal sinn baoghal 'na cheann ní chuirim.	I came to the land which rejects the white grace-giving host; the world had beguiled me overmuch; I know no danger like it.
Fearr bheith thiar ó thigh go tigh do sheirc naomhchuirp Dé dhúiligh ná ríghe 's a bheith a-bhus; don bhreith fhíre do fhéachus.	Better beg from door to door at home for love of the holy Body of the God of the elements than be a king while here; I recognise this judgement of truth.

(Lambert McKenna SJ, *Aithdhioghluim Dána* I, ITS 37 (Dublin, 1939), p.206 (text); *Athdhioghluim Dána* II, ITS 40 (Dublin, 1940), p.120 (translation).

48 Kerney Walsh, '*Destruction by Peace*', pp.207–8.

In 1613 the Scottish Irish connection was underlined in a letter from O'Neill to the Conde de Castro:

> Now or never is the time. . . . All the nobles of the Kingdom of Scotland are on the point of rising against the enemy and await nothing more than to see the fires alight in Ireland, and all that is needed for this in Ireland is the presence of the Earl of Tiron.[49]

When Sir James MacDonald escaped from Edinburgh Castle in 1615, Florence Conry used this event as a pretext for seeking further aid from Spain:

> and now he is in arms with one thousand five hundred soldiers in his territory of the Isle. His lands are at a distance of only three hours' navigation from those of the Earls, to whom the occasion of this revolt would have been of the greatest importance if the Earl of Tiron had been there, for, with very little help, this gentleman could move all Scotland to revolt and they would be of great help to one another in view of their vicinity, their kinship and the strength of their territories.[50]

The following February MacDonald corresponded with Conry: 'Your Lordship knows, and can explain better than I could, who I am and what I am capable of doing to help the catholic cause in Ireland and Scotland'.[51]

MacDonald fled to Ireland and thence to Spain, eventually being recalled from exile and receiving the king's pardon prior to his death in London in 1626. O'Neill's death some ten years earlier had brought a lull to the military plottings of the Irish *émigré* community on the continent. Henceforth its interest in Scotland took on a more missionary aspect. Even though McCaghwell referred to Scotland as the dear daughter of Ireland, and had intended his catechetical work for distribution in the Gaelic areas of Scotland as well as in Ireland, he was, nevertheless, reluctant to have the Irish college in Louvain involved in spearheading a mission to Gaelic Scotland. The question had been mooted since 1615, but a formal request for missionaries was made only in 1618. McCaghwell pointed out *inter alia* that Louvain had difficulty in supplying clergy for the Irish mission let alone that of Scotland, and that this function really pertained to the Scots' colleges at Douai and Rome. It was only on being informed that the pope himself had ordered the release of some members from the Louvain community for the Scottish mission, that McCaghwell eventually

49 ibid, p.316.
50 ibid, pp.365–6.
51 ibid, p.376.

relented. This reluctance was later mirrored in the behaviour of the earl of Antrim who, unwilling to risk the king's displeasure, refused to let his son travel to Scotland, despite being the missionaries' preferred choice as superior.[52] Two Irish priests and a Scottish laybrother set out for Scotland in January 1619 and a second group of three set out in 1624, the mission continuing in rather fitful fashion until 1637.[53] A letter from Cornelius Ward, a member of the second band, reported to McCaghwell in 1626 that the initial group brought about six thousand Scots back to the practice of the catholic faith.[54] When Ward and his *confrère* Patrick Hegarty approached John Campbell, laird of Calder, in 1624, they did so disguised as poet and harper, the former purporting to have composed a piece of eulogistic verse for his host. The ploy proved successful and Campbell, much to the chagrin of the authorities, was won back to the catholic faith. The event is interesting in that it shows the resourcefulness of the friars in taking advantage of the traditional cultural unity between Gaelic Ireland and Gaelic Scotland in order to surmount religious differences,[55] but their task cannot have been helped by the fact that the common vernacular of both countries was now breaking up into two separate languages.[56] The success and heroism of this small mission, however, should not blind us to the fact that the reformed kirk made considerable strides in appointing a remarkable succession of

52 Cathaldus Giblin, OFM, *Irish Franciscan Mission to Scotland 1619–1646* (Dublin, 1964), pp.127–8.

53 Cathaldus Giblin, OFM, 'Hugh McCaghwell, OFM, Archbishop of Armagh (+1626): aspects of his life', *Seanchas Ardmhacha* 11.2 (1985), pp.273–6; *Irish Franciscan Mission.*

54 Giblin, 'Hugh McCaghwell', p.276.

55 J.L. Campbell, 'Review of Cathaldus Giblin, *Irish Franciscan Mission to Scotland, 1619–1646* (Dublin, 1964)', *SGS* 11 (1968), pp.224–6. 'Calder was a man of great importance, but a heretic; it was very difficult to gain access to him; knowing, however, that Calder held poets in high regard, Ward having composed a poem in praise of Calder, disguised himself as an Irish poet; then, accompanied by a singer, carrying a harp, he presented himself before Calder, and was graciously received; Ward continued in the guise of a poet for three days, and then disclosed to Calder who he actually was; he pointed out to Calder the errors contained in the religion he professed, and they argued in private concerning them; satisfied with Ward's reasoning, Calder promised to receive absolution as soon as some non-catholic lairds who were staying with him had taken their departure; later, when, at the direction of Ward, Patrick Hegarty visited Calder, the latter became a catholic as he had promised' (Giblin, *Irish Franciscan Mission*, pp.53–4). In a further submission it was felt that Calder's influence among the members of the Campbell clan would result in many members of the gentry becoming catholics (ibid, pp.79–80).

56 Instructions from the nuncio at Brussels to the Irish missionaries urge them to improve their knowledge of the Scottish tongue: 'In Scotica lingua sedulo cavent proficere' (Giblin, *Irish Franciscan Mission*, pp.26–7).

ministers to a majority of parishes in the Highlands. By the early seventeenth century nearly all of these ministers had been educated at a university in the Lowlands; despite James's insistence on the need to eradicate the barbarism associated with Gaelic culture, care was taken to ensure that these men were sufficiently proficient in the Gaelic tongue to carry out of their pastoral duties.[57]

CONCLUSION

The final twenty years of the sixteenth century mark the evolution of a militant faith and fatherland ideology among the Gaelic Irish, but after the demise of Hugh O'Neill this ideology underwent a major mutation from one of hostility to the English crown to acceptance of it. Orchestrated for religious reasons by the Irish Franciscans of Louvain, this process was facilitated by the ability of the Irish Gaelic poets to furnish an impeccable Gaelic genealogy for the Stewart dynasty, the learned classes having equally pragmatic secular reasons for recognizing James I.[58] The advance of the Reformation in Scotland, however, placed the cultural unity of Irish-Scottish Gaeldom under increasing strain, and notwithstanding the persistence of catholicism in MacDonald territory, one can no longer speak of a common faith. With the Lowland plantation of Kintyre and the almost simultaneous plantation of Ulster, this same crown drove a further wedge between Irish and Scottish Gaels. Despite his Scottish origin and his Gaelic pedigree, the policies of James Stewart were deliberately designed to undermine the alliance between the Gaels of Ireland and western Scotland.

57 J. Kirk, 'The Jacobean church in the Highlands, 1567–1625', in his *Patterns of Reform* (Edinburgh, 1989), pp.449–87; T.P. McCaughey, 'Protestantism and Highland culture', in J.P. Mackey (ed.) *An Introduction to Celtic Christianity* (Edinburgh, 1989), pp.172–205.

58 Breandán Ó Buachalla, 'Na Stíobhartaigh agus an t-aos léinn: Cing Séamas', *PRIA* 83C (1983), pp.81–134; 'Poetry and politics in early modern Ireland', *Eighteenth-century Ireland: iris an dá chultúr*, 8 (1992–3), pp.149–75; 'James our true king: the ideology of Irish royalism in the seventeenth century', pp.7–35, especially pp.7–23.

CHAPTER SEVEN

Gaelic culture in the seventeenth century: polarization and assimilation

Allan Macinnes
University of Aberdeen

The significance of Gaelic poetry as a historical as well as a literary source for the early modern period remains a matter of controversy. Among Irish academics a vigorous debate continues,[1] whereas an inside view suggests that Scottish academics have been primarily concerned with the trenchant issuing of proposition papers.[2] Little has been attempted by way of comparative study, however, although the development of Gaelic culture is now the subject of international discussion.[3] Without laying claim to a comprehensive synthesis or to an expansive knowledge of Irish Gaelic sources, there is undoubtedly scope for an exploratory comparative study of Gaelic culture within the context of political polarization within the three kingdoms and the need to acclimatize to a British political agenda, particularly evident in the opening up of the land-market through colonization, civil wars and debt in the

1 B. Bradshaw, 'Native reaction to the westward enterprise: a case-study in Gaelic ideology', in K.R. Andrew, N.P. Canny and P.E.H. Hair (eds) *The Westward Enterprise* (Liverpool, 1978), pp.65–80; T.J. Dunne, 'The Gaelic response to conquest and colonisation: the evidence of the poetry', *SH* 20 (1982), pp.1–30; N.P. Canny, 'The formation of the Irish mind: religion, politics and Gaelic Irish literature 1580–1750, *P&P* 95 (1982), pp.91–116.

2 J. Macinnes, 'Clan unity and individual freedom', *TGSI* 47 (1971–2), pp.338–73; D. Thomson, *An Introduction to Gaelic Poetry* (London, 1974), pp.99–155; A.I. MacInnes, 'Scottish Gaeldom, 1638–1661: the vernacular response to the Covenanting dynamic', in J. Dwyer, R.A. Mason and A. Murdoch (eds) *New Perspectives in the Politics and Culture of Early Modern Scotland* (Edinburgh, 1982), pp.59–94; W. Gillies, 'Gaelic: the classical tradition', in R.D.S. Jack (ed.) *The History of Scottish Literature, I, Origins to 1660* (Aberdeen, 1988), pp.245–61.

3 A. Dooley, 'Literature and society in early seventeenth-century Ireland: the evaluation of change', and A.I. Macinnes, 'Seventeenth-century Scotland: the undervalued Gaelic perspective', both in C.J. Byrne, M. Harry and P. O'Siadhail (eds) *Celtic Languages and Celtic Peoples* (Halifax, NS, 1992), pp.513–34, 535–55.

seventeenth century. Such a comparison, while drawing primarily on Scottish sources, should provide an alternative point of reference to the prevailing anglocentric view of early modern British history.

CULTURAL DEVELOPMENTS

The ongoing debate about the development of Gaelic culture in the early modern period shares a common awareness of the emergent dynamic of vernacular Irish and Scottish Gaelic from the mid-seventeenth century. The reasons for this vernacular divergence from common classical Gaelic require historical as well as literary analysis. While the emergent vernacular dynamic in both kingdoms drew heavily on classical bardic traditions of eulogy and elegy, significant doubts have been raised about the historical vitality of common Gaelic as against vernacular Gaelic in providing either a political or social critique, far less a Gaelic ideology, to counter the growing commitment of the Irish and Scots to a British political framework in the aftermath of the Union of the Crowns in 1603. By the outset of the seventeenth century, common classical Gaelic, a literary dialect rooted in the educated speech of medieval Gaeldom, had become far removed from the regional and local spoken dialects which had evolved in both Ireland and Scotland.

Although the bardic schools, as the principal proponents of common classical Gaelic, were not entirely unresponsive to intrusive British political, social and commercial influences in the course of the seventeenth century, their historical perspective remained anachronistic, particularist and elitist. Their main concern was not the nationwide permeation of political consciousness but rather retrospective fatalism allied to introspective humiliation for the decline of classical culture and bardic patronage.[4] This decline has been viewed as the cultural product of the Reformation and the planting of Ulster as a wedge between the Irish and Scottish Gaels. Yet the professional bards did not feel that their cultural leadership

4 D.S. Thomson, 'Three seventeenth century bardic poets: Niall Mor, Cathal and Niall MacMhuirich', in A.J. Aitken, M.P. McDiarmid and D.S. Thomson (eds) *Bards and Makars* (Glasgow, 1977),pp.228–34; *Collected Works of Padraic H. Pearse: Songs of the Irish Rebels and Specimens from an Irish Anthology* (Dublin, 1918), pp.36–49; Glasgow University Library, McLagan Collection, GU MSS gen. 1042/189.

was about to be eclipsed at the outset of the seventeenth century. The handful of Scottish schools certainly drew strength from regular intercourse and technical cooperation with their Irish counterparts. This shared contemporaneous perspective was facilitated by the short sea-crossing of the North Channel and by the opportunities to glorify the episodic involvement of clan mercenaries in the Irish wars against Tudor expansionism. No more than thirteen miles separated Antrim and Kintyre, the strongholds of the Clan Donald South, leading patrons of the bardic schools in both kingdoms and foremost contractors for the mercenary *buannachan* (redshanks). As well as commending the epic heroism of the clan elite and the amount of tribute exacted by the *buannachan*, the bardic schools expected not only honour and hospitality for their art, but also an ample share of booty from the Irish forays. At the same time, bardic propaganda heightened clan rivalry over military prowess and amounts of tribute exacted on these excursions, thereby aggravating the feuds that originated in the territorial ambitions of their chiefs and leading gentry, their *fine*.[5]

The escalating response of vernacular poets to intrusive British influences after 1603 was contextually and geographically distinctive, with the Scots Gaels being, perhaps, the more forward in displacing the bardic schools from their pivotal position in Gaelic culture. Vernacular poetry – as the structured, if discursive, representation of spoken Gaelic dialects in both Ireland and Scotland – was both radical and reactionary. It was radical in its use as a polemical medium, vernacular poetry that exhibited an oral vitality, relative immediacy and popular orientation; it was reactionary in its defence of traditional values. Vernacular poetry was not without an awareness of pan-Gaelic affinities in tracing common ancestry across the North Channel, in bestowing nobility on the *fine* through shared kinship by descent and intermarriage and in propagating the racial superiority of the *Gael* over the *Gall* by acclaimed military prowess.[6] There were, however, essential cultural differences in the vernacular response of the Irish and

5 J. MacDonald, 'An elegy for Ruaidhri Mor', *SGS* 8 (1955–7), pp.27–49; W.J. Watson, 'Unpublished Gaelic poetry: IV', *SGS* 3 (1931), pp.139–51; *CSP Scot* XII (1595–7), pp.201–11.

6 D. Hyde, *A Literary History of Ireland* (London, 1967), pp.542–3; J. MacInnes, 'The panegyric code in Gaelic poetry and its historical background', *TGSI* 51 (1978–80), pp.435–98; W.J. Watson, 'Unpublished Gaelic poetry: III', *SGS* 2 (1927), pp.75–91. *Gall* was applied variously to Lowlanders, English or other foreigners.

Scottish Gaels to colonization, civil wars and conquest, differences which magnified as the century unfolded: whereas the vernacular dynamic in Ireland was driven by religion, that in Scotland was driven by politics.

In Ireland the 1630s and to an even greater extent the 1640s witnessed a concerted endeavour by priests and scholars returning from the continent to propagate the Counter-Reformation through vernacular verse and prose. In the process, the promotion of a nationalist ideology through Roman Catholicism served to shape the political consciousness of the Irish Gael. The progressive and popular elements of this concerted endeavour can be exaggerated, however. The mission of the returning exiles to promote a catholic Ireland was primarily evangelical and targeted at the confessional commitment of the Gaelic social elite. Novel vernacular insights of war, conquest and colonization could not paper over animosities – as much territorial as racial – between the native Irish and Old English. The purported political focus for their common catholicism from 1642, the Irish Catholic Confederacy, broke up within seven years under the strain of internal rivalries, chronic underfunding and unrealized objectives. Renewed conquest and reimposed colonialism, resulting from the Cromwellian occupation of Ireland, led to a cultural reversion, fatalism and humiliation, tempered only by religious faith in place of bardic escapism, themes which endured into the Restoration era as calls to restore the traditional social order remained unrequited.[7]

The diminishing appeal of the bardic schools in Scotland coincided with the determined resolve of the crown, initiated under James VI and I and continued by his hapless son Charles I, to 'civilize' the clans, especially those on the western seaboard who had sent *buannachan* to Ireland. In contrast to that in Ireland, however, Gaelic society in Scotland was neither afflicted comprehensively by war nor threatened overtly by conquest and colonization prior to the 1640s. Three clans, all debilitated by internal dissension among their *fine*, were expropriated: namely the MacDonalds of Islay and Kintyre (the Clan Donald South), the MacLeods of Lewis and the MacIains of Ardnamurchan. A fourth, the Clan Gregor, was outlawed and dispersed. The Scottish complement to the plantation of Ulster was not so much a military

7 *The Poems of David O'Bruadair*, ed. J.C. MacEarlean, ITS (3 vols; London, 1910–16), *passim; Collected Works of Padraic H. Pearse*, pp.62–71; N. Canny, *Kingdom and Colony: Ireland in the Atlantic World, 1560–1800* (Baltimore, Md, 1988), pp.41–5, 135–6.

as a legislative offensive. The Statutes of Iona of 1609 – reissued piecemeal in the wake of the abortive rising of Clan Donald South of 1615 – professed to aim for a reformation of religion, manners and customs. Although better resourced and undoubtedly on the ascendant, protestantism, like Roman Catholicism, remained a missionary endeavour within Scottish Gaeldom until the mid-seventeenth century. In substance, the legislative programme concentrated on the redundancy of the *buannachan*, on the imposition of controls on hospitality and vagrancy and, above all, on the inculcation of the work ethic in estate management. Accordingly, legislation had three principal objectives: the commercial reorientation of customary relationships within the clans; the political accountability of the *fine* for the conduct of their clans; and the gradual assimilation of the clan elite into Scottish landed society. The cultural currency of Gaelic, though ostensibly threatened by legislation calling for the extirpation of the language, was only gradually compromised by the promotion of English schools, which remained an optional pursuit for the clan elite until the 1690s. English, or rather Scots, was none the less propagated as the language of instruction and estate management.[8]

Whereas the bardic response to this military and legislative offensive remained muted, elitist and profoundly introspective, the vernacular response – albeit still localized – demonstrated a greater contextual awareness of changing political and social circumstances. The first significant stirring of contemporaneous opinion can be traced to the attempted extirpation of the Clan Gregor. Several anonymous songs from the opening decades of the seventeenth century, though not abounding in pertinent polemics, vividly highlight the precarious existence of outlawed MacGregors hounded by the Clan Campbell, with official backing from the crown.[9] The realignment of the social as well as the political priorities of the *fine* was observed with novel bemusement by Eachann Bacach (Hector Maclean) from Mull. The requirement of central government that the *fine* be annually accountable for the conduct of their clans had led to traditional notions of liberality being altered during the 1630s by the sojourns of his chief, Sir Lachlan Maclean of Duart, in Edinburgh.

8 A.I. Macinnes, 'Crown, clans and *Fine:* the 'civilizing' of Scottish Gaeldom, 1587–1603', *Northern Scotland* 13 (1993) pp.31–55.

9 D.S. Thomson, 'Scottish Gaelic folk poetry ante-1650', *SGS* (1955–8) pp.1–17; W.F. Skene (ed.) *Collectanea de Rebus Albanicis* (Edinburgh, 1847), pp.128–36.

'S ann ded' bheus a bhith sgapadh an òir;
Is nach b'urrainn dod' dhùthaich
Chur ad ghlacaibh de chùinne
Na chosgadh tu chrùintibh mu'n bhòrd.[10]

[It is a custom of yours to dispense gold, while your own land could never put as much money in your hands as the crowns you would spend round the gaming table.]

Though by no means scathing, such comments clearly infer that the *dol sios,* the passing away of the days of glory of the Clan Gillean, was attributable to the conduct of the chief as well as to changed political circumstances since the Union of the Crowns. Sir Lachlan's personal extravagance, allied to his periodic absenteeism, undoubtedly compounded his inherited financial difficulties from the desperate feud his clan had waged with Clan Donald South over lands in Islay at the turn of the seventeenth century. In 1634 Sir Lachlan had been obliged to mortgage part of his estates against a loan from Archibald Campbell, Lord Lorne. Such was the scale of his liabilities that he was obliged within three years to cede the feudal superiority over his estates in the Isle of Jura together with Aros and Brolos in the Isle of Mull to the future marquis of Argyll, who subsequently used his political leadership of the Covenanting movement during the 1640s to the private advantage of his acquisitive house. From the outbreak of the Scottish civil war in 1644, Sir Lachlan, as a royalist, had withheld payments of public dues levied in support of the Covenanting movement. Argyll took over these arrears which, along with Sir Lachlan's private debts, amounted to £31,015 (Scots) by 1647. Having bought out Sir Lachlan's creditors and having raised an action in his own heritable jurisdiction – as hereditary justiciar of Argyll and the Western Isles – the marquis now had the legal pretext to hold courts on Mull to reorientate management of the Duart estates at the expense of the Macleans.[11] Forewarned by Argyll's eviction of Macleans from Jura since 1637, Catriona Maclean, a poetess from Coll, surmised that this judicial action was but the thin end of a wedge to evict her clan from their heritage.

10 *Bardachd Chloinn Ghill-Eathain: Eachann Bacach and Other Maclean Poets,* SGTS (Edinburgh, 1979), pp.xxxix–xl, 6–7.

11 J.R.N. Macphail (ed.) *Highland Papers* I (Edinburgh, 1914), pp.244–5, 320–3; J.T. Clark (ed.) *Genealogical Collections Concerning Families in Scotland Made by Walter Macfarlane, 1750–51* (Edinburgh, 1900), pp.135–6. After the Union of the Crowns, £12 (Scots) was equivalent to £1 (sterling).

Chan a dùthchas bhur n-athar
Tha sibh a'labhairt 'san àm air,
No oighreachd bhur seanar
Tha sibh a'ceangal mu Chaingis,
Ach staid dheagh Mhic Ghilleathain.[12]

[It is not the land of your ancestors that you are discussing at this time, nor is it the estate of your forebears that you are allocating at Whitsun, but the estates of the excellent chief of the Macleans.]

This defence of traditional ordering used two concepts of heritage which marked a profound distinction between the Gaels of Ireland and Scotland. The collective heritage of the clan, their customary *duthchas*, was their prescriptive right to settle territories over which their chiefs and leading gentry provided protection. This concept underwrote the personal authority of the *fine* as trustees for their clan. With the spread of feudal conveyancing from the middle ages, the acquisition of charters by the clan elite – preferably from the crown but also from nobles and other powerful landowners – defined the estates settled by their clans as their titular *oighreachd*. This concept of individual heritage warranted from above the institutionalized authority of the *fine* as landed proprietors. The absence of this latter concept of heritage differentiated the Irish from the Scottish Gael. From the outset of clanship in Scotland, the *fine* strove to be feudal landlords as well as territorial warlords. Accordingly, clanship can be deemed a product of feudalism, kinship and local association.[13] Gaelic society in Ireland, however, historically lacked a corresponding feudal dimension and, by the outset of the seventeenth century, was faced with the alien imposition of English common law – perhaps the most obnoxious feature of the plantation of Ulster.[14]

None the less, the contemporaneous legislative offensive of the Scottish crown on the western seaboard signposted the gradual tilting of the balance away from *duthchas* in favour of *oighreachd* as the *fine* became assimilated into Scottish landed society. In the process, vernacular poetry afforded the Scottish Gael a uniquely forceful means of protest against the political, social and

12 J.A. MacLean, 'The sources, particularly the Celtic sources, for the history of the Highlands in the seventeenth century' (Aberdeen University, PhD thesis, 1939), pp.135–6.

13 A.I. Macinnes, *Clanship, Commerce and the Stuarts* (Edinburgh, 1995).

14 H.S. Pawlisch, *Sir John Davies and the Conquest of Ireland: A Study in Legal Imperialism* (Cambridge, 1985), pp.55–64, 84–100; G. Keating, *The History of Ireland*, ITS (London, 1902), pp.67–71; K.W. Nicholls, *Gaelic and Gaelicised Ireland in the Middle Ages* (Dublin, 1972), pp.21–44, 57–65.

commercial ramifications of intrusive British influences since 1603. In particular, the emergence of the Covenanting movement, which after 1638 imposed constitutional limitations on the monarchy of Charles I, led to the creation of a centralized state which for thirteen years exerted continuous and unprecedented pressures for ideological conformity, financial supply and military recruitment. These centralized pressures not only polarized the clans politically, but also commited them irrevocably to Scottish as against pan-Gaelic politics. Simultaneously these pressures produced a vernacular response throughout Scottish Gaeldom which was essentially political and social, not religious, in associating the traditional values of clanship with the royalist cause of Charles I and, after his execution in 1649, with that of his son, who was crowned as the king of Britain at Scone on 1 January 1651. The vernacular poets who assumed the mantle of cultural leadership within Scottish Gaeldom were drawn predominantly from the clan gentry, though more often fringe rather than foremost members of the *fine*. Although vernacular poetry by no means abandoned celebration of the clan elite, priority was accorded to political propaganda and social comment over stereotyped artistic standards. Topical information was disseminated and public opinion shaped through the *celidh*, the spontaneous folk session, which became the alternative to the literary evening in the great halls of the *fine* as well as the rival to the covenanting pulpits. Grassroots criticism of national leadership extended from covenanters to royalists in the course of the 1640s. As a result, the vernacular poets continued to set the polemical agenda for Scottish Gaeldom for the remainder of the seventeenth century.[15]

POLITICAL POLARIZATION

The political reaction of the Irish and Scottish Gaels to intrusive British influences after 1603 was no more uniform than their distinctive cultural development. Despite an understandable

15 Following on from the stimulus of the Covenanting movement, from 300 to 500 vernacular poems comment on political events or accompanying social changes during the seventeenth century: C. O'Baoill and D. MacAulay, *Scottish Gaelic Vernacular Verse to 1730: A Checklist* (Aberdeen, 1988); MacLean, 'Celtic sources', pp.ii–iii.

historical tendency to view the Gael as the victim of plantation and assimilation, distinction must be drawn between official propaganda and the actual implementation of crown policies in the Irish provinces and the Scottish Highlands and Islands. An underlying counterpoint to the discriminatory propaganda which castigated the Gael for barbarity and incivility was the projected gains to the English and Scottish exchequers, which proved more fictitious than factual.[16]

Notwithstanding episodic fears of concerted Gaelic rebellion requiring continuous policing of the North Channel, the crown lacked the political commitment as well as the financial resources to effect the wholesale transformation of rural settlement within Gaeldom. Even in Ulster, there was limited displacement of the native Irish, a situation not dissimilar to the displacement of the *fine* among the four expropriated Scottish clans.[17]

The principal beneficiaries of expropriation within Scottish Gaeldom were the *fine* of the Campbells and the MacKenzies, respectively headed by the earls of Argyll and Seaforth. In like manner, the Irish branch of the Clan Donald South, the MacDonnells of Antrim, were foremost among the Irish families who retained crown favour as landowners in Ulster. Ennobled as the earls of Antrim, they enjoyed favoured status under both James VI and I and Charles I despite their avowed Roman Catholicism. The social advantage enjoyed by these three noble houses under the early Stewarts cannot be easily translated into political alignment for the crown, however. The emergence of the Covenanting movement having served to trigger the civil Wars of the Three Kingdoms, only the house of Antrim remained unswervingly royalist. Yet, both Randall the first earl and his son, Randall the second earl (later first marquis) of Antrim, had lost out to Archibald Campbell, Lord Lorne, in a territorial dispute over Kintyre during the 1630s.

16 G. O'Brien (ed.) *Advertisements for Ireland* (Dublin, 1923); D. Gregory, *History of the Western Highlands and Isles of Scotland* (Edinburgh, 1881, repr. 1975), pp.275–7, 286–7, 293–4, 313–15, 330–3; ICA transcripts, VIII (1600–10), no.256; IX (1611–20), no.202. Material has been collated from this archive as part of a Major Research Grant from the British Academy which finances my ongoing investigation into the political and cultural influence of the house of Argyll, 1603–1761.

17 BLLP 1602–*c.*1711, Add MSS 32,476 ff9–11; R. Gillespie, 'Explorers, exploiters and entrepreneurs: early modern Ireland and its context, 1500–1700', in B.J. Graham and L.J. Proudfoot (eds) *An Historical Geography of Ireland* (London, 1993), pp.123–57; Canny, *Kingdom and Colony,* pp.44–59; B. Fitzpatrick, *Seventeenth-Century Ireland: The War of Religions* (Dublin, 1988), pp.28–33, 44–6.

Kintyre along with Islay had been secured by the Clan Campbell following the expropriation of Clan Donald South. Archibald Campbell, seventh earl of Argyll, fled as an apostate catholic to the Spanish Netherlands in 1618, and the House of Antrim reasserted its clan's traditional claim to the peninsula; this claim appeared to come to fruition by 1635 when Argyll, still banished from Scotland but rehabilitated at the court of Charles I, and the indebted eldest son of his second marriage, James, Lord Kintyre, agreed to sell out. However, Lorne, as the effective chief of the Clan Campbell and as the undoubted financial manager and feudal superior of the Argyll estates, successfully blocked and then rescinded this purchase by judicious lobbying at Edinburgh and at court. As well as his strong legal case for pre-empting any proposed sale of Kintyre, Lorne, the future first marquis of Argyll, was not disadvantaged by traditional clan affinities to the MacDonnells of Antrim. The house of Antrim, no less than the acquisitive house of Argyll, were advocates of commercial landlordism. Lorne had a better track record as a landlord in the disputed territories, having assiduously cultivated the satellite families who had formerly adhered to the Clan Donald South, whereas Randall, prior to his ennoblement as the first earl, had his lease of Islay revoked in 1613 – in the first year of its operation – after protests by the island's indigenous families against the importation of Ulster practices.[18]

Lord Lorne's success in retaining Kintyre was a reflection of the consummate political adroitness of the house of Argyll in maintaining their Gaelic identity, while projecting themselves in the first rank of Scottish landowners prepared to acclimatize to the changing British situation in the wake of the Union of the Crowns. As early as 1604, the influence at court of Archibald, the seventh earl, was actively cultivated by Richard Burke, fourth earl of Clanricarde, the head of the prominent Old English family who was later acclaimed in both England and Ireland for opposing the plantation of Connaught in his capacity as absentee governor of Galway prior to his death in 1635.[19] Indeed from 1607, the house of Argyll was to the fore in using the terms 'North British' for

18 G. Hill, *An Historical Account of the Macdonnells of Antrim* (Belfast, 1873, repr. 1976), pp.229–30, 237–46; D. Stevenson, *Alasdair MacColla and the Highland Problem in the Seventeenth Century* (Edinburgh, 1980), pp.49–50; Gregory, *History of the Western Highlands*, pp.347–8; ICA bundles 3/60; 3/67; 7/148; transcripts IX, no.209; X (1621–8), nos 7, 20–1, 190; XI (1629–37), nos 243, 264, 633, 637, 643, 653, 664, 666, 712, 714.

19 ICA bundle 63/3; A. Clarke, *The Old English in Ireland 1625–42* (London, 1966), pp.90–110.

Scotland and 'British' for colonists settling in Ulster, terminology which suggests that Scottish settlers were not necessarily all from the Lowlands and that the Gaelic-speaking tenants in Ulster were neither exclusively Irish nor exclusively migrants displaced from the territories of the Clan Donald South.[20] While the house of Antrim has gained notice for importing Lowland Scottish farmers, Lord Lorne was not averse to commissioning British entrepreneurs from Ulster to diversify the economy of his estates, notably through the construction of salt-pans, fuelled by indigenous coal supplies in Kintyre from 1637.[21] In turn, the devastation wreaked in Ulster by the Argyll Regiment serving in the Covenanting expeditionary force during 1642 was not just the wanton perpetuation of their clan feud with Antrim but an integral part of the British suppression of an Irish rebellion.[22]

Clan feuding, however, was a principal theme in the vernacular poets' interpretation of the civil wars of the 1640. Support for the royal house of Stewart was rooted in the traditional values of clanship which were projected nationally on to the political stage. As the chiefs were the protectors of the clan *duthchas*, so were the Stewarts trustees for Scotland; their hereditary entitlement to rule, their *oighreachd*, provided the roots of justice and legitimized the social order. Such traditionalism should not be confused with nationalism, which was no more easily embraced by royalists in Scotland than by royalists or the Catholic Confederacy in Ireland. Charles I certainly enjoyed the support of the majority of the

20 Notwithstanding the lack of standardized orthographies, regional variations in Gaelic pronunciation and corruptions in transcribing from Gaelic to English, surnames cited in periodic population surveys of Ulster suggest not only a considerable settlement of former *buannachan* but also a significant migration of Highland farming and labouring families, particularly from the adjacent shires of Argyll and Bute in the wake of plantation; a migration boosted erratically in the later seventeenth century, evident from the irregular incursions of Gaelic-speaking presbyterian missionaries from Argyllshire by the 1690s: M. Perceval-Maxwell, *The Scottish Migration to Ulster in the Reign of James I* (London, 1973), pp.154–6, 288–9; J.H. Ohlmeyer, *Civil War and Restoration in the Three Stuart Kingdoms: The Career of Randall MacDonnell, Marquis of Antrim, 1609–83* (Cambridge, 1993), pp.24–6, 37–41; BM Add MSS 4770, Muster-Roll of Ulster, *c.*1630–36, ff145–62; S. Pender (ed.) *A 'Census' of Ireland c.1659, with supplementary material from the Poll Money Ordinances, 1660–61* (Dublin, 1939); I am particularly grateful to my former research assistant Fiona MacDonald for providing information on Highland migration to Ulster in the seventeenth century.

21 ICA transcripts VIII, no.256; IX, no.163; XI, no.787; XII (1638–49), nos 111, 141; Perceval-Maxwell, *Scottish Migration to Ulster*, pp.232–3.

22 Hill, *Macdonnells of Antrim*, pp.73–4; D. Stevenson, *Scottish Covenanters and Irish Confederates* (Belfast, 1981), pp.110–15; Fitzpatrick, *Seventeenth-Century Ireland*, pp.70–1, 73–6.

Scottish clans, but this support was essentially reactionary. The royalist clans were fighting less for an absentee monarch and more against the Covenanting movement's unprecedented demands for ideological, financial and military commitment. More especially, clans were reacting against powerful noble houses, pre-eminently the Campbells of Argyll and the Gordons of Sutherland, whose public espousal of the Covenanting cause cloaked their private territorial ambitions. Conversely, aversion to the hitherto pervasive influence of the Gordons of Huntly persuaded some clans in the central Highlands to side with the Covenanters and others to remain neutral. Civil war divided the clans no less than the rest of Scotland. Religious affiliation was a less divisive issue, although the Campbells and other Covenanting clans were in broad sympathy with presbyterianism.[23]

In propagating resistance to the Covenanting movement, the royalist poets drew heavily on the imagery of feuding to make the course of events intelligible to clansmen. Such imagery, which reached its vitriolic apotheosis in the poetry of Iain Lom (John MacDonald) from Keppoch, did not necessarily conform to military circumstances. As well as castigating the Clan Campbell for promoting cultural assimilation with the racially inferior Lowlander, Iain Lom appealed to the strength of tradition within Clan Donald to sustain the military backbone which the various branches of the clan provided for the royalist campaigns of James Graham, first marquis of Montrose and his lieutenant-general, Alasdair MacColla, from 1644 to 1647. His vitriol as a war correspondent is especially evident in his poem celebrating the royalist victory at Inverlochy in Lochaber on 2 February 1645:

'S lìonmhor claidheamh claisghorm còmhnard
Bha bualadh 'n lamhan Chlann Dòmhnaill.
'N uair chruinnich mór dhragh na falachd,
'N am rùsgadh nan greidlean tana,
Bha iongnan Dhuibneach ri talamh
An déidh an luithean a ghearradh.[24]

[Numerous are the blue-fluted, well-balanced swords that were wielded in the hands of Clan Donald. When the great work of blood-letting came to a height at the time of unsheathing slender swords, the claws of the Campbells lay on the ground with sinews severed.]

23 E.M. Furgol, 'The Northern Highland covenanting clans, 1639–1651', *Northern Scotland* 7 (1987), pp.119–31; J.C. Beckett, *The Making of Modern Ireland, 1603–1923* (London, 1978), pp.82–103.

24 A.M. MacKenzie (ed.) *Orain Iain Luim: Songs of John MacDonald, Bard of Keppoch*, SGTS (Edinburgh, 1973), pp.22–3.

Whereas Ian Lom was an exultant eye-witness of the carnage wreaked against the Covenanting Campbells, Florence, the sister of Sir Duncan Campbell of Auchinbreck and wife of John Maclean of Coll, composed a riposte which was not so much a lament for her fallen brother as a hymn for vengeance against the royalist forces, including her husband's clan.

> N' an robh mis' an Inbhir-Lochaidh,
> Is claidheamh da-fhaobhair am dhòrnaibh,
> Is neart agam gu'm mhiann, is eolas,
> Dheanainn fuil ann, dheanainn stròiceadh,
> Air na Leathanaich 's Clann Dòmhnaill;
> Bhiodh na h-Eireannaich gun deò annt,
> Is na Duibhnich bheirinn beò as.[25]

> [Were I at Inverlochy, with a two-edged sword in my hand, all the strength and skill I could desire, I would draw blood there, and I would tear assunder the Macleans and Clan Donald. The Irish would be without life, and I would bring the Campbells back alive.]

The widow of Campbell of Glenfeochan was no more forgiving. The Irish, though ill equipped, were recognized as the driving impetus for Clan Donald and their Scottish associates who deprived her of her husband, her father, her three sons, her four brothers and her nine foster-brothers. She not only lamented her lost kindred, but also directed her parting criticism forcibly against her chief, the marquis of Argyll, who had made his escape by galley:

> Thug MacCailein Mór an linn' air,
> 'S leig e'n sgrìob ud air a chinneadh.[26]

> [The marquis of Argyll took to the loch and let that calamity come upon his kindred.]

Such innovatory criticism of the clan elite has tended to be masked by polemics extolling feuding and solidarity among the Gaels in support of the royalist cause. The Irish contingent involved with the royalist clans composed three regiments of fewer than 2,000 men raised in 1644 from the MacDonnells of Antrim, from their Ulster associates and from their expatriate kinsmen of the Clan Donald South, such as their leader, Alasdair MacColla himself. MacColla's remit, which he pursued successfully for over two years, was to tie up Covenanting troops on the western seaboard and prevent reinforcements being sent to the Covenanting expeditionary force in Ulster. Although the Irish troops were almost exclusively

25 Maclean, 'Celtic sources', p.29.
26 ibid, p.26.

recruited from his estates, Randal MacDonnell, the second earl of Antrim did not join them in Scotland until the summer of 1646, when the royalist cause was all but lost. The anonymous kinsman who welcomed Antrim as a hero of the Wars of the Three Kingdoms hoped that his arrival would serve as much to reverse Covenanting dominance in Scotland as to perpetuate their feud with the Campbells.

> Gheibh gach cealgair mar thail e,
> Theid gach traoitear a smàladh,
> Cha bhi chuing oirnn 'ga giulan,
> 'S chan'n fhaigh luchd diumbaidh an àilein,
> Gun teid luchd nam beul fiara,
> A chur sios fo ar sàilean,
> 'S bidh Clann Domhnuill an uachdar,
> Mar bu dual do'n an àl sin.[27]

> [Every rogue will get what he deserves, every traitor will be snuffed out. We will not have to bear the yoke and the spiteful ones will not get their wishes. The Campbells will be under our heels and Clan Donald will be on top as is the custom of that progeny.]

An Irish vernacular poet, not unsympathetic to Antrim, had certainly viewed this expedition as a means of promoting the interest of the Irish branch of the Clan Donald South. Yet this same anonymous poet had already protested against the repeated absenteeism of the second earl. For Randall MacDonnell, more celebrated as a military entrepreneur than as a political operator, had reputedly allowed his estates to be 'worn spectre-thin' in financing his shuttle diplomacy between Charles I and the Irish Catholic Confederacy to secure sponsorship for the royalist campaign in Scotland.[28] Despite eulogies for the Irish regiments' contribution to the endeavours of the Clan Donald South to reclaim Kintyre and Islay, discerning poets took cognizance of wider political considerations. Her unrequited antipathy to the marquis of Argyll nothwithstanding, it was the brilliant guerrilla campaign that MacColla fashioned with Montrose and his subsequent bridgehead on the western seaboard for Irish reinforcements that caused Dorothy Brown, from the island of Luing, to assert his indispensability to the royalist cause:[29]

27 A. MacDonald and A. MacDonald (eds) *The MacDonald Collection of Gaelic Poetry* (Inverness, 1911), pp.46–7.

28 R. Flower, 'An Irish Gaelic poem on the Montrose Wars', *SGS* 1 (1926), pp.113–18; Ohlmeyer, *Civil War and Restoration*, pp.6–10, 172–83.

29 J. MacKenzie (ed.) *Sar-Obair nam Bard Gaelach: The Beauties of Gaelic Poetry* (Edinburgh, 1872), pp.56–7.

Cha deanar cogadh as t-eughmais,
'S cha deanar sìth gun do réite.

[War cannot be carried on without you, and peace cannot be established without your approval.]

However, the solidarity expressed by the poets on the western seaboard towards the Irish found little tangible support from the royalist clans in the central or northern Highlands. Indeed, Gaelic solidarity sustained little practical impetus from the autumn of 1645, when the Covenanting forces began to reassert their ascendancy. Following the withdrawal of Antrim's relief force at the outset of 1647 and the imminent collapse of royalist resistance on the western seaboard, Angus MacDonald of Glengarry had crossed to Ireland as much to avoid military reprisals as to reciprocate the assistance given by the Irish Gael. However, as the following stricture from Iain Lom bears out, his clansmen gave less than wholehearted support to their chief:

'S ann diubh 'n t-Aonghas òg Glinneach
A ghabh fogradh thar linnidh,
'S truagh gun ròiseal d'a chinneadh 'ga chòir.[30]

[Among them is young Angus of the Glen, who took to flight across the sea; it is a pity that there is not a force of his people with him.]

As Iain Lom realized in the same poem, solidarity among the Gael was effectively laid to rest following the retreat of MacColla from Islay and his subsequent death, in the services of the Catholic Confederacy, at Knocknanuss, County Cork, on 13 November 1647. His reputation for epic heroism proved an enduring legacy for the clans' association with the house of Stewart until the eclipse of Jacobitism in the eighteenth century. However, this reputation was actively propagated to enhance MacColla's standing among the Gael, for MacColla had faced a credibility problem at the outset of the royalist campaigns. He was not a traditional Gaelic warlord. His landed status was tenuous, he was on the fringes of the *fine* of the expatriated Clan Donald South and his dependence on military adventure for his livelihood meant that his campaigns did not enjoy full cooperation from snobbish chiefs of the other leading branches of the Clan Donald. By propagating his undoubted skill and valour on the battlefield, the royalist polemicists furthered his recruiting drives among the clans. Moreover, the poets remained jealously protective of MacColla's reputation, even when the haste of his

30 *Orain Iain Luim*, pp.36–7.

retreat from Kintyre and Islay in the summer of 1647 cast doubts on his abilities as a general in the eyes of both Gael and Lowlander. In his contemptuous dismissal of the Covenanting leadership, Eachann Bacach commemorated MacColla not merely for his resolute stand in battle:

> 'S cha b'e mala na réit e
> Do dh'fhearaibh Dhùn Éideann.[31]

> [And his countenance was not one for compromise with the men of Edinburgh.]

This same leadership had come under sustained poetic opprobrium for their decision to offset escalating public debts by the sale of Charles I to the English parliamentarians in January 1647 for £400,000 (sterling). Although Charles had persistently manifested a lack of commitment to a negotiated conclusion to the first English civil war during the eight months he had spent in the custody of the Covenanting army, his sale was castigated without equivocation by Murchadh MacMhurchaidh (Murdo MacKenzie) from Wester Ross:

> Lach na firinn fòirinn
> Bhi brath an rìgh chionn airgid.[32]

> [The law of truth exposed to danger, betraying the king because of money.]

Criticism of the national leadership was not confined to the Covenanting movement: the Prince of Wales (the future Charles II) was reprimanded by Iain Lom for his tardiness in returning from exile in Holland to claim the Scottish crown following the execution of his father. Having promoted a radical upheaval in the Covenanting leadership, the English regicides were now threatening Scottish independence:

> Nach truagh leat do dhìlsean,
> Gach cill sgìr am bheil clachan,
> bhith air'n dùbladh 'sna cainbibh
> 'N déis an tionndadh aig Sasann?[33]

> [Does it not grieve you that your loyal subjects, in every parish church and kirktown, are trussed up in hempen ropes to which they are consigned by the English?]

31 *Bardachd Chloinn Ghill-Eathain*, pp.20–1.

32 M. Macfarlane (ed.) *Lamh Sgriobhainn Mhic Rath: The Fernaig Manuscript* (Dundee, 1923), pp.119–21.

33 *Orain Iain Luim*, pp.50–1.

Criticism of national leadership could be sophisticated as well as strident. Undoubtedly, the most potent example was composed anonymously by a kinsman or local associate of the MacDonalds of Glengarry which analysed the cost of implementing the Engagement of 1648, whereby conservative elements within the Covenanting movement had escalated the second English civil war on behalf of Charles I. As well as condemning the polarization among the covenanters which had dissipated their armed intervention in England, the poet lambasted the Engagers' efforts to manipulate the Prince of Wales and recorded the feeling of national humiliation throughout Scotland on the news of their ignominious rout by Oliver Cromwell at Preston in Lancashire on 17–19 August. A disillusioned military veteran of the royalist campaigns under MacColla, the poet pleaded for peace and denounced further military adventures throughout the three kingdoms.

> Claidheam geur cha ghiulain mi,
> Ga rusgadh as a thruaill;
> Gu'n tugainn do fhear-saoithreach e
> Chuir faobhair air a thuaigh
> Gu'm b'annsa bhi le caibeachaibh
> Ag ruamhradh geig 's a chluain,
> Na stri ri cogadh leith-cheannach
> 'S ag teich air feadh nam bruach.
>
> [I will not bear a sharp sword to draw it for bondage. I would give it to a working-man to sharpen his axe. I would rather be with spades draining the meadow than striving to be in a foolish war and running away among the banks.]

This protest song is entitled 'An Cobhernandori', literally 'help to the pursuers' but polemically 'help to the Tories'. The label 'Tory', first applied abusively by planters and colonists to the dispossessed native Irish, was attached subsequently by parliamentarian and royalist forces in Ireland to the Catholic Confederacy. The direct Gaelic borrowing of the label, probably through the military association of MacColla's Irish regiments and his clan contingents, predated its English introduction to Scotland by three years, when the rural guerrillas resisting the Cromwellian occupation within Scottish Gaeldom were termed Tories. While the English label was imported to Scotland as a term of abuse, the Gaelic label was more one of reproach to the Engagers: the same politicians were opposed from the other end of the political spectrum by militant radicals from the south-west of Scotland who, for their endeavours to drive the Engagers from office, have won recognition as the first Whigs. The currency of Whig and Tory for propaganda purposes throughout the three kingdoms had to await the Exclusion Crisis in the late 1670s, but the original derivation and coeval application of these rival labels serves to demonstrate that British history is not imposed necessarily from England nor exclusively through the use of English.[34]

The 1650s, however, was a decade in which events in Ireland and Scotland tended to be dictated from England. The reimposition of colonialism and conquest on Ireland and the occupation and eventual annexation of Scotland stirred nationalist ire among vernacular poets throughout Gaeldom. Undoubtedly coloured by civil war perspectives, the Interregnum era in both kingdoms attracted unreserved condemnation as 'the time of the oppressions'. The partiality towards the ruling elite exhibited by the vernacular poets in both countries can be interpreted as equating the defence of the traditional social order with the defence of national interest.[35] Such an interpretation is more superficial than substantial: whereas the Irish grounded their nationalism in their Catholic faith, the Scots projected their nationalism through resurgent royalism.[36] Indeed, the only concerted recourse to arms against the Cromwellian regime throughout the three kingdoms was the ill-fated rising of the clans led initially by William Cunningham, ninth earl of Glencairn, and subsequently by Lieutenant-General John Middleton between the summer of 1653 and the autumn of 1654. In Ireland, Gaelic society was faced not only with political, commercial and religious discrimination but also with the wholesale confiscation of land primarily to benefit financially pressed Cromwellian soldiers together with private English adventurers. In Scotland, confiscation was discriminatory and directed more towards sequestration rather than forfeiture of estates, principally as an inducement for the former Covenanting leadership to make terms with the English regime. The clans, as the mainstays of the four-year guerrilla campaign against the Cromwellian occupation, faced wholesale containment through a series of garrisons littering Scottish Gaeldom. None the less, once General George Monck assumed full responsibility for suppressing the royalist rising in the

34 A.I. Macinnes, 'The first Scottish Tories?', *SHR* 67 (1988), pp.56–66.

35 MacLean, 'Celtic sources', pp.146–51; *Selected Works of Padraic H. Pearse*, pp.62–71; *Poems of David O'Bruadair*, I, pp.18–19, 28–7, 48–51; II, pp.32–3; III, pp.12–25.

36 A point taken up in detail by Barber, Chapter 8 in this volume.

spring of 1654, he extended a policy of piecemeal settlement towards clan chiefs and leading gentry prepared to accept if not collaborate with the Protectorate. Selective favouring for the *fine* included indemnity for past engagements against the Cromwellian forces, discretionary assistance with private debts incurred as a result of political involvement during the 1640s and partial relief from the monthly maintenance levied on the whole of Scotland for the upkeep of the army of occupation. Monck's selective favouring undoubtedly took the edge off the widespread resentment about paying for the army of occupation and for the garrisons which sustained the high military profile of the regime within Scottish Gaeldom.[37] Vernacular poets were further induced to moderate their criticisms of Monck after he proved instrumental in effecting the Restoration of Charles II in 1660. Even the passing of Oliver Cromwell in 1658 had been accepted with resigned tolerance by John MacLachlan of Kilbryde, a member of a learned family long associated with the house of Argyll:

> Ge làidir 's ge neartmhor Protector na rioghachd gu leir
> Cenn-uighe nan gaisgeach 's an taic 's an lòn da reir,
> Ge iomadh tùr chaisteal's gunna praise nan sgal mu chré,
> Cha chumadh sud grabhadh air teachdaire mear mhic Dhe.

> [Though strong and mighty the Protector of the whole kingdom, and although he had many a towered castle and spluttering canon to protect his body, that did not delay God's swift messenger.][38]

By way of contrast, Irish poets neither contemporaneously nor retrospectively moderated their criticisms. Paralleling Monaco's selective initiatives, Major-General Henry Cromwell moved English policy away from coercion towards conciliation following his dispatch as acting commander of the forces in Ireland by his father in 1655. The policy of new plantation in Munster and Leinster as well as Ulster was less successful than expected as new settlers and protestant tenants failed to arrive in sufficient numbers. None the less, Ireland remained a testing ground for reform in the same way that Scotland had served as a political laboratory during the 1630s. At the same time, the capacity of existing British settlers to make purchases from non-resident Cromwellian soldiers ensured that protestants were left holding the bulk of Irish land as well as a

37 BL Lauderdale Papers, Misc. Correspondence, I, 1630–60, Add MSS 23,113 f40; BL Papers of General Desborough, 1651–1660, Egerton 2519 ff21, 23, 25; C.H. Firth, *Scotland and the Protectorate* (Edinburgh, 1899), pp.117–18, 234–7, 269–82, 285–8, 366–81.

38 MacLean, 'Celtic sources', pp.164–7.

monopoly of political and commercial power, a position only slightly modified at the Restoration.[39]

DIVERGENT ACCLIMATIZATION

Ostensibly, the Restoration Settlement in both Ireland and Scotland had similar objectives if markedly different outcomes. Recognized and welcomed by vernacular poets in both countries, the Restoration of Charles II had offered the prospect of restoring the traditional social order to political power. However, the failure of the parliaments in both countries to retain control over votes of supply ensured that the government of Ireland and Scotland was primarily conciliar, a situation in Ireland which intensified its colonial relationship with England and which all but reduced Scotland to the satellite status of an English province. The fluctuations in the vice-royalty, notably the removal in 1669 of James Butler, first duke of Ormond, after nine years and his reappointment for seven years in 1677 had a limited impact on either the efficiency or British perceptions of Irish government. The Restoration regime in Ireland was marked neither by concerted armed dissent nor by sustained religious persecution. Ormond successfully monitored and prevented cooperation between Ulster presbyterians and Scottish covenanters. Following the outbreak of the Popish Plot in 1678, he moderated if not assuaged English fears about Irish involvement – albeit he was obliged to concur in a London trial for the Catholic primate, Oliver Plunkett, archbishop of Armagh. A noted exponent of the wholesale if voluntary exile of the Gaelic Irish, Tory dissidents, Archbishop Plunkett was none the less executed for treason in July 1681. At the same time, the continued intertwining of political and religious discrimination led to a more forceful as well as a more sophisticated phase of vernacular Gaelic poetry, particularly evident in the native Irish reaction to the judicial exposure of the Popish Plot in 1682. As castigated by David O'Bruadair, 'The Plot of perjured rudeness' had threatened Ireland with 'the lance's wounding thrust' as by 'yelling slanders' from whose oppressive sway 'no landed chief escaped'.[40]

39 T.C. Barnard, *Cromwellian Ireland: English Government and Reform in Ireland, 1649–1660* (Oxford, 1975), pp.10–15, 20–3, 297–305; Canny, *Kingdom and Colony*, pp.107–8; L.J. Arnold, 'The Irish Court of Claims of 1663', *IHS* 24 (1985), pp.417–30.

40 *Poems of David O'Bruadair*, pp.263–9; Beckett, *Making of Modern Ireland*, pp.122–38; Fitzpatrick, *Seventeenth-Century Ireland*, pp.231–2, 244–5.

By way of contrast, the ascendancy in Scotland of James Maitland, first duke of Lauderdale, from 1667 to 1679, was marked by the consolidation of a militarized regime intent on implementing absolutism on the cheap. Whereas this prospect alarmed Whiggish interests in England, as well as intimidating religious dissenters in Scotland, Lauderdale's willingness to resort to the military option was not unwelcome among leading Ulster politicians resolved to maintain unfettered Scottish settlement in the province. While the persecution of religious dissent was not an issue of significance within Scottish Gaeldom, enthusiasm for the Restoration, even in former royalist circles, was rapidly diminished by Lauderdale's use of the Highlands as a military training ground for both the standing forces and the militia; by his exploitation of persistent banditry by caterans and reivers to enforce fiscal exactions from the clan elite; and by his ready clientage for the house of Argyll and other acquisitive branches of the Clan Campbell.[41] Indeed, in order to justify the support of government forces, Archibald Campbell, ninth earl of Argyll, was prepared to attest in 1679 that the armed opposition of the Clan Gillean to the attempted expropriation of their chief, Sir John Maclean of Duart, for chronic public and private indebtedness, was a Scottish adjunct of the Popish Plot. These spurious charges served their purpose in securing military backing against the Macleans and their allies among the former royalist clans of Lochaber who had been resisting the territorial ambitions of the Campbell chief since 1674. Albeit Oliver Plunkett had nominally served as the Roman Catholic Prefect for the Highland and Islands from 1669 and Argyll's leading opponent within Scottish Gaeldom was the Catholic courtier Aeneas MacDonnell, Lord MacDonnell and Aros, the Macleans and the bulk of the former royalist clans – including the Camerons of Lochiell and the MacDonalds of Glencoe – were certainly protestant.[42] Although Iain Lom took no cognizance of the spurious charges of Archibald, the ninth earl, his continuing endeavours to check the acquisitive house of Argyll did acknowledge the importance of Lord MacDonnell's political lobbying on behalf of the Macleans on a British basis:

41 BL Lauderdale Papers, XXII, Add MSS 23,134 f23; ICA bundles 45/8; 45/10; 47/5; 70/6; A.I. Macinnes, 'Repression and conciliation: the Highland dimension, 1660–1688', *SHR* 65 (1986), pp.167–95. For caterans and reivers, see the Glossary pp.x, xi.

42 ICA bundles 54/4; 54/334–5; 68/1; 70/4–5; P.F. Anson, *Underground Catholicism in Scotland, 1622–1878* (Montrose, 1970), pp.70–1.

Ach a Mhorair Chlann Dòmhnaill,
Chum thur chòmhdhail gu h-ullamh,
Chaidh thu'n coinne 'n Iarl Adhraich
'N uair a shaoil e bhith 'm Muile;
Bha thur roimhe 'n Dùn Eideann –
Sheas thu 'm feum ud gu duineil;
Is neo-throm leam an cosgadh
On a choisinn thu'n Lunnainn.[43]

[But, Lord MacDonnell, readily did you keep the tryst; you engaged the Inveraray Earl when he thought to lord it in Mull; you were ahead of him in Edinburgh and manfully conducted that business. Trivial do I deem the expenditure involved since you won your point in London.]

Political lobbying on behalf of the Macleans of Duart notwithstanding, the expropriation of their *fine* was accomplished by 1679, likewise the MacLeods of Assynt were removed to the advantage of the house of Seaforth in the following decade. The aggressive resurgence of such acquisitive participation by Scottish Gaelic lords in the land-market stands in stark contrast to the house of Antrim and other Irish Gaelic, landed families who had benefited from the plantation and resettlement of Ulster in the early seventeenth century. Despite the execution and forfeiture of Archibald Campbell, the first marquis of Argyll, for his Covenanting activities in 1661, his son Archibald had been restored fully as ninth earl to the family estates and heritable jurisdictions within four years. Yet Randall MacDonnell, the first marquis of Antrim, who was reduced to the status of *rentier* after his Ulster estates were forfeited by the Cromwellian regime in 1653, was imprisoned rather than indemnified as an innocent Catholic at the Restoration. Although liberated in 1661, he spent the next two years having to prove that his former association with the Catholic Confederacy was specifically directed by Charles I in 1643, before he was pronounced innocent of any malicious intention or rebellion by the Irish Court of Claims. Another two years were to elapse before he was restored to his family estates in Ulster, but even then the judicial rearguard action fought by the Cromwellian soldiers and English adventurers laying claim to his estate ensured no more than a partial restoration.[44]

Bolstering the more assertive and favoured standing of the clan *fine* as Scottish landlords was a pronounced buoyancy in the

43 *Orain Iain Luim*, pp.152–3.

44 Ohlmeyer, *Civil War and Restoration* pp.241–73; Hill, *Macdonnells of Antrim*, pp.280–346; BL Petitions to the Council of State, 1652, Add MSS 34,326 f2; BL Surveys of Properties, 1655–*c.*1661, Add MSS 4765 ff20–1; BL Abstract of the Decrees of the Court of Claims for the Tryall of Innocents, 1662, Egerton 789 ff 32, 61.

Highland economy, despite the common legacy of political disruption and social dislocation from the 1640s. The partial prohibition on importing Irish cattle to England from 1663 that was made comprehensive in 1666, combined with the phenomenal growth of London as Europe's largest city and the continuous imperial demand for salt-beef, led to an upsurge in droving from Scotland. Gaeldom had emerged as the region principally benefiting from the black-cattle trade by the 1680s. Commercially conscious chiefs and clan gentry were thus able to diversify the economy of their estates from a position of relative strength whereas Irish Gaels were obliged to diversify out of necessity. At the same time, profits from droving not only enabled the clan elite to pay off pressing creditors, redeem outstanding debts and justify rent-rises but also, by underwriting absenteeism and conspicuous expenditure, subsidized their assimilation into Scottish landed society. None the less, the consistent but by no means irreversible failure of augmented rentals to keep abreast of public and private indebtedness meant that chiefs and leading gentry had increasing recourse to wadsetting, that is, mortgaging portions of their estates to secure ready supplies of credit. Conversely, the profitability of droving, when allied to more frugal lifestyles and the traditional preference of the clan elite to favour their own kinsmen and local associates in granting leases and wadsets, fuelled a major expansion of landowning among the lesser clan gentry. Lands held customarily under lease were acquired heritably, initially by wadset and subsequently, depending on the scale of indebtedness, by irredeemable feu, a conveyance equivalent to the sale of property.[45] The expansion of an indigenous landowning class, which was a pronounced feature of Scottish rather than Irish Gaeldom,[46] gave

45 ICA bundle 68/2; BL An Abstract of Every Rent per annum in Every Barony in Each County in the Kingdom of Ireland, 1678, Add MSS 15,899; A.I. Macinnes, 'The impact of civil wars and Interregnum: political disruption and social change within Scottish Gaeldom', in R. Mitchison and P. Roebuck (eds) *Economy and Society in Scotland and Ireland, 1500–1939* (Edinburgh, 1988), pp.58–69.

46 There is a manifest need for comparative cadastral studies to scrutinize changes in the land-market on either side of the North Channel, notably in County Antrim and Argyllshire, in the course of the seventeenth century. Whereas cadastral data drawn from valuation rolls and sasines have been processed for Argyllshire, the relevant material for County Antrim is still at the stage of raw data. The Argyllshire data confirm a progressive expansion of landownership to the order of 25 per cent in the course of the seventeenth century, with incomers rising from just over 3 per cent of the total number of landowners in 1629 to no more than 5 per cent of the total of 392 in 1688, when they featured primarily among the smaller landowners. Data from Argyllshire valuation rolls have been processed comprehensively with assistance from the Economic and Social Science Research Council (ESRC), by the

the lesser as well as the leading clan gentry a vested interest in maintaining political stability and curtailing the banditry of caterans. Curbing dissident elements within Gaelic society was thus a disciplinary measure acceptable to an expanded clan elite, not just an extraneous imposition of the church or state.

The process of Gaelic acclimatization to British perspectives diverged markedly in Scotland from Ireland with respect to public policy, commercial opportunity and the land-market. Hence, despite their common appeals to Gaelic tradition, too much should not be made of the apparent similarity of polemical themes evident in the work of the two most celebrated vernacular poets of the Restoration era, David O'Bruadair in Ireland and Iain Lom in Scotland. Both exhibited a shared concern that the Gaelic elite acquired legally secure charters for their estates, that estate management should not be exploitive and that traditional expectations of patronage, protection and hospitality be upheld.[47] However, the main thrust of Irish polemical criticism – albeit the more politically aware in the Restoration era – was anti-colonial in so far as it was directed against external English agencies deemed responsible for the continuing political, religious and commercial as well as landed discrimination against the Gael. Although Iain Lom and the Scottish Gaelic poets were not averse to polemical swipes at the English and the Lowlander, their most dynamic criticism was directed against the political and social conduct of the *fine*, especially negative aspects arising from their assimilation into the Scottish landed classes which occasioned a gradual, if piecemeal, redefinition of customary expectations to support rent-raising and the exploitation of proprietary resources.

After prolonged periods of absenteeism and steadily accumulating debts on account of his sustained campaigning with Scottish royalists and Irish Catholic confederates, Angus MacDonald

---

John Robertson Bequest and by John Burroughs Ltd. The datasets, catalogued as A.I. Macinnes, ARGVAL, can be consulted in the ESRC Data Archives, Essex University. Technical aspects of the datasets and preliminary findings are discussed in A.I. Macinnes, 'From clanship to commercial landlordism: landownership in Argyll from the seventeenth to the nineteenth century', *History and Computing* 2 (1990), pp.176–86. The raw data for County Antrim are primarily contained within the Library of Trinity College, Dublin; The Originals or Authentick copies of the Examinations taken by virtue of Commissions for Inquiring into ye Losses Chiefly of ye British Subjects, ye cruelties etc., committed by ye Irish and English Rebels in 1641 to ye Settlement of this Kingdom by ye Restoration, MSS 838; NAI Books of Survey and distribution, 1636–1703, I, MFS 2/1.

47 cf. *Poems of David O'Bruadair*, II, pp.38–41, 44–5, 204–9; III, pp.12–23, 26–7; *Orain Iain Luim*, pp.72–3, 98–9, 132–5, 142–3, 150–1, 154–5, 162–3.

of Largie seemed disposed to sell his patrimony in Kintyre at the Restoration. He reconsidered only after an anonymous clansman supplicated against what had hitherto been considered unthinkable:

Shaoil mi darach leathann àrd
Tarruing air barr as fhreumh
Gun gluaiste na creagan dilinn
nan dibrid o'n Leirg do threubh.[48]

[I thought of pulling a broad high oak out by the top from its roots, timeless rocks could be moved if your family forsook Largie.]

Notwithstanding this apparent polemical success, vernacular poets in the Restoration era became more accustomed to recollecting past glories than celebrating contemporaneous festivities, hospitality and patronage in the households of chiefs and leading clan gentry who were habitual absentees. Even though his political lobbying at court was occasionally commended, Aeneas, Lord MacDonnell, was repeatedly chided by Iain Lom for neglecting his traditional obligations:

Gur fada leam an Sasann thu,
'S a bhith 'gad chreach le spòrs.
B'fheàrr leam còt' is breacan ort
Na pasbhin chur air cleòc;
Is tu bhith falbh gu h-aigeannach
An triubhas chadaidh clò;
Greis a thoirt air chuariteachadh
Do Ghleanna Cuaich an fheòir.[49]

[You seem to me to be a long time in England, being ruined by gaming. I would prefer you in a coat and plaid than in a cloak which fastens; and that you should walk in a sprightly manner in trews made of tartan cloth and visit for a spell in grassy Glenquoich.]

Lord MacDonnell, who had been designated Angus MacDonald of Glengarry prior to his enoblement at the Restoration, remained impervious to criticisms from his kinsmen about his adoption of the habits and fashions of a courtier, which were supported by a yearly pension of £300 (sterling) until his death in 1680. When not resident at court or in Edinburgh, he preferred to dwell near Inverness rather than among his clansmen in Lochaber. The vernacular poets' stress on the traditional obligations of chiefs and leading gentry to their clansmen did not reverse absenteeism, prevent the accumulation of debts, or check rent-raising

48 *MacDonald Collection of Gaelic Poetry*, pp.59–60.
49 *Orain Iain Luim*, pp.124–5.

throughout Scottish Gaeldom. None the less, vernacular poetry did serve to publicize the commercial reorientation of clanship. Eulogy and elegy were now deployed to defend, not simply to glorify, the traditional ordering of Gaelic society.[50] What made the polemics of the Scottish Gaels more penetrating as well as socially sophisticated was the general willingness of the vernacular poets to identify internal factors contributing to the political and financial difficulties of the clan elite, a critical faculty particularly apparent in polemical attitudes towards the expropriation of the Clan Gillean and the excessive expenditure of the Clan Leod in the later seventeenth century.

Under Archibald, the ninth earl, the restored house of Argyll had embarked upon a credit squeeze within Scottish Gaeldom that revived and expanded the policy of forcing heavily indebted chiefs and leading gentry to accept their feudal superiority. By exploiting the legal technicalities in charters, the insatiable fiscal demands of the Restoration regime and an unfortunate run of minorities in the chiefship of the Macleans of Duart, the ninth earl of Argyll accomplished the expropriation of the *fine* of Clan Gillean from the isles of Tiree and Mull and the adjacent mainland district of Morvern. On account of the unrivalled heritable jurisdiction of the house of Argyll, the chiefs and leading gentry of the Macleans were obliged to answer in a Campbell court for private and public debts in excess of £231,726 (Scots) by 1675. Because the ninth earl's court was a public court, the Macleans' refusal to acknowledge the court's decision that their estates come within the feudal superiority of the house of Argyll was deemed defiance of the crown. Accordingly, the Campbell chief was empowered to mobilize the militia in the shires of Argyll, Bute and Dumbarton as well as his own clansmen to evict the Macleans. However, the territorial losses of the Clan Gillean were regarded by vernacular poets as the product of self-inflicted debilities as well as Campbell legalism. In particular, the failure of Sir John Maclean of Duart to reclaim his inheritance following the rebellion and forfeiture of the ninth earl of Argyll in 1685 was lambasted by his kinsman, Iain MacAilein (John Maclean) from Mull: this failure was made critical by the

50 cf. *Bardachd Chloinn Gill-Eathain*, pp.48–53, 60–7; J.C. Watson (ed.) *Gaelic Songs of Mary MacLeod*, SGTS (Edinburgh, 1965), pp.52–3, 64–5; J. MacInnes, 'Clan unity and individual freedom', *TGSI* 47 (1971–2) p.348; A.M. Sinclair (ed.) *Na Baird Leathanach: The Maclean Bards* (2 vols; Charlottetown, PEI, 1898–1900), I, pp.107–11; W.J. Watson (ed.) *Bardachd Ghaidhlig: Gaelic Poetry, 1550–1900* (Inverness, 1976), pp.120–1.

restoration of the house of Argyll at the Revolution when the Maclean chief opted for exile in France rather than contest the loss of his heritage. In seemingly the first Gaelic riposte to the emergent coffee-house culture in Restoration Britain, Iain MacAilein attributed the fatal political atrophy of his chief to changing social habits.

Gur h-e 'chuir an t-ainfhiach ur-s' ort
Meud do dhùil de'n Ghalltachd
A phoit bheag 'bhith 'n cois an teallaich
'S blas meala air a h-eanraich
A cosg an ni le'n cumadh t'athair
Luchd-taighe le'n armaibh.[51]

[It is your degree of interest in the Lowlands which has plunged you into this new debt, with the small pot being beside the fire and the taste of honey from its brew, spending the resources with which your father maintained in householdmen and their weapons.]

Another chief whose dereliction of duty was criticized by Iain MacAilein and his contemporary poets was that of the Clan Leod of Skye, Harris and Glenelg. Despite inheriting a burden of debt of £115,000 (Scots) in 1664, John MacLeod of Dunvegan, by refraining from unnecessary absenteeism, forsaking political ambition and, above all, mobilizing financial support from his clan gentry, reduced this burden to £41,360 (Scots) in 1693. However, his eldest son and heir as chief of Clan Leod was gaining a reputation as a spendthrift through sojourns noted for their liberality as far afield as London and Paris. The most scathing critic of Roderick the wastrel – who was to run up debts in excess of £45,000 (Scots) prior to his own death in 1699 – was An Clarsair Dall (Roderick Morison). The Blind Harper's evocative assault on the corrosive and corrupting impact of conspicuous expenditure led to his removal from his privileged position in the chief's household for publicly admonishing John MacLeod about his son's conduct:

An uair a thilleas e rìs
a dh'amharc a thìre féin,
'n déis na mìltean chur suas,
gun tig sgrìob air an tuach mu spréidh,
gus an togar na mairt

51 *Na Baird Leathanach*, I, p.171; *Highland Papers*, I, pp.275–320; NLS Campbell Papers 1639–1837, MS 975 ff23, 45, 49; ICA bundle 54/329; P. Hopkins, *Glencoe and the End of the Highland War* (Edinburgh, 1986), pp.44–5, 56–70, 99–104, 362, 374. I am indebted to Dr Steve Pincus, University of Chicago, for the suggestion that the contents of the small pot were more likely to be coffee rather than tea as hitherto accepted.

'n déidh an ciuradh 's an reic air féill:
siod na fiachan ag at,
gus am fiarach ri mhac 'na dhéidh.[52]

[When he returns to view his own country, though thousands (of pounds) have already been sent away, a cattle levy is imposed on the tenantry, and so the marts are exported, after being cured and sold at the market. Thus do the debts increase, to be demanded from his son after him.]

Such trenchant polemical criticism, which reflected the underlying social tensions within a Gaelic society required to acclimatize to a British political agenda, has tended to be masked by polemical Gaelic support for Jacobitism. As with royalism in the 1640s, polemical support for Jacobitism upheld the concept of the house of Stewart as the rightful trustees of Scotland. Moreover, in a sentiment shared with Irish vernacular poets, Jacobitism was seen as a corrective to political, social and commercial deviations from custom. None the less, shared appeals to conserve tradition, which demonstrated an often unappreciated level of polemical sophistication in both Ireland and Scotland, should not detract from the confirmation afforded by Jacobitism to the cultural divergence of the Scottish from the Irish Gael. Despite the common investment of emotional capital in the cause of James VII and II, the political basis of Gaelic support was also distinctive.

Irish poets, such as O'Bruadair, commended James II for his commitment to catholicism, albeit its political basis was more French than Roman; for his favouring of Irish catholics in the military, judiciary and the municipalities as well as central and local government; for his galvanizing of support from all in Ireland who had not collaborated with the Cromwellian regime or countenanced the abortive Scottish rebellion of the ninth earl of Argyll in 1685. Above all, James, commended for his Scottish and French origins, was depicted as the protector of the Irish Gael who offered redress from Cromwellian expropriations, protestant triumphalism and the scattering of Irish manpower, whether as continental mercenaries or into colonial servitude in the West Indies.[53] Yet the Irish Gaels had no first-hand experience of James as a politician until his dispatch by Louis XIV to Ireland in March 1689 to tie up British forces that could otherwise have assisted the

52 W. Matheson (ed.) *The Blind Harper: The Songs of Roderick Morison and his Music*, SGTS (Edinburgh, 1970), pp.70–1; R.C. MacLeod (ed.) *The Book of Dunvegan, 1340–1700* (Aberdeen, 1938), pp.266–7.

53 *Poems of David O'Bruadair*, III, pp.38–45, 78–91, 94–111, 114–15, 119, 128–41.

Dutch army of William of Orange. Apart from the military ineptitude which characterized his sixteen-month stay in Ireland, James demonstrated a limited grasp of Irish catholic aspirations: indeed, the political and military role accorded to the native Irish was subordinate to that of the Old English. In turn, the thirty-month Jacobite campaign in Ireland, which ended with the treaty of Limerick in October 1691, entrenched the political, social and commercial supremacy of the protestant minority, a supremacy which all but excluded the Irish Gael from public life and simultaneously cemented the colonial status of Ireland in the eighteenth century.[54]

The Scottish Gael saw in Jacobitism an opportunity to assert and shape how Scotland should be governed. Jacobitism represented the maintenance of not only a traditional but also a divinely warranted social ordering. Vernacular poets, such as Aonghus MacAlasdair Ruaidh (Angus MacDonald) from Glencoe, upheld the rightful trusteeship of the Stewarts, not the divine right of kings to suspend or dispense with law or custom.

> Chane eil e ceadaicht' dhuinn claonadh
> No'n righ saoghalta mhùcadh
> 's gur e'n t-oighre fiòr dhligheach,
> O'n a ghineadh o thùs e;
> Chan fhaod deifer an crèidimh,
> No neo-chreidimh ar taladh
> 'S gun ùghdaras laghail,
> Is gníomh foilleil dhuinn aìcheadh.[55]

> [It is not permissible for us to turn aside from, or suppress our temporal king. For, from the moment he was first conceived, he was the true rightful heir. No difference of faith, or even lack of faith, may draw us away; without lawful authority, it is a treacherous thing for us to renounce him.]

The sundering of genealogical continuity in the royal house through the displacement of James VII by his daughter Mary and her husband William of Orange imperilled the lawful exercise of government and the maintenance of justice in Scotland, which now, as in Ireland, was underpinned by religious faith. But confessional nationalism in Scotland was rooted in indigenous episcopalianism rather than Roman Catholicism. The spread of episcopalianism among the clans in the Restoration era was of greater religious

54 Fitzpatrick, *Seventeenth-Century Ireland*, pp.246–55; Beckett, *Making of Modern Ireland*, pp.139–61; Canny, *Kingdom and Colony*, pp.128–33.

55 MacLean, 'Celtic sources', pp.255–7.

import than the sporadic catholic missions. Episcopalianism not only provided a religious complement to the hierarchical nature of clanship, but also inculcated a spirit of obedience and submission to royal authority. Duncan MacRae, an episcopalian minister in Wester Ross, railed against William and Mary for breaking the fifth commandment:

Neo-nàdur a'bheart so
Do neach a ghabh baisteadh
Ann an ainm nan trì pearson tha shuas.[56]

[This is an unnatural act for one who received baptism in the name of the Trinity.]

The most pronounced political difference with the Irish was that the Scottish Gaels had direct and favourable experience of James when he was dispatched north during the Exclusion Crisis. As duke of York, he promoted conciliation in place of repression. His involvement of clan *fine* on the commissions of justiciary to pacify the Highlands between 1682 and 1684 added a *de jure* dimension to their *de facto* role as local government agents. The suppression of the ninth earl of Argyll's rebellion in 1685 – albeit achieved by the over-enthusiastic participation of former royalist clans – indicated the depth of his support among the clans, a support further encouraged by his unfulfilled promise to curb the abusive exercise of feudal superiorities within Scottish Gaeldom. None the less, Jacobitism, like royalism during the 1640s, occasioned civil war in Scotland and among the clans, with a small presbyterian core headed by Clan Campbell committed to the Revolution of 1689–90 as earlier to the Covenanting movement. Their principled commitment was dismissed by An Clarsair Dall as a betrayal of traditional kingship:

Thug iad stràc cho mallaichte
's gur annamh e r' a luaidh –
gràdh thoirt do rìgh annasach
's an ceannas a chur uath'.[57]

[They struck a blow so accursed that the like has seldom been told – to give their love to an alien king and to disown the true sovereignty.]

James, however, no more helped his own cause in Scotland than in Ireland. For although Ireland became the major battleground

56 *Lamh Sgriobhainn Mhic Rath*, p.187.

57 *Blind Harper*, pp.26–7; A.I. Macinnes 'Jacobitism', in J. Wormald (ed.) *Scotland Revisited* (London, 1991), pp.129–41.

during the first Jacobite campaign, this was as much by default as by the direction of Louis XIV. James failed to appreciate the depth of Scottish commitment to his cause and, in turn, failed to provide adequate backing for the Jacobite clans after their victory at Killiecrankie, on 27 July 1689, was marred by the fatal wounding of their commander, John Graham, first Viscount Dundee. Indeed, the Scottish campaign exhibited considerable tensions between the clans and their Irish allies. Unlike the 1640s when the Irish forces accompanying Alasdair MacColla were enthusiastically welcomed on the western seaboard, the smaller Irish Gaelic contingent, mainly from the Isle of Rathlin, who fought with the clans at Killiecrankie, were regarded with some trepidation, bordering on loathing, by the Clan Donald poet, Alasdair MacAlasdair Ruaidh:

> Cha bu ghealtachd 'bhi 'gan seachnadh,
> Cha robh am faicinn boìdheach
> An léintean paisgte fo'n da achlais,
> 'S an casan gun bhrògan,
> Boineid dhaithte dìon an claiginn,
> 'S an gruaig 'na pasgan fòtha;
> Bu chos mhuile 'n gléus ri trotan bhéistean
> Na rì buchd-céille còire.[58]

> [It was not cowardice to shun them, they were not a pleasant sight to see; their shirts were folded up under their armpits, and their feet were shoeless; coloured bonnets were on their heads, with their hair gathered under; their charge was more like the stampede of cattle, than the charge of a beloved and related people.]

Because Kenneth MacKenzie, fourth earl of Seaforth was considered to have dallied overlong with James on his Irish campaign, he faced far from muted criticism from his clansmen, who remained reluctant to rally to his banner after he returned to Scotland in June 1690. Despite polemical admonitions against failing the cause and forsaking honour, the continuing reluctance of the MacKenzies in Wester Ross and the Isle of Lewis to support their errant chief obliged him within four months to surrender to the Whig forces loyal to William of Orange.[59] The Jacobite campaign in Scotland stuttered on until the peace concluded at Achallader in June 1691. The dilatoriness of the clans in accepting the offered indemnity by the prescribed deadline of 31 January

58 MacLean, 'Celtic sources', pp.301–3; J. MacKnight (ed.) *Memoirs of Sir Ewen Cameron of Lochiel* (Edinburgh, 1842), pp.250–63.

59 MacLean, 'Celtic sources', pp.320–30; Hopkins, *Glencoe and the End of the Highland War*, pp.233–48.

resulted in the Whig regime condoning and executing the salutary, but infamous, massacre of the MacDonalds of Glencoe on 13 February 1692. With the restored Presbyterian Church of Scotland as well as the Whig regime becoming so distinctly anti-Gaelic as well as anti-clanship in their public policy pronouncements, Iain Lom was uncompromisingly prophetic in vilifying William:

> Sgios gun iarmad gun duilleach,
> Chan iarrainn tuille am dhàn duibh,
> Gun sliochd a dh'iadhach mu t'uilinn
> De ghnìomh bruinne droch Mhàiri.[60]

> [Destruction without posterity, without green leaf on your family tree – I would not ask for better on your behalf in my song, with no offspring to gather round your elbow from the fruits of evil Mary's womb.]

Glencoe and anti-Gaelic bias notwithstanding, the clans like other Scottish Jacobites escaped the swingeing political, commercial and religious discrimination and the permanent forfeitures meted out to their Irish counterparts. However, the comparative dearth of political deterrents cannot wholly or even primarily explain why Jacobitism remained a significant force in Scottish politics until the mid-eighteenth century. Jacobitism in Scotland, which operated within a different constitutional framework from that of Ireland, was undoubtedly revitalized by the political, commercial and religious grievances arising from the treaty of Union. At the same time, no protestant supremacy excluded the Scottish Gael from public life. Despite continuing political differences between Jacobites and Whigs, the clan elite, like other members of the Scottish landed classes, shared a common ideological commitment to property, progress and prosperity within an imperial rather than a colonial framework in the aftermath of Union.

CONCLUSION

Gaeldom in both Ireland and Scotland was dominated increasingly by a British rather than an English or Scottish political agenda in the course of the seventeenth century. It was the vernacular rather than the common classical Gaelic response to this evolving agenda which exhibited the greater cultural dynamism and critical

60 *Orain Iain Luim*, pp.208–9.

divergence as evident in the poets' reaction to plantation and expropriation, to civil wars and Cromwellian occupation, and to the Restoration and Jacobitism. This divergence was the product of the different constitutional experience affecting British acclimatization in Scotland from Ireland. The clan *fine* remained *de facto* agents of local government throughout the seventeenth century as they assimilated politically, commercial and socially with the Scottish landed classes. The Gaelic elite in Ireland, after a century of displacement and dislocation, were progressively divorced from the development of commercially landlordism. While the Irish experience politically, socially and commercially was undoubtedly more susceptible to a colonial analysis,[61] the Gaels in both countries were, unlike the American Indians, considered part, albeit a problematic part, of the governmental fabric in the three kingdoms. Irish and Scottish Gaels made not an insignificant contribution to the shaping as well as the disruption of this fabric in the seventeenth century. But Gaelic polarization during the civil wars of the 1640s, reaffirmed by the civil wars of 1689–91, had demonstrated that Gaeldom as a cohesive political and cultural concept was no longer attainable. Support from Scottish, if not Irish, Gaeldom ensured that Jacobitism continued to disrupt the British political agenda in the eighteenth century. But in identifying the very survival of Gaeldom with Jacobitism, the Scottish Gaels were not so much following on from Irish tradition as belatedly coming to terms with a lost cause.

61 W.J. Smyth, 'The making of Ireland: agendas and perspectives in cultural Geography', in B.J. Graham and L.J. Proudfoot (eds) *An Historical Geography of Ireland*, (London, 1993) pp.420–7; Canny, *Kingdom and Colony*, pp.140–1.

CHAPTER EIGHT

Scotland and Ireland under the Commonwealth: a question of loyalty

Sarah Barber
University of Lancaster

A study of the fashioning of a concept of 'Britain' covers a two hundred year span but it may nevertheless seem odd that there is no chapter which deals with the period of the 1640s. Students could be directed to any number of specialist books on the period. The omission of one of the central events in the history of these islands is not intended to skew the overall contents: on the contrary, a spotlight on the 1640s may, in itself, be a distorting factor. Wars, revolutions and upheaval always have an eager audience and our interest in them demarcates our view of the world in general. Revolutionary jolts to the system are seen either as the culmination of a process or as the catalyst of further change. Inserting the crisis of the 1640s into the centre would make the other chapters dance either an anticipatory or a consequential dance to its tune.

The 1640s have acquired many sobriquets, dependent on the historiographical stance of commentators. To the Whigs of the latter half of the nineteenth century, the 1640s marked the climax of a long struggle between representative authority and royal prerogative, both of which focused on London and sought, in different ways, to speak for the English people. The period 1642 to 1649 was 'the English civil war', or likewise, the 'English Revolution'.[1] A refinement of this notion regarded the conflicts in the plural, in order to take account of the shifting power relations within English politics. The second civil war was fought on a

1 This is the legacy of Samuel Gardiner, Charles Firth and the scholars of the early twentieth century. More recently, studies have appeared such as R. Ashton, *English Civil War: Conservation and Revolution 1603–1649* (London, 1978); J.H. Hexter (ed.) *Parliament and Liberty from the Reign of Elizabeth to the English Civil War* (Stanford, Calif., 1992); M. Ashley, *The English Civil War* (London, 1974).

different agenda from and with the factions differently grouped than in the first.

Subsequently, revisions have been made to the metropolitan view of English politics. Regionalism has drawn attention both to the continuing struggle of the royalists and to those who chose to be neutral or to take arms to defend their communities against the ravages of both armies.[2] The idea of religious struggle has been revived and due attention has finally been paid to the symbiotic and interlinked roles of the four nations which make up the 'Atlantic archipelago'.[3] Initially, this was done at a superficial level. It was deemed proper to look at the influence that politics in Edinburgh and Dublin, and to a lesser extent inside Wales, exerted over the political stance of those in London. This expanded to begin an overdue examination of the ways in which politics and society within the four nations cannot be disentangled; although each has a separate existence, all four also have an interlocking and reinforcing history.

This chapter concentrates on the politics of the earlier 1650s, to point to those who resisted the seemingly inexorable drive towards the further integration of the four nations. In the ultimate irony of the mid-seventeenth century, the pressures of war and the nature of the politics of the Commonwealth dictated that for these politicians, closer and more institutionalized union became a reality, something which their own political ethos resisted. In tracing the ideology of the protagonists of republicanism, it is necessary to retrace some aspects of wartime politics, for their attitude towards Scotland and Ireland was not only a central tenet of their thought but also a reaction to the events of the 1640s.

Conrad Russell has rightly drawn attention to the isolationist attitude of English people in the early seventeenth century, a reaction which was to be writ large in the characters of our protagonists. Perhaps, therefore, he argues, we have a reason for the bewilderment of the English political nation when faced with the collapse of authority in 1642. The 'War of the Three Kingdoms' has become a new way of explaining the revisionist picture in which

2 R. Hutton, *The Royalist War Effort, 1642–1646* (London, 1982); A. Hughes, *Politics, Society and Civil War in Warwickshire, 1620–1660* (Cambridge, 1987); J. Morrill, *Cheshire, 1630–1660: County Government and Society during the English Civil War* (Oxford, 1974); D. Underdown, *Somerset in the Civil War and Interregnum* (Newton Abbot, 1973).

3 The revision of the religious aspects of the wars has never been fully realized but a contribution has been made by P. White, *Predestination, Policy and Polemic: Conflict and Consensus in the English Church from the Reformation to the Civil War* (Cambridge, 1992).

there was relative stability prior to 1642 and the slide to war was far from inevitable. In England, 'few of the participants remembered a country deeply enough divided to justify the fate which fell on it'.[4] There was no road to war, merely a governmental path beneath which, unbeknownst to the politicians of Whitehall, Irish and Scottish malcontents were burying land-mines. Charles I's support for Arminianism meant that his authority was at its lowest in Scotland, where the covenanters laid the trap of the wars of 1639–40.[5] Irish politics was essentially quiet in the later 1630s: the explosion of the early 1640s was more a reaction to English events – the attainder of Strafford and obsessional English fears of catholicism – than the sudden and violent upheaval of naturally rebellious subjects.[6] The Bishops' Wars, the covenant in Scotland and the rebellion in Ireland were actions that closed doors to the continued peaceful coexistence within and between the three kingdoms.[7]

The War of the Three Kingdoms was not one narrative, based on London, into which Scotland, Ireland and Wales appeared in bit parts. It could be read as four concurrent and interrelated chronicles: more of a soap opera than a classic serial. Russell managed in over five hundred pages to tell five years of this saga, and it is beyond the scope of one chapter to complete his work. Rather, this chapter will trace the careers of a group of Englishmen, those who were to form the central core of government in 1649, and demonstrate how their attitudes towards Scotland and Ireland influenced the philosophy which was ultimately to lead to the conquest of both the Celtic nations and their closer integration – albeit temporarily – into the British polity, an outcome which, it will be argued here, was the mirror image of that which these protagonists wished. This is hardly a narrative at all, but a study of the impact of four nations' politics on the formation of a political identity and ideology.

Many of the characters identified by Russell – Marten, Rigby, Strode, Cromwell, Pyne, Cooke, Harley, Penington and Venn – turn up here. Three stand out at first: Henry Marten, Alexander Rigby

4 C. Russell, *The Fall of the British Monarchies 1637–1642* (Oxford, 1991), p.525.

5 A. Macinnes, *Charles I and the Making of the Covenanting Movement 1625–1641* (Edinburgh, 1991).

6 A. Clarke, 'Ireland and the general crisis', *P&P* 48 (1970), pp.79–99; A. Clarke 'Genesis of the Ulster Rising of 1641', in P. Roebuck and J.L. McCracken (eds) *Plantation to Partition* (Belfast, 1981).

7 Russell, *British Monarchies*, p.398.

and John Pyne. They were blessed with a common background of county gentryism. To this group could be added the four Thomases, Grey,[8] Chaloner, Scot and Rainsborough, along with extra-parliamentary figures such as John Wildman, Edward Sexby, Maximilian Petty and William Wetton.[9] They shared several similar political reactions,[10] but this chapter will examine just one: ultimate rejection of the link between England and Scotland, of the idea of common interest between the two polities and their obsessive dislike of those sections of the Scottish political nation which fought to keep the link intact.[11]

Militant resistance by the Scots was the trigger for the recall of parliament in 1640 and the inability of the parliament and the king to agree on measures to tackle the Irish rebellion was a trigger to joint Anglo-Scottish action to settle the question of control of the militia. There were common ecclesiastical concerns among those 'to whom the cause of reformation was never one which had stopped in 1559' and there were those who shared the religious outlook of the covenanting Scots. Some welcomed the Scots because they recognized their religious vision and some, who let Cromwell stand as representative, welcomed the Scots because the Stewart state presented a threat to protestant ecumenicism. The blood of irenic brotherhood was thicker than the waters of the River Tweed.

8 Thomas, Lord Grey of Groby, is the only aristocratic figure to appear here, and for the purposes of this chapter he assumes the status of honorary gentleman. He is in many ways an enigma, not least because most of his family papers have been lost, and he has a more noble lineage than any of the others, being part of the Bradgate Greys who produced the unfortunate Lady Jane. His politics, however, are atypical of his social standing, as were his religious views, which were millenarian to the point of his joining with Fifth Monarchists, and his political stance was more akin to that of his gentry allies than that of his noble fellows, a fact underscored by his single aristocratic signature at the head of Charles I's death warrant.

9 Wetton was the fourth, rather overlooked Leveller to be named to the committee of sixteen to draw up a second *Agreement of the People.* All of the non-parliamentary and most of the Members cited here can be found to have a personal and political link with Henry Marten.

10 This chapter forms a small part of ongoing work to demonstrate a form of republicanism, christened 'gentry republicanism' which predated the regicide and which was superseded by the now well-known concept of aristocratic, classical republicanism identified by Blair Worden, 'Classical republicanism and the puritan revolution', in H. Lloyd-Jones, V. Pearl and B. Worden (eds) *History and Imagination: Essays in Honour of H.R. Trevor-Roper* (London, 1981).

11 The shared political ethos that this group possessed went beyond a hatred of Scottish interference in English politics. It was rather a parochial, introspective philosophy which ran parallel to the Leveller concern for 'England's liberties'. It was not necessarily that the liberties of English people were of greater importance than those of others, but that it was such a central task that they be secured that other concerns must be subsumed to this national interest.

Marten supposedly stands alone as one who was uninterested in religious reformation. For him, the Scots provided expedient political aid. But when all of these ultimately anti-Scottish republicans – and in this Cromwell is the odd man out – supported the 1643 alliance with the Scots, they were all subsuming political doubts about calvinistic covenanting to the demands of political expediency.[12] In 1643 the parliamentarians needed the Scots and their army. Over the following two or three years, the English army was recreated, pacific aristocratic commanders were ousted by committed professionals, and the parliamentarians achieved control over their own national destiny. Thus, the Scots' involvement could be reappraised. The group that emerged as engineers of the republican settlement of 1649 swung away, for a mixture of religious and political reasons, from an initially joyous welcome of the Scots to open hostility which, in part, defined their stance. There was a common desire to 'bind an untrustworthy king in chains'.[13]

THE ROOTS OF REPUBLICANISM

During the first civil war, republican sentiment was very much a minority taste. The leaders of the parliamentary war effort put themselves through all manner of constitutional contortions in order to demonstrate that they remained ultimately loyal to the crown while they faced Charles and his forces across the battlefield. The anti-royalist outbursts of Henry Marten were isolated and, at first, easily contained. The parliament took his financial contributions, which he believed earned him the right to express his divergent views. Instead, John Pym waited his opportunity and then had him barred from the House.

12 Cromwell's enthusiasm for religious toleration led him to oppose the malingering of the Scottish commissioners in England, but it is hard to trace for him a similar road from pro-Scots' war party support to republican firebrand.

13 Russell, *British Monarchies*, p.529. Russell identifies Marten as pro-Scottish for parliamentary purposes, and thus one who lived in uneasy alliance with the single representative of Scottish republicanism, Johnston of Wariston. Indeed, objection to the Stewarts was the only thing they had in common, but it was an ideological stance which overrode Marten's more polished political standpoint of opposition to the conclusion of the Anglo-Scottish alliance.

When Marten returned in 1646 he launched a new onslaught.[14] He joined the like-minded Thomas Chaloner, whose speech on the peace proposals offered to Charles at Newcastle sparked off a campaign. The peace proposals were approaching the anodyne: the fire that Chaloner ignited under them altered the course of radical politics. Chaloner's contribution was dubbed the 'speech without doors'. It expressed sentiments which could not possibly be countenanced were it not for the protection of parliamentary privilege and it encouraged a whole host of minor scribblers to contribute to the debate beyond the hallowed portals of Westminster. Chaloner's main objection to the Propositions of Newcastle was the continuing presence of the Scottish commissioners and the views which they wanted to enshrine within the peace settlement. The speech was therefore the first indication of a paradigm shift in the attitude of some English parliamentarians towards the Scots. In 1642 the Scots had been necessary and generally welcome allies. By 1646 they were a persistent, insistent and increasingly loathed irritant. The Scottish commissioners were forceful in their demands for a Scottish-style Presbyterian Church settlement and reiterated their demand that parliament treat with Charles both as a king and as a man of dignity, allowing him to return, ironically, to the English capital. It was as a reaction to Scottish demands that a small faction of radicals, both inside and outside the Commons, first openly voiced republican sentiments.

The pro-Chaloner pamphleteers sought to establish the autonomy of England and Scotland, despite their dual monarchy. Charles being in England, they argued, the Scots had 'nothing at all to doe to dispose of the Person of the King'.[15] This author took great delight in echoing the Scots' own controversialist, Samuel Rutherford, who in *Lex Rex*, 'an elaborate Booke written by one very neere and deere to some of the Scottish Commissioners', had made a distinction between the office of king *in abstracto* and the person

14 The return of Marten to the Commons is somewhat confusing. He was barred in 1643 for unparliamentary phrases about the king, and was supposed to have been banned for three years. However, in 1645, his brother-in-law, Sir George Stonehouse, was disabled for his royalism to sit for Abingdon, and Marten seems to have returned in a recruiter election. When the three years expired the following year, he resumed his seat for Berkshire and the like-minded William Ball of Barkham was chosen in his place. When Ball died in 1648, Marten secured the seat for his republican friend, Henry Nevile.

15 *The Justification of a safe and wel-grounded Answer to the Scotch Papers, printed under the name of Master Chaloner his Speech*, Th.26 Oct. 1646, E363(11), p.3. References to pamphlets in the Thomason Collection at the British Library are given with a date on which Thomason noted his receipt of the tract ('Th.') and a BL classmark, 'E'.

of the king *in concreto.* Chaloner also threw back at the Scots a reminder of the past treatment they had meted out to their monarchs. Charles was in England as the king of England, not of Scotland, '[for] if he were here in the capacity of a King of *Scotland* he were a Subject, and then you might know well enough what should become of the King of *Scotland,* as you have formerly done of some of them, who yet have plotted lesse then others have acted'.[16]

Marten was less circumspect in his language, probably because his support of Chaloner was anonymous; he was cautious that having but recently returned to parliament, he should not earn another ban. The pamphleteering style, however, is unmistakably his and set the tone for the republican rhetoric of anti-Scottishness which formed one of its distinctive characteristics for the next six years: 'the Parliament were better to be without your [the Scottish commissioners'] service & resolution; and indeed for all your boasting, 'tis thought you have been and are but a back-friend, that you row one way and looke another; which in plain English (if not in Scotch) is to play the disembling hypocrite'.[17] Charles was given such lenient terms at Newcastle that he was likely to escape 'scot-free'. Marten even went as far as to claim a false imprimatur, that of the king's Scottish printer in Edinburgh, Evan Tyler. The same trick was practisèd by the author of *An Unhappy Game at Scotch and English,* who argued that English 'Lawes Lives and Liberties' were 'more pretious, then to be prostitute to the exhorbitant boundlesse *will* of any mortall *Steuart* under the Sun'.[18] England and Scotland were so separate, sovereign and foreign to each other that the Scottish commissioners were the equivalent of ambassadors: 'I would wee were all at home Jockey, & I a currying of my Masters horse, a better conditioned Jack by half'.[19]

Parliamentarians whose radicalism was religiously driven, such as Edmund Ludlow, John Pyne and Lord Grey of Groby, were unsettled by the Scots' insistence on a presbyterian settlement.

16 ibid, p.10.

17 [Henry Marten], *A Corrector of the Answerer to the Speech out of Doores,* Th.26 Oct, 1646, BL E364(9), p.3.

18 *An Unhappy Game at Scotch and English,* Th. 30 Nov. 1646, BL E364(3), p.10.

19 At the time of writing the more political portion of the Marten manuscripts were held by Sotheby's, whose generosity in letting me transcribe them I should like to acknowledge. They are now in the public domain at the British Library. This is a fragment of a reply to the Scottish commissioners, in Marten's hand, and is MSS 71532 11. Marten's contempt for the commissioners is clear in his repeated, ribald use of 'Jockey' throughout.

What binds the group which Russell identified as proponents of religious reformation in 1642 was their congregational, sectarian and, in the circumstances of the mid-1640s, tolerationist line. The prospect of calvinist imposition turned them away from their Scottish allies and into English retrenchment. Those who were guided by Marten and Chaloner were more concerned with a secular settlement and were alarmed at the gravity with which the Scottish commissioners imbued their role as guardians of the personal functions of the king. The alarm of both religious and secular radicals was encapsulated in the document which had cemented Anglo-Scottish relations in arms; the Solemn League and Covenant, 'for Reformation and Defence of Religion, the honour and happiness of the King, and the peace and safety of the three kingdoms of England, Scotland and Ireland'.[20] For a small group of radicals, the speech without doors controversy marked the abandonment of the covenant. As one such, G.G., 'a lover of his country' (that is, England), maintained, 'the Scots make the person of the King the only thing now in dispute, but wee are by Covenant oblieged to mayntayn as well the Law of the Land, as the person of the King'.[21]

The Solemn League and Covenant contained within it several hints at a wider and more permanent union. England, Ireland and Scotland were 'by the providence of God living under one King' and were 'of one reformed religion'. Furthermore, 'whereas the happiness of a blessed peace between these kingdoms, denied in former times to our progenitors, is by the good providence of God granted to us, and hath been lately concluded and settled by both Parliaments: we shall . . . endeavour that they may remain conjoined in a firm peace and union to all posterity'.[22] Such mutuality was reinforced by Argyll in a speech to the committee of parliament in June 1646:

> let us hold fast that union which is happily established between us; and let nothing make us again two, who are in so many ways one; all of one language, in one island, all under one King, one in religion, yea, one in Covenant, so that in effect we differ in nothing but in name – as

20 S.R. Gardiner, *Constitutional Documents of the Puritan Revolution, 1625–1660* (Oxford, 1979), pp.267–71.

21 G.G., *Intituled, A Reply to a Namelesse Pamphlet, An Answer to a Speech without Doors*, &c, Th.26 Oct. 1646, BL E362(26), p.3.

22 *Solemn League and Covenant* preamble and clause v, Gardiner, *Constitutional Documents.*

> brethren do – which I wish were also removed that we might be altogether one, if the two kingdoms shall think fit.[23]

The direction of anti-Stewart policy which was forming around the speech without doors controversy, and which was to shape the nature of republicanism in the late 1640s, was parochial, nationalistic, self-interested and virulently anti-Scottish. Several key figures approached this view from a materialist and localist standpoint. Both Thomas Chaloner, the Buckinghamshire Member of Parliament (MP) whose family estates lay around Guisborough, and Alexander Rigby, the MP for Wigan, moved from a pro- to a violently anti-Scottish position during the middle years of the 1640s, partly because their lands were occupied by Scottish forces, where a policy of 'Scottishization', especially in ecclesiastical affairs, had made good headway.[24] There was a particularly poignant cry from the author of *The Justification* that the person of the king was at Newcastle in England, 'though some of the Army there date thei[r] Letters from Newcastle in *Scotland*'.[25]

By 1648 there was emerging a republican platform that could draw individuals together from the otherwise disparate concerns of religious and constitutional radicalism. In January 1648 the republican position crystallized around opposition to the Scots' continued influence in English affairs and the presbyterians' growing loyalism towards Charles. The king was becoming the focus of both loyalty and hatred. Crisis point was reached early in 1648. Parties of Scottish loyalists signed an Engagement with Charles, which had the effect of uniting the Hamiltonian party, the committee of estates and the Scottish parliament and of stealing the fire from Argyll's kirk faction by calling for greater civil cooperation between the Scots and a reborn Stewart England. The Scottish Engagers were pursuing an entirely consistent policy. They swore to uphold the terms of the covenant which guaranteed the protection of the king's person and to foster the 'reformed' religion by stamping out 'Anti-Trinitarians, Anabaptists, Antinomians, Arminians, Familists, Brownists, Separatists, Independents, Libertines, and Seekers'[26] – an all-embracing description of the leaders of English military and parliamentary radicalism. In the English parliament, the numbers who were trying to disengage from the

23 Cited in W. Ferguson, *Scotland's Relations with England: A Survey to 1707* (Edinburgh, 1977), p.131.

24 Russell, *British Monarchies*, p.195.

25 *The Justification*, p.10.

26 Gardiner, *Constitutional Documents*, p.348.

union with the Scottish army and abandon the covenant were swelled by those who were outraged at the Scots' role in the Engagement. A shaky alliance coalesced between a radical parliamentary faction and the ranks of the New Model Army, forced to return to the horrors of battle, having believed that reconstruction was about to begin. The shock of a new war pushed swelling numbers of soldiers to the realization that they were fighting 'Charles Stuart, that man of blood'.[27] The king was charged with sacrilege, because he had ignored the verdict of God at Naseby, and the Scots were his impious abettors who, in crossing the border, were wilfully attempting to reverse providence.

Henry Marten made a couple of forays into pamphlet literature, in response to the increasingly close links between Charles and the Scots, and Westminster's rejoinder, a vote of no further addresses to the king. He set up the provincial, parochial, patriotic concerns of the republican firebrands. It was important to maintain 'England's Independency':

> There is some alteration in the condition of affairs: So long as we needed the assistance of your Country-men [the Scots] in the Field, we might have occasion to give you meetings at *Derby House*, and now and then in the *Painted Chamber*, it being likely that the Kingdom of *Scotland* might then have a fellow-feeling with us of the wholesomeness or perniciousness of your counsels; whereas now since we are able (by Gods blessing) to protect our selves, we may surely (with his holy direction) be sufficient to teach our selves how to go about our own business, at least without your tutoring, who have nothing in your considerations to look upon, but either your particular advantage, or that of the Kingdom whence you are.

The English parliament was justified in voting through a vote of no further addresses to the king, 'notwithstanding the advice of the Scottish Commissioners'.[28] Marten went off to his estates in Berkshire in order to raise a republican regiment, the better to defend his home against the royalists and the Scots. Thomas, Lord Grey of Groby, raised a similar force, boasting to Major-General Skippon and to the nation at large that 'Old English blood' was 'boyling afresh in Leicestershire men: Occasioned by the late barbarous invasion of the Scots'.[29] Alexander Rigby defeated his

27 P. Crawford, 'Charles Stuart, that Man of Blood', *JBS* 13.1 (1973), pp.21–43.

28 Henry Marten, *The Independency of England Endeavoured to be Maintained against the Scots Commissioners*, Th.11 Jan. 1648, BL E422(16), p.21; *The Parliament's Proceedings Justified...* Th.7 Feb. 1648, BL E422(2).

29 Thomas, Lord Grey of Groby, *Old English Blood Boyling afresh in Leicestershire men*, Th.28 Aug. 1648, BL E461(7).

former allies at Preston. When the combined forces of the presbyterians, royalists and Scots had been vanquished, the settlement that was completed between the soldiers and the politicians traded 'condign punishment' on the single author of the Wars of the Three Kingdoms for support for a radical experiment in government.

REPUBLICANS IN POWER

As soon as the new English republic was born, its actions and its concerns were dictated from outside. The earliest months of the government were dominated by the declaration made in Scotland on 5 February 1649, which announced Charles Stewart the younger to be 'King of Great Britain, France and Ireland'.[30] Charles was given the blessing of the elite in Scotland to lay claim to the throne in England, having already accepted his Scottish crown, by recognizing presbyterian ecclesiastical control. This declaration came the day after he had received the news of his father's execution, and just six days since bitterness, expediency and the lack of any clear alternative had driven the Rump of the English parliament to the act of regicide. In one theatrical, climactic action, the Rumpers hoped to bring down the curtain on the long-running obsession which the English people had with the Stewart family and cure them of their thraldom to monarchism. They had taken the only possible action that would appease the rank and file of the New Model Army and prevent further rallies by the royalist forces.[31] The fledgling and insecure government also laid itself open to an onslaught from publicists, clerics and foreign governments of such vehemence that its adherents who looked to the Bible for their solace and inspiration must have felt justified in their self-image as the prosecuted remnant of God's children. The republican regime called Charles Stewart 'young Tarquin', the king of Scots.[32]

The wave of revulsion and belligerence that greeted the regicide concentrated republican minds on political survival. For those who

30 *Acts of Parliament of Scotland* vi/ii 157.

31 I. Gentles, *The New Model Army in England, Ireland and Scotland, 1645–1653* (Oxford, 1992).

32 For example in *A Perfect Account* published by order, 29 Jan. to 5 Feb. 1651/2, BL E623(3); *Mercurius Politicus* 5 4–11 July 1650, in Robin Jeffs (gen. ed.) *The English Revolution III: Newsbooks 5* (London, 1971), p.81.

had led the coup of December 1648 and now shaped the structure of the resultant regime, political durability was inextricably tied to their personal hold on power. Many of these men had lost any chance of reprieve from the royalist regime almost as soon as the war had begun. For them the Commonwealth had to be a success, and as such, their first task was to protect and buttress the republicanism of the new England. It was no wonder, therefore, that they were obsessed with the Scots, since the northern kingdom had provided the issues around which the republican coterie had begun to cohere during the late 1640s.

There was little change in the policy of either the English parliament towards the Scots, or the Engagers towards the Independents as a consequence of the regicide. The English republicans felt that their mistrust of the Scots was fully justified and their anti-Scottish policy in 1649 was a continuation of that which had characterized republicanism throughout the later 1640s. The Engagers' alliance continued in its campaign to uphold the terms of the Solemn League and Covenant. The belief which was held among some Englishmen, that Scottishness was a byword for perfidy and malignancy, was confirmed with even more conviction. Contrary to the jibes which had been made in Scotland that the Stewart monarchs had deserted their native land for English wealth and influence, the English resurrected the idea that Charles Stewart had taken wealth abroad to 'his native Kingdome of Scotland'.[33] Pro-government newsletters used an argument derived from the theory of the Norman Yoke and laced it with contempt for the formality of the presbytery:

> The Parliament sit here [Edinburgh] daily, the Priests and they are at as much variance as the parl. and rigid presbytery of England, so fearfull are they that their outward call, and foolish fopperies of the stool of repentance, can stand of no legs, when the inward call is given to Gods people, and then how odious will they appear, in that they have hidden the light of the Gospel from them for so many years together. They bring us all to the stool of repentance that were in the last invasion of England, to acknowledge their errour . . . in a word they act their own designs upon their own interest; . . . They much lament the losse of their Country man *Charles Stewart*, but more the loße of their Revenue out of the Crowne of England, which was half the support of this poor Nation. The parl. here is in great fear, and therefore hath almost as strong a Guard as the Parl with you: parties

33 *The Armies Modest Intelligencer* 25 Jan. to 1 Feb. 1649, BL E541(2).

> here seeme many and violent, but all will joyne unanimously against the Sectaries of England, or in any design for ruining the Godly party of that Nation.[34]

For their part, the royalists used the same argument of self-interest to lambast the Commonwealth. Noting the design of the new great seal, which emerged from a committee chaired by Marten, *Mercurius Elencticus* railed:

> instead of the *Kings Armes* &c. they have put on the one side the *Mapp* of *England* and *Ireland*, with the *Islands* adjoyning. A *Crosse* (ô horrible) for the *Armes* of *England*, and a *Harp* for *Ireland*, . . . but neither the Armes of *Scotland* or *France*, for they are willing . . . to quit those interests, so they may quietly enjoy the other two.[35]

The war dictated that England could not ignore Scotland. Early publicists of the Commonwealth government picked up the anti-Scottish language which had been a feature of 1640s republicanism and embellished it with the ribald sarcasm that is born of fear. Scotland was the major threat to the peace, security and republicanness of the new regime. It represented the old enemy, and Scottish preparations for a royalist invasion were just another manifestation of the Scots' untrustworthiness and implacable hatred of the Commonwealth. Cromwell was boasting of 'a more easy conquest . . . than al the English Kings ever had'.[36] Although *The Kingdomes Faithfull and Impartiall Scout* was under the impression that there were few in Scotland who would not 'embrace . . . and cast a smiling countenance' on Charles Stewart, the Commonwealth's man in Hamburg was

> partly of Opinion our Army gone Northwards will have a great Influence upon ye Scotts, to sett them at odds with their King, & that if they can tell how to doe it, they will declyne him: if they doe not, they are ye veriest fooles in ye World; & if they doe, they are ye veriest Knaves, they have so ye Woolfe by the Eares, I beleeve you will shortly heare of their Complianc[e] with ye Parlem^t^ of England, in wch there's more danger, then all ye force they & their King can raise.[37]

Bradshaw was another who had had experience of the Scottish

34 *The Perfect Weekly Account* 31 Jan. to 7 Feb. 1649, BL E541(24), pp.378–789 (misnumbered). See also *The Armies Modest Intelligencer* 1–8 Feb. 1649 BL E541(28), p.5. Reference to the 'stool of repentance' was also made by Bradshaw, the envoy to Hamburg.

35 *Mercurius Elencticus* 36, 6–13 Feb. 1649, BL E542(13).

36 D. Laing (ed.) *The Letters and Journals of Robert Baillie* (3 vols; Edinburgh, 1842), III, p.68.

37 Richard Bradshaw to Strickland, 21 June 1650, Lancashire CRO, Bradshaw MSS, DDF411 5/unfol.

army. His language to describe the Scots was offensive, stereotyped and entirely in keeping with the opinions of those at the head of the government: 'a Scott knowes how to make a virtue of Necessity. I hope o^{r} Generall will know how to deale with them if they come oute to a Treaty. We have experience what Fayth they keep: the Proverb sayeth, They are good serv^{ts} but bad Masters'.[38]

The military campaign of Oliver Cromwell, on behalf of his masters in London, went first to Ireland, where the activities of Michael Jones had already weakened the resistance of the Confederate army. In 1649 the Irish lords, Ormond and Inchiquin, joined Argyll in the lists of those who had turned on the English state because it had taken the decision to execute their king. It therefore became imperative that the republicans defeat the Anglo-Irish lords, although they had displayed an ambivalent attitude to the war in Ireland in the past. Dire warnings to the rebels in Ireland had been a feature of English anti-royalist discourse during the 1640s, but they had emanated mainly from the ranks of the presbyterian faction. Some of the puritans in the 1649 government felt that Ireland was unfinished business: vengeance was due to those who had killed the 'innocent' English in 1641. There were members of the government who wished to put an end to the pernicious influence of catholic priests. In the main, however, the radicals, who had exhibited such venom towards the Scots, were more tolerant and flexible in their approach to Ireland. There was evidence that this attitude was quite widespread within the admittedly small coterie that now made up the English political centre. Disagreements within the ranks of the Rump about the future of Ireland were tied up in the reluctance of the army rank and file to serve across the water, and the different perspectives which those at the core of power brought to their task in 1649. In May the *Moderate Intelligencer* was pushed into starting a whole series of editorials on the rightness of Irish reconquest, not because of external opposition to the regime, 'the rather because in discourse, the same Queries have been put by some very active and eminant in the present Government'.[39]

38 ibid, no. 22, 3 Sept. 1650, punctuation added.

39 *Moderate Intelligencer*, 2 May 1649, BL E552(26). Unfortunately, there is some confusion about the political persuasions of those who expressed doubts about the role of the army in Ireland. Army Council minutes suggest it may have been New Model stalwarts, Cromwell and Whalley, who were anxious: see Norah Carlin, 'The Levellers and the conquest of Ireland in 1649', *HJ* 30 (1987) pp.269–88, 276. I am grateful to Dr Carlin for help on these points.

At the same time as his vitriolic attacks on the Scots were going to the presses, Henry Marten was drafting a pamphlet on Ireland. With the end of the first civil war, the presbyterian-dominated parliament had turned its attention to the conquest of Ireland. A vital secondary motivation behind sending the army to Ireland was to reduce its ability to radicalize politics in England. The parliament decided that now was the time to dispatch the lord deputy, Lord Lisle: Marten's pamphlet was designed as an attempt to influence the policy which Lisle would implement on behalf of his masters in Whitehall. Marten called on the Irish to lay down their arms and on the English to negotiate. It cannot be said that he altogether opposed the reconquest of Ireland, for Lisle was to use force if the Irish refused a cease-fire, but he came very close to it:

> He that would state the quarrell in Ireland upon religion & thinkes this way to make all Christendome a protestant is descended sure from those gallant ancestors that ly buryed in Palestine whither they were carryed with a fervent desire to recover the holy land & beat the wholl world into Christianity.[40]

The arguments against the disbandment and dispersal of the New Model Army in Ireland which had been used in 1646 were dusted down at the end of the second civil war and reappeared wearing much the same garb. In 1647 disbandment had been a way of silencing an increasingly fractious, uppity and politicized army. In 1649 the army was less vocal, but it had established a tradition of direct political intervention which the Rump was anxious to forestall. Central government felt that the soldiers had fulfilled their role in influencing policy. The continuing war in Ireland provided both a useful way of ridding England of unpaid, under-resourced and mutinous soldiers and of demonstrating to Ireland and the world the new rigour of the Commonwealth military. The soldiers who opposed the posting in Ireland attempted delaying tactics, calling for full payment of their arrears before embarkation. Some went as far as to oppose the posting altogether. They had fought for freedom of conscience, they declared: how could they now impose anglicization on the Irish?[41] This implication behind the most extreme viewpoint, put forward by Leveller-influenced soldiers who had looked to Henry Marten for support, was that recognition of 'England's liberties' ought to imply

40 Marten Loder MSS, Brotherton Library, University of Leeds, box 78/11.

41 Carlin, 'Levellers and the conquest of Ireland'; C. Durston, ' "Let Ireland be quiet": opposition in England to the Cromwellian conquest of Ireland', *History Workshop Journal* 21 (Sept. 1986), pp.105–12.

a parallel 'Irish liberty'. It is difficult to find an individual at the centre of government in 1649 who had a similar concept of Scottish liberties.

THE CROMWELLIAN CONQUEST

The view taken by the leadership of the army was often directed by Oliver Cromwell, supposedly a servant of the state, albeit an influential one, but one who has come to overshadow the historiography of the Commonwealth regime.[42] Accounts of his career prior to 1653 or 1654 have been tinged by hindsight. Aware of the emergence of the Protectorate, Dow was led to talk of a 'Cromwellian Scotland' which began in 1651 and Barnard of 'Cromwellian Ireland', starting in 1649, more than four years before the general officially gained supreme power.[43] Those who provided the extra-parliamentary support to the republicans, such as Edmund Chillenden, Edward Sexby, Maximilian Petty and John Wildman, had always questioned the grandees' political intentions and those of Cromwell in particular. The leaders of the republican state had also learned to mistrust him, but army support had been necessary in order to bring about the coup of December 1648, and the state continued to need Cromwell and the army while the Engagers and the kirk party in Scotland and Ormond and the confederates in Ireland were waging war against the Commonwealth.[44] It is important to gauge how far Cromwell's military influence in Ireland and Scotland was able to incline government policy.

Cromwell displayed a difference of approach towards Scotland and Ireland. He regarded Scotland as a nation overly fond of presbytery and thus limited by legalistic formalities. It was also in

42 Recent studies include R.C. Richardson (ed.) *Images of Oliver Cromwell* (Manchester, 1993); J.-P. Poussou, *Cromwell: La Révolution d'Angleterre et la guerre civile* (Paris, 1993); B. Coward, *Cromwell* (London, 1991).

43 F.D. Dow, *Cromwellian Scotland, 1651–1660* (Edinburgh, 1979); T. Barnard, *Cromwellian Ireland* (Oxford, 1975). B. Levack in *The Formation of the British State: England, Scotland and the Union, 1603–1707* (Oxford, 1987), hardly mentions the republic, and it does not appear in the index except as it is subsumed within the Protectorate.

44 Though, admittedly with hindsight, they still did not trust Cromwell: see Edmund Ludlow, *The Memoirs of Edmund Ludlow*, ed. C.H. Firth (2 vols; Oxford, 1894), II, pp.241–2.

open rebellion. However, Cromwell's personal philosophy was so tied to his faith and was so shaped by religious concerns, that it was also important that the Scots were protestants, misled and misinterpreting, but fundamentally godly. There was 'such a witness amongst them, as if it work not yet there is that conviction upon them that will undoubtedly bear fruit in time'.[45] It was Cromwell who pressed that policy towards Scotland should combine military might with a policy of political persuasion, designed to separate the ultra-protestant Protester party from the royal cause.[46] There was plenty of evidence that the Scots could be divided, for as Robert Baillie lamented, 'It wer to be wished that men of all sydes wald now learne to deny themselfs, if they would approve their former professions for Religion, King, Countrey'.[47] The fall of the kirk faction in 1651 resulted in a vacuum in Scottish politics which sucked in ever increasing draughts of monarchism and during that summer Charles II of Scotland was 'stronger than at any other time since his accession'.[48] During 1651, therefore, the conditions of Scottish politics changed in a way which was to have repercussions in Whitehall. The factionalism of Scottish politics enabled the English forces to turn the tide in their favour. With the kind of irony in which the Commonwealth was often double bound, at the same point at which the monarchism of Scottish politics peaked, the radical republicanism of 1649 collapsed. When the Commonwealth leaders ought to have been able to rally England to republicanism because of Charles's power and the fear of invasion, military success became important for its own sake and not for the political consequences that accompanied it. With it came a revival of the army commanders' opportunity to influence civilian affairs and they drew in civilian allies. The year 1652 saw the rise of different characters. Republican sympathizers, who had been alienated from politics in England by the events of December 1648 and January 1649, were encouraged by the sort of military success that could be achieved by a republican government to re-enter the political arena.

45 W.C. Abbott, *Writings and Speeches of Oliver Cromwell* (4 vols; Cambridge, Mass., 1939), II, pp.275–468, esp. 'To the General Assembly of the Kirk of Scotland', pp.302–3.

46 *The Remonstrance of the Presbyterie of Sterling against the present conjunction with the Malignant Party to the Commission of the Kirk at St Johnstons* Edinburgh 4 Feb. 1651/2, BL E623(1); Dow, *Cromwellian Scotland*, p.9.

47 Laing (ed.) *Letters*, III, p.69.

48 Dow, *Cromwellian Scotland*, p.10.

With parallel irony, at the point at which Charles's power was at its zenith, Scottish resistance collapsed. The divisions within Scottish politics, and especially the failure of the zealous religious factions to work with those whom they regarded as malignant, enabled the general and his forces to transform what had previously looked like a losing position into a heroic conquest.[49] Dissension within the Scottish ranks allowed Cromwell the mighty victory at Dunbar, followed by a rout of the combined royalist forces at Worcester. Such victories, apparently guided by the merciful hand of God, contributed to a private reputation which Cromwell had previously not enjoyed. The New Model Army as a whole had been lauded, but the victories at Dunbar and Worcester personalized the glory.

Cromwell regarded the Irish as rebellious papists and beyond recall. He was at the head of a mission to avenge innocent protestant deaths during the civil wars, and to stamp out the supposedly pernicious influence of the catholic priests. The English general's legacy in Ireland was the massacres of Drogheda and Wexford. He regarded the routs as a just judgment on the wilful resistance of such 'barbarous wretches'. Drogheda was the verdict of God on the anti-Christian practices of the catholic Irish:

> It is remarkable that these people, at the first, set up the mass in some places of the town that had been monasteries; but afterwards grew so insolent that, the last Lord's day before the storm, the Protestants were thrust out of the great Church called St. Peter's, and they had public mass there: and in this very place near one thousand of them were put to the sword.[50]

Cromwell and his fellow soldiers tended to view their battles in sectarian terms: Scotland had provided them with a moral dilemma: protestant against protestant. The soldiers who went to Scotland were acutely aware of the fact that they were fighting co-religionists, who had formerly been their allies.[51] Ireland was a far clearer case of good versus evil. Cromwell and Marten illustrate the priorities with which different sections of the English ruling classes viewed the problems of the three kingdoms. Cromwell's famous maxim was

49 Dow, *Cromwellian Scotland*, p.8; D. Stevenson (ed.) *The Government of Scotland under the Covenanters, 1637–1651* (Edinburgh, 1982), p.xxxii; Sir Archibald Johnston of Wariston, *Diary of Sir Archibald Johnston of Wariston*, ed. D. Hay Fleming (Edinburgh, 1919), p.26.

50 Abbot, *Writings and Speeches*, II, pp.127, 128.

51 J.P. Kenyon, *The Stuart Constitution* (1st edn, London, 1966), *Declaration of the army of England upon their march into Scotland to all that are saints, and partakers of the faith of God's elect, in Scotland*, 19 July 1650, 'out of our tenderness towards you, whom we look upon as our brethren, and our desire to make a distinction and separation of you from the rest'.

'I had rather be overrun with a Cavalierish interest [than] of a Scotch interest; I had rather be overrun with a Scotch interest than an Irish interest; and I thinke of all, this is most dangerous'.[52] Marten regarded the royalists as the greatest threat; the Irish, the least.[53]

For those who were primarily republicans, the religious standpoints of the Scots and the Irish were of importance, but as Ferguson pointed out, political differences proved more decisive than religious ones.[54] Nevertheless, the altercations about political policy towards Scotland and Ireland were about the political consequences of differing attitudes towards religion. Compare two statements by republican supporters of the Commonwealth. The former is by Cornet John Baynes. In the early 1650s he was a junior officer fighting with the New Model Army, but when the Rump was reinstated in 1659, he was to become Receiver-General of the Revenues in Scotland and was cited as a leading republican plotter the following year. His opinion of Scotland was that 'the Kirk and the Cavalier cannot endure one another . . . the latter is more rationally convinced'.[55] Like many of these republicans, he would rather have dealt with monarchists, whose position was diametrical to his. They came from the same starting-point, were concerned with the same issues, and thus were more comprehensible than those, such as the calvinists, whose values he could not understand. Henry Marten's spies, operating within the royalist court in France, where Ormond and Inchiquin were active for the Stewart cause, reported that 'nothing can undo [the Irish] but by L[ieutenant] G[eneral] Iretons giving them conditions of favour for their religion which will make an end of that quarrel'.[56] The difference

52 William Clarke, *The Clarke Papers*, ed. A. Woolrych (2 vols; 1992), II, p.205; Gentles, *New Model Army*, p.351.

53 Marten Loder MSS, Brotherton Collection, University of Leeds, box 78/12: 'The Kings rebellion in England was farr more high then that of y<e> Irish rebells . . . much more daungerous (being within our bowells) more uniust . . . more chargeable'.

54 Ferguson, *Scotland's Relations*, p. 135.

55 The brother of the Yorkshire captain, Adam Baynes, whose career was also one of a spectacular riser and was another whose initial success was temporarily halted by republican opposition to Cromwell: see G.E. Aylmer, *The State's Servants: The Civil Service of the English Republic, 1649–1660* (London, 1973), pp.233–4 and *passim.*

56 Marten Loder, MSS, Brotherton Collection, University of Leeds, box 67/122. Research is coming to show that the anonymous letters and those which carried an alias, which were sent to Marten from France, were penned by Edward Sexby. I am grateful to John Smith of Durham University, whose work on the Fronde in Bordeaux unearthed this discovery.

between these two approaches was that in Scotland it was the vanquished who refused to let the issue of religious homogeneity slip from the agenda; in Ireland, the Rump were prepared to allow limited toleration for catholicism in order to secure an overriding allegiance to the state.

FACTION AND SETTLEMENT

This comparison was also evident in the respective Acts of Settlement for Scotland and Ireland. The settlement for Scotland of February 1652 was for a union of the commonwealths, designed to protect individual liberties and thus religious toleration. The lands of those who had been in opposition to the state were to be confiscated, but those who declared loyalty to the English regime were to be spared. The power of the Scottish landed classes was to be neutralized, for the republicans viewed Scotland as a society of over-mighty aristocrats, who had long had designs on English noble land. As Marchamont Nedham reviled both in 1650, 'there's not a Royalist in England but dream of an office (*Sir Reverence*) . . . if his nose be not put out of joynt by Some hot-metalled *Laird*, or *nine peny Scotchman*'.[57] The Scottish settlement would therefore free the lesser orders from the 'vassalage, and oppressions' of their lords. Representatives of the saints in Scotland were to be consulted as to the nature of the settlement. This description of the Act represented a considerable softening of the proposals at first offered by the leaders of the republican regime. Edmund Ludlow complained 'how great a condescension it was in the Parliament of England to permit a people they had conquered to have a part in the legislative process'.[58] The original plan had envisaged the confiscation of Scottish lands without compensation and control of the land by the state. Gradually, the potentially swingeing effects of the Act were ameliorated. The land was given to officers, and in most cases eventually found its way back to its original owners. The sympathetic attitude towards the Scots was continued and

57 *Mercurius Politicus* 5 p.65, 4–11 July 1650, in Jeffs, *English Revolution III: Newsbooks 5*, p.81.

58 Ludlow, *Memoirs* p.310, where Ludlow was convinced that the Scottish settlement had been pressed on the English parliament by ambitious grandees. Quotation cited from pp.298–9.

confirmed by the Cromwellian Act of Grace and Pardon, issued in 1654, by which only twenty-four Scottish lords were to lose their estates. Those who had opposed closer ties between England and Scotland during the 1640s were forced, by the nature of Scottish resistance and the need to send in the army to make the victory complete and the humiliation total, to a settlement in which Scotland was bound in total submission to the English state. Those who acted out their policy of conquest were anxious to reward the past cooperation which common sainthood had bestowed and pressed for continued mutual involvement in the framing of the vanquished's submission.

The passage of the Irish Act of Settlement worked in reverse. The Commonwealth commissioners, three out of four of whom could be described as republican supporters of the regime,[59] had pressed for relatively generous terms to be offered to the Irish rebels as an incentive to submit and turn state evidence against their fellows. This tactic was repeatedly opposed within the highest ranks of the New Model Army as evidence that there was a 'general aptness to leniency with this enemy'.[60] In line with the policy suggested by Marten's spy, relatively flexible terms were held out to the Irish, provided that they were prepared to recognize their allegiance and leave the fledgling republic in peace. The first draft of the Act of Settlement for Ireland, in April 1651, named only nine Irish lords liable to the severest punishment. The army pressed for blanket retribution, since 'these barbarous, cruel, murthers [were in] generall joined in and since justified by the whole nation'. By April 1652, after heavy lobbying from within the army and consequent changes of personnel on the relevant committee, the number of named Irish rebels had mushroomed to 104.[61] With the dissolution of the Rump, control of the Irish and Scotch Committee in Barebone's parliament fell to the army officers. It was they who proposed that the catholic Irish should be cleared from the areas which they wanted for themselves and sent to the barren lands of Connaught and Clare.[62]

59 The commissioners were Edmund Ludlow, Miles Corbet, John Weaver and John Jones. Only the last of these could be described as a sceptic about the Commonwealth government, being one of those influenced by Welsh evangelicalism and, in 1654, a supporter of Cromwell.

60 Ludlow, *Memoirs*, I, pp.512–13.

61 Commissioners for Ireland to Sydney, 23 Oct. 1652, in R. Dunlop, (ed.) *Ireland under the Commonwealth*, II (Manchester, 1913), p.290.

62 S. Barber, 'Irish undercurrents to the politics of April 1653', *Historical Research* 65.4 (1992), pp.315–35.

The process by which the treatment of Scotland was gradually ameliorated, and that towards Ireland became more uncompromising, reflected the shift in power-relations and ideologies going on within the Commonwealth regime. During the years 1649 to 1651 the republican radicals were in power. Marten, Chaloner, Pyne, Ludlow, Grey of Groby and their acolytes dictated the direction of policy and were concerned with the mechanisms by which the republican ethos that powered the new regime could be encouraged on a wider scale. Men such as Marten and his supporters within the Leveller movement were anxious to give some substance to phrases which had acted as rallying calls during the 1640s and which had now to become more than empty rhetoric. They had to provide a practical demonstration of the implications of 'English liberties', 'the sovereignty of the people' and 'the people's representatives'.

The complexities of relations between England and Scotland and Ireland had ramifications for this policy which stretched far beyond the bald declarations of war by former allies like Ormond and Argyll. A continuing war north of the Tweed and beyond the Irish Sea necessitated an executive committee to oversee hostilities. The civil wars of 1642 to 1648 had witnessed the growth of the powers of the Committee of Both Kingdoms to become the centralized Derby House Committee. In 1649 the Derby House committee was replaced by the council of state, meeting in Derby House. The most important and interconnected functions of the council of state were to 'oppose and suppress whomsoever shall endeavour or go about to set up or maintain the pretended title of Charles Stuart' and to prevent all tumults and insurrections.[63] As such, an executive body was created which undermined the representativeness of the Commons. Moves were made to try to increase the accountability of the council, but these, such as rotating the chair, were soon abandoned for reasons of impracticality. The army rank and file, which had looked to Marten and his associates in its campaign to stop the grandees' march to power, believed that the new government was tarred with the same brush as that of the Stewarts. The mechanisms that were necessary to perpetuate the War of the Three Kingdoms were similar to those which the agitating soldiers had found distasteful during the war in England. The former

63 Gardiner, *Constitutional Documents*, pp.381–3. At this stage, prior to the declaration of Charles Stewart as king, the crucial role of Scotland was not mentioned in this Act. The Commonwealth was at pains to remind the world that Scotland was a foreign country.

fighters, who referred to themselves as the 'five small beagles', hunted the foxes which they had unearthed in Newmarket and Triploe Heath to the corridors of power at Whitehall. Now they were railing against 'the introduction of an absolute platform of Tyranie, long since hatched by Ireton; for it was he who first offered the expedient of Government by way of a Councel of State. . . . But no sooner was this Monster born into the world, but it devours up half the Parliament of England, and now it is about adorning itself with all Regal magnificence'.[64] The councillors were 'Tyrants Triumphant'. Lilburne, Prince and Overton, who had announced the death of parliamentary government as soon as the army stepped into the political arena, were disappointed in the Commonwealth. The grandees had marginalized worthy parliamentarians, among whom they named Marten, Ludlow and Rigby, and after twice purging Westminster, they had set up their own mock parliament at Windsor, consisting of Cromwell, Fairfax, Ireton, Harrison, Fleetwood, Rich, Ingoldsby, Haselrig, Constable, Fenwick, Walton and Allen.[65]

The republican activists who had come to power on the back of Pride's Purge may well have lost their power as soon as the council of state was formed. It is less clear that the army grandees were able to gain power by creating the council. The overtly military nominations of Ireton and Harrison were rejected and the members of the council of state during the first three years of its life were overwhelmingly of the radical persuasion. The radicals were undoubtedly aided by war in the north and the west which kept the soldiers focused on military and not civil affairs, even though they were anxious to intervene to redirect the government's objectives.

When the wars in Scotland and Ireland came to a close, during the last months of 1651 and the first half of 1652, a change was underway, directly echoed by the changes that were being wrought to the Acts of Settlement for Scotland and Ireland. The generals were no longer engaged in combat, but were demanding a say in the structure of the peace. Thus they re-entered the political arena with gusto. The policy of conquest over Scotland was giving way to a

64 Robert Ward, Thomas Watson, Simon Graunt, George Jellis and William Sawyer, *The Hunting of the Foxes from New-Market and Triploe Heaths to Whitehall, by Five Small beagles, late of the Army*, Th.21 March 1649, BL E348(7), p.8.

65 *Tyrants Triumphant or the High Court of State*, 669.f14(47), Lilburne, Overton, Prince, *The Picture of the Councel of State, held forth to the Free People of England*, 28 March 1649, BL E550(14).

revival of the idea of incorporation into the Commonwealth. Ironically, this was partly as a result of the success of the military conquest. There was a fresh confidence in the idea of a republic and men returned to government who had kept a low profile following the execution of Charles and the rebuilding of authority. The policy which had sent out the army to do the service of the state, thus taking them away from political interference, returned to haunt the leaders on the council of state. The army was anxious to recover its arrears of pay, primarily in the form of the reallocation of Irish land. In Scotland, the movement was away from the contemptuous ribaldry of 1649 and 1650 and towards a fresh recognition of the Scots' ultimate dignity. Scotland was more suited to a commonwealth than conquest, according to Algernon Sidney, one of those who returned to government during 1652.[66]

A UNIONIST CONCLUSION?

To a large extent, it is not possible to piece together the type of administration that the Rump envisaged for Scotland[67] and Ireland. The continuation of the war in the north and the west made it impossible for it to act without reference to the neighbouring countries, so the dream of a proud, independent and stable republic was stymied. The need to carry on the fighting made it impossible to implement anything. The respective histories of Scotland and Ireland provided the republicans with an excuse for a hardline attitude towards the former and a certain sympathy towards the latter. The Commonwealth downgraded the religious issue, since it was more important to them that the peoples of Ireland and Scotland lived in peaceful allegiance to a republican regime, under which, they rather naively believed, individual liberties would be protected. It would be to state the point too forcefully to say that they found catholicism less offensive than presbyterianism, but at least catholicism had the advantage of being the faith of the underdog. It was a negative way of looking at it, but the presbyterians were more heinous offenders against liberty. The republicans had tasted life under calvinism. The most radical of them could justify repressing the Scots, not because of their

66 J. Scott, *Algernon Sidney and the English Republic* I (Cambridge, 1988), p.100.
67 C. Stanford Terry (ed.) *The Cromwellian Union* (Edinburgh, 1902), p.xvii.

religion, but because their religion dictated an anti-republican, anti-libertarian stance. The presbyterians, and particularly the calvinist nobility, had actively demonstrated their hostility to republicanism. As Ludlow put it, the Scots 'by publick protestation bound themselves to impose that government upon us, which we had found necessary to abolish'.[68] It was less easy to justify repression of the Irish on religious grounds: the Irish were calling for liberty of conscience.

In its Bill for a New Representative, the Rump decided that thirty MPs from Scotland and thirty from Ireland should sit in the new parliament. Modern historiographical studies have concluded that the qualifications for voting which the Rump had envisaged would have barred all but the most dedicated supporters of the republic from participation in the franchise. It would seem likely that the same qualifications would apply to the conquered nations.[69] As such, Ireland and Scotland were part of a redivision of landed and political power from which the Cromwellians complained they were excluded. It is difficult to see how this type of union would have benefited the newly integrated countries. It is also a matter of conjecture how the union of commonwealths would guarantee their liberty, except in the most negative sense that those who accepted the regime and signed an oath of loyalty would be entitled to all of the rights enshrined in the constitution, while everybody else would not.

Within the republican junto which never achieved a representative number of members, there was sharp disagreement over union. The main difference in approach hinged on the motivation behind its introduction. The dominant strain of English nationalism which characterized the early Commonwealth, including hatred of the Scots and ambivalence towards Irish reconquest, dictated that the Rump's reasons for union tended to be negative. Union was designed to impose the Commonwealths-men's will on Scotland and a modicum of peace in Ireland, but the Rumpers' paramount concern was their English republic. The Rump parliament failed to agree an Act of Union and implementation was left to the Protectorate.[70] Cromwell operated with a more intense dynamic. Union with Ireland would quicken the pace of catholic land-clearance, plantation, the propagation of

68 Ludlow, *Memoirs*, I, p.243.

69 B. Worden, 'The bill for a new representative', *EHR* 86, (1971), pp.473–96; A. Woolrych, *Commonwealth to Protectorate* (Oxford, 1982).

70 Levack, *Formation of the British State*, pp.9–10.

the gospel and social and legal reforms. Union in Scotland would glorify the idea of protestant ecumenicism and quicken the pace of Highland clearance. The Act of Union with Scotland, introduced by the Cromwellian Protectorate on 12 April 1654, made reference to a precedent established by the Rump, which had intended to unite the symbols of government and to call representatives to Westminster. Cromwell, however, went further, by abolishing feudal tenures and establishing a common economic and trading structure.

There was also a constitutional difference between the Commonwealthsmen – both of 1649 and of 1652 – and the Cromwellians. The former believed in creating structures that would prevent concentrations of power. They believed that voting should take place at regular intervals; offices must be regularly elected and magistracy subject to rotation. Union, which would draw Scotland and Ireland towards the centre of power did not fit this model any better than it fitted a concept of English national independence. However, as David Stevenson has pointed out, it created a seamless fit within the Cromwellian governmental framework, which operated by extending personal power to the periphery.

Republican experiments to dismantle personal power were reversed by the Lord Protector. The office of Lord Deputy of Ireland, abolished in 1651, was re-established in 1654. A council of state was established in Dublin in 1654 and in Scotland in 1655. Scotland was given a lord deputy in all but name. English authority was thus established in Scotland and Ireland at a very meagre return of sixty representatives in Westminster. According to Stevenson,

> the establishment of two outlying councils, replacing former parliamentary commissioners in both cases, seemed to imply a degree both of decentralisation and of recognition that more permanent and formal arrangements than in the past should be made for governing Ireland and Scotland separately from England. Furthermore, just as executive power had been to some extent concentrated in the hands of one man at the centre, the Lord Protector, so such individuals, subordinate to him, should be established in the peripheral capitals.[71]

In fact, Cromwell, by replacing the commissioners with councils and inviting sixty men to Westminster, was securing the ability of London to control Edinburgh and Dublin. The administrations of

71 D. Stevenson, 'Cromwell, Scotland and Ireland', in J. Morrill (ed.) *Oliver Cromwell and the English Revolution* (London, 1990).

Scotland and Ireland could hardly be said to be more responsive to the interests of local people as a result of Cromwellianization.[72]

The vitality of politics in Ireland and Scotland had brought down Charles I. Their facility for independent action, despite Stewart attempts at integration, had caused too many fissures in the royal regime. The attempt to assert power and orthodoxy was at the heart of both royal and Cromwellian policy. It was the defeats of Scotland and Ireland that confirmed Cromwell's reputation and contributed to the fall of the Commonwealth: maintaining control over the defeated territories was vital if Cromwell was to keep his prestige. The Commonwealth had not been a dress rehearsal for Cromwellian policies. Commonwealth politicians had been more concerned to consolidate control of England: they had had a hard enough struggle to establish a national republican interest. Retrenchment was part of the package when the majority of people in all three nations believed their very existence to be illegitimate.

72 Levack, *Formation of the British State*, p.202.

CHAPTER NINE

The origins of a British aristocracy: integration and its limitations before the treaty of Union

Keith M. Brown
University of Stirling

INTEGRATION, ANGLICIZATION AND XENOPHOBIA

Elite integration provides a useful means of exploring state formation in the early modern era. One reason for the success of the British state in the eighteenth and nineteenth centuries was the homogenization of the aristocracies of the constituent parts of the state.[1] However, there is a tendency among historians to exaggerate the pace of the process and to underestimate its complexity; the experience of Wales is instructive in underlining just how long it took before even elite integration was successful.[2] In Scotland there is no doubt that by the early nineteenth century the aristocracy was thoroughly integrated with its English counterpart; it might even be appropriate to describe the peerage as anglicized, and it was positively supportive of the British state. What is less clear is the extent to which the experience of regal union – the period between 1603 and 1707 – eroded the Scottish identity of the aristocracy and predisposed it towards the idea of a British state. In other words, did a significant degree of elite integration take place before the formation of a British state, in the halfway house of the regal union?

1 L. Colley, *Britons: Forging the Nation 1707–1837* (London, 1992). While Colley does argue that there was a strong popular side to the development of a British identity, there is little doubt that the process was encouraged by the elites.
2 P. Jenkins, *A History of Modern Wales 1536–1990* (London, 1992), pp.57–77.

In spite of the early optimism of James VI and I and his unionist supporters, the period between the Union of the Crowns in 1603 and the outbreak of the Covenanting revolution in 1637 demonstrated that Anglo-Scottish union was unlikely to proceed much beyond the initial sharing of a Stewart monarch. The king's great project for a union of parliaments collapsed due to opposition in both kingdoms.[3] While there was intergovernmental cooperation on matters such as the policing of the borders, Ulster and the western highlands of Scotland, and while there was some mixing of the privy councillors of the two realms, the governments of England and Scotland remained distinct. Efforts by James VI and I and Charles I to employ the church as a means towards drawing these two kingdoms closer together had some success, but ultimately had the effect of driving the Scots towards revolution and causing the disintegration of the multiple monarchy in Britain.[4] There was some progress towards the creation of a British aristocracy grouped around the court, but even here the 'union of hearts and minds' towards which King James had worked was of little substance. By the 1630s there were Scottish noblemen who had points of contact with English and Irish noble families, and had something of a nascent British identity, but even among those who were most comfortable in this surrounding, men like the third marquis of Hamilton, the pull of roots remained strong. Outside of a court where anglicization was insignificant and a sense of Britishness was underdeveloped, the great majority of Scottish noblemen was largely untouched by English influences, or by notions of a British identity.[5] Furthermore, the court aristocracy was out of touch with feelings in Scotland, and it proved wholly ineffective in preventing the surge of national outrage which overwhelmed Charles I in 1637–41.[6] Among Irish noblemen, the second earl of Antrim was,

3 B.P. Levack, *The Formation of the British State: England, Scotland and the Union 1603–1707* (Oxford, 1987); B. Galloway, *The Union of England and Scotland 1603–1608* (Edinburgh, 1986).

4 D.G. Mullan, *Episcopacy in Scotland: The History of an Idea, 1560–1638* (Edinburgh, 1986); W. Makey, 'Presbyterian and Canterburian in the Scottish revolution', in N. Macdougall (ed.) *Church, Politics and Society in Scotland, 1408–1929* (Edinburgh, 1983), pp.151–66.

5 K.M. Brown, 'Aristocracy, anglicisation and the court, 1603–37' *HJ* 36 (1993), pp.543–76. For an exhaustive study of a Scottish courtier who was not anglicized, see J.J. Scally, 'The political career of James, third marquis and first duke of Hamilton (1606–1647) to 1643', (Cambridge University, Ph D thesis, 1993).

6 K.M. Brown, 'Courtiers and cavaliers: service, anglicisation and loyalty among the royalist nobility', in J. Morrill (ed.) *The Scottish National Covenant in its British Context 1638–1651* (Edinburgh, 1990), pp.155–92.

like Hamilton, able to project different images of himself as tribal chief or British aristocrat depending on whether he was at home or at court.[7] The impact of colonization on Ireland, creating a new wave of English and Scottish elites who were in competition with the native Irish and Old English elites, created a fragmented Irish aristocracy, but one which did, nevertheless, find some common Anglo-Irish identity.[8] As for the English, while a greater number of noblemen acquired Irish lands than previously, and some embraced Scottish in-laws, the notion that these aristocrats were anything other than English would have been regarded as insulting.[9] By the time political crisis broke in the summer of 1637 elite integration was in decline from the high-point of James VI and I's early years, and the experience of the next two decades did little to convince people to halt that retreat.

During the 1640s and 1650s the absence of a British royal court removed the single biggest catalyst towards integration. However, the experience of fighting in British civil wars and having to think about British solutions to political problems created new opportunities for contacts to be made. The military involvement of the Scots in the north of England is reflected in a number of Anglo-Scottish marriages such as those between the earl of Leven's daughter and a Northumberland gentleman in 1642, and his son and a sister of the earl of Carlisle, whose own father had been a Scottish immigrant in the reign of James VI and I.[10] There were, however, few marriages between the victorious governing elites of the two kingdoms in the 1650s. One of Oliver Cromwell's nieces married Sir William Lockhart, who was then appointed ambassador to France, but the Protectorate court was an English institution in which the only Scottish office-holder was Sir Oliver Fleming whose

7 J.H. Ohlmeyer, *Civil War and Restoration in the Three Stuart Kingdoms: The career of Randal MacDonnell, Marquis of Antrim, 1609–1684* (Cambridge, 1993).

8 N. Canny, 'The formation of the Irish mind: religion, politics and Gaelic Irish literature 1580–1750', *P&P* 95 (1982), pp.91–117; N. Canny, 'Identity formation in Ireland: the emergence of the Anglo-Irish', in N. Canny and A. Pagden (eds) *Colonial Identity in the Atlantic World 1500–1800* (Princeton, NJ, 1987), pp.159–212.

9 The question of national identity does not even arise in L. Stone, *The Crisis of the Aristocracy 1558–1641* (Oxford, 1965).

10 *The Scots Peerage*, ed. J.B. Paul (9 vols; Edinburgh, 1904–14), V, p.378; *The Complete Peerage*, ed. G.E. Cockayne (13 vols; London, 1910–59), VII, pp.617–18. Leven's successor as commander of the army of the covenant, David Leslie (Lord Newark in 1660) was another Scottish nobleman who found a wife among the daughters of the Yorkshire gentry, as did his nephew, James Leslie, third Lord Lindores: Leslie, *Scots Peerage*, VI, pp.440–2; *Complete Peerage*, IX, pp.505–6; Lindores, *Scots Peerage*, V, p.385; *Complete Peerage*, VIII, p.3.

'Scottish birth exposes him to the present unpopularity of his whole nation'.[11] The defeated royalist communities produced a handful of marital alliances such as that in 1657 between John Campbell of Glenorchy and Mary Rich, the daughter of the first earl of Holland,[12] or in 1659 between John Murray, second earl of Atholl, and Amelia Stanley, daughter and heiress of the executed seventh earl of Derby.[13] Therefore, interaction between English and Scottish noblemen throughout the middle decades of the century was not limited to that of a military nature and other examples of marriage, residence and political involvement can be found. However, the Scottish invasions of England in the 1640s convinced the English of the need to keep the Scots out of their affairs, and the earl of Clarendon rightly observed that by 1647 the whole of England had 'a great detestation of the Scots'.[14] At the same time the military occupation of the 1650s left many Scots resentful of their neighbours, and as English garrisons were withdrawn from towns like Stirling the mob attacked the soldiers screaming 'kill the rogues, kill the rogues'.[15]

It is against this background of deep-seated prejudice that one can approach the last five decades of the regal union. Andrew Marvell appealed for 'No more discurse of Scotch or English race', but his sentiments found little favour in either kingdom and seemed old-fashioned in the more aggressively nationalist England of the later seventeenth century.[16] The gravest threat to a British identity always had come from the 'notoriously xenophobic' nature of the English, particularly in London.[17] That fear of foreigners was a common refrain throughout the century whether those aliens were the Scots in the 1600s, the Irish in the 1640s, or the Dutch in the 1690s. For example, around 1684 an anonymous Whig scribbler gave vent to this anxiety with the hope that

11 C. Hill, *God's Englishman* (Harmondsworth, 1975), p.145; R. Sherwood, *The Court of Oliver Cromwell* (Cambridge, 1989), p.89.

12 *Scots Peerage*, II, pp.203–5; *Complete Peerage*, II, pp.290–2.

13 *Scots Peerage*, I, pp.473–5; *Complete Peerage*, I, pp.315–16.

14 E. Hyde, Earl of Clarendon, *History of the Rebellion* (6 vols; Oxford, 1888), IV, p.307.

15 F. Dow, *Cromwellian Scotland, 1651–1660* (Edinburgh, 1979), p.276.

16 Marvell also wrote in 'The Loyal Scot' that 'The world in all it does but two nations bear,/ The Good, the Bad, and those mixed everywhere', *Andrew Marvell: The Complete Poems* (Harmondsworth, 1972), pp.185, 189.

17 R.M. Smuts, *Court Culture and the Origins of a Royalist Tradition in Early Stuart England* (Philadelphia, Pa, 1987), p.287.

Scotch Vermin, *Irish* Frogs, *French* Locusts: all
That swarm both at *St James* and Whitehall;
Though now advanced to all trust, all command,
All offices enjoy by sea or land,
Shall, when this sun is set, no more appear
Within the confines of our hemisphere.[18]

In the later seventeenth century many Englishmen continued to view the Scots with something approaching hysteria, as avaricious and aggressive bigots who threatened England and its interests. A 1667 memorandum criticizing Clarendon's Irish settlement argued that the Irish should be preferred to the Cromwellian settlers as the latter had proved unable to stem the flow of Scots 'so numerous, so needy, and so new to Ireland, so cunning, close and confederated that some of our statesmen apprehend they may soon possess themselves of the whole island'.[19] As always, there was the picture of the Scottish nobleman as poor, grasping and mercenary, a caricature not entirely without foundation because of the problem that Scots faced in overcoming a disadvantageous exchange rate. Sir Edward Seymour made the well-known jibe in January 1700 that a union with Scotland would be like a man marrying some poor woman, and consequently 'if he married a beggar he should have a louse for a portion'.[20] Clearly little had changed since Sir Anthony Weldon had made his notorious attack on Scotland during the reign of James VI and I.[21] This kind of arrogance was reinforced by ignorance of a country that was less familiar to the English than Ireland and visited even less often by English noblemen than it had been in the earlier seventeenth century when royal progresses had taken them there. By the reign of Queen Anne a leading English politician, Robert Harley, was admitting that he knew 'no more of Scotch business than of Jappan'.[22]

18 'The Metamorphosis', in *State Poems; Continued . . . to This Present Year 1697* (London, 1697), pp.159–60.

19 *CSP Ire 1666–69* ed. R.P. Mahaffy (London, 1908), p.558. Even if this was a deliberate piece of scaremongering the point is that the official who wrote it believed the picture he was presenting was credible.

20 G.P.R. James (ed.) *The Vernon Letters* (3 vols; London, 1841), II, p.408. Not surprisingly 'This the Scotch have heard and are very angry'. However, comparative wealth was often a matter of perception, and the comment that 'The nobility . . . are poor, weak, and destitute of authority' was made by Magalotti of the English nobility in 1668, *Lorenzo Magalotti at the Court of Charles II: His Relazione d'Inghilterra of 1668*, ed. W.E.K. Middleton (Waterloo, Canada, 1980), p.20.

21 Sir A. Weldon, 'A perfect description of the people and country of Scotland', in W. Scott (ed.) *The Secret History of the Court of James the First* (2 vols; Edinburgh, 1811), II, 75–89.

22 W. Ferguson, *Scotland's Relations with England: A Survey to 1707* (Edinburgh, 1979), p.210.

MARRIAGE AND THE FAMILY

One very obvious way in which this prejudice and ignorance might be broken down was interracial marriage. Integration through marriage had been one of James VI's hopes for the regal union, but the peerages of all three kingdoms remained conservative in their marriage patterns. Only three English peers (1.9 per cent) married an Irish or Scottish wife during 1600–69, and between 1670–1759 that figure rose only to thirty-six marriages (5.8 per cent).[23] However, a sizeable minority of Scottish peers did find wives in England over the course of the seventeenth century. While there were fluctuations in the rate of these marriages, the overall pattern is fairly steady with an average of around one marriage per year, a total of ninety-six for the period 1603–1707. The relatively small numbers involved and the fact that the dates of a number of marriages are uncertain make any close analysis of marriage patterns highly problematic, but the rate of Anglo-Scottish marriages was at its greatest before 1642, when almost a quarter of all marriages involving Scottish peers or their heirs were to English brides, and at its lowest between 1642 and 1660.[24] After 1660 there was an increase in the rate of these British marriages, and between the Restoration and the treaty of Union forty-one Scottish peers or heirs of peers married Englishwomen.[25]

In the mid- and later seventeenth century a number of Scottish families that had moved into England and the English marriage market in the reign of James VI reinforced their new identity. The Bruce family further entrenched themselves in England with a marriage in 1646 between Robert, second earl of Elgin, and a daughter of the first earl of Stamford. In 1676 the son and heir of this marriage, Thomas, third earl of Elgin and second earl of Ailesbury, married Elizabeth Seymour, heiress to the duke of Somerset. With an English grandmother, mother, wife and all six of his sisters married to English gentlemen, the anglicization of Elgin's family was complete.[26] Commenting on the fifth duke of Lennox in

23 J. Cannon, *Aristocratic Century* (Cambridge, 1984), pp.87–8. In 1603 the number of peers in the two kingdoms was roughly the same, but by 1700 the Scots constituted less than 10 per cent of the total number of peers in Britain: ibid, pp.31–2.

24 By 1700 the Scots peerage numbered 135 in a total of 1,546 peers throughout Britain: ibid, pp.31–2.

25 In addition, 15.7 per cent of the daughters of Scottish peers married an Englishman in the period 1690–1740: ibid, p.88.

26 *Scots Peerage*, III, pp.478–80; *Complete Peerage* I, pp.58–60.

1668, Magalotti wrote, 'his family became English about sixty years ago', and the last of the Scottish estates were sold off to one of Queen Anne's doctors in 1703.[27] This process of absorption into the English aristocracy was repeated in a handful of other cases, such as the earls of Stirling, Dysart and Newburgh. However, in all these cases the family had little territorial stake in Scotland, and had ceased to play any role in Scottish affairs long before the end of the century. They had, in effect, gone native.

The post-Restoration courts also threw up opportunities for aristocratic elites to meet and form relationships and alliances shaped by the political and economic circumstances of the new era. After 1660 the major territorial interests in Scotland were represented by the heads of the Murray, Campbell, Gordon, Douglas and Hamilton families, all five of whom formed English marriage alliances during this period. The examples of two of these families, the Campbells and Hamiltons, gives an indication of the British dimension to their marriages. In 1678 Archibald Campbell, Lord Lorne, eldest son and heir to the earl of Argyll, married Elizabeth Tollemache, daughter of Sir Lionel Tollemache of Helmingham in Suffolk and his Scottish wife, Elizabeth Murray, countess of Dysart. Their son, John, second duke of Argyll, married an English lady in 1702, Mary Brown, daughter of John Brown of St James's, Westminster. The principal Campbell cadet, John Campbell of Glenorchy, also contracted English marriages for himself and his son.[28] In 1687 James, earl of Arran, heir to the third duke of Hamilton, married Anne Spencer, eldest daughter of Robert Spencer, second earl of Sunderland, in an alliance that cost the latter £2,000 (sterling). Following her death, Arran married another English woman around 1689, this time a daughter of the fifth Lord Gerard who eventually brought Arran substantial estates in Lancaster. Arran's younger brothers also found English wives. In 1695 George, earl of Orkney, married a daughter of Sir Edward Villiers, knight marshall of England. Elizabeth Villiers had been King William's mistress, and the Hamilton family objected to this particular English match, but George replied that 'there is no doubt she has a blot but she has a merite capable to wash that away'. The merit was her social connections and an income estimated at between £800 and £1,000 (sterling) per year. In 1701

27 Magalotti, *Relazione*, p.116; W. Fraser, *The Earls of Cromartie* (2 vols; Edinburgh, 1876), I., p.224.

28 *Scots Peerage* I, pp.368–76; II, pp.203–5; *Complete Peerage*, I, pp.205–08; II, pp.290–2.

another brother, John, earl of Ruglen, married as his second wife Elizabeth Hutcheson, who was the daughter of a Nottinghamshire gentleman and the widow of John, Lord Kennedy.[29] Similar patterns of marriage into the English aristocracy are found among the Murrays, Gordons and Douglases.[30]

As can be seen in the Hamilton cases, financial considerations played a big role in choosing a bride, and an English marriage could bring a substantial sum of sterling. Only very rarely, as in the Hamilton–Gerard alliance, did marriage allow Scots to gain access to English estates. John Campbell of Glenorchy's opportunism in 1657, when he married Mary Rich, daughter of Henry, first earl of Holland, eventually brought this highland laird both wealth and considerable social cachet. Glenorchy rose to become earl of Breadalbane in 1677, and his eldest son, John, married Frances Cavendish, daughter of Henry Cavendish, second duke of Newcastle.[31] Yet if the general impression is of Scots noblemen on the hunt for English heiresses, the bargaining did not always go their way. In December 1667 John Middleton, first earl of

29 *Scots Peerage*, IV, pp.383–4; VI, pp.578–80; VIII, pp.361–2; *Complete Peerage* VI, pp.266–9; IX, pp.106–9; XI, pp.230–1. Details of the Hamilton–Spencer marriage contract are found in a letter from the duchess of Hamilton to her daughter, Lady Murray, SRO NRA 234/29/I/5/42. For George Hamilton's letter, SRO NRA 234/29/I/7/177–9.

30 The 1659 marriage between the second earl of Atholl and Amelia Stanley produced a number of children, of whom Charles Murray, first earl of Dunmore, married (without his father's permission) an English heiress, Katherine, daughter of Richard Watts of Great Munden, Hertfordshire. A daughter of Atholl's also married in England, *Scots Peerage*, I, pp.473–5; III, pp.383–7; *Complete Peerage*, I, pp.315–16; IV, pp.542–3. Dunmore met his wife at court where Katherine's grandfather, Colonel Werdyn, was controller of the duke of York's household, *Chronicles of the Atholl and Tullibardine Families*, ed. John Murray, seventh duke of Atholl (5 vols; Edinburgh, 1908), I, pp.181–2. The great north-east Gordon clan made its way into the English marriage market in 1676 when George, fourth marquis of Huntly, married Elizabeth Howard, daughter of the duke of Norfolk, uniting the two leading catholic families in Britain. However, the marriage ended in a legal separation in 1707. Huntly's kinsman, John, Lord Strathnaver, heir to the earl of Sutherland, married as his second wife Catherine Tollemache, another of Sir Lionel Tollemache's daughters. For Gordon, *Scots Peerage* IV, pp.549–51; *Complete Peerage*, VI, pp.3–4: Sutherland, *Scots Peerage*, VIII, pp.353–5; *Complete Peerage*, XII, pt 1, pp.559–61. Among the Douglases, a younger son of the marquis of Douglas, George Douglas, first earl of Dumbarton, married a daughter of Sir Robert Wheatley of Bracknell in Berkshire. However, political leadership of the Douglases passed to the Queensberry house and the heir of the first duke of Queensberry, James, Lord Drumlangrig, married Mary Boyle, daughter of the Anglo-Irish peer Viscount Dungarvan in 1685, *Scots Peerage*, III, pp.216–17; VII, pp.140–3; *Complete Peerage*, IV, p.515; IX, pp.694–6.

31 *Scots Peerage*, II, pp.203–7; *Complete Peerage*, II, pp.290–2. Following the death of his first wife, Breadalbane's son remarried in 1695 to Henrietta Villiers, another daughter of Sir Edward Villiers.

Middleton, married Lady Martha Carey, a daughter of the late earl of Monmouth, having agreed that he would settle all his Scottish estates in trust for his new wife and any male issue of the marriage, thus disinheriting Lord Clermont, his son and heir by a previous marriage. However, if he purchased lands within forty miles of London worth £40,000 (sterling) then Clermont would inherit the Scottish estates.[32] Yet not all these marriages were cold, calculated arrangements. Amelia Stanley recorded in her diary on the day of her marriage to the earl of Atholl on 5 May 1659 that 'I was made the hapiest creature alive in being maried', and the warm correspondence between these two people over the next forty-four years suggests that they remained very much in love.[33]

It is doubtful if the wider interpretation of nationality created by the judgment in Calvin's case in 1608, when the English judges decided that subjects of James VI and I born after the Union of Crowns had rights of naturalization in any and all of his kingdoms, made a great deal of difference to how people felt about their national identity. However, for some individuals who were the product of a mixed marriage and who were born in England, that identity was probably more perplexing. The two eldest sons of the Atholl–Stanley marriage, John and Charles, were born in 1660–1 at Knowsley in Lancashire, the principal residence of the Stanley family. In the 1680s and 1690s three of the children of Charles Murray and his English wife were born in Whitehall and another three in St James's Palace. The eldest, if not all the children, were baptized in St Martin-in-the-Fields church, close to the court in central London. But an English marriage was not a straightforward route to anglicization. Nine of Amelia Stanley's children attained adulthood, of whom seven married Scots, including her eldest son and eldest daughter. In spite of his early exposure to English influences, John Murray, first duke of Atholl, married a Scottish wife, lived on his Perthshire estates, carved out for himself a career in Scottish politics, and opposed the treaty of Union.[34] Anna,

32 G.H. Jones, *Charles Middleton: Life and Times of a Restoration Politician* (Chicago, 1958), pp.9, 11. For examples of other Anglo-Scottish marriage contracts see SRO GD 25/iv/1/2/5/775 for an article of agreement on 9 November 1698 between John Kennedy, seventh earl of Cassillis and Mary Fox, daughter of the late John Fox of St Giles-in-the-Field (and a high-class whore) and GD 25/iv/1/1/18/108a for the articles of agreement followed by a marriage contract on 15 June and 5 September 1698 between John, Lord Kennedy, and Elizabeth Hutcheson, daughter of Charles Hutcheson of Outhorp, Nottinghamshire.

33 SRO NRA 234/1687.

34 *Scots Peerage*, I, pp.473–5; III, pp.383–7; *Complete Peerage*, I, pp.315–16; IV, pp.542–3.

duchess of Buccleuch, was twice married, both times to an Englishman, but when it came to finding a wife for her grandson in 1720, she wrote to her agent in Edinburgh about one prospective bride, 'I think her person verie agreeabill, and my great projectt of having my grandson no stranger to his own country, is in all liklyhood not to be disapointed by marying a Scotts lady'.[35]

One reason that Anglo-Scottish marriages were less important in changing aristocratic society in Scotland was that, as in the earlier seventeenth century, many of the Scottish peers who married Englishwomen were entering a second or third marriage and already had an heir. Consequently, the children of these marriages were less important than those of earlier Scottish marriages, and indeed many of these unions were issueless, reflecting the older age of the partners. Besides, the common assumption in early modern society was that a wife would take on the values and identity of her husband. The only Scottish peers with English fathers were Henry Scott, earl of Deloraine, son of the duke of Monmouth, and Lionel Tollemache, third earl of Dysart. The overwhelming majority of the issue of mixed marriages had Scottish fathers and English mothers. Within the group of some thirty-one Scottish peers with English mothers the process of integration was carried one step further in that thirteen of them married Englishwomen, but this is a very small number and only four peers came into this category in 1707.[36] The balance of status also made it more likely that the children of these parents would be brought up as Scots. Between 1603 and 1707 only nine daughters of English peers or their heirs gave birth to sons who inherited or were created Scottish peers. It is not very surprising to find that William Boyd, first earl of Kilmarnock, was no different from the provincial nobility of the west of Scotland simply because his mother was English. She was Catherine Crayke, the daughter of a York citizen who had been disinherited by his father, a pedigree that pales into insignificance beside that of the Boyds who had held their peerage since the mid-fifteenth century and had a longer noble ancestry.[37] Nor is there much evidence that these English wives played the role of the eleventh-century Queen Margaret, introducing the Scots to more 'civilized' English manners and fashions. Elizabeth Howard, duchess

35 W. Fraser, *The Scotts of Buccleuch* (2 vols; Edinburgh, 1878), II, p.372.

36 The four peers with English mothers and English wives were the first earl of Dunmore, the fifth earl of Stirling, the second duke of Argyll and the sixth earl of Abercorn (who was Irish by descent and birth).

37 *Scots Peerage*, V, pp.172–3; *Complete Peerage*, II, p.263.

of Gordon, sent her friend Mary, countess of Traquair, a secret recipe for Sanatifera, and on another occasion described how to make a 'leaden plaister' that was in her opinion 'the best in Britain'.[38] Such housewifery was unlikely to threaten Scottish culture. Hiberno-Scots marriages produced even fewer multinational families, although Mary Moore, daughter of the first earl of Drogheda, produced the third Lord Bellenden and the fourth and fifth earls of Dalhousie in her two Scottish marriages.[39] However, the Abercorn branch of the Hamiltons did maintain a court presence in England, retained an interest in Scotland, and was well established as major Irish landowners who had married into the Anglo-Irish aristocracy.[40]

EDUCATION AND CULTURE

When Francis Vernon recorded Ralph Montagu's ambassadorial entry into Paris in the spring of 1669, he wrote 'with my lord, of *English* gentlemen, the principal were my Lord of Rochester, Lord Arlington, the Marquis of Huntly, and Lord Clermont'.[41] Obviously it never occurred to Vernon that two of this party were Scots. This pressure to become Englishmen and to conform to the cultural norms of the south of England was particularly prevalent among the court aristocracy. John Dryden enthused that 'if any ask me whence it is that our conversation is so much refined, I must freely, and without flattery, ascribe it to the Court', but the very low profile of Scots at court greatly reduced its role as a cultural trendsetter.[42] The slow spread of English among the nobility and gentry of Wales, most of whom continued to speak Welsh down to 1700 – it took three generations of earls of Pembroke to become Englishmen – is a significant demonstration of the fact that even with political control of a culture that lacked its own universities and whose bardic tradition was in steady decline, it took time to change the language of its elites.[43] In Ireland it again proved difficult to make

38 W. Fraser, *The Book of Carlaverock* (2 vols; Edinburgh, 1873), II, p.163.

39 *Scots Peerage*, II, pp.72–3; III, p.101; *Complete Peerage*, II, p.99; IV, p.32.

40 *Scots Peerage*, I, pp.40–59; *Complete Peerage*, I, pp.2–6.

41 Jones, *Middleton*, p.12; my italics.

42 G. Parry, *The Seventeenth Century: The Intellectual and Cultural Context of English Literature, 1603–1700* (Harlow, 1989), pp.117–18.

43 Jenkins, *History of Modern Wales*, pp.57–77; W.O. Williams, 'The survival of the Welsh language after the union of England and Wales: the first phase, 1536–1642', *WHR* (1964), pp.69–93.

much headway, although something like an Anglo-Irish Protestant identity was in the making by the later seventeenth century.[44] Yet there is little evidence to suggest that the Scottish nobility was culturally anglicized. Scottish accents, like those from Wales, Ireland and the English regions, continued to draw English criticism until the late eighteenth century when an entrepreneurial Irish dramatist, Richard Sheridan, was able to make money teaching English pronunciation to the Scottish nobility. Furthermore, the correspondence of the aristocracy was peppered with Scots vocabulary and grammar, although there is no doubt this was decreasing. The duchess of Buccleuch, who was given to quoting old Scots proverbs in the letters she wrote home from London, was aware of the linguistic choices she faced. In one letter to Sir George Mackenzie, Lord Royston, about a land purchase on which he was advising her, the duchess wrote 'I own I long (that is Inglish), but I green (that's Scotts) to hear more of this proposell'.[45] In preserving their linguistic identity, the Scots' own commitment to an impressive educational system was crucial, and aristocratic parents of the later seventeenth century were little different from earlier generations in preferring Scottish schools and universities to those in England. If a spell of further education was required, they were more likely to send their sons to Holland rather than bother with Oxbridge. Robert Dalzell, sixth earl of Carnwath, was one of the very few who attended Cambridge in the early 1700s,[46] while William Colville, third Lord Colville, appears to have been the only Scot to attend Trinity College, Dublin, where he died and was buried in 1656.[47] A number of Scots received honorary degrees, like the earl of Middleton, who was admitted to a MA at Oxford on 5 October 1663, no mean feat for a rough old soldier with little formal learning; Lauderdale received a LL D from Cambridge in 1676.[48] However, all this demonstrated was Oxbridge's willingness to ingratiate itself with powerful Scots. One or two noblemen were educated wholly or partly in England. Charles Murray, the son of the earl of Atholl, wrote from England to his mother around 1670, when he was about 9 years old, telling her of his studies under the

44 Canny, 'Formation of the Irish mind'; Canny, 'Identity formation in Ireland'; T.C. Barnard, 'Crises of identity among the Irish Protestants 1641–1685', *P&P* 127 (1990), pp.39–83.

45 Fraser, *Buccleuch*, II, p.387.

46 *Scots Peerage*, II, pp.415–17; *Complete Peerage*, III, p.51.

47 *Scots Peerage*, II, p.559; *Complete Peerage*, III, p.382.

48 Jones, *Middleton*, p.7; *Scots Peerage*, V, pp.303–6; *Complete Peerage*, VII, pp.488–50.

watchful eye of his aunt, Lady Dorchester,[49] and the anglicized fourth earl of Stirling sent his eldest son, Henry, to Eton in 1678.[50] In September 1693 John, Lord Murray, wrote to his wife about his efforts to find a suitable school for their son in England, informing her that he liked one in Hackney where it would be possible for the boy to hear the sermons of a Dr Bates. The school cost £15 0s 6d per quarter and included writing, dancing and French in its curriculum. Lord Murray went ahead and entered his son on the school roll, and he received a first progress report in January 1694.[51] However, this example is unusual; there is no doubt that the exposure of the Scottish aristocracy to an English education came long after the political union of 1707.

While the drawing power of London was considerable, absenteeism among the aristocracy was less common than one might expect. A handful of families did settle down permanently in England, the Alexander earls of Stirling, for example, were settled in the south throughout the latter half of the century.[52] Yet while two-thirds of English peers owned or leased property in London by the 1630s, very few Scots owned property there.[53] The Scottish aristocracy did not participate in the London building boom that followed the Restoration when the great town houses like Clarendon, Berkley and Burlington were erected. The second duke of Ormond bought a massive complex of rooms in St James's Square in 1682 for which he was congratulated by his son, who told this great Irish courtier 'how ill it would look now you are an English duke to have no house there'. Ormond's neighbours included a galaxy of English court and government officers like the earls of Conway, Devonshire, Suffolk, and even the vice-treasurer of Ireland, the earl of Ranelagh, but no Scots. London continued to attract Scottish architects: Sir David Cunningham's designs were among the best in prewar London, and pre-eminently there was Colin Campbell, author of *Vitruvius Britannicus*, who drew up plans for Archibald Campbell, earl of Islay, in the early eighteenth century. The house was never built, however, and the first Scottish aristocrat to erect his own palace in the city was the third duke of

49 SRO NRA 234/29/1/3a/4.

50 *Scots Peerage*, VIII, p.182; *Complete Peerage* XII, pt 1, pp.284–5.

51 SRO NRA 234/29/I/7/31.

52 *Scots Peerage*, VIII, pp.181–2; *Complete Peerage*, XII, pt 1, pp.282–5.

53 Smuts, *Court Culture*, pp.54–5; Brown, 'Aristocracy, anglicization and the court', pp.559–60.

Queensberry, work on whose house began in 1721.[54] Instead, most Scottish noblemen rented accommodation, and only a very few were fortunate enough to be given rooms at the crown's expense. In the 1660s Lauderdale had lodgings in the privy garden at Whitehall, but he also had Lauderdale House in Highgate and property at St Pancras. In addition, Lauderdale lived at Ham House out at Petersham, which had been granted in 1636 to his wife's father by Charles I.[55] In the mid-1680s the second earl of Middleton had a house at Winchester and another at Goodwood in Sussex, but unlike Lauderdale he had very little property in Scotland, and like most of those who had English property he belonged on the margins of the Scottish peerage.[56] Apart from London, there was little else to attract Scots to England, there being a perfectly adequate provincial centre in Edinburgh. The exception was perhaps Bath, which drew people from all over Britain to take the waters. The earl of Traquair was there in May 1706, but was a little disappointed to find that 'ther is but few of our country men here at present'.[57]

The overwhelming majority of Scottish noblemen did not spend much time in London at all, since it was too expensive and too far from their local political interests, estates and families, or from Edinburgh where their legal business was conducted. A journey to England continued to require a travel pass, such as that issued by Chancellor Aberdeen for Charles Erskine, fifth earl of Mar, on 28 August 1683, so that he could repair to court.[58] Getting to London remained a major problem as Lady Murray discovered in 1693 when she paid £12 (sterling) for two seats on what would be a long and bumpy coach ride from Scotland to London.[59] Complaints about the cost of living in London were commonplace. Lady Dundonald bemoaned this fact to her sister Lady Murray in a letter in July 1695;[60] a series of account books belonging to the earl and countess of Roxburghe between 1697 and 1703 amply demonstrates

54 In fact the work was begun by the earl of Darnley: C.S. Sykes, *Private Palaces: Life in the Great London Houses* (New York, 1986), pp.23–76, 80; S. van Raaij and P. Spies, *The Royal Progresses of William and Mary* (Amsterdam, 1988), pp.91–2.

55 SRO NRA 832A/i/54–5; SRO NRA(5) 832A.

56 Jones, *Middleton*, p.242.

57 Fraser, *Book of Carlaverock*, II, p.168.

58 SRO GD 124/10/411.

59 SRO NRA 234/29/I/7/36. She told her husband that she was trying to negotiate a share arrangement with some other ladies and book the entire coach at a cost of £30.

60 SRO NRA 234/29/I/7/154.

the cost of their travels to London, Bath and Scarborough.[61] One reason for this expense was the unfavourable 12:1 exchange rate and the commission charged on the exchange. In May 1678 the countess of Atholl's agent wrote to Sir Thomas Stewart of Grandtully asking 'iff you could afford hir the soume in Inglish money, it would bee a great kyndnes, for their is none to be had att Edinbrough, and it wold save the exchange, which is now six per cent'.[62] In January 1696 Lord Murray advised his wife that Scots money was acceptable as far south as Newcastle, but that she should buy up as much English coin as possible, even small denominations. Three months later she wrote to him from London, saying that the rate of exchange on Scots coin was so poor that she was at a loss for money.[63] The experience was far from unique, and when Lord Balcaskie wrote from Windsor in 1685 that 'I beginne to weary here allready, for money melts away lyke snow before the sun', he was voicing the frustrations of most of his countrymen.[64] In 1661 James, Lord Drummond, suggested that his brother John's money problems might be solved if he were 'to lower zour fancie and resolve to be a Scots mane' by returning home.[65] The fifteenth earl of Sutherland came to the same conclusion in 1705 after long service in the army and at court

> I have (I thank God) a competency to live a retired life upon, though the soldier trade by not being justly payed (the publicks not paying me), and being so much att court (London) hes impaired my fortune not a litle. Soe that now, unles to serve my queen, country, or freind, I resolve never to star out of Sutherland.[66]

Usually wives and children were left at home in order to reduce expenses, although this could result in husbands being sent a shopping list such as that received about 1671 by the earl of Atholl in which his wife asked him to buy serge for a bed and suggested he take a trip around the 'Indian shops when sometimes one may meete with prittie things and cheap'.[67] Cost and distance therefore made London prohibitive for all but the richest nobles, and the fact that Luttrell found the comings and goings of the 'Scotch' nobility

61 SRO NRA 1100/264–9.
62 W. Fraser, *The Red Book of Grandtully* (2 vols; Edinburgh, 1868), II, p.236.
63 SRO NRA 234/29/I/8/18; NRA 234/29/I/8/107.
64 Fraser, *Grandtully*, II, p.275.
65 Fraser, *Grandtully*, II, p.168.
66 W. Fraser, *The Sutherland Book* (2 vols; Edinburgh, 1892), II, p.200.
67 SRO NRA 234/29/I/3/21–2. Earlier on in their marriage it was the countess of Atholl who could be found living in London while her husband remained 'in this solitary please Bleare Castell' anxiously awaiting her return, NRA 234/29/I/3/3.

a matter worth noting in his diary suggests that they were not ordinarily in the city.[68]

Besides, there is no reason to suppose that noblemen particularly wanted to spend much time in London. The boom in country house building in Scotland and the investment in estate improvements and purchases there suggests otherwise.[69] Although she went south to marry some sixty years earlier, the duchess of Buccleuch continued to take a very keen interest in her Scottish estates in the 1720s. She had strong views on the improvements to Dalkeith Palace, advised on the choice of a schoolmaster – 'one qualifeed for the place as a scholar, and one who is not high floun upon any account' – or a chamberlain, and she intimated her willingness to increase ministerial stipends 'providing ther is no powr claimed by thos good men, but what they have a right to'. The duchess was also a very aggressive buyer in the land-market, joking with her agent that 'I find you are resolved to purches half Scotland. I own it will be for my cridet, when I am dead, that I have improved my esteat'. Yet that improving was seen within a traditional framework of mutual obligations and responsibilities, and the duchess opposed the introduction of new farming methods since 'I think it would rewin the tenants or else I am sure opress them, which I will never do'.[70] This was not the voice of the absentee court *rentier*. Nevertheless, the duchess of Buccleuch was an absentee, and was very conscious of and even embarrassed by it. In 1700, when finally she got around to planning a return to Scotland, she wrote that 'I am the greatest stranger ever waint to ther own countray'. She was also nettled by any suggestion that she was not interested in returning home: 'som popall has indevored to make it thought I never desir to be acquainted with my own countray'.[71] Instructions in testaments to return the bodies of the deceased to Scotland for burial similarly suggest that the pull of roots remained strong. Thus when the duke of Lauderdale died at Tunbridge Wells in August 1682, his corpse was embalmed at Ham

68 For example in February 1692 'Divers of the Scotch nobility are come to town to represent the present affairs of that kingdome to his magestie': N. Luttrell, *A Brief Historical Relation of State Affairs* (6 vols; Oxford, 1857), II, p.365; see also I, pp.175, 584; II, p.365.

69 I. Whyte, *Agriculture and Society in Seventeenth-Century Scotland* (Edinburgh, 1979), esp. ch. 5; J. Macaulay, *The Classical Country House in Scotland 1660–1800* (London, 1987), pp.1–54.

70 Fraser, *Buccleuch*, II, pp.372, 384–8.

71 Fraser, *Buccleuch*, II, pp.374, 376.

House before being transported home to Scotland.[72] Similarly, the eighth earl of Eglinton, who lived in Yorkshire for most of the time between the first of his English marriages in 1679 and his death in 1701, was buried in the family vault at Kilwinning.[73]

Not surprisingly, therefore, Scots were not greatly involved in court culture. The court of Charles II and his successors was an English court in which Scots played a minimal role as either patrons of or contributors to court culture. The smart set of the Restoration court – Buckingham, Rochester, Mulgrave, Dorset, Buckhurst and Sir Charles Sedley – were all English, and there were no significant Scottish poets or artists at court. Nor were Scottish noblemen inclined to patronize court culture, unlike the Irish duke of Ormond and his son, the earl of Ossery, who both patronized John Dryden, a leading exponent of the new English triumphalism. Lauderdale, by contrast, could be both crude and a philistine, complaining that 'he would rather hear a cat mew, than the best musique in the world'. Yet he was also a serious scholar, especially of history, and was rightly recognized as 'a man very national and truly the honour of our Scots nation for wit and parts'.[74] The only other Scot at Charles II's court to receive Magalotti's attention was the equally patriotic and brilliant Sir Robert Murray, one of the founder members of the Royal Society, a body that included John Hay, second earl of Tweeddale.[75] However, the Whiggish Kit Kat Club which played such a prominent role in artistic patronage in the 1700s had an entirely English membership, and it was increasingly the English aristocracy themselves in their clubs and country houses rather than the royal court that was shaping the dominant culture of Britain.[76] Yet given the opportunity to respond to a court culture defined by Scottish ideas, as occurred in Edinburgh during the duke of York's residence there in 1679–81, the Scots were enormously enthusiastic. Lord Wharton noted that 'all the Scotch nobility in London are preparing to go, I do not know of one that stays'.[77] Scottish pride in the revival of the Royal Company of Archers in 1676 and the Order of the Thistle in 1687,

72 Luttrell, *Brief Historical Relation*, I, p.215.

73 *Scots Peerage*, III, pp.452–4; *Complete Peerage*, V, pp.22–3.

74 M. Lee, *The Cabal* (Urbana, Ill., 1965), p.30. For Magalotti's comments, *Relazione*, pp.55–6.

75 Magalotti, *Relazione*, pp.46–7.

76 R.J. Allan, 'The Kit Kat Club and the theatre', *Review of English Studies* 8 (1931), pp.56–61.

77 Jones, *Middleton*, p.46.

and the redecoration of Holyrood Palace, indicate a desire to re-emphasize the Scottish origins of the Stewart dynasty.[78] At much the same time there was enormous enthusiasm in Scottish heraldry and ancestry, evidenced in the armorial registrations in the Lord Lyon's Court. Sir John Dalrymple of Stair's *Institutions of the Laws of Scotland* (1681) provided a self-confident, rational and philosophic basis for Scots Law, the legal system that in large measure defined the principles upon which landed power in Scotland was based. Edinburgh already was becoming a centre of scientific and medical excellence, the Advocates Library was founded in 1680, and there was a strong native emphasis on intellectual if not artistic achievement, in which the aristocracy played a useful role as patrons and participants.[79] There is little evidence that the trade boom of the 1670s brought with it an overwhelming influx of English ideas, tastes or fashions, and both French and Dutch luxury imports continued to be favoured.[80] Country house culture continued to place an emphasis on indigenous baronial styles, or was influenced by new ideas which were predominantly French or Italian in their origins. The best examples of the latter were expressed in the buildings of Sir William Bruce at Hopetoun House, an early Palladian construction that directly drew on Italian ideas, or the early work of William Adam.[81] In short, there was neither a crisis in confidence, nor a slavish following after the English, but instead the Scottish nobility remained rooted in their own culture, looking outward to Europe, and discerning in their attitude to what England had on offer.

OFFICE-HOLDING AND HONOURS

One attraction held out by the court and the English state was office and its rewards. The dominance which Scots had enjoyed at

78 H. Ouston, 'York in Edinburgh: James VII and the patronage of learning in Scotland, 1679–1688', in J. Dwyer, R.A. Mason and A. Murdoch (eds) *New Perspectives in the Politics and Culture of Early Modern Scotland* (Edinburgh, 1982), pp.133–55.

79 R. Cant, 'Origins of the Enlightenment in Scotland: the universities', in R.H. Campbell and A.S. Skinner (eds) *The Origins and Nature of the Scottish Enlightenment* (Edinburgh, 1982), pp.42–64.

80 This is a topic that requires much greater investigation, but for a taste of the enduring nature of French influences on Scotland see the Royal Scottish Museum's *French Connection: Scotland and the Art of France* (Edinburgh, 1985).

81 Macaulay, *Classical Country House*, pp.1–86; J. Gifford, *William Adam 1689–1748* (Edinburgh, 1989).

court throughout the first two decades of regal union could not be repeated after 1660, and contemporary narratives of court life, such as those of Magalotti or Grammond, scarcely mention any Scots at Charles II's court.[82] When Charles arrived in England from Breda he brought a household that included twenty-eight men of rank. All were English apart from Ormond and his two sons who provided the Irish contingent, and two Scots, Viscount Newburgh, who was appointed as captain of the guard, and Sir William Fleming, a gentleman usher. All seven of the duke of York's household servants were Englishmen.[83] The once very powerful bedchamber from which James VI and I's Scottish friends and servants exercised such influence was described by Edward Chamberlayne in 1677 as being staffed by 'the prime nobility of England'.[84] He was almost right. Lauderdale was the first Scot to be appointed a gentleman of Charles II's bedchamber, and the only others to gain access to what still was an influential and lucrative office were the earl of Arran in 1679 and the second earl of Middleton in 1682. The earls of Ossory and Ranelagh were the only Irish gentlemen of the bedchamber, and the one important court office not to be in English hands, that of lord steward, was held by Ormond. A scattering of Scots and Irish were found on the lower rungs of court office: the fourth earl of Roscommon was master of the horse to the duchess of York and captain of the gentlemen pensioners during 1674–7, while Charles, Lord Murray was master of the horse to Princess Anne.[85] James VII and II's court contained a few more powerful Scots like Melfort and Middleton, while Arran was retained in the bedchamber and in July 1687 James added the first earl of Dumbarton, one of his military cronies.[86] Under William II and III there were too many Dutchmen and English Whigs demanding rewards, but while the bedchamber was relatively cosmopolitan with Dutch, English, Irish (the earls of Arran and Cork), Scottish (the earls of Drumlangrig and Selkirk)

82 Magalotti, *Relazione;* A. Hamilton, Count of Grammond, *Memoirs of the Court of Charles the Second* (London, 1859).

83 Sir E. Walker, *A Circumstantial Account of the Preparations for the Coronation of His Majesty King Charles the Second* (London, 1820), pp.12–14.

84 E. Chamberlayne, *Angliae Notitiae* (London, 1677), p.154.

85 E.S. de Beer, 'A list of the department of the lord chamberlain of the household, autumn 1663', *BIHR* 19 (1942), pp.13–24; Chamberlayne, *Angliae Notitiae* (London, 1674, 1677, 1684); G.T. Beatson, *A Political Index to the Histories of Great Britain and Ireland* (Edinburgh, 1786), pt II, pp.1–25; Luttrell, *Brief Historical Relation,* I, pp.5, 215; R.H. Kearsley, *His Majesty's Bodyguard of the Honourable Corps of Gentlemen at Arms* (London, 1937), pp.233–4. A handful of Scots and Irish names appear among the grooms of the bedchamber.

86 *CSP Dom James II,* I, pp.38, 101, 148, 577, 616, 678, 1382, 1484, 1800: II, pp.120, 1,441–2; III, p.130; Luttrell, *Brief Historical Relation,* I, pp.408–9.

and a French member, no court offices went to Scots or Irishmen.[87] Anne's court was dominated by English Tory families and the Scottish presence was reduced to two doctors. It was little wonder that Godolphin wrote to the earl of Seafield in 1705 that 'as to the argument of English influence, how can the Queen but bee influenced by her English servants when she has no Scots servants near her person'.[88] The fact that from the early 1680s court offices were being cut back by financial exigencies meant there was even less likelihood of the Scots breaking into the circle of court families.[89]

Elsewhere in government there was little evidence of integration. The experiments in creating a British parliament in the 1650s did little to foster a desire for union between England and Scotland, and the small number of Scottish and Irish members of the Commonwealth and Protectorate parliaments were so obviously agents of the English government – many in fact were Englishmen – that the very idea of union was discredited by the experience.[90] After 1660 no Englishman holding a Scottish peerage attempted to vote in the Scottish parliament.[91] In spite of the earl of Rochester's complaint that the English Cavalier parliament was 'a Parliament of Knaves and Scots' there were in fact very few Scottish members.[92] Between 1660 and 1690 only thirteen members of the English House of Commons were Scottish peers or their sons, but most of these men were Englishmen or very anglicized Scots. For example, Charles Kerr, second earl of Ancram, who was returned for Mitchell in 1647, Thirsk in 1660 and sat five times for Wigan between 1681 and 1685 had an English mother, resided at Kew, was related to the earl of Derby (whose patronage secured the Wigan seat) and at

87 Chamberlayne, *Angliae Notitiae* (London, 1694) pt 1, pp.209–76; (London, 1700), pp.485–522; Beatson, *Political Index*, pt 2, pp.1–25; Luttrell, *Brief Historical Relation*, I, pp.505, 568; Raaij and Spies, *Progresses of William and Mary*, pp.17–18.

88 R.O. Bucholz, 'The court in the reign of Queen Anne' (University of Oxford, D Phil thesis, 1987), pp.123–4. The duchesses of Queensberry and Ormond were members of the all-female bedchamber, but the former was Irish and the latter English.

89 Bucholz, 'The court in the reign of Queen Anne', pp.1–39; E.A. Reitan, 'From revenue to civil list, 1689–1702: The revolution settlement and the "mixed and balanced constitution"', *HJ* 13 (1970), pp.571–88. By the reign of George I there were thirty posts worth over £1,000 (sterling) per year and another 100 worth over £200 (sterling) per year: J.H. Beattie, *The English Court in the Reign of George I* (London, 1967), p.5. The court was also becoming more socially exlusive: ibid, p.153.

90 P.J. Pinckney, 'The Scottish representation in the Cromwellian parliament of 1656', *SHR* 46 (1967), pp.95–114; J.A. Casada, 'The Scottish representation in Richard Cromwell's parliament', *SHR* 51 (1974), pp.124–47.

91 Landless English peers had been disqualified in 1640, and a similar measure was passed in 1704: R.S. Rait, *The Parliaments of Scotland* (Glasgow, 1924), pp.185–7.

92 C.V. Wedgwood, *Poetry and Politics under the Stuarts* (Cambridge, 1960), p.151.

various times he served as a justice of the peace in nine different English counties. By contrast he had no land or interests in Scotland.[93] During these three decades another thirty-one Members of Parliament (MPs) were sons of Irish peers, although in their case the English identity was even stronger.[94] There is little evidence that these men brought a British dimension to Westminster, or that they had much individual impact, although Lauderdale took some part in the House of Lords and the second earl of Middleton and the half Scottish Viscount Preston were appointed by James VII and II to manage the House of Commons in 1685.[95] After the Revolution there was a reduction in the number of Scots or Irish MPs at Westminster.[96] When the Scots did return in 1707, they found that they were so small in number – forty-five in the Commons and sixteen in the Lords – and so despised by English Members that the best way to make the system work in their interests was to play the role of crown lobby-fodder expected of them.[97]

While there had been some overlap in the personnel of the three privy councils of the British Isles during the reigns of James VI and I and Charles I, the institutions themselves had not been merged, and their independence was one of the weaknesses of the British monarchy.[98] After 1660 Clarendon argued for a Whitehall council containing English and Scottish councillors to handle Scottish affairs, and this body did wield considerable influence until his fall in 1667, after which meetings of councillors in London were more *ad-hoc* occasions from which the English were largely excluded.[99] The English privy council did at times consider Scottish

93 B.D. Henning, *The History of Parliament, the House of Commons, 1660–1690* (3 vols; London, 1983), I, pp.16–17; II, pp.677–8. For Ancram, *Scots Peerage*, V, pp.467–8; *Complete Peerage*, I, pp.132. The Wigan seat then passed into the hands of another of the Derby family's Scottish in-laws, Charles Murray, son of the earl of Atholl.

94 Henning, *History of Parliament*, I, pp.16–17.

95 Jones, *Middleton*, p.88.

96 In 1695 there were no Scots – although two English Members held Scottish peerages – and only a few Irish peers: *Members of Parliament return two orders of the . . . House of Commons* (3 parts, London 1878–1961), I, pp.572–8.

97 C. Jones, 'The "Scheme Lords, the necessitous Lords and the Scots Lords": the Earl of Oxford's management of the "Party of the Crown" in the House of Lords', in C. Jones (ed.) *Party and Management in Parliament 1660–1784* (Leicester, 1984), pp.12–51.

98 Brown, 'Aristocracy, anglicization and the court', pp.555–6; K.M. Brown, *Kingdom or Province? Scotland and the Regal Union 1603–1715* (Basingstoke, 1992), ch.1 for Scottish political institutions.

99 For example on 22 October 1683 Charles II sat along with the duke of York, who was something of an expert on Scottish affairs, nine Scots, and the earl of Sunderland, the sole Englishman, *The Register of the Privy Council of Scotland,* 3rd ser. ed. P.H. Brown et al. (Edinburgh, 1908–70), VIII, p.268.

affairs but it was careful to observe a due respect for the separation of powers and responsibilities. Thus in 1668 the English privy council's committee on trade, of which Lauderdale was a member, was authorized to discuss Scottish and Irish affairs, but 'only relating to either of those kingdoms as properly belong to the cognisance of the Council Board'.[100] However, while there had been no Scots on the English privy council in 1660, and Ormond was the only Irishman, some overlap of personnel between the different councils did develop. A few London-based Scots like the earls of Rothes, Lauderdale or Moray were co-opted on to the English privy council, and James VII and II had six Scots and three Irish members on his English council.[101] After 1688–9 there were no Scots on the English privy council, but the practice of appointing Scottish or Irish members was given tacit recognition in the 1701 Act of Settlement where it was stated that only native subjects of England, Scotland or Ireland could serve as English privy councillors.[102]

One obvious reason for the lack of career mobility between Scotland and England was the fact that Scots Law remained distinct. Therefore there was limited opportunity for Scottish officials to operate effectively outside their own native jurisdictions, unlike Welsh judges or lawyers who had no difficulty in practising in English courts. In Ireland too the common law was very close to that in England. However, Scotland's legal elite, which was overwhelmingly aristocratic, remained a potent patriotic interest determined to preserve the national identity of their own legal system from the kind of imperialism that the English were extending to Gaelic Ireland or in some American colonies.[103] Furthermore, while the English were enthusiastic in their efforts to extend the anglicization of the Irish administration and legal system into areas previously dominated by Gaelic norms, and were

100 J.P. Kenyon, *The Stuart Constitution* (Cambridge, 1966), p.483.

101 Kenyon, *Stuart Constitution* pp.478, 491; E.R. Turner, *The Privy Council of England in the Seventeenth and Eighteenth Centuries* (2 vols; Baltimore, Md, 1930–2), I, pp.375–6, 424–5, 428–9, 438; G. Davies, 'Council and cabinet, 1679–1688', *EHR* 38 (1922), pp.47–9.

102 Turner, *Privy Council*, II, p.102.

103 G. Donaldson, 'The legal profession in Scottish society in the sixteenth and seventeenth centuries', *Juridical Review* ns 21 (1976), pp.1–19; A. Murdoch, 'The advocates, the law and the nation in early modern Scotland', in W. Prest (ed.) *Lawyers in Early Modern Europe and America* (London, 1981), pp.147–63; N.T. Phillipson, 'The social structure of the faculty of advocates in Scotland, 1661–1840', in A. Harding (ed.) *Law Making and Law Makers in British History* (London, 1980), pp.146–56.

determined to keep the Scots out of Ireland,[104] Scotland was unpopular with English officials and lawyers during the 1650s and all vestiges of the colonial administration was expunged by the Scots after 1660.[105]

The Scots were no more welcome in English government where their numbers never again recovered to the pre-1642 levels, when the non-English personnel in Caroline government may have been as high as 10 per cent.[106] After 1660 it is difficult to find any Scots in the English treasury, secretary of state's department, board of trade or admiralty, other than very powerful figures like Lauderdale or Middleton.[107] Lauderdale served on a range of commissions and privy council committees, while Middleton became secretary of state for the north of England in 1684 and held the more influential office of secretary of state for the south in 1688. However, Middleton later expressed the view that such high offices in the English state should be held by capable Englishmen, familiar with the constitution and owning large English estates since 'all that told against me'.[108] There was a handful of middle-ranking officials like John Brisbane who worked his way up from the diplomatic service into the admiralty and by 1683 was secretary to the admiralty commission, but the number of Scots in what was a rapidly expanding bureaucracy was negligible.[109] Certainly there were too few to make any difference to the decidedly English tone of the state machinery. Even in the diplomatic service, an area of government that was British rather than English, the numbers of Scots was low, seven among the one hundred and eighteen men employed by the crown between 1660 and 1688, three under

104 N. Canny, 'Dominant minorities: English settlers in Ireland and Virginia, 1550–1650', in A.C. Hepburn (ed.) *Minorities in History* (London, 1978), pp.51–2; T.C. Barnard, 'Lawyers and the law in later seventeenth-century Ireland', *IHS* 28 (1993), pp.256–82.

105 Dow, *Cromwellian Scotland.*

106 G.E. Aylmer, *The King's Servants: The Civil Service of Charles I 1625–1642* (London, 1974), p.24. Predictably the numbers of non-English personnel decreased during the 1650s: G.E. Aylmer, *The State's Servants: The Civil Service of the English Republic 1649–1660* (London, 1973), pp.183–4.

107 J.C. Sainty, *Treasury Officials, 1660–1870* (London, 1972); J.C. Sainty, *Officials of the Secretaries of State, 1660–1782* (London, 1973); J.C. Sainty, *Officials of the Board of Trade 1660–1870* (London, 1974); J.C. Sainty, *Admiralty Officials 1660–1870* (London, 1975).

108 Jones, *Middleton,* p.271.

109 *Scots Peerage* VI, pp.427–8; G. Holmes, *Augustan England: Professions, State and Society, 1680–1730* (London, 1982), pp.239–61; J. Brewer, *The Sinews of Power: War, Money and the English State 1688–1783* (London, 1989).

William II and III, and six under Queen Anne.[110] It was in the armed forces that integration was most successful. Although Scotland and Ireland had their own military establishments, it was increasingly common for regiments from these kingdoms to be placed on the English establishment. Scottish officers like the first earl of Dumbarton already were prominent in James VII and II's army, but it was the massive increase in the size and role of the armed forces between 1689 and 1713 which accelerated the creation of a British army. At the battle of Blenheim in 1704 the duke of Marlborough commanded an army in which seven regimental colonelcies were held by Englishmen, five by Scots and four by Irish officers, while only half his general staff was English. The aristocratic officer corps in fact provided one of the most staunch pro-union interest groups in the Scottish parliament with eighteen of the nineteen serving officers voting for the treaty of Union.[111]

While a number of powerful Scottish courtiers held English county lieutenancies before 1642, and the Scottish localities were subject to English oversight in the 1650s, there was at a local level virtually no evidence of integration among English and Scottish office-holders after 1660. Again the Bruces can provide a model of how an immigrant Scottish family made its way into the upper levels of county society in Bedfordshire, where the second earl of Elgin variously held the offices of Member of Parliament, lord lieutenant, justice of the peace and *custos rotulorum*, but he was a third generation immigrant.[112] Less spectacularly the earls of Newburgh built up a minor influence in Gloucestershire after 1660, but again this is an example of an anglicized immigrant family doing well rather than a Scottish family straddling its interests in both kingdoms.[113] It is perhaps only with the expansion of Hamilton influence into Lancashire in the 1700s that one finds a Scottish

110 It was not until the first decade of George I's reign that the Scottish presence among British diplomats doubled to a more respectable 11 per cent of available postings: P.S. Lachs, *The Diplomatic Corps under Charles II and James II* (New Brunswick, NJ, 1965), pp.52–3, 189–202; D.B. Horn, *The British Diplomatic Service 1689–1789* (Oxford, 1961), pp.85–122.

111 I have discussed this at more length in K.M. Brown, 'From Scottish lords to British officers: state building, elite integration and the army in the seventeenth century', in N. Macdougall (ed.) *Scotland and War AD79–1918* (Edinburgh, 1991), pp.133–69.

112 *Scots Peerage*, III, pp.478–9; *Complete Peerage*, I, pp.58–9; *List of Lieutenants of Counties of England and Wales 1660–1974*, compiled by J.C. Sainty (List and Index Society, Special Series vol. 12, 1979), p.55.

113 *Scots Peerage*, VI, p.453; *Complete Peerage*, IX, p.514.

magnate with sufficient English lands to be appointed to local office.[114]

James VI and I and Charles I had been careful not to indulge in too generous mingling of the English and Scottish peerages, and by 1660 there was little remaining evidence of a mixed honours system.[115] Between 1660 and 1707 little attempt was made by successive monarchs to increase the integration of honours. Charles II dumped two of his bastards on the Scottish peerage (the duke of Buccleuch in 1663 and the duke of Lennox in 1675) and there were five other creations of Scottish peerages for Englishmen between 1661 and 1682.[116] Two more Englishmen bought Nova Scotia bannerets out of the 182 created between 1649 and 1707; as with the earlier batch in the 1630s, neither had any interest in Scotland but were looking for cheap honours.[117] Robert Bruce, second earl of Elgin, was raised to an earl in the English peerage in 1664 as earl of Ailesbury, but the only Scots to receive English peerages before 1707 were Lauderdale, who was created earl of Guildford in 1674, a title that died with him in 1682, and the second duke of Argyll, who was created earl of Greenwich in 1705, making him the only Scot with an English title at the time of the union.[118] The only Scots to be rewarded with a Garter knighthood

114 The fourth duke of Hamilton was appointed master forester and steward of Lancashire Forests in 1710: R. Sommerville, *Office Holding in the Duchy and County Palatine of Lancaster* (London, 1972), p.144.

115 Only two of those English titles granted to Scots were extant and both holders were descendants of Scottish immigrants in 1603: Thomas Bruce, first earl of Elgin, who had been created Lord Bruce of Wharton in 1641, and Charles Stewart, sixth duke of Lennox and third duke of Richmond. Of the seven English men and one woman who had been granted Scottish peerages, six titles remained extant at the Restoration, and most of the eighteen English title-holders of Scottish bannerets also remained extant: *The Complete Baronetage*, ed. G.E. Cockayne (7 vols; Exeter, 1900–9), II, pp.277–454; III, pp.324–52. Irish peers such as Lord Castlestuart, Viscount Montgomery and Viscount Clandeboye were all descended from Scottish planters, but in effect had gone native.

116 The five were Robert Spencer, Viscount Teviot in 1661, Henry Ingram, Viscount Irvine in 1661, Sir Thomas Osborne of Kiverton, Viscount Osborne in 1673, Charles Cheyne, Viscount Newhaven in 1681, and John Churchill, Lord Churchill in 1682. None of these men or their families had any connection with Scotland other than their titles: *Scots Peerage*, II, p.532; III, pp.301–2; V, p.13; VI, pp.466–7; VIII, pp.366–7.

117 *Complete Baronetage*, III, pp.324–52; IV, pp.242–448. They were John Pretyman of Lodington, Gloucestershire in 1660, and Sir Thomas Temple, Buckinghamshire in 1662.

118 Even after the union there was no flood of British peerages for Scots and those like Queensberry and Hamilton who were rewarded soon ran into English prejudices: G.S. Holmes, 'The Hamilton affair of 1711–12: a crisis in Anglo-Scottish relations', *EHR* 77 (1962), pp.257–82.

before 1707 were Lauderdale in 1672, the first new Scottish face to take up his stall in the order since 1633, the third duke of Hamilton in 1682, and the second duke of Queensberry in 1701, but there was never more than one Scot at a time in the order.[119] No Scots were made Knights of the Bath and the restoration of the Order of the Thistle in 1687 provided the crown with a means to reward Scots without intruding on the English honours system; of the twenty creations between 1687 and 1707 all but one was a Scot, the exception being the Irish peer Charles Boyle, fourth earl of Orrery.[120]

INTEGRATION AND UNION

What then of the accusation that unionists in the early-eighteenth-century Scottish parliament were an English interest? Contemporaries such as Andrew Fletcher of Saltoun who made this point actually meant that government ministers took their orders from the English ministers at court, in other words that they were placemen.[121] However, it might be useful to ask if they and their families had in fact been anglicized to the extent that their patriotic instincts were blurred by other loyalties and interests. What one finds is very unimpressive. Queensberry had an Anglo-Irish wife, was a Knight of the Garter, and had a long association with the court; Argyll had an English mother, an English wife, he was an English peer and his career was in the British army, while his brother, Islay, was born in England of the same mother; the earl of Sutherland was married to an Englishwoman, he had served in the army and his son was an officer at the time of the union; the earl of Dunmore had been born in England of an English mother, he in turn found an English wife, his children were all born in England, he had sat in the English House of Commons and at one time was a justice of the peace for Lancashire, he too had been a soldier and now had two sons in the army; the earl of Roseberry was married to the daughter of a Yorkshire gentleman; the earl of

119 N.H. Nicolas, *History of the Orders of Knighthood in the British Empire* (4 vols; London, 1842), I, lxv–lxxiii. Nor was there any great change after 1707 with only three Scots receiving this award before 1760: ibid, III, appendix A, xiv–xvii.

120 Nicolas, *Orders of Knighthood*, III, appendix A, xxxi–xxxii.

121 W. Ferguson, *Scotland: 1689 to the Present* (Edinburgh, 1975), p.39. See also W. Ferguson, *Scotland's Relations with England: A Survey to 1707* (Edinburgh, 1977), pp.197ff; P.W.J. Riley, *The Union of England and Scotland* (Manchester, 1978); P.H. Scott, *Andrew Fletcher of Saltoun and the Treaty of Union* (Edinburgh, 1992).

Deloraine was the son of the executed duke of Monmouth, his wife was an English lady, and he too commanded a regiment in the British army; the earl of Marchmont's eldest son, Lord Polwarth, was serving in the British army and had a Scots-Irish wife, while another son was married to a daughter of a Northumberland gentleman of Scottish extraction; and the Anglo-Irish earl of Abercorn was also a supporter of the union. This adds up to nine peers who were either sons of English mothers, married to Englishwomen, held a British court or military office, or whose sons held such an office, or held an English peerage or honour. The remaining forty peers who supported the union by voting for it had no discernible English connection. Furthermore, six peers who came into the same category as the above list voted against the union: the duke of Hamilton and his brother, the earl of Selkirk, the duke of Atholl, and the earls of Buchan, Home, and Strathmore all had English wives and other strong points of contact with England. One can safely conclude that not only was there very little evidence of anglicization in the Scottish parliament in 1706, but also at least in the case of birth, marriage, office (the exception being military office) and honours, such contacts with England did not even guarantee support for union.

Over the course of the seventeenth century, therefore, there were one or two families who were thoroughly anglicized, and a few experienced a degree of integration with the English aristocracy while retaining their Scottish identity. However, most Scottish noblemen and their families were brought into contact with England and English society that was transient and superficial; what Robert Evans, writing about the relationship between the national elites who mixed at the Habsburg imperial court in Vienna, described as 'juxtaposition not integration'.[122] Furthermore, since this chapter concerns those noblemen who did have some form of intercourse with the English, it is worth underlining that a great many, even of the peerage, had little or no involvement with England and the English. Powerful local families like the Cunningham earls of Glencairn were untouched by any form of observable anglicization, and the Ayrshire peerage as a whole remained very provincial without ever becoming irrelevant. In case after case, family papers turn up little evidence of interest in

122 R.J.W. Evans, 'The Austrian Hapsburgs: the dynasty as a political institution', in A.G.D. Dickens (ed.) *The Courts of Europe: Politics, Patronage and Royalty 1400–1800* (London, 1977), p.123.

England or contact with English people. This can be true even of politically prominent families such as the Erskine earls of Mar. The second earl of Mar was one of the handful of men who ensured that James VI's accession to the English crown went smoothly, and he was rewarded with English lands while he and his kinsmen were often to be found at the London court. Yet all the land was sold and within a generation the Erskines were back home. The extensive Mar archive for the latter half of the seventeenth century contains state and private letters, contracts, land transactions, testaments, genealogical material, legal and ecclesiastical records and other miscellaneous documents, almost none of which relates to England. Like so many other family archives, this one can be read with little sense of there being a regal union at all.[123]

What is clear is that the Scottish aristocracy retained a very strong attachment to their own national identity. A distinct aristocratic Scottish culture did not simply roll over and die in 1603, or even in 1707. The treaty of Union itself guaranteed that Scots Law, a Scottish education, the Presbyterian Church of Scotland and the heritable rights of the nobility would all continue to ensure that Scotland's aristocratic elite remained sufficiently distinct for Samuel Johnson to find material for his anti-Scottish jokes two generations later. Furthermore, after 1625 successive monarchs showed little interest in promoting integration among the different aristocratic elites of their British kingdoms. Forty years after leaving Scotland to marry the duke of Monmouth, the duchess of Buccleuch wrote in 1720, 'tho' I have lived the greatest part of my life in England, you see I am not croupted so as to love any part of the worald so well as my native country. The Scotts hart is the same I brought to England, and will never chang, as I find by long expirience'.[124] That experience was shared widely in the aristocratic society in which she moved.[125]

123 SRO GD 124/1–4. A brief examination of the family correspondence in almost any of Sir William Fraser's volumes reveals a similar lack of interest in or contact with England. See e.g. W. Fraser, *The Annandale Family Book of the Johnstones* (2 vols; Edinburgh, 1894).

124 Fraser, *Buccleuch*, II, p.382.

125 Compared to my investigation of elite integration in the early seventeenth century this chapter is less deeply researched, and I would not be surprised if a later and more thorough inquiry turned up additional evidence of Scottish activity in England. Certainly the question of aristocratic economic interests in England needs to be explored, particularly if the Alien Act is to be fully understood. However, I think that the broad argument I have presented here, that the aristocracy was not anglicized and was only superficially integrated, is on the right tracks.

CHAPTER TEN

Scotland and Ireland in the later Stewart monarchy

Toby Barnard
Hertford College Oxford

Historians of seventeenth-century England, while investigating the Stewarts' composite monarchy, have recently stumbled on Scotland and Ireland. Earlier analysts of the 'War of the Three Kingdoms' in the 1640s, such as S.R. Gardiner, understood the interdependence of events in the three countries. Thus in 1884 Gardiner wrote, 'the connection between Irish history of 1643 and the English is very close and ought to be brought out in any story of the English civil war', and then proceeded to do so.[1] The enthusiastic conversion of some late-twentieth-century scholars to what has long been axiomatic for most who write on early modern Scotland and Ireland, and was once common to historians of Stewart England – that their histories gain from British, European or Atlantic contexts – is not all profit. Sorties into seventeenth-century Scotland and Ireland, valued in proportion as they unravel the 'British problem', can perpetuate a patronizing anglocentrism. Moments when Scotland or Ireland impinged dramatically on England, as before and during the civil wars, overshadow the longer periods of irritable but unsensational co-existence. Yet between 1689 and 1691, when Ireland was battled over by James VII and II, William III and Louis XIV, the fact that this struggle remained a war of three kings rather than of three kingdoms meant that it did not detain the interrogators of the British problem for long.[2]

1 R.M. Gilbert, *The Life of Sir John T. Gilbert* (London, 1905), p.308; S.R. Gardiner, *History of the Great Civil War* (3 vols; London, 1886–91); S.R. Gardiner, *History of the Commonwealth and Protectorate, 1649–60* (3 vols; London, 1894–1901); C.H. Firth, *The Last Years of the Protectorate, 1656–58* (2 vols; London, 1909–10).

2 For example W.A. Speck, *Reluctant Revolutionaries: Englishmen and the Revolution of 1688* (Oxford, 1988), esp. pp.14–15 and n.25.

More surprisingly, although historians argue about the intentions of Charles II and James VII and II – whether simply for greater authority, arbitrariness or absolutism – the evidence of their activities in the two smaller kingdoms has been enlisted only intermittently.[3] Similarly, some but not all grand schemes for comprehending Hanoverian England, as an awesome 'fiscal-military' state; as a polite and prospering society; as a confessional state in which the ideology and experience of protestantism, skilfully transmuted into 'Britishness', assisted unity; or as an *ancien régime* akin to those throughout Europe, have been tested in Scottish and Irish conditions. Keith Brown has also warned lest the craze for British history revitalize the history of the English state.[4] Regrettably, in reverting to such traditional staples as constitutional relationships, the politics and politicization of elites and the military organization of the separate kingdoms, we miss what has lately been achieved in the local histories of Scotland and Ireland: the exact and sensitive reconstruction of society and economy, together with the investigation of collective and individual mentalities.[5] Moreover, despite strictures to the contrary, historians of Scotland and Ireland have been readier than 'British historians . . . to apply the insights on state formation' offered by analysts of continental monarchies.[6]

3 J. Childs, '1688', *History* 73 (1988), pp.399–423; G.S. Holmes, *The Making of a Great Power: Later Stuart and Early Georgian Britain 1660–1722* (London, 1993); R. Hutton, *Charles II* (Oxford, 1989); J. Miller, 'The potential for "absolutism" in late Stuart England', *History* 69 (1984), pp.187–207; J. Miller, 'Britain', in J. Miller (ed.) *Absolutism in Seventeenth-Century Europe* (London, 1990), pp.195–224; J.R. Western, *Monarchy and Revolution: The English State in the 1680s* (London, 1972), pp.146–54.

4 K.M. Brown, 'British history: a sceptical comment', in R.G. Asch (ed.) *Three Nations: A Common history? England, Scotland, Ireland and British History, c.1600–1920* (Bochum, 1993), p.127.

5 Some of this work is surveyed in J.C.D. Clark, 'English history's forgotten context: Scotland, Ireland, Wales', *HJ* 32 (1989), pp.211–28; T.C. Barnard, 'Farewell to Old Ireland', *HJ* 36 (1993), pp.909–28.

6 L. Colley, 'Britishness and otherness: an argument', *JBS* 31 (1992), p.312, n.9. See e.g. K.M. Brown, 'From Scottish lords to British officers: state building, elite integration and the army in the seventeenth century', in N. MacDougall (ed.) *Scotland and War AD79–1918* (Edinburgh, 1991), pp.133–69; A. Clarke, 'Ireland: the general crisis', *P&P* 48 (1970), pp.79–99; J. Goodacre, 'The nobility and the absolutist state in Scotland, 1584–1638', *History* 78 (1993), pp.162–82; M. Lee, 'Scotland and the "general crisis" of the seventeenth century', *SHR* 63 (1984), pp.136–54.

ELITES AND PATRONAGE

Received wisdom portrays Charles II, cautioned by the unpopularity of conquest and enforced union of England, Scotland and Ireland during the 1650s, retreating into an economical minimalism. The king, content to rule each kingdom separately, returned each to its traditional, prewar rulers. These arrangements pleased Charles II so long as neither of the satellites seriously bothered him. Immediately after the Restoration, competitors for office skirmished fiercely: unsullied cavaliers fresh from exile wrestled with the agile collaborators from the Interregnum. The outcome varied. In Ireland those who had worked with Cromwell, Albermarle (the former George Monck) and Robartes were at first appointed, to be helped on the spot by such local quislings as Orrery and Mountrath. But late in 1661 Albermarle and Robartes were supplanted by the *echt* cavalier, Ormond.[7] In Scotland, the ideological equivalents of Ormond and the king's chief minister in England, Clarendon – Glencairn, Middleton and Newburgh – by 1663 had been trounced by Lauderdale.[8] The latter, through his unprincipled dexterity and frank relish for the profits of power, resembled the rapacious Irish settlers like Orrery and Mountrath. These appointments early in the 1660s lessened the prospect of any coordinated approach throughout the three kingdoms. Indeed, the antipathy between Ormond and Lauderdale impeded direct communications between Edinburgh and Dublin and so prevented a joint response to the dangers of the North Channel between Ulster and Scotland, easily and often traversed by Gaelic and presbyterian malcontents.[9]

Different ways of ruling Restoration Ireland and Scotland went beyond the personnel, or their backgrounds, beliefs and English contacts. The varied arrangements reflected and accentuated the status of Scotland as an independent, and Ireland as a dependent, kingdom, and their divergent experiences of English rule

7 *CSP Ire 1660–2*, p.v; Hutton, *Charles II*, p.189; W.D. Macray (ed.) *Notes which Passed at Meetings of the Privy Council between Charles II and the Earl of Clarendon, 1660–1667* (London, 1896), pp.5–6.

8 K.M. Brown, *Kingdom or Province? Scotland and the Regal Union, 1603–1715* (Basingstoke, 1992), pp.146–7; Hutton, *Charles II*, pp.141–4, 190–2, 197, 205–7; J. Patrick, '"A union broken": Restoration politics in Scotland', in J. Wormald (ed.) *Scotland Revisited* (London, 1991), pp.119–22.

9 Bodl Carte MSS 49, f131; 53, f290; 146, pp.31, 102; 214, ff264, 371; Archbishop Michael Boyle to Orrery, 24 Oct. 1677 (Petworth House, West Sussex, Orrery MSS, gen. ser.29): HMC *Ormonde MSS*, iv, p.61.

throughout the century. The Stewarts, as a Scottish dynasty, although they periodically outraged Scottish sensitivities, retained a link that brought them back, when, as in 1641, 1650–1 and 1679, English difficulties mounted.[10] In contrast, and notwithstanding ingenious efforts to invent links, the Irish lacked any earlier intimacy with the Stewarts.[11] Only *in extremis* did James VII and II, panicked from England and dethroned in Scotland, voyage to Ireland (the first of its kings since Richard II to do so), hopeful that his third kingdom would enable him to recover the other two. Throughout the seventeenth century, Ireland, a bystander in the dynastic games across the water, accepted whichever monarch that battle, usurpation or genetic accident delivered. Neither in 1603, nor in 1660, not even (more surprisingly perhaps) in 1688–91, did the elites within Ireland influence who became their ruler. Scotland, on the other hand, not only supplied a king in 1603, but also ensnared his successors with conditions in 1651, 1689 and 1703. The Irish had to acquiesce because protestant Ireland was too puny to survive without England (or Scotland), while a catholic Ireland independent of the English sovereign, occasionally mooted, foundered for want of a plausible alternative ruler either inside or outside Ireland.[12]

Even before the Cromwellian reconquest of 1649–52, Irish institutions – the state church, the law, central and local administration and the armed forces – unlike those in Scotland, were modelled closely after English prototypes, and opened the island to easier control. In addition, newcomers from England, Wales and Scotland had been substituted systematically for the indigenous landowners and office-holders. During the Interregnum, as the ratchet was twisted tighter, catholic survivors were squeezed from their last possessions. These measures, creating an embryonic protestant ascendancy, sometimes orginated with and were eagerly

10 The account on which I have relied heavily is Brown, *Kingdom or Province?* See also J. Wormald, 'The creation of Britain: multiple kingdoms or core and colonies?', *TRHS* 6th ser.2 (1992), pp.175–94.

11 B. Ó Buachalla, 'James our true king: the ideology of Irish royalism in the seventeenth century', in D.G. Boyce, R. Eccleshall and V. Geoghegan (eds) *Political Thought in Ireland since the Seventeenth Century* (London, 1993), pp.9–14, 23–30; 'A series of eight anonymous and confidential letters to James II about the state of Ireland', *Notes and Queries* 6th ser.6 (1882), p.21.

12 T.C. Barnard, 'Settling and unsettling Ireland, 1649–1688', in J. Ohlmeyer (ed.) *From Independence to Occupation* (Cambridge, 1995); J. Miller, 'The earl of Tyrconnel and James II's Irish policy, 1685–1688', *HJ* 20 (1977), pp.820–2; T. Ó Fiaich, 'Republicanism and separatism in the seventeenth century', *Leachtaí Cholm Cille* 2 (1971), pp.74–87.

approved by protestants in Ireland, but depended on decisions taken in London, and as a result obliged all interested in Ireland's future to operate there – after 1660 no less than before.[13]

After 1660, a few innovations in Scotland spoke of a bureaucratic zeal for uniformity between England and Scotland, and closer English supervision. The treasury commission between 1667 and 1682, revived in 1686, and a short-lived advisory council for Scotland which Clarendon established in London, belong in this category.[14] In the main, however, Scotland continued to be governed and administered from Edinburgh. Lauderdale accepted, dominated and defended the devolved government. In the secretaryship for Scotland there existed an office, the importance of which Lauderdale realized and soon enhanced. Through it he controlled policy and the access of other Scots to the king. So long as he kept Scotland reasonably quiescent, he retained the king's confidence and was allowed to treat the kingdom as his own fief, the spoils of which he could digest without the constant English meddling that bedevilled the administration of Ireland. Lauderdale's survival in power until 1679, if it testified to his unscrupulous suppleness, also reflected the inherent stabilities of Scottish society and institutions, and his skill in exploiting them.[15] In Ireland, new measures, decided in London and in accordance with English needs, meant new men. Ormond had to give way as viceroy to Robartes in 1669; Berkeley to Essex in 1672; then Ormond returned in 1677.[16] In Scotland, meanwhile, Lauderdale astutely foresaw the changing requirements of royal policy, and so when his measures were discredited and jettisoned, only his underlings and associates fell.

In Ireland no officer equivalent to the secretary for Scotland filtered local concerns and relayed royal commands. A tentative scheme early in the 1660s to create an advisory council of Irish

13 T.C. Barnard, 'Crises of identity among Irish Protestants, 1641–85', *P&P* 127 (1990), pp.39–83; T.C. Barnard, 'The protestant interest, 1640–1660', in Ohlmeyer (ed.) *From Independence to Occupation*; K.S. Bottigheimer, *English Money and Irish Land* (Oxford, 1971), pp.30–53, 76–114.

14 A.L. Murray, 'The Scottish treasury, 1667–1708', *SHR* 45 (1966), pp.89–104; Patrick, '"A union broken"', pp.121–2.

15 Brown, *Kingdom or Province?*, pp.142–61; W.C. Mackenzie, *The Life and Times of John Maitland Duke of Lauderdale (1616–1682)* (London, 1923).

16 J.C. Beckett, 'The Irish viceroyalty in the Restoration period', *TRHS* 5th ser.20 (1970), reprinted in Beckett, *Confrontations: Studies in Irish History* (London, 1972), pp.67–86; D. Dickson, *New Foundations: Ireland 1660–1800* (Dublin, 1987), p.17; Hutton, *Charles II*, p.340; J.I. McGuire, 'Why was Ormonde dismissed in 1669?', *IHS* 18 (1973), pp.295–312.

peers in London, similar to that for Scotland, was still-born.[17] A viceroy, not blessed with the gift of bilocation, when in Dublin risked political assassination in council and court, and, if in London defending himself, lost his grip on Ireland. In 1670, for example, the irascible lord deputy, Robartes, maligned by the henchmen of his predecessor, Ormond, petulantly resigned; his successor, Berkeley of Stratton, was lamed early in his tour of duty, 'when they once found him to fail of his interests at court'.[18] Successive governors never controlled the access of those from Ireland to the king; they were unable even to establish themselves as the sole conduit for Irish business. Instead, Irish matters, the trivial and the vital, high policy and the allocation of booty, leaked into a bewildering delta of channels that led ultimately to the monarch. The lord lieutenant, told to communicate with the English government only through the principal secretary of state, soon found that other office-holders, like the lord treasurer, Danby, were expected to handle Irish affairs.[19] These administrative confusions added to the hazards and haphazardness of governing Ireland. They were, moreover, symptomatic of the practical dependence of the Irish on the English administration, and of the better integration of Irish politics into those of England.

Since 1541, office as well as land in Ireland had been colonized by the English and Scots. As a result, the distribution of jobs, from that of the lord lieutenancy itself to a captaincy of horse or a tide-waiter's place in a misty Donegal creek, was contested by English politicians and courtiers. Functionally, the Irish administration now belonged to the English patronage system. As one lord lieutenant lamented, there was no post in Ireland, 'be it ever so small, but endeavours are used to get recommendations out of England for it'.[20] Even offices formally in the viceroy's gift were bestowed without reference to him and at the behest of rivals in England, with the result that the incumbent governor was frequently and publicly humiliated. In addition, the English council and court were crowded with those concerned directly with Ireland,

17 Bodl Carte MS 44, f466; for the informal consultation of Irish grandees in London: Chatsworth, diary of second earl of Cork, 11 April 1673; NLI MS 16974, pp.131, 229; *CSP Ire 1660–2* p.v.

18 Bodl Add MS C34, ff121v, 157v, 160, 164v; Robartes to Bridgeman, 6, 21 and 23 Oct. 1669; Bridgeman to Robartes, 23 Nov. 1669 (Staffordshire CRO D1287/18/3).

19 BL Stowe MSS 201, ff107, 162; 207, f282v; Bodl Add MS C33, ff42v, 74, 106v; C34, ff90, 95, 106v, 110, 127v, 164; *CSP Ire 1660–2* p.xxxix; G. Davies, 'Council and cabinet, 1679–88', *EHR* 37 (1922), pp.53, 55.

20 Bodl Add MS C34, f152v; cf. Bowood House, Wiltshire, Petty Papers, 6, ser.ii, 23 (these papers are now in the BL); BL Add MSS 28053, f78.

either as new landowners or self-appointed experts. Albermarle, Arlington, Buckingham, Lady Cleveland and, above all, the duke of York had won extensive Irish estates in the latest lottery.[21] Thereby they acquired opportunities for patronage in Ireland, as well as a lively interest in the shape and detail of the impending settlement. Simultaneously, because Irish business was conducted at Whitehall, the powerful from Ireland were more continuously active in London than ever before. These suitors supplemented those who had already infiltrated the households of the king, the duke of York, Henrietta Maria, Catherine of Braganza and Mary of Modena.[22] Irish protestants also entered the upper reaches of the Whitehall bureaucracy, the English council and the high offices of state. Thus, Ormond served as lord steward, Anglesey as privy councillor and lord privy seal, Conway as secretary of state and Ranelagh as courtier and councillor. Elsewhere, in the purlieux of Whitehall, Sir Robert Southwell, Sir Richard Bellings and Sir William Temple enriched and distinguished themselves. Other Irish protestants sat in the English parliament. Through such means, and at elevated levels, the English of Ireland, their sense of themselves as Englishmen already sharp, were better assimilated to the values and ethos of the later Stewart monarchy.[23] The Scots, if still present at court, were less conspicuous than they had been earlier in the century. For most, politics could be satisfactorily and satisfyingly played out in Edinburgh, where parliament met regularly and the council and courts deliberated, or in their shires.[24] For the local

21 Pearse St Public Library, Dublin, Gilbert MS 207, p.10; Guildford Muniment Room, Brodrick MSS 1248/1, ff111, 124; L.J. Arnold, *The Restoration Land Settlement in County Dublin* (Dublin, 1993), pp.50, 60–1, 72–84; H. O'Sullivan, 'Landownership changes in the county of Louth in the seventeenth century' (Trinity College, Dublin, PhD thesis, 2 vols, 1991), I, pp.200–36.

22 Arnold, *Restoration Land Settlement*, pp.65–85, 131; T.C. Barnard, 'Land and the limits of loyalty: the second earl of Burlington and first earl of Cork (1612–98)', in T.C. Barnard and J. Clark (eds) *Lord Burlington: Architecture, Art and Life* (London, 1995); D.F. Cregan, 'An Irish cavalier: Daniel O'Neill in exile and restoration 1651–1664', *SH* 5 (1965), pp.42–76; D.B. Henning, *The House of Commons 1660–1690* (3 vols; London, 1983), I, pp.16, 17, 536–8, 539–40, 544, 570–1, 619–20, 632–3, 700–3, 721, 755–7; P.H. Kelly, '"A light to the blind": the voice of the dispossessed elite after the defeat at Limerick', *IHS* 34 (1985), p.441; J. Ohlmeyer, *Civil War and Restoration in the Three Stuart Kingdoms: The Career of Randal MacDonnell, Marquis of Antrim 1609–83* (Cambridge, 1993), pp.259–73.

23 The theme of elite integration, illuminated by Keith Brown, has generally occupied historians of Ireland after 1660 little. Other than Antrim, Granard and Orrery, 'notoriously conspicuous to the three kingdoms' (Cambridge University Library, MS 4353, pp.4–5), few operated successfully in all three Stewart kingdoms. This subject is discussed more fully in T.C. Barnard, *The Protestant Ascendancy* (forthcoming).

24 Brown, *Kingdom or Province?*, pp.10–12.

and national leaders of Ireland, while much was still transacted in Dublin and the provinces, more of importance was settled at Whitehall or Windsor. There, either in person or through surrogates, they must be: even more so after 1666 when the querulous Dublin parliament was shut down.

The mechanisms through which Scotland and Ireland were ruled might differ strikingly, but the plans for each kingdom were of a piece. Power was to be delegated to the customary rulers, who, within ill-defined limits, then ruled. Lauderdale after 1663 was free to strike whatever opportunist deals would best preserve Scotland's peace and his own power. His canny instincts for survival intensified the aristocratic reaction which, most agree, marked Restoration Scotland. Peers regained their old pre-eminence in government, the council and Court of Session; the initiatives of parliament were curtailed by the Lords of the Articles; the laity and, from 1669, the king better directed the church; and, while the part in politics of professional and urban groups declined, that of the soldiery ominously increased.[25] This situation reveals the resilience or revival of the power of the traditional rulers, the more remarkable after recent upheavals which had loosened feudal ties and added to the indebtedness of many magnates. Keith Brown has convincingly suggested how the notables regained their hold, because, adaptable and resourceful, they colonized the apparatus of the expanding state, and used new powers and relationships based on the army, bureaucracy, law courts and the church to repair or replace older bonds.[26] In Ireland, too, there occurred a similar process through which the institutions of the English-style state were annexed. However, the Irish beneficiaries, mainly protestants lately substituted for the catholics, were more shallowly rooted in indigenous society than their Scottish counterparts.[27]

The different structures and characteristics of the dominant hierarchies in the two kingdoms cry out for more probing.[28]

25 ibid, pp.33–41, 53–4; J. Buckroyd, 'Bridging the gap: Scotland 1659–1660', *SHR* 66 (1987), pp.1–24.

26 Brown, *Kingdom or Province?*, p.42.

27 One element is considered in T.C. Barnard, 'Lawyers and the law in later seventeenth-century Ireland', *IHS* 28 (1993), pp.254–82.

28 Two accounts which offer sustained comparison between Scotland and Ireland are L.M. Cullen, 'Incomes, social classes and economic growth in Ireland and Scotland, 1600–1900', in T.M. Devine and D. Dickson (eds) *Ireland and Scotland 1600–1850: Parallels and Contrasts in Economic and Social Development* (Edinburgh, 1983), pp.248–59; R.G. Gillespie, 'Landed society and the Interregnum in Ireland and Scotland', in P. Roebuck and R. Mitchison (eds) *Economy and Society in Scotland and Ireland 1500–1939* (Edinburgh, 1988), pp.38–47.

Connected with them was the essential singularity of Scotland and Ireland: the former an equal and independent realm of the English monarch; the latter, conquered and dependent, indeed in some opinions, 'by the king's prerogative . . . at his disposal independently of the Parliament of England'.[29] Charles II and James VII and II in regard to Ireland regressed to an antediluvian era of modest ambitions and resources not seen since the 1530s. In selecting as viceroys Irish landowners, first Ormond and then Richard Talbot (from 1685 earl of Tyrconnell), the Stewarts abandoned the practice followed since 1541 of deputing an English peer or politician to rule Ireland on their behalf. As in the later middle ages, the island was to be left to its baronial lineages.[30] Ormond, a ferocious dynast who, no less than Lauderdale, treated the government as outrelief for himself, his extended family and his numerous clients, was too steeped in the culture of the Stewart court to impersonate the over-mighty subject. Contemporaries, nevertheless, complained that he confused self- with public interest. Furthermore, in the provinces, local representatives all too easily amassed economic, administrative and military powers with which they might oppose the English sovereign.[31] Qualms about returning so much authority, both in Scotland and Ireland, to those who had so lately disputed the Stewarts' policies were justified by events in and after 1688 when some at least turned their local strength against James VII and II.

UNIFORMITY AND ITS DANGERS

After 1660 the centripetal and centrifugal forces in Scotland, Ireland and England were balanced in an uneasy equilibrium. The

29 A. Clarke, 'Colonial constitutional attitudes in Ireland, 1640–1660', *PRIA* 90C (1990), pp.357–75; M. Perceval-Maxwell, 'Ireland and the monarchy in the early Stuart multiple kingdom', *HJ* 34 (1991), pp.285–95; 'A series of eight anonymous and confidential letters', *Notes & Queries* 6th ser.5 (1882), p.402; Wormald, 'Creation of Britain'.

30 S.G. Ellis, *Reform and Revival: English Government in Ireland 1470–1534* (Woodbridge, 1986).

31 Buckingham to unknown, 16 Oct. 1668 (Staffordshire CRO D1787/10/1/9); Bodl Add MS C33, ff17v, 29v; T.C. Barnard, 'Sir William Petty, Irish landowner', in H. Lloyd-Jones, V. Pearl and B. Worden (eds) *History and Imagination: Essays in Honour of H.R. Trevor-Roper* (London, 1981), p. 211; Barnard, 'Land and the limits of loyalty'. On the Butler affinities: W. Smyth, 'Property, patronage and population: reconstructing the human geography of mid-seventeenth century county Tipperary', in W. Nolan and T. McGrath (eds) *Tipperary: History and Society* (Dublin, 1985), pp.104–38.

formal unionism of the Interregnum had been discredited by what were taken to be its inevitable adjuncts: occupying armies and high taxes. In 1661 Scotland and Ireland regained their own parliaments. The former, guided by the Lords of the Articles, though ruffled in the 1670s by mounting aristocratic hostility to Lauderdale's regime, did not alter the essentials of policy, and was successfully managed.[32] By 1666 the success with which Irish protestants in the Dublin assembly had unpicked measures conceived in England led to its demise; sessions projected in the 1670s were abandoned lest they release dangerous opposition. Denied any institutional outlet in Ireland for communal anxieties, a few toyed again with union. Sir William Petty, an indefatigable projector, proposed that Ireland elect 270 Members of Parliament (MPs), 90 of whom would sit in Dublin, allowing the other 180 to travel to England, where the English towns and cities would select half to join an imperial parliament at Westminster (60 Scots would assist in this legislature). As with much else which Petty devised, this scheme occupied an idle hour and stood no chance of being adopted.[33] Only James VII and II, short of solid supporters among the protestant Anglo-Irish, encouraged Petty. Yet, if Petty represented an idiosyncratic and impracticable unionism, others of his contemporaries identified problems common to all three kingdoms, and were accordingly tempted into unitary policies. Erstwhile protégés of Wentworth and Laud, internationalized and sometimes catholicized by exile on the continent in the 1650s, together with the young *ultras* of the 1680s, soldiers, bureaucrats and churchmen, constituted the imperial chancellery of the later Stewarts. Alert to how the issues of religion, security and royal reputation interlocked, they coordinated measures between England, Scotland and Ireland. Charles II had at first been hobbled by caution and meagre funds. By the early 1680s, however, as his confidence, acumen, revenues and impatience with critics grew, so too did his taste for greater freedom.[34] After James VII and II's accession, the king's wish to help his fellow catholics, if not to rule absolutely, prompted better synchronization between

32 J. Patrick, 'The origins of the opposition to Lauderdale in the Scottish Parliament of 1673', *SHR* 53 (1974), pp.1–21.

33 Bowood House, Petty Papers, C53; *The Economic Writings of Sir William Petty*, ed. C.H. Hull (2 vols; Cambridge, 1899), I, pp.159, 220; cf. J.S. Kelly, 'The origins of the Act of Union: an examination of unionist opinion in Britain and Ireland, 1650–1800', *IHS* 25 (1987), pp.236–63.

34 Childs, '1688', pp.404–5, 411; Holmes, *The Making of a Great Power*, pp.167–74; Hutton *Charles II*, pp. 404–45; P. Seaward, *The Restoration 1660–1688* (Basingstoke, 1991), pp.101–22; Western, *Monarchy and Revolution*, pp.46–81.

the three kingdoms, and dreams that the two satellites could furnish the resources with which to cow the recalcitrant English, and laboratories in which policies for all three countries could be tested and perfected.[35]

In each sphere – religion, the military, and an increase in monarchical authority – yearnings for uniformity or congruity foundered on the awkward individualism of each state. In 1660 religion seemed to lend itself most readily to a common approach. How, otherwise, could the unexpected decision in each of the kingdoms to reintroduce episcopacy be explained? The determined in the three capitals of Dublin, Edinburgh and London hustled the cautious and agnostic into a conservative and exclusive settlement. In all three kingdoms, dislike of the recent confusion, affection for tradition and order, and lay impatience with clerical domineering swung the parliamentary classes behind the bishops. Furthermore, the conventional saw that religious pluralism could destroy civil polity – amply proved by recent history – wrecked schemes of comprehension or legal indulgence.[36] Yet the requirement of conformity created a serious problem of dissent: worst in numbers and rebelliousness in Scotland; unsettling enough in England and Ireland.[37] Nonconformity in religion, and the penalties that it incurred, might lead the scrupulous to question the laws, and those who had made and now enforced them, and so fed political dissent.

35 Gilbert Burnet, *History of his own Time* (6 vols; Oxford, 1833), III, p.72; T. Ranger, 'Strafford in Ireland: a revaluation', in T. Aston (ed.) *Crisis in Europe 1560–1660* (London, 1965), p.281; 'A series of eight anonymous and confidential letters', p.4.

36 For evidence of coordination: Glasgow University Library, Wodrow MSS, MS gen. 210, pp.40–2, 47, 51, 82, 98–9; NLI MS 32, f14; D. Dickson and R. Douglas to Orrery, 28 March and 30 April 1660 (Petworth, Orrery MSS, gen. ser. 28); *CSP Ire 1660–2* p.224; *Journals of the House of Commons of the Kingdom of Ireland*, I, p.649; Sir George Mackenzie, *Memoirs of the Affairs of Scotland*, ed. Thomas Thomson (Edinburgh, 1821), p.58. On the vexed question of the settlement: R.A. Beddard, 'The Restoration Church', in J.R. Jones (ed.) *The Restored Monarchy 1660–1688* (London, 1979), pp.155–75; J. Buckroyd, *Church and State in Scotland 1660–1681* (Edinburgh, 1980), pp.22–40; I. Green, *The Re-Establishment of the Church of England 1660–1663* (Oxford, 1978); J.I. McGuire, 'The Dublin convention, the protestant community and the emergence of an ecclesiastical settlement in 1660', in A. Cosgrove and J.I. McGuire (eds) *Parliament and Community: Historical Studies XIV* (Belfast, 1983), pp.121–46; P. Seaward, *The Cavalier Parliament and the Reconstruction of the Old Regime, 1661–1667* (Cambridge, 1989), pp.166–95.

37 For the problems of dissent; Buckroyd, *Church and State*, pp.57–136; T. Harris, 'Introduction: revising the Restoration', in T. Harris, P. Seaward and M. Goldie (eds) *The Politics of Religion in Restoration England* (Oxford, 1990), pp.1–28; P. Kilroy, 'Protestant dissent and controversy in Ireland, 1660–1711', (Trinity College, Dublin, PhD thesis, 1991); A Whiteman, 'Introduction', in E.A.O. Whiteman with M. Clappison (eds) *The Compton Census of 1676* (Oxford, 1986).

The shared grievance against bishops stimulated a common hostility.[38] Dissent travelled well: it took the easy passages between south-western Scotland – the stronghold of Remonstrant and conventicling defiance of the new order – and eastern Ulster heavily settled with Scots and the seat since 1659 of five presbyteries.[39] Both in Scotland and Ulster, obstinate presbyterians suffered most from the rigorous enforcement of conformity. Even so, the lack of any sustained cooperation between Edinburgh and Dublin ensured that when persecution waxed in Scotland it often waned in Ulster. Presbyterianism survived and even thrived.[40] Outside Ulster and Scotland, the nonconforming congregations, identified by the English government as cover for, and links in, an international terrorist movement directed from republican Holland, were too fragile and timid to organize opposition to the restored monarchy and church. At worst, the network of congregations and sympathizers allowed conspirators to move clandestinely between the three kingdoms.[41]

Scottish and Irish enemies of episcopacy, as of other facets of later Stewart rule, knew that policy would be modified only by decisions in London. English help had to be enlisted if concessions were to be granted; to achieve this, critics described what they endured locally as a problem which encompassed all three countries. In religion this was indeed so. The Stewarts, for all their initial minimalism, could hardly permit each kingdom to choose its own distinctive religion. As a result, episcopacy returned to all three. But the congruity behind the façade of bishops was more

38 Harris, 'Revising the Restoration', pp.1–28; T. Harris, *London Crowds in the Reign of Charles II* (Cambridge, 1987), pp.62–95.

39 Kilroy, 'Protestant dissent', pp.7–49.

40 Bodl Carte MSS 37, f79; 146, pp.2–4, 33; 221, ff137, 141, 170; BL Stowe MS 200, ff184v, 235, 287, 301, 334; NLI MSS 2490, f226; 2505, f189; Archbishop Michael Boyle to Orrery, 24 Oct. 1677 (Petworth, Orrery MS, gen. ser. 29); Massareene to Orrery, 9 Feb. 1660[1] (ibid, 28); PRONI D562/19, 33; Victoria & Albert Museum, London, Orrery Letters, ii, f11; I.B. Cowan, *The Scottish Covenanters 1660–88* (London, 1976), pp.65, 95, 132; *CSP Ire 1669–70* pp.225–7; R. Gillespie, 'The presbyterian revolution in Ulster 1660–1690', in W.J. Shiels and D. Wood (eds) *The Churches, Ireland and the Irish* (Oxford, 1989), pp.160–70; C.J. Stranks, *The Life and Writings of Jeremy Taylor* (London, 1952), pp.240–3; C.S. Terry, *The Pentland Rising and Rullion Green* (Glasgow, 1905), pp.37, 71–2.

41 S.J. Connolly, *Religion, Law and Power: The Making of Protestant Ireland* (Oxford, 1992), pp.24–32; R.L. Greaves, *Deliver us from Evil: The Radical Underground in Britain 1660–1663* (Oxford, 1986); R.L. Greaves, *Enemies under his Feet: Radicals and Nonconformists in Britain 1664–1677* (Stanford, Calif., 1990); R.L. Greaves, *Secrets of the Kingdom: British Radicals from the Popish Plot to the Revolution of 1688–89* (Stanford, Calif., 1992); K. Herlihy, 'The Irish Baptists, 1650–1780' (Trinity College, Dublin, PhD thesis, 1992); Kilroy, 'Protestant dissent', pp.51–134.

nominal than real. In Scotland, the bishops were grafted on to a stock still composed of kirk sessions and presbyteries.[42] In Ireland, as befitted its dependent and conquered condition, the Restoration finished what Bramhall (now primate) had started in the 1630s. Through a series of declarations, proclamations and bishops' visitations, and then in 1666 with an Act of Uniformity, the Irish parliament and convocation voluntarily bartered an independent national church for one on the English model, and accepted the revised *Book of Common Prayer.*[43] Such a surrender, at odds with the touchily independent and erastian mood of the Irish parliament in 1661–6, becomes more comprehensible when we discover that the Act of Uniformity was not the main means by which religious conformity was secured. Vigorous bishops and magistrates, especially in Ulster, spurred on by the Dublin government, achieved this between 1661 and 1663.[44] By 1666, when uniformity was enacted, its rigidities were at variance with the muddled generosity now preferred by the English and Irish administrations, so that much of the machinery of the Act was left to rust. Also, the latitude of some bishops, coupled with the seigneurial nature of Irish protestantism, militated against any standardized approach to worship and doctrine.[45] In Ireland, no less than in Scotland and England, secular calculations had persuaded the powerful laity to agree to the bishops' return, but equally would defeat the clergy's hopes of economic and institutional independence.

42 Buckroyd, *Church and State;* J. Buckroyd, *The Life of James Sharp, Archbishop of St Andrews, 1618–1679: A Political Biography* (Edinburgh 1987); C. Kidd, 'Religious realignment between the Restoration and Union' (forthcoming). I am most grateful to Dr Kidd for allowing me to read this and another unpublished paper of his.

43 The evolution of this measure needs proper study. For the moment its hesitant progress can be traced in TCD MS 1038, ff32v–3, 48v, 53v, 61, 75v; Bodl Clarendon SP 76, ff179, 205–8; Chatsworth, Lismore MSS 31/117; 32/1; Anglesey to Orrery, 20 May 1662 (Petworth, Orrery MSS, gen. ser. 22); *CSP Ire 1663–5* p.397; *Journal of the House of Commons,* I, pp.649, 696, 700–1, 703, 705, 710, 741, 742; *A Declaration of the Lords Spiritual, and Temporal, and the Commons, concerning ecclesiastical government, and the Book of Common Prayer* (Dublin, 1661); *His Majesties Declaration to all his loving subjects, December 26, 1662* (Dublin, 1662); HMC *Hastings MSS* iv, pp.131–3; R.H. Murray, 'The Church of the Restoration, 1660–1685', in W.A. Phillips (ed.) *History of the Church of Ireland* (3 vols; Oxford, 1933), III, pp.117–47, esp. p.132, n.2.

44 Bodl Carte MSS 49, f312v; 214, f394; 221, f170; J. Gorges to G. Lane, 24 Nov. 1661, (NLI MS 8643); P. Adair, *A True Narrative,* ed. W.D. Killen (Belfast, 1866), pp. 245–52, 276–85; HMC *Hastings MSS,* iv, pp.127–8; T.W. Moody and J.G. Simms (eds) *The Bishopric of Derry and the Irish Society of London, 1602–1705* (2 vols; Dublin, 1968–83), I, pp.326–31.

45 Bodl Carte MSS 37, f3v; 48, f70v; BL Add MS 23134, f23; Stowe MS 202, f1; Castle Forbes, County Longford, Granard MSS H1/5/18; HMC *Hastings MSS* iv, p.134; *Autobiography of the Rev. Devereux Spratt* (London, 1886), pp.14–15, 17, 30.

The distinctive confessional composition of each kingdom weakened any English quest for strict conformity. The vitality of presbyterianism in the Scottish burghs and Lowlands and in eastern Ulster; the persistence of dissent throughout England; and an Ireland where 80 per cent of the inhabitants were probably catholics: all might suggest that the unitary dreams of Charles II and James VII and II – to edge towards indulgence and toleration – better accorded with the realities. Unhappily, the kings' policies, a volatile blend of whim, cynicism and altruism, veered unpredictably between repression and leniency. In regard to religious policy, Ireland posed intractable difficulties. Its shrewder governors knew that it would be stabilized only if a *modus vivendi* with the catholic majority were to be established. The problem, if unique in the Stewarts' dominions, nevertheless was analogous to that which the presbyterians posed Lauderdale.[46] But where the latter drew the bulk of the presbyterians into the new state church, and isolated and more or less contained the irreconcilables (albeit at great cost), Ormond, the consistent advocate of a pact with the Irish catholics, failed. Since the 1640s when he had first served as the king's lord lieutenant in Ireland, he had favoured a royalist coalition indifferent to race and religion, but organized around the principle of loyalty to the Stewart king of Ireland. After 1660, such an alliance, with power shared between protestants and papists, enraged those protestants, headed by Orrery, who had so lately and so precariously gained a monopoly over Irish government. In the event, Ormond's overtures were rejected because a majority of the catholic clergy still preferred, at least in public, to obey the Pope rather than the king.[47] Ormond's schemes had always carried dangers, for they were the seventeenth-century equivalent of talking to terrorists, and when they were seen to fail excited similar opprobrium. Ormond, thanks to his extended and largely catholic affinity and his years on the continent, was plausibly accused of favouring the papists.[48] Yet he acknowledged what few of his Irish

46 Buckroyd, *Church and State;* Buckroyd, *Life of James Sharp.*

47 Barnard, 'The protestant interest'; J. Brennan, 'A Gallican interlude in Ireland', *Irish Theological Quarterly* 24 (1957), pp.219–37, 283–309; Peter Walsh, *The History and Vindication of the Loyal Formulary of the Irish Remonstrance* (np, 1674).

48 For hostility to Ormond, see e.g. Dr William's Library, London, Morice MS, Entr'ing book, ii, pp.71, 284; Stafford CRO D1787/10/1/9. Recent accounts with contrasted verdicts are J.C. Beckett, *The Cavalier Duke: A Life of James Butler, 1st duke of Ormond* (Belfast, 1991); W. Kelly, '"Most illustrious cavalier" or "Unkinde Desertor": James Butler, first duke of Ormonde, 1610–1688', *History Ireland* 1.2 (1993), pp.18–22.

protestant critics would concede: that unless a substantial section of the catholic population was engaged actively to support the Stewarts, a regime reliant on the fragile protestant minority might crumble in a new crisis. Militant Irish protestants furiously rejected this warning, and asked instead for tougher anti-catholic measures. But as a viceroy patiently explained, even to expel the catholic priests (as was demanded in 1673) required an army of 20,000: a return, in short, to the militarized state of the Cromwellians when, for the first and only time, such draconian action had been taken.[49]

Because catholics were so numerous, and some retained or recovered influence and property after 1660, anti-catholicism functioned rather differently in Ireland than in England or Scotland, at least until the 1680s.[50] If in the other two, predominantly protestant, countries it served as emotive slogan or abstract problem, in Restoration Ireland it best expressed the essence of recent protestant history – massacre, spoliation, dispossession and exile – and, after 1660, fears of a catholic revival abetted by the sympathetic Stewarts.[51] The latter's seeming indifference to these worries, all too reminiscent of Charles I's supposed behaviour in 1641, strained Irish protestant loyalty, and by the 1670s impelled some from Ireland into the English campaigns against royal ministers and policies. From England, it looked as if too many Irish protestants deserved their reputations in royalist demonologies as Cromwellian veterans, gathered in conventicles and in league with republican subversives elsewhere. In an age of conspiracies and plots, the mischievous and devious, both in government and opposition, could kindle and fan fires which might suddenly catch hold and run through the land. A long sequence of disturbances, from Venner's in 1661, a northern rising, a plot to seize Dublin Castle in 1663, the Pentland rising, army mutinies, Blood's escapades, the Popish and Rye House Plots, the attempts of Monmouth and Argyll, embraced the three kingdoms,

49 Bodl. Add MS C34, f11.

50 On this subject in Ireland before 1641: R.G. Asch, 'Antipopery and ecclesiastical policy in early seventeenth-century Ireland', *Archiv für Reformationsgeschichte* 83 (1992), pp.258–301; A. Clarke, 'The 1641 Rebellion and anti-popery in Ireland', B. Mac Cuarta (ed.) *Ulster 1641: Aspects of the Rising* (Belfast, 1993); in England after 1660: J. Miller, *Popery and Politics in England 1660–1688* (Cambridge, 1973).

51 T.C. Barnard, '1641: a bibliographical essay', in Mac Cuarta (ed.) *Ulster 1641*; Barnard, 'Settling and unsettling Ireland'; T.C. Barnard, 'The uses of 23 October 1641 and Irish Protestant celebrations', *EHR* 106 (1991), pp.889–920.

hinted at common causes and invited a unified reaction.[52] All the disturbances were suppressed, but their frequency and growing seriousness convinced alarmists that they had uncovered a supranational or international movement. Thus, if calculating ministers fabricated and manipulated the panics, others worried how to maintain the fragile regime in the face of such danger. However they acted, they would be criticized. In the 1670s Lauderdale, playing up the threat from the Highlands or the Covenanting south-west, was condemned for brutality which, so his Scottish adversaries argued, portended what England might soon suffer.[53] In contrast, Ormond, thanks to his casualness, risked delivering up Ireland to England's papist enemies. The Stewarts' anxious advisers concluded that the three kingdoms were best treated as a single military unit, in which the regular army, with its increasingly professional and impeccably royalist officers, would keep the peace.[54] So, in the later Stewart monarchy, the army, and not as earlier the church, would hold the unstable federation together. Religious harmonization, other than the formal façade of bishops, was no longer practicable. However, the greater role envisaged for the army would also cause difficulties.

THE RICHES TO BE MADE FROM IRELAND AND SCOTLAND

Ministers who aspired to intimidate troublemakers and lessen dependence on the services of testy local elites needed more money to pay extra soldiers. In England, the excesses of the exclusionists between 1678 and 1681 engendered a reaction in the king's favour.

52 BL Egerton MS 2542, f370; Barnard, 'Settling and unsettling Ireland'; Connolly, *Religion, Law and Power*, pp.25–6; Greaves, *Deliver us from Evil*; Greaves, *Enemies under his Feet*; Greaves, *Secrets of the Kingdom*; T. Harris, *Politics under the Later Stuarts: Party Conflict in a Divided Society 1660–1715* (London, 1993), pp.1–116.

53 *An Accompt of Scotlands Grievances by reason of the D of Lauderdales Ministrie* (np, 1674); *A Dialogue between Duke Lauderdale and the Lord Danby* (np, 1678); *The Impeachment of the Duke and Duchess of Lauderdale with their brother Lord Hatton* (np, 1678); A.I. Macinnes, 'Repression and conciliation: the Highland dimension, 1660–1688', *SHR* 65 (1986), pp.167–95.

54 Childs, '1688', pp.399–409; S.S. Webb, *The Governors-General: The English Army and the Definition of Empire* (Williamsburg, Va, 1979); S.S. Webb, '"Brave men and servants to his royal highness": the household of James Stuart and the evolution of English imperialism', *Perspectives in American History* 8 (1974), pp.55–60; Western, *Monarchy and Revolution*, pp.121–39.

Tory loyalists were stuffed into the ministry, the council and local government. Moreover, Charles II, assisted by the larger yield of the taxes bestowed at the Restoration, ruled without parliament after 1681. Similar currents were running in the sovereign's favour in his other kingdoms. In Edinburgh, the presence of the duke of Albany and York focused and fortified the Scots' sense of the Stewarts as their own dynasty.[55] In protestant Ireland, willing accessories acquiesced in a Tory reaction which subordinated the administration, the finances and the army more firmly to England.[56]

During the Interregnum the armies of conquest and occupation were paid from the high taxes which added greatly to the unpopularity of the shotgun unions of Scotland and Ireland with England. In England itself, the union, because it was costly, had been disliked.[57] The reduced ambitions after 1660 told of parsimony. Ireland's and Scotland's new rulers earned easy popularity by paring down the forces and lowering taxes. Nevertheless, each country had still to be defended. Thus in Scotland, while the English soldiers were quickly sent home and the Cromwellian citadels knocked down, a regular army of about 2,000 was retained.[58] The excise and customs failed to meet the expenses, and so the Scottish parliament, already bountiful in voting the king a notional annual revenue of £480,000 (Scots), authorized more. The fresh exactions were resisted. The crude profiteering of Lauderdale's cronies from the salt, brandy and tobacco duties discredited the fiscal regime, and soon soldiers were required to help collect the money: a relapse that echoed the militarized administration of the Cromwellians. Under the new arrangements, at least the troops were Scots and commanded by landowners who themselves shared in the mulcts.[59]

55 Hugh Ouston, 'York in Edinburgh: James VII and the patronage of learning in Scotland, 1679–1688', in J. Dwyer, R.A. Mason and A. Murdoch (eds) *New Perspectives in the Politics and Culture of Early Modern Scotland* (Edinburgh, 1982), pp.133–55.

56 Edward Richardson, 'An enquiry into the dissatisfaction of the people, with an endeavour to undeceive them' (NLI MS 2491, f351); J.E. Ayledotte, 'The duke of Ormonde and English government in Ireland, 1677–85' (Iowa University, PhD thesis, 1975); Dickson, *New Foundations*, pp.21–2.

57 Derek Hirst, 'Experiencing Britain' (unpublished paper), cited by J. Morrill, 'The Britishness of the English revolution 1640–60', in Asch (ed.) *Three Nations: A Common History*? p.110.

58 B. Lenman, 'Militia, fencible men, and home defence, 1660–1797', in MacDougall, *The Scots and War*, pp.172–8; Mackenzie, *Memoirs*, pp.24–5.

59 G. Donaldson, *Scotland: James V to James VII* (Edinburgh, 1965), p.360; Lenman, 'Militia, fencible men', pp.176–84; Patrick, 'The origins of the opposition to Lauderdale', p.20.

After 1660 England longed to stop subsidizing Ireland's government. Yet in 1662 £100,000 (sterling) had to be dispatched, and in 1663 another £60,000. In Dublin, no less than in Edinburgh, the country's representatives acted generously, and voted the king a new hearth tax, the excise, customs and quit rents.[60] The continuing deficit and consequent need for English subventions irritated English officials, who attributed much to local mismanagement. Certainly Irish grandees, accustomed before 1649 to raid the state's resources, after 1660 gorged themselves like beasts released on to spring pastures after a hard winter. Lord Cork, installed in his father's post as lord high treasurer, repaid old and created new obligations by a liberal distribution of sinecures in the customs. His brother, Orrery, slavered over the prospect of licensing alehouses and farming the inland excise, and in his imagination had spent the proceeds before he learned they were not to be his.[61] Lord Anglesey as vice-treasurer merrily cheated the kingdom of thousands. Arran, Ormond's son, sought a licence literally to coin money with a patent to mint farthings.[62] In Ireland, then, the crown had cheerfully restored the easy-going alliance with the local elites, ruptured first by Wentworth and more recently by the Cromwellians. Soon enough English observers saw that the deal was not working, since it cost England too much. Yet until the 1680s the racketeers parried greater English interference by offering the king a share of the lucre.

Charles II assented to the Irish revenue being managed by a consortium headed by an ambitious Irish peer, Ranelagh, which would cut out the Dublin government and itself receive and disburse the money.[63] A sweetener of £50,000 for the king in 1671–2 was a foretaste of more to follow. Charles blew much of the cash, not on the military, but on embellishing the interior of Windsor Castle as a baroque celebration of his dynasty.[64] Ranelagh's

60 C.D. Chandaman, *The English Public Revenue 1660–1688* (Oxford, 1975), p.264, n.2; J.G. Simms, 'The Restoration, 1660–85', in T.W. Moody, F.J. Byrne and F.X. Martin (eds) *A New History of Ireland, III, Early Modern Ireland 1534–1691* (Oxford, 1976), pp.439–41.

61 Chatsworth, diary of second earl of Cork, 21 and 29 Nov., 1 Dec. 1660, 4, 15 and 21 Jan., 20 Feb. 1660[1], 30 March, 10 July, 22 Aug., 1 and 3 Oct. 1661, 2 and 27 April 1663; Lismore MS 32/113–15.

62 Staffordshire CRO D1778/I/i/618; D1778/iii/0/19 (R. Aylward to G. Legge, 3 Sept. 1678).

63 S. Egan, 'Finance and the government of Ireland 1660–1688' (Trinity College, Dublin, PhD thesis, 2 vols, 1983), I, pp.240–2; II, pp.7, 29–71.

64 H.M. Colvin (ed.) *The History of the King's Works, V, 1660–1782* (London, 1976), pp.312, 322–8.

scheme had also seduced the lord treasurer, Danby, with the promise of Irish supplements to royal income: he expected £130,000 from Ireland in 1676, and an annual £60,000 thereafter. In the event, neither the king nor his government profited from the project as much as Ranelagh and his partners. In 1680 Ranelagh slipped out, £210,000 to the good, owing the Irish administration nearly £100,000, and admirably qualified for the post to which William III would appoint him – paymaster-general of the forces. The English treasury now asserted itself: from 1682 Irish finances were overseen by a commission. Superficially it resembled the body through which the Scottish treasury had been surbordinated to better English control. The Irish commission, however, in tune with Ireland's dependence, though fronted by an Irish peer, Longford, was staffed with English officials and run from Whitehall.[65]

These developments have been seen as belonging to, and deepening, English mastery of Ireland. The usurpation of financial control by London, clear in the Ranelagh syndicate and the 1682 commission, angered viceroys who could no longer decide the priorities for spending. Rumours that Ireland's specie was draining away to England appalled Irish patriots.[66] Yet the latter, denied a parliament of their own, could only urge English MPs to link these abuses with Danby's and Lauderdale's efforts to introduce arbitrary government throughout the other kingdoms. In practice, these fiscal and administrative devices continued long-standing English ambitions for Ireland, and merely varied, rather than ended, the mutually advantageous alliance between a few in Ireland and the monarchy. The fortunate in Ireland, allied with English courtiers and projectors, had long creamed off Ireland's wealth, through revenue farms as well as grants and patents.[67] Ranelagh's venture still enriched some from Ireland, notably himself. Over a longer period, the hearth tax, farmed county by county, attracted local undertakers who calculated, sometimes wrongly, that the direct and

65 Bowood House, Petty Papers, C14; Chandaman; *English Public Revenue*, pp.235, n.1, 237; Egan, 'Finance and the government of Ireland', II, pp.118–32, 145–79, 199–207.

66 Bodl Carte MS 69, f141; Archbishop Michael Boyle to Orrery, 2 Oct. 1677 (Petworth, Orrery MSS gen. ser. 29); T.C. Barnard, 'The political, material and mental culture of the Cork settlers, *c.*1650–1700', in P. O'Flanagan and N.G. Buttimer (eds) *Cork: History and Society* (Dublin, 1993), p.320.

67 H.F. Kearney, *Strafford in Ireland 1633–41: A Study in Absolutism* (Manchester, 1959), pp.159–68; V. Treadwell, 'The establishment of the farm of the Irish customs, 1603–13', *EHR* 93 (1978), pp.580–602.

indirect rewards exceeded the perils.[68] The dispositions of the 1670s and 1680s reflected the new prominence of Anglo-Irish notables at court. Losers and winners alike came from the small coterie which still handled so much of the profitable business of Ireland. The gains of Ranelagh and Longford were matched by the chagrin of the former's uncle, Cork, whose prestige, patronage and profits as lord treasurer were summarily reduced. Even the arch exponent of English treasury supremacy, Laurence Hyde, future earl of Rochester and Irish lord lieutenant, was Cork's favourite son-in-law and recipient of a mysterious pension of £1,600 yearly on the Irish civil list.[69] So, while a few were mortified, the spoils of the revenue percolated through provincial Ireland, and helped to bind petty functionaries to the distant regimes in Dublin and London. As in many other spheres, the apparent subordination of Ireland to England through the fiscal, administrative and military innovations after 1660 should not be mistaken for a loss of practical autonomy.[70]

Ireland, despite the demographic and political disasters of the mid-century and subsequent commercial discrimination by the Westminster parliament, was more populous and wealthier than Scotland. In consequence it could offer men and money. Its resilient economy was translated in the buoyant 1680s into an annual Irish revenue of between £250,000 and £300,000.[71] Once again Ireland might reasonably be expected to top up English funds. And indeed, from 1684, a modest £30,000 was sent over each year. As a tip for the extravagant king it was welcomed. But in an English budget of over £2 million the extra could hardly make the difference between constitutional and authoritarian monarchy.[72] Nevertheless, the financial argument, that a properly governed

68 Christ Church, Oxford, Evelyn MSS, box VI, 'Computation of hearth money 1685–94' with names of farmers; NLI MS 4908, ff65, 76; Pearse St Public Library, Gilbert MS 207, pp.30–2; L.A. Clarkson and E.M. Crawford, *Ways to Wealth: The Cust Family of Eighteenth-Century Armagh* (Belfast, 1985), pp.25–6, 33–43; D. Dickson, C. Ó Gráda and S. Daultrey, 'Hearth tax, household size and Irish population change, 1672–1821', *PRIA 82C* (1982), pp.156–8; J. Miller, 'Thomas Sheridan (1646–1712) and his "Narrative"', *IHS* 20 (1976), pp.107, 111–14.

69 Bodl Carte MS 59, f653v.

70 Others have read rather more into Dr Egan's findings: Dickson, *New Foundations*, p.198, n.4; P.H. Kelly, 'Ireland and the Glorious Revolution: from kingdom to colony', in R.A. Beddard (ed.) *The Revolutions of 1668* (Oxford, 1991), p.167.

71 Dickson, *New Foundations* p.25; R.G. Gillespie, 'James II and the Irish Protestants', *IHS* 28 (1992), pp.127, 129; Miller, 'Tyrconnel', p.815.

72 Chandaman, *English Public Revenue*, pp.332–3, 360–1.

Ireland could assist the king in England and Scotland, was frequently advanced by those such as Tyrconnell who sought to capture Irish policy. The Stewarts, greedy for more money, were beguiled by such visions, and promoted the visionaries. In 1687 Tyrconnell, the sorcerer who would conjure so much from his catholic countrymen, was entrusted with the Irish government.

MILITARY UNITY

Monarchies, if they were to be secure, let alone absolute, needed to monopolize the means of violence. Standing armies best guaranteed such a monopoly. The Cromwellian interlude, sustained by costly and unpopular soldiers in all three countries, bequeathed hostility to armies, especially when they meddled in politics. Yet Charles II, insecure at home and abroad, required soldiers.[73] In Scotland a regular contingent of 2,000 was kept. Then in 1663 an amenable parliament sanctioned a militia of 20,000 foot and 2,000 horse, for service not only at home but also when necessary in Ireland or England. No compunction here about the resources of one kingdom being used to humble another: a view that had earlier assisted Strafford to the scaffold. Soon enough, in 1666, when the Pentland Rising coincided in time and (some supposed) in aim with the alert over the second Anglo-Dutch War, it was mustered. Piecemeal, in districts loyal to the regime and under trusty nobles, this militia came into being. It was unleashed against dissidents: in the Highlands, among the covenanters and reluctant taxpayers, and in the 1680s against Argyll's followers. The government named the quarries. But since the government was run by partisans of Lauderdale, it was suspected that dangers were identified – or even created – to buttress Lauderdale's position, and to permit favoured nobles to pursue traditional enemies now conveniently designated as enemies of the state. The monarchy might not have surrendered its monopoly over violence, but by deputing it to others, in the recent past often adversaries of the Stewarts, it concentrated

73 H.M. Reece, 'The military presence in England, 1649–1660' (Oxford University, D Phil thesis, 1981); A. Woolrych, 'The Cromwellian Protectorate: a military dictatorship?', *History* 75 (1990), pp.208–30.

military strength in those who might again defy the crown.[74]

The larger English army in Ireland was not so easily stood down at the Restoration. Arrears of pay had still to be satisfied. Many officers, lately metamorphosed into Irish landowners, awaited the new land settlement. In addition, Ireland, perhaps more urgently than England or Scotland, had to be protected. So an army of between 5,000 and 7,000 remained.[75] For Ormond appointments in the army offered wonderful opportunities to gratify the king and English friends, to recompense his own affinity and to buy support within the Irish elites. Through the distribution of commands, and even in the location of garrisons and forts, the same mutually advantageous bargain between the crown and landowners in England and Scotland was struck. In 1664 twenty-nine commanders of Irish troops were peers, their sons or brothers, twenty-one of whom were in the thirty cavalry companies. Ormond packed his own chums and relations into the elite corps quartered around Dublin. At the lower levels, and in distant stations, there survived many for whom the Cromwellian collaborator, Orrery, obligingly vouched.[76] This use of the army to pamper local notables, if it placated the restless protestant community, undermined military preparedness. In 1669 the new lord deputy, Robartes, thundered against 'a painted army, such cheating in dead payers and false mustering of men'.[77] But the corrupt commanders, high in status and ready to scuttle over to England with their grumbles, fended off reformers.

By the early 1670s, as royal policy was more loudly disputed, the political tractability of the regular forces encouraged Charles II and his advisers to regard army officers as reliable agents of a supranational monarchy. All three kingdoms, together with overseas outposts, were increasingly organized as a single military unit through and between which men were freely moved. In 1674, for example, twenty-five English troops, for the moment superfluous

74 *An Accompt of Scotlands Grievances,* p.4; Brown, 'From Scottish lords to British officers', pp.142–8; Lenman, 'Militia, fencible men', p.172; J. Robertson, *The Scottish Enlightenment and the Militia Issue* (Edinburgh, 1985), pp.5–6.

75 J.C. Beckett, 'The Irish armed forces 1660–1685', in J. Bossy and P.J. Jupp (eds), *Essays Presented to Michael Roberts* (Belfast, 1976), pp.41–53; K.P. Ferguson, 'The army in Ireland from the Restoration to the Union' (Trinity College, Dublin, PhD thesis, 1981), pp.9–22; P.A. Morris, 'Ormond's army: the Irish standing army 1640–69' (Vanderbilt University, PhD thesis, 1980).

76 Bodl Carte MS 59, ff595–6, 610–15; Robartes to Bridgeman, 6 Oct. 1669, Staffordshire CRO D1287/18/3; D1778/I/i/109.

77 Robartes to Bridgeman, 19 and 23 Oct. 1669, Staffordshire CRO D1287/18/3.

with the ending of the Anglo-Dutch War, were dumped in Ireland. By 1684 five Scottish companies were stationed there and paid from the Irish revenues, while four Irish regiments garrisoned Tangiers.[78] In 1666 and again in 1678 Irish contingents were marched into eastern Ulster, either to intimidate or to serve in Scotland. On this occasion transnational cooperation was not tested. Instead Lauderdale and Ormond wrangled over who should pick up the tab, since each of the kingdoms baulked at financing operations outside its own confines.[79]

Because the Irish soldiery might help outside their own island, English ministers interested themselves closely in Ireland's military as well as financial potential. Ormond, who saw the army as his personal preserve, resisted, but he was edged aside by the malleable Irish peers, Longford and Granard. Even before Charles II's death, the stranglehold of aristocratic commanders and the nominees of the tight clique which now directed Irish affairs in London and Dublin was loosened. The new king encouraged his old companion, Tyrconnell, to elbow aside Ormond, and to transform the force into an overwhelmingly catholic one: by 1688, 90 per cent of the soldiers were papists.[80]

This rapid change was the more alarming because it was attended by the dismantling of the militia. As in Scotland and England, so in Ireland, the militia offered a cheap and less menacing alternative to the regulars.[81] In the 1660s the Irish parliament had not copied the Scottish assembly by authorizing a militia, perhaps because a large army still existed.[82] Invasion scares during the second Anglo-Dutch War obliged a reluctant Ormond to muster the militia. During the next decade it was revived and

78 Bodl Carte MS 59, ff645–6; Beckett, 'Irish armed forces', pp.50–2; J. Childs, *The Army of Charles II* (London, 1976), pp.203–4; Egan, 'Finance and the government of Ireland', II, pp.4–5, 26.

79 Bodl Carte MS 146, p.43; Victoria & Albert Museum, Ormonde MSS i, ff101v, 103, 111v–12, 117v; HMC *Ormonde MSS* iv, pp.66, 68–9, 72–3, 102, 522.

80 Bodl Carte MSS 53, f653; 59, ff645–6; Childs, *Army of Charles II*, pp.207–9; J. Childs, *The Army, James II and the Glorious Revolution* (Manchester, 1980), pp.58–76; Miller, 'Tyrconnel', pp.817–19; J.G. Simms, *Jacobite Ireland 1685–91* (London, 1969), pp.18, 24–5.

81 A. Coleby, *Central Government and the Localities: Hampshire 1649–1689* (Cambridge, 1987), pp.104–13; A. Fletcher, *Reform in the Provinces: The Government of Stuart England* (New Haven, Conn., 1986), pp.323–48; J. Miller, 'The militia and the army in the reign of James II', *HJ* 16 (1973), pp.659–78; J.R. Western, *The English Militia in the Eighteenth Century* (London, 1965).

82 Bodl Carte MS 48, f49; G.J. Hand, 'The constitutional position of the Irish military establishment from the Restoration to the Union', *Irish Jurist* 3 (1968), pp.330–5.

enlarged. Successive lords lieutenant suspected that its existence and growth not only perpetuated the military ethos and origins of Irish protestant settlements, especially in Ulster and Munster, but also concentrated power dangerously in the hands of those there who headed the 'Protestant Interest'. As in Scotland, the privatization of the use of force threatened the government should it ever find itself at odds with these local notables.[83] Tyrconnell, aware of the risk, first disarmed and then suppressed the militia. Horrified protestants readily grasped how these reversals prefigured Tyrconnell's complete review of how Ireland fitted into and could contribute to James VII and II's system.[84]

TYRCONNELL AND THE FAILURE OF UNITY

Tyrconnell, in common with James VII and II (and Ormond), saw matters with the simplicity and clarity of a soldier. He accepted the premise on which Stewart power since 1660 had been grounded, that is, to restore authority to the localities where the landowners, under closer supervision from the centre, should govern. What he could also demonstrate was that in Ireland, unlike in Scotland and England, no such alliance had been reconstructed. Instead, craven advisers, headed by those inveterate opponents of the Irish catholics (and Tyrconnell) Clarendon and Ormond, cobbled together a feeble protestant coalition of returned cavaliers and others riddled still with republican and seditious principles. So far from stabilizing Ireland, Tyrconnell contended, this new order, artificially created by the Cromwellian conquest and maintained only by an unjust land and religious settlement, endangered the Stewarts' hold over the island. He counselled that the kingdom be brought belatedly into proper congruity with England and Scotland by restoring power to its natural local rulers, the Catholics.[85]

James VII and II was captivated by this promise of an Ireland loyal and docile. Tyrconnell, like others before him who had made their careers in Ireland, insisted that what he could accomplish

83 Barnard, 'Settling and unsettling Ireland'.

84 T.C. Barnard, 'Athlone 1685; Limerick 1710: religious riots or charivaris?', *SH* 27 (1993) pp.61–71.

85 Miller, 'Tyrconnel', pp.804–23; 'A series of eight anonymous and confidential letters', pp.2–4; Simms, *Jacobite Ireland*, pp.39–43.

there, notably larger supplies of money and troops, showed what might soon be done elsewhere. Tyrconnell's opponents, like Wentworth's in the 1630s or Lauderdale's in the 1670s, agreed that this venture possessed British implications, for how, other than through English or Scottish intervention, could his sinister design be halted? The interdependence of Irish and English affairs meant that no Irish policy, no matter how sensitively it catered to the unique confessional and social conditions of Ireland, could be detached from the larger, British dimension. Moreover, Tyrconnell, like Strafford during the 1630s, made good his boasts: the country was passive; the displaced protestants, though edgy, merely moped; Ireland did indeed send cash and, in the autumn of 1688, soldiers to aid James in England.[86] But, as in the past, what Ireland contributed was not commensurate with the resultant political disquiet, popular pandemonium and damage to the king's reputation.[87] In addition, if regiments were shipped to England, and others paid with Irish taxes, Ireland could never add enough to the Stewarts' resources to free them from the constraints imposed by England and Scotland. After 1689 Ireland, though appealed to by James, could not lever him back on to his other thrones; indeed, it failed even to preserve him as its own catholic king.

Thus, for all that Tyrconnell dressed up his as a British programme, with Ireland as the model and underwriter of catholic absolutism, his prototype would hardly export to England or Scotland. In fact his plan, so frighteningly innovative to its likely victims, asked only that Ireland be ruled in accordance with tradition. That constitutional legalism and conservatism, clear in the earlier Confederation of Kilkenny and in the provincial particularism of rebellious elites throughout seventeenth-century Europe, so much in tune with the thinking behind the Tory reaction of the 1680s, animated the Irish catholics' campaign since 1660 to retrieve their lost rights and property. Tyrconnell, far from exporting to Britain, wished to import into Ireland the deals which had successfully returned power in England and Scotland to the familiar elites. His misfortune was that Ireland's government was returned to members of the catholic majority at the very moment

86 Childs, *The Army, James II and the Glorious Revolution*, pp.6, 58–60, 68; Gillespie, 'James II and the Irish Protestants', pp.124–33; Simms, *Jacobite Ireland*, pp.42–3.

87 G.H. Jones, 'The Irish fright of 1688', *BIHR* 55 (1982), pp.423–35; P. Melvin, 'The Irish army and the Revolution of 1688', *Irish Sword* 9 (1969–70), pp.295–307. Tyrconnell planned to recruit the Irish force to nearly 40,000 men: BL Add MS 28938, f291; Simms, *Jacobite Ireland*, pp.49, 53.

when in England and Scotland James switched power to untried minorities. Once more, Ireland marched out of step with the Stewarts' other dominions. That it did so suggested that Ireland's value as a laboratory in which to refine a unitary policy appropriate to all three kingdoms had been overstated; so too what it could contribute to the later Stewarts' ambitions. Despite some halting steps towards congruence, integration and anglicization, a feeble trickle of cash and a noisy stream of soldiers, Ireland still played Bohemia to England's Austria and Scotland's Hungary in the composite monarchy of the later seventeenth century.

CHAPTER ELEVEN

Constitutional experiments and political expediency, 1689–1725

David Hayton
Queen's University, Belfast

UNION: END OR MEANS?

At first glance the three decades after the Glorious Revolution seem to mark a closing stage in the forging of a multinational British state. The parliamentary union of England and Scotland in 1707, and the accompanying measure of administrative integration, finally realized the implications present since the Union of the Crowns, while persistent obscurities in the constitutional relationship between England and Ireland were dispelled in a different but equally decisive manner by the English Declaratory Act of 1720, which confirmed the provisions of Poynings' Law and dismissed the pretensions of the Irish parliament to anything more than a strictly subordinate role in the government of the island. If we look to statute therefore, and only to statute, to define the political relationship of the three kingdoms we are presented with a neat finish to a process of state formation. In that case the purpose of this chapter would be simply to describe how the terminus had been reached; more specifically perhaps, to explain why legislative union had been seen as the answer to the Scottish question but not to the Irish.

There has been a vigorous, and occasionally vituperative, debate over the making of the treaty of 1707, between those, like the great Whig historian G.M. Trevelyan,[1] who saw Anglo-Scottish union as a statesmanlike (and on the whole sensible) solution to chronic

1 G.M. Trevelyan, *England under Queen Anne, vol.II, Ramillies and the Union with Scotland* (London, 1932).

problems of political insecurity and economic dysfunction – inclining to accept politicians as honourable and merchants and economists as disinterested – and more recent revisionists, determined cynics like Patrick Riley or staunch Scottish nationalists like William Ferguson, for whom union was a political job carried through by bribery and with no higher object than personal or party-political advantage.[2] Much of the disagreement has seemed to hinge on interpretations of character: are we to regard parliamentarians on either side of the border as far-sighted and principled, or myopic and corrupt; should we take their public statements at face value, or scratch for the private interests that may have lain underneath? Such fundamental differences of opinion between historians are often insoluble, but in the case of the union the detailed evidence presented in Riley's studies of Anglo-Scottish politics between 1689 and 1707 leaves little room to question the justice of his severe judgement, at least in so far as the timing of the treaty is concerned.

The need felt among the majority of the political classes in both England and Scotland for a means of safeguarding the Revolution settlement and the protestant succession probably made a union inevitable, but the fact that consummation occurred in 1707 rather than in 1689 or 1702 was a function of high-political manoeuvring at Westminster, as the lord treasurer, Godolphin, and the Whig politicians with whom he was in uneasy alliance each succeeded in convincing themselves that they stood to profit by the arrangement. As Riley observed, the key to union was to be found in England. After the Revolution the Scots could probably have been brought to agree to a treaty at any time. Besides the votes that might be purchased through bribes to individuals or party leaders, there was a strong element of principled pro-unionist opinion in Scotland, and especially in the Scottish parliament. Consistent advocates of union were joined by others who became persuaded that this was

2 W. Ferguson, 'The making of the Treaty of Union of 1707', *SHR* 43 (1964), pp.89–110; W. Ferguson, *Scotland's Relations with England: A Survey to 1707* (Edinburgh, 1977); T.C. Smout, 'The road to union', in G. Holmes (ed.) *Britain after the Glorious Revolution 1689–1714* (London, 1969), pp.176–96; P.W.J. Riley, 'The union of 1707 as an episode in English politics', *EHR* 74 (1969), pp.498–527; P.W.J. Riley, *The Union of England and Scotland: A Study in Anglo-Scottish Politics of the Eighteenth Century* (Manchester, 1978); G. Holmes, *British Politics in the Age of Anne* (2nd edn, London, 1987), pp.xxxiv-xxxv; G. Holmes, *The Making of a Great Power: Late Stuart and Early Georgian Britain 1660–1722* (Harlow, 1993), ch.20.

now the only feasible way to uplift the struggling Scottish economy.[3] Opposition remained, among Jacobite cavaliers, bitter patriots like Andrew Fletcher of Saltoun, the radical presbyterians of the south-west and the urban populace, but, as the events of 1706–7 were to prove, voting strength in the Scottish parliament lay with a coalition of committed unionists and pliant politicians, and the host of the venal.[4] The failure of the negotiations in 1702 was not the result of Scottish hesitancy so much as English indifference and a mounting ministerial apprehension, understandable in the circumstances, that Scottish Members elected to a united parliament would be resistant to court direction.

By extension Riley's thesis also provides a convincing answer to the question of why there should have been no Anglo-Irish union. The Irish parliament could also have been brought to union at the bidding of the English ministry. Some among the protestant elite actively canvassed for constitutional integration, on similar grounds to their Scottish counterparts, namely as a means of securing the protestant establishment and fostering economic development; this strain of opinion seems to have become predominant during the early years of Queen Anne's reign, for while negotiations were under way between the English and the Scots the Irish parliament expressed concern lest the country miss out on any benefits, and even perhaps suffer commercial discrimination.[5] A violently patriotic opposition would have been improbable. As yet the Anglo-Irish did not possess a sufficiently strong sense of national identity, and in any case, the normal operations of patronage and influence would presumably have guaranteed the purchase of a majority. However, no English administration was tempted to trust to the likely behaviour of Irish MPs sent to Westminster, except for a moment in 1697 when the Whig junto fell under the impression

3 For pro-unionist opinion in general, Riley, *Union* ch.VI and esp. pp.233–9; *Anglo-Scottish Tracts 1701–1714*, comp. W.R. McLeod and V.B. McLeod (Lawrence, Kansas, 1979), pp.165, 198. For particular examples, [George Mackenzie,] *Parainesis Pacifica* . . . (Edinburgh, 1702); [William Seton,] *The Interest of Scotland in Three Essays* . . . (Edinburgh, 1702), pp.37–63; Sir William Fraser, *The Earls of Cromartie: Their Kindred, Country and Correspondence* (2 vols; Edinburgh, 1876), I, pp.161–3, 296; II, pp.1–2; Douglas-Home MSS (Lord Home, the Hirsel, Berwicks) box 21, folder 4, Sir David Dalrymple to Lord Home, 20 Sept. 1702; *Correspondence of George Baillie of Jerviswood* . . ., ed. Earl of Minto, Bannatyne Club 72 (Edinburgh, 1842), p.21.

4 *The Lord Belhaven's Speech in Parliament* . . . (1706); Andrew Fletcher, *Selected Political Writings and Speeches*, ed. D. Daiches (Edinburgh, 1979); P.H. Scott, *Andrew Fletcher and the Treaty of Union* (Edinburgh, 1992); see also note 41 below.

5 J. Kelly, 'The origins of the Act of Union: an examination of unionist opinion in Britain and Ireland, 1650–1800', *IHS* 25 (1986–7), pp.241–4; J. Smyth, '"Like amphibious animals": Irish Protestants, Ancient Britons', *HJ* 36 (1993), pp.785–97.

that Irish parliamentary elections would naturally produce an influx into their midst of ultra-Protestant and therefore Whiggishly inclined MPs. At that point a timely outburst of Irish protestant 'patriotism' showed up, for the benefit of even the most obtuse, some of the drawbacks of a legislative union.[6] In general an Anglo-Irish union would have offered too many risks to English political equilibrium, and as it was inessential in terms of statecraft the subject remained beneath ministerial consideration.

But to formulate the question in such a way fails to do justice to the complexity of the problems involved in governing the three kingdoms. It seems to embody two false assumptions: that the union constituted the end of a political process rather than a step along the road, and that it can be wholly understood in an Anglo-Scottish context. Looked at differently, the union appears in another form, as an expedient to which ministers resorted in order to overcome difficulties in political management, difficulties common to the government of Scotland and Ireland, and even of England itself. It was not the only means employed, nor by itself did it provide all the answers.

If we take as our guiding theme not the establishment of a unitary eighteenth-century state from the potential multiple monarchy of the Stewarts, but the continuing responsibility of monarchs and their English ministers to effect the political management of Scotland and Ireland, a different configuration falls on the landscape. Constitutional innovations, of which the union was one among many, have to be set against the re-emergence of an historic method of administering remote and dependent territories: the contracting-out of political management to locally based magnates. By the mid-1720s there had evolved a system of governing Scotland and Ireland through native political interests, in Scotland the great house of Argyll, and in Ireland the less grand but equally effective parliamentary undertakers such as William Conolly or Henry Boyle: a system whose parliamentary trappings would have been alien, but whose inner rationale would have been familiar enough to the barons of the medieval marches.

Behind the legislative experiments that mark the period can be found traditional calculations of political expediency, and the

6 TCD MS 750/1 (King letterbooks), p.79, Archbishop King to Sir Robert Southwell, 19 July 1697, cited in D. Szechi and D. Hayton, 'John Bull's other kingdoms': the English government of Scotland and Ireland', in C. Jones (ed.) *Britain in the First Age of Party 1680–1750: Essays Presented to Geoffrey Holmes* (London, 1987), p.268.

interplay between the two shaped the settlements which emerged. The necessity for additional taxation to finance European military commitments, and a simultaneous retreat from pro-active domestic policies, induced the post-Revolution monarchy to seek the cooperation of representative institutions in all three kingdoms in the hope of securing government by consensus. Instead, these various assemblies brought forth turbulence and disharmony, so that crown and ministers looked for ways to reduce them to discipline, even in the last resort by dispensing with them altogether. The Scottish parliament was submerged in the English; the Irish parliament suffered a reinforced limitation of its powers. This ministerial reaction did not go so far as to deprive parliaments of any part to play in improving the political cohesion of Scotland and Ireland, but what was left was a role of reduced importance, the provision of a further means, beyond the working of governmental patronage, through which grievances might be met and vested interests satisfied.

THE RISE OF PARLIAMENTS

However Whiggish it may seem to say so, it remains true that the years after the Glorious Revolution witnessed a remarkable flowering of representative institutions across the three kingdoms. The Westminster parliament attained institutional status, meeting regularly and for longer periods than before, doing much more business, and as a result elaborating its procedure and expanding its bureaucracy.[7] Even more spectacular were the advances made in Ireland, where no parliament had been called since 1667. After a somewhat erratic history under William and Anne the Irish parliament settled into its classic eighteenth-century pattern of biennial sessions.[8] The Scottish estates had met more frequently since the Restoration, but there had none the less been long stretches – between 1663 and 1672, for example, and from 1673 to 1681 – punctuated by only the briefest of sessions. After 1689 such

7 A. McInnes, 'When was the English Revolution?' *History* 67 (1982), pp.387–92; J. Brewer, *The Sinews of Power: War, Money and the English State 1688–1783* (London, 1989); Kathryn M. Ellis, 'The practice and procedure of the House of Commons, 1660–1714' (University of Wales, PhD thesis, 1993).

8 D.W. Hayton, 'Ireland and the English ministers, 1707–16' (Oxford University, DPhil thesis, 1975), pp.90–102.

short sittings were exceptional; more important, the abolition of the Lords of the Articles (the crown-nominated committee responsible for the introduction of business) gave scope for initiative and a more genuine participation on the part of barons and burgh commissioners.[9]

But it was not only parliaments that flourished. In 1701 the convocation of Canterbury entered on an unexpected Indian summer, meeting alongside parliament to debate questions of ecclesiastical reform; three years later clerical pressure led to the resumption of the convocation of the Church of Ireland, for the first time since 1666.[10] The Presbyterian church settlement in Scotland had already involved the recall of the general assembly after a gap of forty years.[11] Even the convocation of the stannaries in Cornwall, the so-called 'parliament of tinners' which voted the pre-emption of the tin duty, reappeared in 1702 to take on some of the qualities of the parliament proper at Westminster, to which its more prominent members also belonged, with elections fiercely contested and the proceedings infected by the plague of party politics.[12]

What would be unacceptably Whiggish would be to depict this widespread and complex phenomenon simply as a function of the triumph of parliament at the Glorious Revolution. Certainly 'Revolution principles' were a factor in obliging King William to work through representative institutions in establishing his authority. The king's statements of intent had included promises to the English and Scots that he would summon parliaments, and in response the Declaration of Rights in England and the Claim of Right in Scotland had each required a guarantee of frequent and free elections.[13] Even in Ireland it was assumed by king and

9 R.S. Rait, *The Parliaments of Scotland* (Glasgow, 1924), pp.75–125, 386–92, 506–7.

10 N. Sykes, *William Wake, Archbishop of Canterbury 1657–1737* (2 vols; Cambridge, 1957), I, ch.2; G.V. Bennett, *The Tory Crisis in Church and State 1688–1730 . . .* (Oxford, 1975) chs III–VII; J.C. Beckett, 'The government and the Church of Ireland under William III and Anne', *IHS* 2 (1940–1), pp.291–7; S.J. Connolly, *Religion, Law and Power: The Making of Protestant Ireland 1660–1760* (Oxford, 1992), pp.172–3, 187–8.

11 I.B. Cowan, 'Church and state reformed? The Revolution of 1688–9 in Scotland', in J.I. Israel (ed.), *The Anglo-Dutch Moment: Essays on the Glorious Revolution and its World Impact* (Cambridge, 1991), pp.177–83.

12 E. Cruickshanks, 'The convocation of the stannaries of Cornwall: the Parliament of Tinners 1703–1752', *Parliaments, Estates and Representation* 6 (1986), pp.59–67.

13 L.G. Schwoerer, *The Declaration of Rights, 1689* (Baltimore, Md, 1981), pp.112–14, 296–7; *Acts of the Parliament of Scotland* (12 vols; London, 1844–75), IX, pp.9, 38–40.

ministers that once the wartime emergency had come to an end the further steps necessary to secure the regime would be taken in an Irish parliament.[14] The lord lieutenant, Sidney, although speaking in terms of privilege, declared in the parliament in Dublin in 1692 that the kingdom 'can no way be so well restored to any degree of settlement, as by a Parliament thus legally constituted and assembled, which . . . is a blessing that for many years you have been deprived of'.[15]

But William himself was no Whig, nor were his ministers always men distinguished by a strict adherence to constitutional propriety. The principal reason that he and his successors continued to summon parliaments was the need for subsidies: to fight costly continental wars, to maintain in peacetime the strategic military reserves that diplomatic ambitions demanded, and ultimately to service the fiscal deficits that this new foreign policy had created.[16] The Irish parliament furnishes perhaps the best example, if only because from time to time the tempestuous course of Anglo-Irish relations made ministers yearn for a return to what were treasured in retrospect as the peaceful, parliament-free, years of Charles II's reign. After the fiasco of the short-lived parliament of 1692, dissolved without a vote of 'additional' duties to supplement the crown's hereditary revenue, the Irish government tottered towards bankruptcy. The treasury stood empty, depleted by years of civil war, and payments were stopped.[17] Despite the unpopularity of royal policies and officials in Dublin, the lord deputy, Capel, had no option but to summon a new parliament and come to terms with opposition leaders in order to obtain a temporary additional supply.[18] By 1699 the recovery of the Irish public revenue permitted the suspension of parliamentary sessions again during stormy political weather. But not for long; payments were soon being interrupted once more, the lords justices in Dublin followed Queen

14 Nottingham University Library, Portland (Bentinck) MSS, PwA 299b–c, Lords Sidney and Coningsby to Portland, 27 Sept. 1690; HMC *Finch MSS*, IV, 54–5; *CSP Dom 1691–2*, pp.55, 65–70; J.I. McGuire, 'The Parliament of 1692', in T. Bartlett and D.W. Hayton (eds) *Penal Era and Golden Age: Essays in Irish History 1690–1800* (Belfast, 1979), pp.2–9.

15 *Journals of the House of Commons of the Kingdom of Ireland 1613–1776* (19 vols; Dublin, 1753–76), II, p.576.

16 D.W. Jones, *War and Economy in the Age of William III and Marlborough* (Oxford, 1988); Brewer, *Sinews of Power*, chs 4–5; P.G.M. Dickson, *The Financial Revolution in England: A Study in the Development of Public Credit* (2nd edn, London, 1993), chs 3–4.

17 HMC *Buccleuch MSS*, II, 99.

18 Hayton, 'Ireland and the English ministers', pp.90–1; W. Troost, *William III and the Treaty of Limerick (1691–1697)* (Leiden, 1983), chs III–IV.

Anne's accession with a call for a further subsidy, and parliament duly resumed in 1703.[19] Under George I the Irish administration immediately slipped into a permanent financial deficit, when the excise voted in 1715 yielded far less than had been anticipated, because of stockpiling by Irish merchants after the expiry of additional duties at Christmas 1713.[20] It was now harder than ever for the crown to subsist without parliamentary assistance, and under the Hanoverians a series of limited grants of additional duties guaranteed regular sessions.

There were other needs which parliaments could best satisfy. After 1689 the English monarchy, preoccupied with European diplomacy and requiring no more from its domestic governance than the virtues of order, stability and high taxation, abandoned the initiative in social and economic policy to interest-groups. Even in matters of religion, in which previous Stewart kings had taken a personal, and often disastrous, interest, the stimulus to radical change came now from outside the court, from High Churchmen keen to impose a new uniformity or dissenters anxious to break it, while William and his successors behaved as well-meaning but unassertive referees. Moreover, the commercial and financial revolutions had produced new and complex problems in the regulation of economy and society which conciliar government was not fully equipped to solve.[21] Parliaments (and convocations) offered the most attractive alternative, given that monarchs and ministers seem to have wished to proceed as far as possible by consensus rather than by proclamation, and that they lacked both the reliable statistical information necessary to gauge the scope of economic and social problems and an ideology sufficiently sophisticated to enable them to understand the mechanics of change. In these circumstances the local knowledge to which Members of Parliament could lay claim acquired a sovereign authority in debate. Legislation became an instrument of vested interests; and so useful an instrument that the province of statute expanded dramatically. The volume of local and private Bills now

19 *CSP Dom 1700–2*, p.326; *1702–3*, p.563.

20 Hayton, 'Ireland and the English ministers', pp.92–3; TCD MS 2536 (King letterbooks), pp.239–240, King to Frederick Hamilton, 12 April 1715; MS 750/13 (King letterbooks), p.43, King to Joseph Addison, 14 April 1715.

21 L.K. Davison, 'Public policy in an age of economic expansion: the search for commercial accountability in England, 1690–1750' (Harvard University, PhD thesis, 1990); L. Davison, T. Hitchcock, T. Keirn and R.B. Shoemaker (eds) *Stilling the Grumbling Hive: The Response to Social and Economic Problems in England, 1689–1750* (Stroud, 1992), introduction.

being presented to the English House of Commons necessitated repeated efforts to restrict the flow in order that government business should not be choked.[22] A rapid survey of the published record would suggest an equally sharp and sustained rise in the legislative activity of the Irish parliament, even though the requirements of Poynings' Law made the legislative process in Ireland cumbersome and expensive, so that for Irishmen in pursuit of private Bills the Westminster parliament continued to be used as a viable, and sometimes cheaper, alternative.[23]

It was, therefore, very much in the interests of the post-Revolution monarchy to encourage the development of representative institutions in its dominions. Parliaments were essential in financial terms. They were also highly desirable politically, in that they offered the possibility of proceeding towards a settlement of general questions of domestic governance through agreement and through making use of the most reliable sources of information, while at the same time gratifying local interests and settling local grievances.

CRISES OF FACTION

Such was the theory; practice was often very different. Factional conflicts disrupted the smooth running of parliamentary business, sometimes so badly that, as in Ireland in 1692 and 1713, or Scotland in 1700, sessions could not continue. Occasionally the government found itself pushed off course, even having to accept a diminution of royal powers: King William was obliged to assent to the English Triennial Act of 1694 and a year later his lord deputy tacitly acknowledged the Irish House of Commons' unjustified assumption of a 'sole right' to initiate money Bills.[24] The fact that each of the three kingdoms possessed its own representative

22 P. Langford, 'Property and virtual representation in eighteenth-century England', *HJ* 31 (1988), pp.83–115; P. Langford, *Public Life and the Propertied Englishman 1689–1798* (Oxford, 1991) ch.3; Brewer, *Sinews of Power,* ch.8; S. Handley, 'Local legislative initiatives for economic and social development in Lancashire, 1689–1731', *PH* 9 (1991), pp.14–37; S. Lambert, *Bills and Acts: Legislative Procedure in Eighteenth-Century England* (Cambridge, 1971), pp.52–5.

23 TCD MS 3821/117 (Crosbie MSS), Maurice Fitzgerald to [David Crosbie], 4 July 1709; *Journals of the House of Commons* XV, 530.

24 H. Horwitz, *Parliament, Policy and Politics in the Reign of William III* (Manchester, 1977), pp.110–11, 114, 124–5, 137–9; F.G. James, *Ireland in the Empire 1688–1730,* Harvard Historical Monographs 68 (Cambridge, Mass., 1973), pp.32–5; McGuire, 'Parliament of 1692', pp.19–22, 24–5, 29.

institutions brought the additional hazard of different national parliaments pressing conflicting interests, even so far as to quarrel with each other and imperil essential measures, as happened in 1698–9 when the English parliament decided to take a strong line against imports of Irish woollens.[25] Alternatively, discontented elements in different kingdoms might combine their attacks on administration into a common front of opposition: a rarer prospect but one that materialized as early as 1693, when Whigs in England opened an inquiry into alleged misgovernment in Ireland and imported as their witnesses the leading 'troublemakers' in the dissolved Irish parliament.[26]

Traced in outline the political histories of the three kingdoms in this period exhibit remarkably similar patterns. Early confusion in the aftermath of the Revolution, with 'moderate' or mixed ministries under attack from the more extreme elements on both sides, ended in the establishment in about 1694–5 of more settled and successful administrations in the 'Revolution' interest which, directly or indirectly, produced men and money for the war effort: the Whig junto in England, their party colleague Capel in Ireland assisted by local Whig politicians such as the Brodrick brothers, and in Scotland the ministry headed by the secretary, Johnston.[27] In each kingdom, however, the settlement proved short-lived. In England from 1698 onwards the junto was hounded from office but not effectively replaced since its Tory opponents were divided among themselves and unable to restrain the 'Country' enthusiasms of their rank and file.[28] In Ireland popular resentment over the English Woollen Act and the forfeitures resumption deterred ministers from putting their management to the test after 1699; when parliament was eventually recalled the Court party was forced to stomach a series of 'Country' inquiries and resolutions.[29]

25 H.F. Kearney, 'The political background to English mercantilism, 1695–1700', *EcHR* 2nd ser.11 (1959), pp.484–96; P. Kelly, 'The Irish Woollen Export Prohibition Act of 1699: Kearney revisited', *IESH* 7 (1980), pp.22–44.

26 *Journals of the House of Commons* X, 826–33; *The Parliamentary Diary of Narcissus Luttrell 1691–1693*, ed. H. Horwitz (Oxford, 1972), pp.438–43.

27 Horwitz, *Parliament, Policy and Politics*, chs VI–IX; Troost, *William III and the Treaty of Limerick* chs III–IV; D. Hayton, 'The beginnings of the "undertaker system"', in Bartlett and Hayton (eds) *Penal Era and Golden Age*, pp.40–1; P.W.J. Riley, *King William and the Scottish Politicians* (Edinburgh, 1979), chs 1–4.

28 B.W. Hill, *The Growth of Parliamentary Parties 1689–1742* (London, 1976), chs 4–5; Horwitz, *Parliament, Policy and Politics*, chs XI–XII.

29 James, *Ireland in the Empire*, pp.51–9; Szechi and Hayton, 'John Bull's other kingdoms', pp.267–8; *CSP Dom 1703–4*, pp.130–2, 140–1, 146, 149–50, 157–8, 163–4, 169–71; NAI, Frazer MSS 207/331, minute book of Irish House of Commons Committee of Public Accounts 1703–17 (unfol.).

Simultaneously, in Scotland Johnston's position was undermined by a resurgence of magnate influence that eventually brought to power the duke of Queensberry, who in his turn proved unable to restrain the violence of the Scottish 'Country' party in the parliaments of 1700–2.[30] Order was restored only when Godolphin and Marlborough established in England a settled administration with Whig support, a model which was extended to Ireland under Lord Wharton, and even to Scotland, where Queensberry's revived Court party, in uneasy alliance with Argyll and the Squadrone, carried the union.[31] The Whig defeat in 1710 undermined this stability, though the political skills of the new lord treasurer, Robert Harley, postponed a collapse until 1713. Then Tory divisions deprived him of a majority in the British parliament, the Scottish peers and MPs moved for repeal of the union, and Irish management foundered in a calamitous parliament.[32] After the Hanoverian succession, jealousies among the victorious Whigs in all three kingdoms again produced a general political crisis, coming to a head after 1720 with a reinvigorated opposition in the British parliament, and in Ireland a bout of high-political infighting accompanied by patriotic disturbances.[33] By 1726 this last crisis was over, however, and in each kingdom tensions were resolved and the violence of popular feeling abated.

The fact that politics in the three kingdoms ran such closely parallel courses suggests the presence of common factors. Admittedly some of the difficulties in which administrations found themselves are attributable to specific local causes, whether it be the grievous financial losses sustained in Scotland as a result of the Darien disaster, or the resentment among Scots in 1713 against the imposition of the malt tax.[34] They might also be the consequence

30 Riley, *King William and the Scottish Politicians*, chs 5–8.

31 Hill, *Growth of Parliamentary Parties*, chs 6–7; Holmes, *British Politics*, chs 11–12; L.A. Dralle, 'Kingdom in reversion: the Irish viceroyalty of the earl of Wharton, 1708–10', *HLQ* 15 (1951–2), pp.393–431; Riley, *Union*, chs IV–V, VII.

32 G. Holmes and C. Jones, 'Trade, the Scots and the parliamentary crisis of 1713', *PH* 1 (1982), pp.47–77; D. Hayton, 'The crisis in Ireland and the disintegration of Queen Anne's last ministry', *IHS* 22 (1980–1), pp.193–215.

33 J.H. Plumb, *Sir Robert Walpole: The Making of a Statesman* (London, 1956), chs VII–X; Hill, *Growth of Parliamentary Parties*, chs 9–10; P.W.J. Riley, *The English Ministers and Scotland, 1707–1727*, University of London Historical Studies 15 (London, 1964), pp.262–74; W. Ferguson, *Scotland 1689 to the Present* (Edinburgh, 1968), pp.137–43; R.E. Burns, *Irish Parliamentary Politics in the Eighteenth Century* (2 vols; Washington, DC, 1989), I, chs II–IV; Joseph Griffin, 'Parliamentary politics in Ireland during the reign of George I' (National University of Ireland, MA thesis, 1977).

34 *The Darien Papers . . . 1695–1700*, ed. John Hill Burton, Bannatyne Club 90 (Edinburgh, 1849), pp.371–417; J. Prebble, *The Darien Disaster* (Edinburgh, 1978),

of particular failures in management, such as the duke of Shrewsbury's ill-advised 'middling scheme' in Ireland in 1713.[35] But there were also underlying causes of a more general nature. Some were economic: there can be little doubt that the widespread troubles of the later 1690s were at least exacerbated by a serious economic depression consequent upon the over-straining of the British and Irish economies during the Nine Years War. A similar explanation might help to account for the collapse of political management at the end of the War of the Spanish Succession, while ministerial tribulations in the early 1720s cannot have been unconnected with the anxiety over public credit induced by the bursting of the South Sea Bubble and in Ireland a further manifestation of a recurring crisis over the coinage.[36] Other general causes were clearly political in nature, deriving from uncertainties over the succession to the throne or the continuance in office of the leading ministers, the strength or weakness of the court in England being reflected in the relative standing enjoyed by royal representatives in Scotland and Ireland.

The interrelationship between the political systems of the three kingdoms could thus pose various kinds of problems for the monarchy. The greatest danger arose when a 'patriotic' opposition in Scotland or Ireland began to identify as its enemy not corrupt ministers of the crown, nor even corrupt *English* ministers, but England itself and the English connection. This was the train of thought followed by Scots Jacobites after the union, and the more so after the Hanoverian succession: however, relatively few committed Jacobites held parliamentary seats before 1715, and none thereafter. In a parliamentary context, such centrifugal forces were perhaps most strongly felt in the political crisis that engulfed all three kingdoms at the end of William's reign, a crisis whose British dimension has not been fully appreciated by historians but which was to have a profound effect on the ways in which English ministers subsequently perceived their Scottish and Irish problems.

---

ch.5; Holmes and Jones, 'Trade, the Scots and the parliamentary crisis of 1713', pp.52–4; *Letters of George Lockhart of Carnwath 1698–1732*, ed. D. Szechi, Scottish History Society, 5th ser.2 (Edinburgh, 1989), pp.74–82; B. Lenman, 'Scotland between the '15 and the '45', in J. Black (ed.) *Britain in the Age of Walpole* (London, 1984), pp.80–1, 86–7.

35 Hayton, 'Crisis in Ireland and disintegration of Queen Anne's last ministry'.

36 Jones, *War and Economy*; J. Carswell, *The South Sea Bubble* (London, 1961); Lenman, 'Scotland between the '15 and the '45', pp.80–1; J. Johnston, *Bishop Berkeley's Querist in Historical Perspective* (Dundalk, 1970), p.32; M. Ryder, 'The Bank of Ireland, 1721: land, credit and dependency', *HJ* 25 (1982), pp.557–82.

Actual legislative interference by the English parliament in Irish affairs, and presumed English trading interference in the business of the Company of Scotland, combined to raise the temperature of both Anglo-Irish and Anglo-Scottish relations to fever pitch. The landed elites in both Anglo-Ireland and Lowland Scotland became politicized to an unusual degree: in Ireland opponents of the resumption of the forfeited estates mounted a campaign of county addresses to the king, the so-called 'national remonstrance',[37] while in Scotland the parliamentary elections of 1702 were marked by a high number of contests and the appearance in some counties of the practice of 'instructing' MPs in the details of a 'Country' party manifesto for reform.[38] In both countries the debate at quarter sessions or freeholders' court and in the press revolved around the relationship with England: Irish protestants followed the lead given by William Molyneux in his celebrated *Case* and disputed the right of the English parliament to legislate unilaterally for Ireland; Scotsmen questioned the purpose of their contribution to the war effort when it was the English and Dutch who reaped the rewards, and demanded that any union of the kingdoms or settlement of the Scottish succession be made conditional on guarantees of future protection from English economic oppression. The xenophobic arrogance of the English response, a high-handed dismissal of Irish pretensions, and, among Tories in particular, a contemptuous rejection of Scottish overtures, served to fan the flames of resentment.[39]

A further eruption of popular revulsion in Scotland was provoked by the union itself, which prompted addresses of protest from burghs and county communities to the doomed Scottish parliament and mob demonstrations in Edinburgh and other

37 J.G. Simms, *The Williamite Confiscation in Ireland, 1690–1703*, Studies in Irish History (London, 1956), pp.124–5; *Journals of the House of Commons* XIII, 718–19, 744–6; BL Add Ch 19526–38.

38 A list of controverted elections may be found at NLS MS 14498 (Yester MSS), ff82–3. For the 'instructions' in Berwickshire, see Duns Library, Berwickshire Local History Collection, f9, folder 36, electoral court minutes, 1702. For those in neighbouring Roxburghshire, SRO GD 6/1061/2, 6 (Biel MSS), speech to head court, 'heads' of instructions, 1702; GD 6/1062/b, electoral court minutes, 1702. The background to the latter is explained in Roxburghe MSS (Duke of Roxburghe, Floors Castle, Roxburghshire), bundle 726, William Bennet to [the Countess of Roxburghe], 8 Oct. 1702. I am grateful to the Duke of Roxburghe for permission to consult his family papers.

39 Bodl MS Eng. hist. C289, f277; Riley, *Union*, p.25; D. Hayton, 'The "Country" interest and the party system, 1689–*c*.1720', in C. Jones (ed.) *Party and Management in Parliament, 1660–1784* (Leicester, 1984), pp.60–3; D. Hayton, 'From barbarian to burlesque: English images of the Irish, *c*. 1660–1750', *IESH* 15 (1988), pp.24–5.

towns.[40] But once the deed was done, and, more important, the abortive Jacobite invasion attempt of 1708 had underlined the purpose and the value of the union, the majority of the Scottish political nation lowered its patriotic sights. Thus the motion of 1713 to repeal the union was in reality not much more than a shadow-play, a piece of mischief hatched by frustrated Tory back-benchers and the embittered duke of Argyll, and encouraged by the English Whigs and their Scottish allies in the hope of party-political advantage.[41] Although no self-respecting Scot dare oppose it in public, only a few took the motion in deadly earnest. When popular hatred of the malt tax at length burst out again, in the Shawfield riots of 1725, there was no such accompanying parliamentary campaign, for the Scots who remained in parliament were staunch adherents of the Revolution settlement and the Hanoverian succession, and had been thoroughly frightened by the Fifteen into regarding the union as sacrosanct. In the mean time, irreconcilable anti-unionism had become the preserve of Jacobites. The proposed county addresses in the winter of 1714–15 urging the dissolution of the union were Jacobite in inspiration, and while the great patriotic hero, Fletcher, always remained a resolute Hanoverian, a younger but equally passionate devotee of the national cause, Sir Alexander Murray of Stanhope, swallowed his presbyterian prejudices and came out in the Fifteen.[42]

Compromised by its identification with Jacobitism (a development that reached its apogee in the lionizing of the rugged presbyterian Fletcher in the Jacobite George Lockhart's provocative *Memoirs*), the strong national feeling which had animated Scottish politics at the turn of the century became enervated, and in the hands of a new generation of polite propagandists, of whom the virtuoso, Sir John Clerk of Penicuik, is the epitome, became subsumed under (though not entirely superseded by) an affected 'Britishness'. By contrast, the 'patriotism' of the protestant, Anglo-Irish ascendancy, actually became more vigorous under the

40 *Acts of the Parliament of Scotland* XI, 345–69 *passim*; [George Lockhart,] *Memoirs Concerning the Affairs of Scotland* . . . (3rd edn, London, 1714), pp.273–85, 341–7; Daniel Defoe, *The History of the Union* . . . (London, 1786), pp.218–84; Hume, *Diary*, pp.187–8.

41 Holmes and Jones, 'Trade, the Scots and the parliamentary crisis of 1713'.

42 *The Lockhart Papers* . . . , ed. Anthony Aufrere (2 vols; London, 1817), I, pp.574–88; HMC *Mar and Kellie MSS*, pp.509–10; NLS MS 10285 (Spottiswoode MSS) ff7, 9; B. Lenman, *The Jacobite Risings in Britain 1689–1746* (London, 1980), pp.105–6; BL Add MSS 70249, Murray to Lord Oxford, 31 May 1713; NLS, Advocates' MSS 29.1.1 (Murray Papers), I, ff120–1; III, ff1–21.

Hanoverians. Reassured by the passivity of the Irish catholic population as a whole during the Jacobite rising, and even more so by the Pretender's evident indifference to Ireland, the protestants slowly grew in confidence and began to assume a sense of Irishness alongside, and sometimes in place of, their traditional self-image as 'the king's English subjects of Ireland'.[43] In consequence their determination to seek just treatment from England in any point at issue between the two kingdoms was redoubled, especially in disputes over trade: thus the violence of the furore against Wood's Halfpence. But at the same time their constitutional demands, though forcibly expressed, remained relatively modest, aimed at the restriction or removal of English parliamentary jurisdiction rather than a denial of English government control over the Irish administration and legislature.

None the less, the unchanging view from Westminster was that any furiously 'patriotic' opposition was a danger to the political stability of the three kingdoms, because of the implicit tendency towards separatism.[44] It might therefore be assumed that an alternative form of political discourse in Scotland and Ireland would have been safer, one in which the polarities were not 'Court' and 'Country' but, as in Queen Anne's reign, 'Whig' and 'Tory' in the English style; in other words, a situation in which the party structures of the three kingdoms were as effectively integrated as those of England and Wales. Some anthropologists have argued the paradox that a society in which there is constant competition for power may nevertheless be regarded as fundamentally stable, since what is in dispute is not the legitimacy of institutions of government but the right to control them.[45] This is a theory which Linda Colley has applied to the so-called 'divided society' of Queen Anne's England, to make the case that the alleged instability of the first age

43 [Lockhart,] *Memoirs*, pp.68–72; I.G. Brown, 'Sir John Clerk of Penicuik (1676–1755): aspects of a virtuoso life' (Cambridge University, PhD thesis, 1980), pp.116–30; D.W. Hayton, 'Anglo-Irish attitudes: changing perceptions of national identity among the protestant ascendancy in Ireland, ca. 1690–1750', *Studies in Eighteenth-Century Culture* 17 (1987), pp.145–57; N. Canny, 'Identity formation in Ireland: the emergence of the Anglo-Irish', in N. Canny and A. Pagden (eds) *Colonial Identity in the Atlantic World 1500–1800* (Princeton, NJ, 1987), pp.202–10. Further enlightenment on this point may be found in Gerard McCoy, 'Local political culture in the Hanoverian empire: the case of the Anglo-Irish' (Oxford University, DPhil thesis, 1994).

44 *CSP Dom 1695* and Addenda, p.217; E. Gregg, *Queen Anne* (London, 1980), p.130; William Coxe, *Memoirs of the Life and Administration of Sir Robert Walpole . . .* (3 vols; London, 1798), II, p.350.

45 M. Gluckman, *Politics, Law and Ritual in Tribal Society* (Oxford, 1967), ch.IV.

of party was more apparent than real.[46] Similarly, Alison Olson, in reflections on Anglo-American politics, explained the absence of separatist tendencies among early-eighteenth-century planters by reference to the appearance in their assemblies of English-style party politics.[47]

The Irish experience might suggest a further use for this argument. Certainly the fading out of 'patriotic' issues from parliamentary debate in Ireland after 1703 coincided with the transplantation to Ireland of Whig and Tory parties, while the later re-emergence of such 'patriotic' grievances as the gift of places and pensions to English absentees and the exercise by the British House of Lords of an appellate jurisdiction over Irish causes followed closely on the Hanoverian succession and the return to a system of parliamentary politics in which the standing division was between 'Court' and 'Country'.[48] The different terrain of Scottish politics offered less scope for the growth of parties, but after 1710 the emergence of a popular 'Tory' (largely episcopalian) interest in Scotland, and the identification of the Squadrone and the remains of Queensberry's outgoing Court group with the Whig opposition, briefly held out the prospect of a two-party system there. Scottish MPs were drawn into the partisan conflicts of their English colleagues and addresses from burgh councils and county meetings began to adopt the abusive slogans of Whig and Tory invective.[49] But the impact of the Fifteen, in which a number of hitherto vociferous and prominent Tories involved themselves, destroyed the electoral credibility of Toryism north of the border.

The spread of English party politics to Ireland and Scotland produced damaging side-effects, however. Religion, the principal issue dividing Whigs from Tories, exercised an even greater emotive power in the other two kingdoms than in England itself. The higher visibility of the Catholic and Jacobite threat from native Irish and Highland Scots made Whiggism in Ireland and Scotland correspondingly more violent, while the resentment of the excluded episcopalian minority in Scotland and the fears of a Church of

46 L. Colley, *In Defiance of Oligarchy: The Tory Party 1714–60* (Cambridge, 1982), pp.11–20.

47 A.G. Olson, *Anglo-American Politics 1660–1775: The Relationship between Parties in England and Colonial America* (Oxford, 1973). See also R.R. Johnson, *Adjustment to Empire: The New England Colonies 1675–1775* (Leicester, 1981), ch.VI.

48 Szechi and Hayton, 'John Bull's other kingdoms', pp.267–8, 273.

49 Scottish Catholic Archives, Blairs College MSS; BL 2/168/4, James Carnegy to the Scots College, 4 Feb. 1711 (a reference that I owe to Professor Daniel Szechi); *Scots Courant* 23 July 1712 to 12 May 1714, *passim*.

Ireland establishment under challenge from the expanding presbyterian synod in Ulster gave Toryism in both kingdoms, when it eventually arose, a sharper edge. Party animosities could thus undermine political stability in a different way, by exacerbating the conflicts within Scottish and Irish society, a phenomenon seen most clearly at the local level, as Scottish episcopalians became more pronouncedly Anglican in their liturgical observance after the union, ventured in some parishes to 'rabble' intruding presbyterian ministers, and eventually rose in numbers in Jacobite revolt;[50] or in the increasingly bitter disputes between church and presbytery in Ireland, dividing borough corporations, turning magistrates into rabid persecutors, and occasionally provoking mob violence.[51] But even where it did not produce social disruption the integration of party systems spelt trouble for ministers, who thereby lost at least some of their freedom of manoeuvre on issues of patronage and policy to the demands of party solidarity. The extent to which partisan tail could wag ministerial dog may be seen in the history of the Tory administration from 1710 to 1714, in which a prolonged rearguard action by the lord treasurer, Oxford, failed to restrain the more vigorous elements among Scottish and Irish Tories from the pursuit of measures to relieve Scots episcopalians and harass Ulster presbyterians.[52]

The collapse of parliamentary Toryism in Scotland and Ireland after the Fifteen, so much more complete than in England, broke this direct connection between the different national party systems. Although the new configurations of Scottish and Irish politics, with the Whig interest split into contending factions, paralleled the Whig Schism in England, the nature of the correspondence between English politics and the politics of the outlying kingdoms had altered significantly. The divisions between English Whigs, between

50 Tristram Clarke, 'The Scottish Episcopalians 1688–1720' (Edinburgh University, PhD thesis, 1987), pp.186–90, 351–8, 368, 423; Robert Wodrow, *Analecta . . .*, Maitland Club 60 (4 vols; Edinburgh, 1842–3), I, p.328; II, pp.74, 256; SRO GD 305 add/bundle xiv (Cromartie MSS), George Mackenzie to [Cromarty], 21 Sept. 1711; Lenman, *Jacobite Risings*, ch.6; Bruce Lenman, 'The Scottish Episcopal clergy and the ideology of Jacobitism', in E. Cruickshanks (ed.) *Ideology and Conspiracy: Aspects of Jacobitism 1689–1759* (Edinburgh, 1982), pp.36–48.

51 Hayton, 'Ireland and the English ministers', pp.127–30, 300–1; PRONI Ant. 4/1/1, County Antrim grand jury presentment book, 23 April 1712.

52 Hayton, 'Ireland and the English ministers', pp.278–86; D. Szechi, *Jacobitism and Tory Politics 1710–14* (Edinburgh, 1984), pp.85–8, 102, 110–12, 157–8; D. Szechi, 'The politics of "persecution": Scots Episcopalian toleration and the Harley ministry, 1710–12', in W.E. Sheils (ed.) *Persecution and Toleration*, Studies in Church History 21 (Oxford, 1984), pp.275–87.

the Squadrone and Argyll in Scotland, and between the factions led by Lord Chancellor Brodrick and Speaker Conolly in Ireland were personal in nature rather than being grounded in differences of principle and were therefore not so deeply entrenched. In consequence, schemes of management were no longer predetermined by the iron logic of party, but could be adjusted to the balance of forces within Scottish or Irish politics. From 1717 to 1725 alliances between English and Irish factions underwent several shifts, usually on the initiative of the viceroy, who, as with Bolton in 1719, could switch his favour from one politician to another in anticipation of more effective parliamentary assistance.[53] A similar fluidity prevailed in Anglo-Scottish politics. The obverse of Lord Oxford's predicament was the condescension exercised by Stanhope and Sunderland in 1718, permitting the duke of Argyll to crawl back into favour on their terms, or the freedom of action enjoyed by Walpole in 1725, again at the expense of the incoming Argyll, whose ambition of a clean sweep of Scottish offices Walpole was able, temporarily at least, to frustrate.[54] To that extent, therefore, a return to the politics of 'Court' and 'Country' held out some advantages to ministers, always provided that their navigation kept clear of the most dangerous reefs of national *amour propre.*

MINISTERIAL RESPONSES: STRATEGIES OF MANAGEMENT

The political disruption that parliaments could engender meant that if they were to continue some attempt would have to be made at management, and sheer financial necessity left the crown with little choice. In England, at least, the response had been a determined improvement in managerial techniques at all levels, so much so that the Augustan period may justifiably be reckoned as a critical phase in the history of parliamentary management. In the Commons, Danby's method of building a permanent Court party from placemen and pensioners was refined, and lines of communication between front- and back-benchers were brought to a new level of sophistication through the activities of political clubs

53 Coxe, *Walpole,* II pp.172–4; Griffin, 'Parliamentary politics', pp.60–76, 94.

54 J.M. Simpson, 'Who steered the gravy train, 1707–1766?', in N.T. Phillipson and R. Mitchison (eds) *Scotland in the Age of Improvement* . . . (Edinburgh, 1970), p.52; Riley, *English ministers and Scotland,* p.256.

and the institution of formal briefings.[55] In the Lords too, ministers transformed dependent office-holders, the so-called 'poor lords', and the bishops into lobby-fodder, a 'system' which was to form the basis of government control over the upper House for over a century.[56] Not even the clergy in convocation were left to go their own way without guidance from the court.[57] In Ireland and Scotland, the partial forfeiture of direct governmental control over legislation was partly offset by importing English techniques of management: a systematic use of patronage to cement the court's following, the advance planning of sessional strategy and the preconcerting of debating tactics by cabals of court managers.

However, as was amply illustrated by the chequered fortunes of Court parties in all three parliaments under William and Anne, management of this kind did not guarantee success; after 1714 the Whig ascendancy, lacking inhibitions over constitutional custom and corporate privilege, began to alter the ground rules, for example by prolonging the lifespan of the British parliament from three to seven years, and even dispensing altogether with those non-parliamentary assemblies whose naturally Tory complexion made them mouthpieces for rancorous opposition, the convocations of Canterbury and Ireland, and the Cornish 'parliament of tinners'.[58] The increasing volume of patriotic protest in early Hanoverian Ireland made the parliament in Dublin another candidate for suspension. This was a delicate matter, involving the prospect of not only financial hardship but also political embarrassment: the premature dissolutions of 1693 and 1714 had each resulted in a damaging propaganda defeat for the adminis-

55 A. Browning, *Thomas Osborne Earl of Danby and Duke of Leeds 1632–1712* (3 vols; Glasgow, 1944–51), I, pp.151–2, 166–73, 191–3, 205–7, 273–7, 422–3, 466–8, 482–4, 500–1; III, pp.33–51, 164–217; Basil Duke Henning, *The House of Commons 1660–1690* (3 vols; London, 1983), I, pp.32–6; Horwitz, *Parliament, Policy and Politics*, pp.208–10; Holmes, *British Politics*, ch.9; C. Jones, 'The parliamentary organization of the Whig junto in the reign of Queen Anne: the evidence of Lord Ossulston's diary', *PH* 10 (1991), pp.164–82.

56 C. Jones, '"The scheme Lords, the necessitous Lords, and the Scots Lords": the earl of Oxford's management and the "Party of the Crown" in the House of Lords, 1711–14', in Jones (ed.) *Party and Management*, pp.123–67; C. Jones, 'The House of Lords and the growth of parliamentary stability, 1701–1742', in Jones (ed.) *Britain in the First Age of Party*, pp.96–101.

57 Bennett, *Tory Crisis in Church and State*, pp.57–61, 67–8, 71–5, 84–8, 99–101, 125–8; cf. Dralle, 'Kingdom in reversion', pp.412–13.

58 Sykes, *William Wake*, I, pp.137–49; II, pp.235–7; Bennett, *Tory Crisis in Church and State*, pp.214–15; P. Langford, 'Convocation and the Tory clergy, 1717–61', in E. Cruickshanks and J. Black (eds) *The Jacobite Challenge* (Edinburgh, 1988), pp.107–22; Connolly, *Religion, Law and Power*, p.188; Cruickshanks, 'Convocation of the stannaries', p.64.

tration.[59] In general the alternatives to summoning an Irish parliament were never properly discussed; ministers lurched into periods of non-parliamentary government without taking full cognizance of what they were doing. The exception occurred in 1720, when anxiety at the possible reaction in Ireland against the Declaratory Act was such that a unique summit conference was held to discuss strategic options, the choicest being a plan to resurrect the farm of the Irish revenue in order to raise sufficient funds to cover a retrenched budget. Having stopped themselves at the brink, probably from no more elevated a motive than the wish to perpetuate the possibilities for intrigue which Irish parliamentary sessions offered to the rivals in a divided English administration, ministers then found that their fears had been unfounded. Irish MPs declined to rise to the snub, a surprising show of restraint which reassured ministers and removed the stimulus to further constitutional speculation.[60]

Action had of course already been taken to terminate the separate existence of the Scottish parliament. It was one of the most important effects of the union to deprive the Scots of the opportunity for independent parliamentary action, not only to settle their succession on an alternative claimant, but also, if they so wished, to withhold taxes, embroil themselves in a trade war or even embark upon a constitutional conflict with another parliament. In a combined House of Commons in which Scotsmen were outnumbered by over ten to one, Scottish voices were easily overborne if acting on their own in pursuit of a national interest. None the less, the Scottish representation in the united parliament still required close attention. From time to time the Court majority in either House was so slender as to afford Scotsmen the power to turn the scale, as Oxford found to his cost when struggling for the acceptance by the Lords of his peace policy in the winter of 1711–12 and for the ratification of the treaty of commerce with France a year later.[61]

59 BL Add MSS 70017, f1, [Edward Harley?] to Sir Edward Harley, Jan. 1692[–3]; Bodl Carte MS 130, f345, Robert Price to the Duke of Beaufort, 25 Feb. 1692[–3]; Hayton, 'Crisis in Ireland and the disintegration of Queen Anne's last ministry', pp.207–8.

60 D. Hayton, 'Walpole and Ireland', in Black (ed.) *Britain in the Age of Walpole*, p.102; Burns, *Irish Parliamentary Politics*, II, pp.114–17.

61 G.S. Holmes, 'The Hamilton Affair of 1711–12: a crisis in Anglo-Scottish relations', *EHR* 77 (1962), pp.257–82; Holmes and Jones, 'Trade, the Scots and the parliamentary crisis of 1713'. See also C. Jones, '"Venice preserv'd; or a plot discovered": the political and social context of the Peerage Bill of 1719', in C. Jones (ed.), *A Pillar of the Constitution: The House of Lords in British Politics 1640–1784* (London, 1989), pp.84–7.

It was a truism that management of a separate Irish or Scottish parliament would have to be entrusted to men of local knowledge and local influence. Historically, the bypassing of native political interests in favour of an English nominee (a policy which had been employed in Ireland if not in Scotland) had meant rule by force rather than consultation, a military rather than a political option. In neither kingdom was there a 'Court' party substantial enough to confer a parliamentary majority on an incoming English governor. Thus far the two kingdoms were alike. But of course they differed sharply in many other respects: in their institutions of government, constitutional law, political traditions and social structure, and in the nature of their relationship with England.

Not only was Ireland governed by a viceroy appointed from Westminster, but also it was at least customary for the viceroy to be English, owing to the lack of resident magnates. Before the Hanoverian succession there had been only two Irish candidates, and afterwards there were none. The duke of Ormond actually served as viceroy from 1703 to 1707 and again from 1710 to 1713, and Arthur Annesley, earl of Anglesey, although he lacked the lustre of Ormond's name, nevertheless possessed the talent and the English political connections to have been able to succeed after the duke's second spell in office had the turn of circumstances been different.[62] But for all that Anglesey was a self-proclaimed Hanoverian, he was also a Tory of the hotter variety, and the arrival of King George consigned him to the wilderness just as surely as it ended the official career of the Jacobite Ormond. As for the rest, the various Boyles were either ineffectual, otherwise preoccupied or absentee; Abercorn, despite developing a minor electoral empire in north-west Ulster, was too eccentric. In general the relative constitutional unimportance of the Irish House of Lords was reflected in the political feebleness of the Irish peerage. The single most important borough-monger in early-eighteenth-century Ireland was not a peer at all but a commoner, William Conolly, and the chief political 'interests' were not aristocratic affinities but regional groupings headed by prominent Members of the House of Commons: Conolly in north-west Ulster, the St Georges in Connaught, and the Brodricks with their 'Cork squadron' which Henry Boyle was to inherit.[63]

62 Holmes, *British Politics*, pp.278–9; Hayton, 'Crisis in Ireland and disintegration of Queen Anne's last ministry', pp.200, 211–14; BL Add MSS 47087, f57.

63 Hayton, 'Ireland and the English ministers', pp.112–19; Hayton, 'Walpole and Ireland', pp.114–17.

The nature of the viceroyalty, however, imposed strict limitations on the role its occupant could play in parliamentary politics.[64] An English appointee would know little of his new domain, and the chief secretary who accompanied him would be equally ill informed, a transient incumbent of an office which was regarded as a political apprenticeship. Nor was the administration in Dublin castle staffed by men of sufficient political weight to constitute a 'treasury bench' in the Irish House of Commons. The court was thus obliged to rely upon such Irish politicians as it was able to recruit, and not only for counsel in kitchen cabinet and leadership in debate, but also for bringing in votes to fill out the otherwise puny corps of 'King's friends'. Of course, some viceroys were more energetic than others; Wharton for one flung himself into the fray. But this strenuous lobbying was no more than an adjunct to the real work being done on the court's behalf by Commons 'undertakers', men who ever since Capel's rapprochement with the opposition in 1695 had customarily been entrusted with carrying through government business, in return for a generous slice of patronage and a loud voice in the making of policy.

In Scotland, by contrast, there was no shortage of resident magnates; quite the reverse. Scottish politics was magnate-ridden, as contemporary commentators bewailed, and the unicameral structure of the Scottish parliament enabled the magnates to dominate proceedings there.[65] The problem for King William was not how to find a Scottish nobleman to act as parliamentary commissioner, or to head the administration in Edinburgh, but how to cope with an embarrassment of eligible candidates, and to arrange matters so as to minimize offence. More specifically, a way had to be found to accommodate the ambitions of the greatest magnates, Argyll, Atholl, Hamilton and Queensberry, a bristling collection of super-egos whose envy generally prevented them from cooperating except in opposition, where their joint forces were powerful enough to wreck any administration. The history of Scottish political management in William's reign has been interpreted as a series of attempts to square the circle, either by

64 For what follows, Hayton, 'Beginnings of the "undertaker system"'.

65 Riley, *King William and the Scottish Politicians*, p.3; J.S. Shaw, *The Management of Scottish Society 1707–1764 . . .* (Edinburgh, 1983), ch.1; B.P. Lenman, 'The Scottish nobility and the Revolution of 1688', in R. Beddard (ed.) *The Revolutions of 1688* (Oxford, 1991), pp.137–62; for contemporary comment, *Spottiswoode Miscellany*, I, 233; SRO GD 305/1/165/87, speech 'against luxury', 1705; Defoe, *History of the Union*, pp.312–16; Riley, *Union*, pp.233–4.

constructing a viable coalition of lesser interests or by alighting upon some alliance of magnates that would remain stable.[66] None of these schemes lasted long, although they did yield two important by-products: the aggrandizement of the duke of Queensberry, who in the years after 1698 grew to become the most important of the magnates; and the fusion of the Tweeddale-Roxburghe and Marchmont connections under Johnston's ministry into the nucleus of the 'new party' or Squadrone Volante which, with the eventual adhesion of the duke of Montrose, came to acquire a kind of collective magnate status. It was to be a fortuitous convergence of Queensberry, Argyll and the Squadrone in 1706–7 which finally brought about union, but only after a further succession of parliamentary failures under Anne had reduced commentators in Scotland and in England to despair at what they regarded as the perennial hopelessness of Scottish factionalism.

Union seemed to offer a way out. In the long term there was the prospect of Scottish MPs becoming integrated into the English party system, which would remove the necessity for separate schemes of management. (Indeed, this process began under the Tory ministry of 1710–14 but brought with it different, and equally unpleasant, problems, and in any case ground to a halt in 1715.) More immediate was the hope of diminishing the magnates by enlarging the pool in which they were wallowing: a line of argument developed in unionist propaganda.[67] Circumstances conspired to assist the process: Queensberry expired from colic in 1711, leaving successors who proved unable to maintain his overblown influence; Hamilton fell to Lord Mohun's sword a year later and was followed by a long minority; Atholl's influence finally succumbed to terminal equivocation. That left only Argyll, the loyalty of whose followers had been sorely tested by their chieftain's support for union and by his opportunist antics thereafter; the Squadrone, who after some tergiversation in 1708–10 had now committed themselves to the Whigs; and the somewhat dubious figure of Lord Mar, a former ally of Queensberry who was looking to establish himself as a power in his own right. In these circumstances Lord Oxford was able to embark between 1711 and 1713 on an experiment in 'direct rule', abolishing the office of secretary of state for Scotland, which Queensberry had enjoyed after the union, and putting control over Scottish patronage into

66 Riley, *King William and the Scottish Politicians, passim.*
67 See references cited in note 65.

English hands, that is to say his own. Unfortunately, Oxford's habitual procrastination, especially in the payment of salaries, and the conflict within his ministry engineered by the intrigues of Bolingbroke, undermined his 'Scottish system' and at last, after repeated parliamentary embarrassments at the hands of the Scots, he was forced to revive the Scottish secretaryship in 1713 for the gimcrack magnate Lord Mar.[68]

The readoption of the strategy of employing Scottish politicians to govern Scotland, and to manage the Scottish representation in parliament, was carried on by the Whigs after 1714, but its full implications were not realized for over a decade. Just as in Ireland, where the two opposing Whig factions, led by Lord Chancellor Brodrick and Speaker Conolly respectively, pursued their quarrels within the Court party, so in Scottish politics the Squadrone, who took over leadership of the Scottish administration from Mar, were forced to coexist in government with their greatest rivals, the brothers Argyll and Ilay. This did not represent a conscious policy of 'divide and rule' on the part of successive English ministries, so much as a reflection of the confusions and uncertainties of English (and Irish and Scottish) politics. It came to an end once stability had been reimposed in England through the establishment of the Walpolean hegemony. Walpole did not turn his attention immediately to Ireland and Scotland, but the disturbances in 1724–5 over Wood's Halfpence and the malt tax sparked a reappraisal of Irish and Scottish policies. A change of viceroy in Dublin brought a final decision between the 'two great men' there, and the exclusion of the Brodricks from office; while in Scotland Walpole was able to act directly, dismissing the duke of Roxburghe, the Scottish secretary, and most of the Squadrone, and installing Argyll and Ilay as principal Scottish managers.[69]

Walpole seems to have been well aware of the danger of creating 'over-mighty subjects' in Dublin and Edinburgh, and in both cases he and his colleagues, in particular Newcastle, made simultaneous efforts to restrict the influence of their Irish and Scottish managers. In Ireland loyal Englishmen were named to the places of lord chancellor and archbishop of Armagh, in order to establish in Dublin Castle a permanent 'English interest' which would offer an alternative source of information and an alternative channel of

68 Riley, *English Ministers and Scotland*, chs XI–XV.

69 Hayton, 'Walpole and Ireland', pp.103–8; Riley, *English Ministers and Scotland*, pp.270–86; Simpson, 'Who steered the gravy train?', pp.52–5.

patronage to the Commons 'undertakers'. In Scotland Walpole, following Oxford's example in this as in so much else, took the opportunity to suppress the Scottish secretaryship again, and to restore some areas of patronage, notably in the Scottish customs, to English supervision. He also made sure that the Argyllites did not achieve their immediate intention to purge their enemies from all Scottish offices.[70]

Yet the fact remained that in both kingdoms the English ministry was now exercising its authority through the medium of local political interests; through local 'undertakers', to use the Irish terminology, men who were able to deliver votes, whether in the Irish parliament or among the Scots at Westminster, in return for delegated power. These Irish and Scottish 'undertakers' obviously differed in one major respect, that whereas in Ireland Conolly and his ilk worked for a succession of English lords lieutenant, a Scottish chief minister like Argyll in the late 1720s, or even Queensberry before him under Queen Anne, would be to all intents and purposes his own viceroy. But their essential similarity can be recognized in their shared requirements from any English ministry: that enough patronage should be made available to satisfy their followers; and that it should be clearly apparent at all times that they, and they alone, enjoyed royal and ministerial favour.

The Irish 'undertakers' did not demand a monopoly over patronage, realizing that places in the higher echelons of government, the law, or the church, would often be reserved for English nominees. They did expect to be consulted on these more significant appointments and for their advice to be listened to, but in general it was not the plums of patronage so much as the everyday disposal of minor places which they regarded as their province: if an undertaker's promise could not be made good for some lowly applicant, offence would quickly be taken and veiled threats uttered concerning the mortal damage that had thereby been inflicted on the undertaker's 'credit' and 'interest', and by extension the credit and interest of government. Moreover, in the most fruitful field of patronage – the rapidly expanding bureaucracy of the Dublin customs house – undertakers had established something approaching a property. The office of 'first

70 On Ireland, J.L. McCracken, 'The undertakers in Ireland and their relations with the lords lieutenant 1724–71' (Queen's University, Belfast, MA thesis, 1941), ch.III; Griffin, 'Irish parliamentary politics', pp.168ff; Hayton, 'Walpole and Ireland', pp.108–11. On Scotland, Riley, *English Ministers and Scotland*, pp.273–94; Simpson, 'Who steered the gravy train?', pp.54–5.

commissioner' of the revenue, which was usually occupied by one of the government's principal parliamentary managers, carried with it a *de facto* control over the admission and promotion of revenue officers. Since the customs commissioners were responsible to the British treasury rather than to the viceroy or his deputies in Dublin they were able to fend off interference from above by reference to their own superior local knowledge or the arcane rules of the service, or even by invoking the god of administrative efficiency, a method honed to perfection by William Conolly, who as first commissioner from 1714 onwards transformed the revenue into a personal fief.[71]

Scottish 'undertakers' like Queensberry or Argyll, even though they might behave viceregally, were obliged to settle for much the same conditions in their negotiations over patronage.[72] Not every Scottish place could be reserved for their disposal: the occasional grant might even go to an Englishman. Queensberry recognized that there were others besides himself with requests to make, notably Godolphin's great friend Lord Seafield. Argyll after 1725 had to accept the continuance in office of Scotsmen of neutral, even of Squadrone, leanings. But it was expected that the general run of appointments would go as the 'undertaker' intended, and that this fact would be publicly known. Where the line of Court favour was obscure, government could not function properly, as Queensberry had soon discovered after the union, when conflicting messages reached Scotland as to the relative standing at court of his party and the Squadrone.[73]

After 1725 the balance in the relationship between English ministry and Scottish 'undertaker' was to shift in favour of the latter. The Argathelian party extended its influence to the point where it did come close to establishing a monopoly over Scottish patronage. This was the work not of the second duke of Argyll himself, a selfish, insensitive and petulant *grand seigneur*, but of his much abler brother Archibald, earl of Ilay (later to succeed as third

71 Previous studies of the subject have now been superseded by Patrick McNally, 'Patronage and politics in Ireland 1714–1727' (Queen's University, Belfast, PhD thesis, 1993), ch.3 of which deals specifically with the Irish revenue service.

72 For what follows, Riley, *English Ministers and Scotland*, pp.285–94; Simpson, 'Who steered the gravy train?', pp.54–61; Shaw, *Management of Scottish Society*, esp. ch.6; A. Murdoch, *'The People Above': Politics and Administration in Eighteenth-Century Scotland* (Edinburgh, 1980), ch.1.

73 Riley, *English Ministers and Scotland*, chs VII–VIII; C. Jones, 'Godolphin, the Whig junto and the Scots: a new Lord's division list from 1709', *SHR* 58 (1979), pp.158–74.

duke). The recovery of Argyll's influence from its nadir in 1708 had been Ilay's doing, as he recruited new clients from among his brother's military connections, from hitherto unattached presbyterian lairds, and lawyers like Forbes of Culloden, and after 1715 from ex-Queensberryites and moderate, non-Jacobite Tories like Seafield, who had been excluded from the charmed circle of the Squadrone. Under his guidance the Argyll interest grew silently and inexorably, like a pike in a tank of goldfish. By the 1727 election it had become undeniably predominant in Scotland. All that remained was to settle matters with Walpole, who had been persuaded by his Irish and Scottish experiences in 1724–5 of the danger of over-reliance on local politicians in situations where unpopularity was the price of doing the king's bidding. Ministerial resistance to a purge of the Squadrone and Walpole's continued reliance on the advice of an English official, John Scrope, in the administration of the Scottish customs (which was kept under much stricter control from Whitehall than was the Irish revenue commission) was eventually overcome through the establishment of a close personal relationship between Walpole and Ilay. The prime minister came to trust his Scottish manager to an unprecedented extent, even more than Godolphin had trusted Seafield. Stationed almost permanently at court, Ilay presided in the 1730s over a formidable political machine, run for him in Edinburgh by his highly capable and influential factotum, Lord Milton (ironically, a nephew of Fletcher of Saltoun), with the assistance of a number of talented under-managers, including Forbes, Charles Areskine, George Drummond, and the burgh election agent Henry Cunningham of Boquhan.[74] So effective was this machine that, as John Shaw has written, it appears as if before Ilay Scotland had simply not been managed at all.[75]

74 On the poor state of the Argyll interest in 1707–8, SRO GD 112/39/204/8–9 (Breadalbane MSS), Campbell of Auchinbreck to [Breadalbane], 10, 14 Feb. 1707; GD 112/39/210/13, Campbell of Mamore to [same], 1707. On the interest in its prime, two decades later, see Shaw, *Management of Scottish Society, passim,* esp. chs4–7; R.M. Sunter, *Patronage and Politics in Scotland 1707–1832* (Edinburgh, 1986), ch.12; Murdoch, *'People Above',* ch.1. As yet the story of the intervening period remains unwritten.

75 Shaw, *Management of Scottish Society,* p.86.

CONCLUSION: THE EMERGENCE OF A BRITISH STATE?

The late seventeenth and early eighteenth centuries were marked by their own 'crisis of parliaments'. In each of the three kingdoms representative institutions became firmly established and extended their scope through offering essential subsidies and a means of solving a range of economic and social problems. However, the unrestricted exercise of parliamentary power could undermine political stability in each of the three kingdoms and, as in 1698–1703, even seem to threaten the connections between them. In response English ministers developed various strategies for more efficient political management, and in some cases dispensed with representative institutions altogether. The union of 1707 was a compromise between these two approaches: the Scottish parliament was absorbed into the English and thus prevented from taking radical or precipitate action on its own account. The Irish parliament retained a separate identity: although in theory MPs at Westminster could legislate for Ireland, in practice this power was exercised for the most part on private business and as a means of offering to Irish protestants another form of legislative relief.

Which of the two kingdoms benefited more from these constitutional arrangements is an open question. Research into the legislation of the British and Irish parliaments in the eighteenth century has not progressed far enough to enable a meaningful comparison to be made. But it appears as if the Irish enjoyed greater legislative opportunities, the programme at Westminster being rather too crowded with other items to allow much time for the Scots to introduce their own measures. Nor did the presence of a Scottish contingent in both the Commons and Lords necessarily mean that the British parliament would side with Scotland in any dispute with the Irish. There was an active Irish lobby at Westminster, often abetted by the lord lieutenant and his representatives, which on such matters as the encouragement of the Irish linen industry could block, even if it could not defeat, Scottish proposals.[76] In return for what became a more complete autonomy in matters of patronage, the Scots may have forfeited some capacity to secure legislative redress of national grievances.

This brings us back to the question of what kind of British state

76 F.G. James, 'The Irish lobby in the early eighteenth century', *EHR* 81 (1966), pp.543–57; James, *Ireland in the Empire*, pp.154–8; Szechi and Hayton, 'John Bull's other kingdoms', p.248.

was in existence by the late 1720s. Constitutionally England and Scotland had been integrated, but in terms of political management they were still separate, and indeed the management of Scotland had reverted to a system of contracting-out to a powerful local magnate able to bespeak appointments to many crown offices. Constitutionally Ireland was also more closely under English control, and governed now invariably by an English lord lieutenant. But under the lord lieutenant the political management of the kingdom was shared out between English officials and Irish parliamentary 'undertakers' who made powerful claims on the disposal of patronage and the determination of aspects of government policy. Nor was there yet a very strong sense of 'British' national identity. Some unionist Scots had sought to promote the notion of an umbrella 'Britishness' under which their national pride could take shelter, but the real emergence of 'Britishness' had to wait until later in the century.[77] For their part, the protestant Irish had been travelling in the opposite direction, discarding their old sense of identity as 'the King's English subjects of Ireland' in favour of a new and vigorous Irish patriotism, and rejecting any notion of being 'British' since that would have implied a community of interest with the despised Ulster Scots.[78]

Moves towards the constitutional incorporation of Ireland into the British state did not really begin until the 1760s, when for a variety of reasons, the most important connected with events in India and across the Atlantic, English ministers started to think of Ireland in an imperial context and to cast their 'Irish question' afresh.[79] All this suggests that perhaps we should be looking to the later eighteenth century rather than the later seventeenth to mark the emergence of a British state. Even in political terms the long-delayed re-emergence of something approaching English party systems in Scotland and Ireland in the 1770s suggests a new level of integration. But even then the process was not all one-way, for the rise of empire and the rise of party broadly coincided with the epiphany in Scotland of another great political magnate, the

77 Brown, 'Clerk of Penicuik', ch.5; Murdoch, *'People Above'*, p.91; L. Colley, *Britons: Forging the Nation, 1707–1837* (New Haven, Conn., 1992); L. Colley, 'Britishness and otherness: an argument', *JBS* 31 (1992), pp.309–29. Of central importance to this theme is Colin C. Kidd, 'Scottish Whig historiography and the creation of Anglo-British identity, 1698–*c.*1800' (Oxford University, DPhil thesis, 1992).

78 Hayton, 'Anglo-Irish attitudes'; Connolly, *Religion, Law and Power*, pp.114–24.

79 An argument implicit in J. Kelly, *Prelude to Union: Anglo-Irish Politics in the 1780s* (Cork, 1992), esp. ch.1.

ultimate successor to Lord Ilay, in the establishment of what a recent historian has described as the 'despotism' of Henry Dundas.[80]

Acknowledgements

No foray into Scottish history would have been possible without the generous assistance afforded me by staff at the National Library of Scotland, the National Register of Archives (Scotland), and especially the Scottish Record Office, where I have been fortunate indeed to have enjoyed the expert advice of David Brown, Tristram Clarke and John Shaw. I have also to thank colleagues at the *History of Parliament:* Stuart Handley and Andrew Hanham, for making available their specialized knowledge; Perry Gauci and, especially, Linda Clark, for reading through an earlier draft and helping me to express my meaning more clearly. My greatest debt, however, is to my undergraduate tutor, the late Patrick Riley, to whose memory this chapter is dedicated. Needless to say, the errors, infelicities and omissions are entirely my own responsibility.

80 M. Fry, *The Dundas Despotism* (Edinburgh, 1992).

CONCLUSION

A state of Britishness?

Sarah Barber
University of Lancaster

If the mark of a study is its ability to be as challenging at the end as it was at its opening, then David Hayton's warning that perhaps a notion of Britishness has to wait until the latter half of the eighteenth century is a reflection of the complexities and subtleties involved here. His observation that the strangled cry of infant Britain was born of the turmoil in the imperial spheres of India and America should also make us think about the possibility that identity develops as much, if not more, from one's perception of the other as it does from a discovery of self – a process of internationalization rather than internalization. The loss of the colonies in America and the generation of a compensatory concept of imperial greatness in the east produced a notion of Britishness because it forced the peoples of the Atlantic archipelago to think about the nature of the 'British empire'. There was a need for unity abroad which, from this account of the making of Britain, was establishing itself slowly and painfully within these shores. Britons abroad had a clearer sense of the cultural and political oxygen of which, in the heat and humidity of the tropics, they believed they were deprived.

In the high middle ages, England attempted to keep a toe-hold in its continental empire, but Richard II tackled the fourteenth-century equivalent of the Irish problem, losing his English throne as a consequence; Edward III and Henry IV looked to Wales; and a succession of English and Scottish monarchs tried to define their mutual border rivalry through recourse to arms. Finally, as York and Lancaster played out an aristocratic power game, England was, for over one hundred years, more concerned with its own internal stability. As such, at the start of the period under discussion here, two parallel movements were underway. In the first, England was relatively inward looking, having abandoned an earlier concentration on that defining period of European colonization described by Robert Bartlett.[1] At the opening of the sixteenth century, Bartlett's statement about the development of a concept of Europeanness can be reshaped – replacing the word 'Europe' with 'Britain' – and is strikingly apposite: '"internal expansion" – the intensification of settlement and reorganization of society within western and central Europe – was as important as external expansion; and hence the problem of describing and explaining these expansionary movements is not distinct from the problem of describing and explaining the nature of European society itself'. The English state in the early sixteenth century had failed to establish authority in Ireland and was following a policy of containment in the wild counties of the north and the Welsh marches, ably described, both here and elsewhere, by Steven Ellis. 'Colonialism' was a process by which the south-eastern, agrarian society established its control over the remote corners of these islands.

In Scotland, however, the renaissance came early. The Scottish political nation was not a central concern of the powers on the continental mainland, but at least Scotland had an outward-looking state, links with France and, in its pursuit of Reformation ideas, was fed by the fervour of the 'calvinist Rome' – Geneva – which gave it scholars and politicians of international repute. During the reign of Mary Tudor, when the tie with Rome and Spain was an attempt to drag England back to European politics as much as a means to re-establish catholicism, the net result was to confirm England's isolation. The loss of Calais deprived England of the last vestige of the continental empire of Edward III's vision. In England the Marian martyrs were a more private concern. Cranmer may have died a romantic death, immortalized by Foxe's martyrology, but his services to religion were to define a peculiarly English form of worship and to contribute to the poetry of the English tongue. The Scottish scholars to emerge from continental exile gave Scotland a wider status. John Knox was a figure of international significance, not least for the part he played in tying Scottish politics to those of England. Indeed, as Jane Dawson has outlined, this was one moment in which a viable Anglo-Scottish culture could take on

1 R. Bartlett, *The Making of Europe: Conquest, Colonization and Cultural Change, 950–1350* (London, 1993).

some characteristics of Britishness. The parallel process by which religious practice and expression was defined seemed a way to forge a shared island culture. When Scotland succumbed to civil war, its southern neighbour was just beginning to participate in a late flowering of art and letters in which the cultural process begun by Cranmer was magnified by Shakespeare, Sidney and Bacon. Ironically, by the time the Scottish monarchy was ready to take up its birthright in the other three kingdoms, circumstances had come to dictate that it was post-Elizabethan England which was the dominant nation among the four.

The wider interests of the Welsh, Scots and Irish were often defined during the seventeenth century by their exclusion from the direction of the English state. The other three peoples did not abandon their wider concerns, but they took up the politics of exile. Scottish mercenaries were a valued component of the mighty Swedish army commanded by Gustav Adolph during the Thirty Years War. Welsh sectaries found a new life in the Americas.[2] The Irish people were particularly diasporic. In most Spanish cities there is an area called O'Donnell and behind the magnificent Counter-Reformation baroque of the cathedral in Cádiz lies a little street called Conde de O Reilly, much to the amusement of the visiting English who are unaware of the role that the Wild Geese played in the formation of the international profile of other states. Studies have examined the part played by the Irish in Spain and Spanish Flanders.[3] The range of the Irish experience in the colonies covered everything from transportation as criminalized traitors to the English state, to the day-to-day oversight of post-Restoration, royalist England's flagship colony in the Carolinas.[4] As Robert Stradling has pointed out, however, they were valuable abroad as they were England's enemies. They did not lose their sense of indignation at their treatment, and this resulted in many serving as

2 B.J. Levy, 'Notable settlements of radical domesticity: northwest British Quakers in rural Pennyslvania, 1681–1780', in R. Bennett (ed.) *Settlements in the Americas: Cross-Cultural Perspectives* (Newark, Del. 1993).

3 R.A. Stradling, *The Spanish Monarchy and Irish Mercenaries: The Wild Geese in Spain, 1618–68* (Dublin, 1994); G. Henry, *The Irish Military Community in Flanders, 1586–1621* (Dublin, 1992); P. Gouhier, 'Mercenaires irlandais au service de la France (1635–64)', *Irish Sword* 7 (1965–6), pp.58–75.

4 Among the leading landholders in the newly founded colony of Carolina in 1672 were Captain Florence O'Sullivan, executor of the estate of Michael Moran, along with several other prominent names of Irish descent; 'warrants for land in South Carolina', Columbia Record Office, SC, 'Documents relating to the Irish in the West Indies' in A. Gwynn (ed.), *Analecta Hibernica* 4 (Oct. 1932), pp.139–286.

mercenaries for France or Spain or participating in the first anti-British slave rebellion on Barbados.[5]

Nevertheless, the dominant strain of the history of the four nations in this period is one of increasing anglicization. According to Ciarán Brady, the upper echelons of Welsh society connived at a process of greater integration into the English state apparatus, whereas in Ireland, the former English elite was hostile to the increasingly heavy hand of centralized bureaucracy. The response in Ireland might bear comparison with religiously motivated, localized reactions in England, such as the Pilgrimage of Grace, or with the reaction of local elites to the centralizing states of France or Spain as they attempted to replaced local custom and tradition with a new standardized loyalty.[6] Perhaps a good place to start would be the Revolt of the Netherlands, which passed through several phases, but which began with a disgruntled Netherlandish aristocracy, kicking against the imposition of hispanization.

As Philip Jenkins has shown, the Welsh gave a welcoming response to protestant proselytism in the vernacular. By contrast, historians of the Irish situation are still debating the aptness of the question of religious success or failure.[7] As language is both a means of cultural expression and a tool of colonial suppression, the failure of the English to take full advantage of proselytism in the Irish tongue, and the completeness with which the vernacular was seen as evidence of foreignness or otherness, hint at a half-hearted attempt at cultural imperialism. The English settled, rather, for security, in other words, for containment, sometimes military, sometimes geographical, increasingly political. Both Mícheál Mag Craith and Allan Macinnes tell tales of opportunities for integration, assimilation and mutual growth which were missed by

5 Stradling, *Spanish Monarchy and Irish Mercenaries*, p.159; C. Hill, 'Radical pirates?', in C. Hill, *People and Ideas in Seventeenth-Century England: The Collected Essays of Christopher Hill* (Brighton, 1986), III; H. Beckles, *White Servitude and Black Slavery in Barbados, 1627–1715* (Knoxville, Tenn. 1989).

6 M.E. James, 'Obedience and dissent in Henrician England: the Lincolnshire rebellion 1536', *P&P* 48 (1970), pp.3–78; M.E. James, 'The concept of order and the Northern rising', *P&P* 60 (1973), pp.49–83 among numerous studies of Tudor England; R. Bonney, *The European Dynastic States, 1494–1660* (Oxford, 1991); R. Forster and J.P. Greene (eds) *Preconditions of Revolution in Early Modern Europe* (Baltimore, Md, 1970).

7 N. Canny 'Why the Reformation failed in Ireland: une question mal posée', *JEH* 30 (1979), pp.423–50, K.S. Bottigheimer, 'The failure of the Reformation in Ireland: une question bien posée', *JEH* 36 (1985), pp.196–207; A. Ford, *The Protestant Reformation in Ireland 1590–1641* (Frankfurt am Main, 1985); S.G. Ellis, 'Economic problems of the church: why the Reformation failed in Ireland', *JEH* 41 (1990), pp.239–65.

all the parties involved. Both Scottish and Irish Gaels used the vernacular to express national pragmatism: the local tongue was not a weapon with which to lash the foreign invader. Indeed, the survival of the vernacular in Scotland was as much part of internal criticism at the weakness of highland opposition to the process of assimilation. Keith Brown has outlined how the Scottish aristocracy were largely unintegrated into the English cultural scene, because as British became increasingly identified with London-based society, London could afford to marginalize them. The republican Commonwealth regime was forced by its own isolation into a policy of aggressive conquest and consequent union, but remained sceptical of the value of national integration. The Cromwellian government's union could not be said to have been any more than re-establishing English overlordship. Toby Barnard and David Hayton's accounts of the four nations' political mechanisms at the end of the seventeenth century show how the English polity was in a position to ignore those of its Scottish and Irish subjects who did not play by its rules.

The process of four nations' integration, therefore, is multi-layered, but one in which the cross-fertilization worked faster in one direction than in the other, with the cultural totems of the hegemonic English widening their spell. How far on a road towards a concept of Britishness had the four nations come during the two hundred year span examined here? The answer: not very far. However, if we take the notions of nation and state that John Morrill, wittily and provocatively, set up at the start, there is a sense in which Britain has emerged. There is a state infrastructure, a bureaucracy, a multi-kingdom monarchy, a unitary army and civil service. Within a situation of continuing cultural diversity lurked new agents of codification and orthodoxy. Other Europeans recognized a British state, with its new international focus. There were no longer two weak monarchies, concerned with internal reconstruction, but an efficient governmental apparatus which looked acquisitively outwards. In this, the peoples of the British islands were participating in a Europe-wide process. There is a sense in which a state could tackle the experience of meeting a totally new culture only when it had a more centralized and homogenized view of itself. Spain became a colonial power as it reunited its diverse kingdoms and expelled its non-Christian subjects. The Netherlands emerged as a major player in international economics once it had freed itself of the overlordship of Spain. Sweden could boast an internationally reputed military once it had established what it was to be Swedish, geographically, religiously and politically. Once the British state had established its identity, it looked beyond Europe to the riches of east and west. With the usual sense of loss, it was only once the sun started to set on parts of the empire that it chose to examine what this entailed culturally.

Notes on Contributors

Sarah Barber is a lecturer in History at Lancaster University, having studied in Dublin. She is the author of several articles on Irish and English history of the seventeenth century and co-editor of *Aspects of Irish Studies*. She is currently completing a study of Henry Marten.

Toby Barnard returned to Oxford in 1976 as fellow and tutor in modern history at Hertford College, having previously taught in the universities of Exeter and London. He is the author of *Cromwellian Ireland* (1975) and *The English Republic* (1982), as well as of numerous articles on English and Irish history in the seventeenth and eighteenth centuries. He also edited, with Jane Clark, *Lord Burlington: Architecture, Art and Life* (1995).

Ciarán Brady is Senior Lecturer in Modern History at Trinity College, Dublin. He is the author of *The Chief Governors: the Rise and Fall of Reform Government in Tudor Ireland* (1994) and editor of *Interpreting Irish History: the Debate on Historical Revisionism* (1994). He has edited several volumes of essays and published a number of articles on early modern Irish history. He is currently joint-editor of the periodical *Irish Historical Studies*.

Keith M. Brown is a Lecturer in History at the University of Stirling. He is the author of *Bloodfeud in Scotland 1573–1625* (1986) and *Kingdom or Province? Scotland and the Regal Union 1603–1715* (1992). He has also written a large number of essays on the early modern Scottish nobility, and is currently writing a book on that subject.

Jane Dawson is the John Laing Lecturer in the History and Theology of the Reformation at the University of Edinburgh. She has published numerous articles on Scottish history and on the relations between the different countries of mainland Britain and Ireland during the sixteenth century. She is finishing a book on *The First British Politician? The Career of the Fifth Earl of Argyll (c. 1530–73).*

Steven G. Ellis is Professor of History at University College Galway. His many books and articles on British and Irish history include *Tudor Ireland: Crown, Community and the Conflict of Cultures, 1470–1603* (1985) and *Tudor Frontiers and Noble Power: the Making of the British State* (1995).

David Hayton is Lecturer in Modern Irish History at the Queen's University of Belfast. He previously worked for many years as a research assistant, and then as editor, on the 1690–1715 section of the *History of Parliament,* and has written a number of articles and essays on British and Irish politics in the late seventeenth and early eighteenth centuries.

Philip Jenkins is Professor of History and Religious Studies at the Pennsylvania State University. His publications include *A History of Modern Wales 1536–1990* (1992); *Intimate Enemies: Moral Panics in Contemporary Great Britain* (1992); and *Using Murder: The Social Construction of Serial Homicide* (1994).

Mícheál Mac Craith is a Franciscan priest who lectures in Modern Irish in University College, Galway. His published works include *Lorg na hiasachta ar na Dánta Grá* (1989), an examination of foreign influences on Gaelic courtly love poetry; and *Oileán rúin agus muir an dáin* (1993), a study of the modern Gaelic poet Máirtín Ó Direán. He has published numerous articles on Gaelic literature from the Renaissance to the present day.

Allan I. Macinnes holds the Burnett-Fletcher Chair of History at the University of Aberdeen. Professor Macinnes has published extensively on covenants, clans and clearances. He is the author of *Charles I and the Making of the Covenanting Movement, 1625–41.* His next book, to be published in the spring of 1995 by Canongate Academic, Edinburgh, will be *Clanship, Commerce and the House of Stuart, 1603–1788.*

John Morrill is Reader in Early Modern History at Cambridge and is a Fellow and Vice Master of Selwyn College. He has written and edited fifteen books, and Longman has published a collection of twenty of his more important essays as *The Nature of the English Revolution* (1993). He is now writing a book provisionally entitled *British Reformations: Religious Culture in the Three Kingdoms, 1559–1720.*

Maps

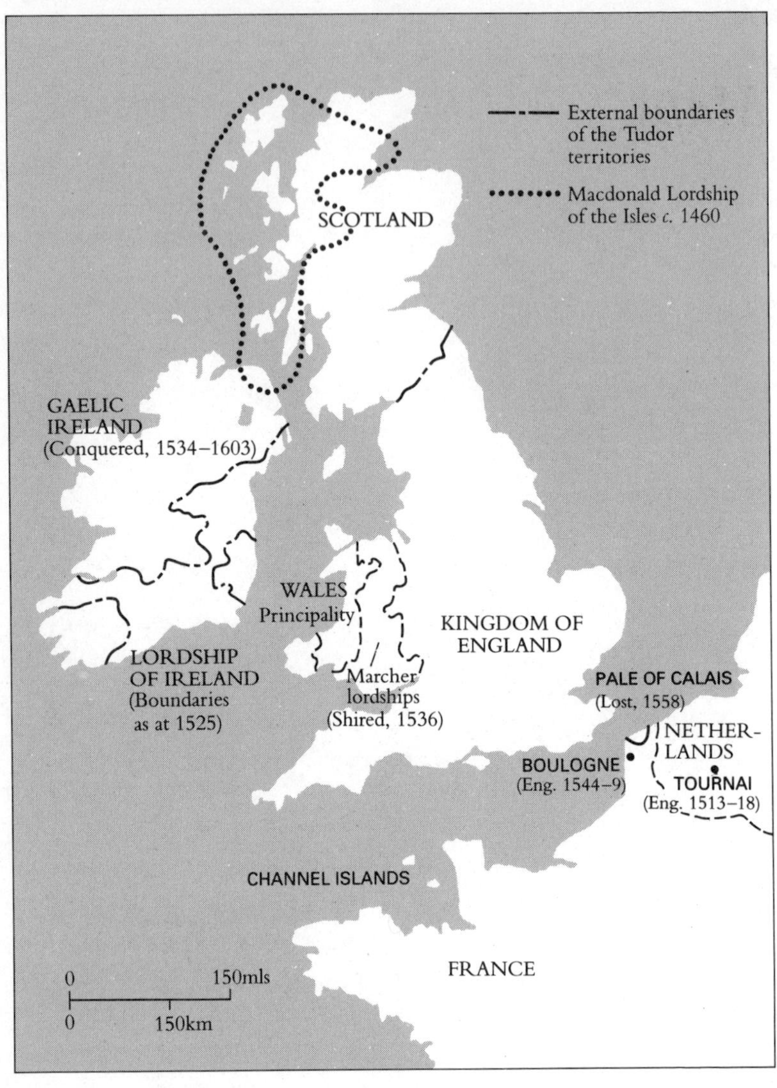

1. The British Isles 1460–1603

2. Linguistic boundaries of the British Isles *c.* 1500

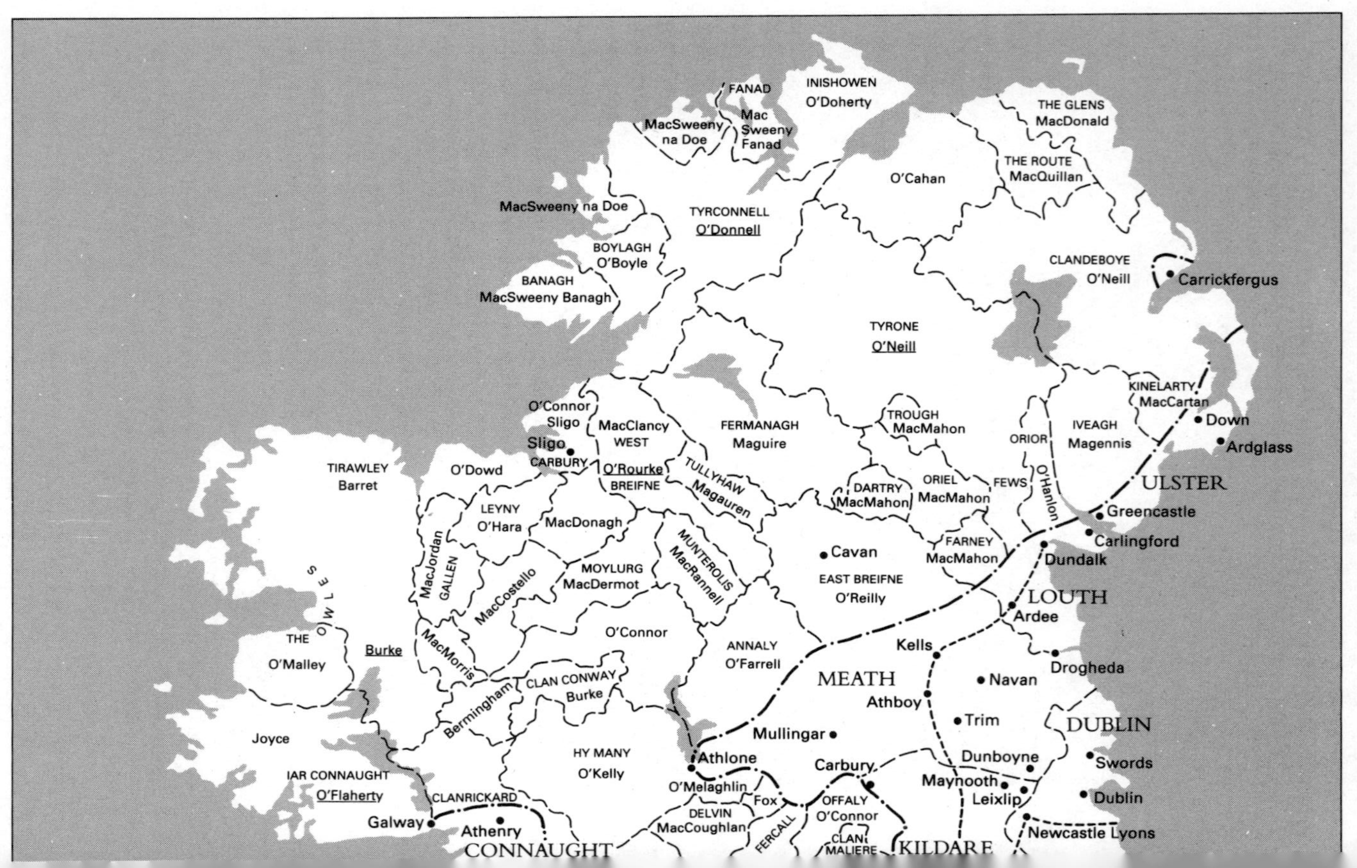
INISHOWEN
O'Doherty
FANAD
Mac
Sweeny
Fanad
MacSweeny
na Doe
THE GLENS
MacDonald
THE ROUTE
MacQuillan
O'Cahan
MacSweeny na Doe
TYRCONNELL
O'Donnell
BOYLAGH
O'Boyle
BANAGH
MacSweeny Banagh
CLANDEBOYE
O'Neill
Carrickfergus
TYRONE
O'Neill
KINELARTY
MacCartan
Down
Ardglass
O'Connor
Sligo
Sligo
CARBURY
MacClancy
WEST
O'Rourke
BREIFNE
FERMANAGH
Maguire
TROUGH
MacMahon
ORIOR
IVEAGH
Magennis
ULSTER
TIRAWLEY
Barret
O'Dowd
TULLYHAW
Magauren
DARTRY
MacMahon
ORIEL
MacMahon
FEWS
O'Hanlon
Greencastle
Carlingford
Dundalk
LEYNY
O'Hara
MacDonagh
MacJordan
GALLEN
MacCostello
MOYLURG
MacDermot
MUNTEROLIS
MacRannell
Cavan
EAST BREIFNE
O'Reilly
FARNEY
MacMahon
LOUTH
Ardee
THE
OWLES
O'Malley
Burke
MacMorris
O'Connor
ANNALY
O'Farrell
Kells
MEATH
Navan
Drogheda
CLAN CONWAY
Burke
Bermingham
Athboy
Trim
DUBLIN
Joyce
Mullingar
HY MANY
O'Kelly
Athlone
Carbury
Dunboyne
Swords
IAR CONNAUGHT
O'Flaherty
CLANRICKARD
Galway
Athenry
CONNAUGHT
O'Melaghlin
Fox
DELVIN
MacCoughlan
FERCALL
OFFALY
O'Connor
CLAN
MALIERE
KILDARE
Maynooth
Leixlip
Dublin
Newcastle Lyons

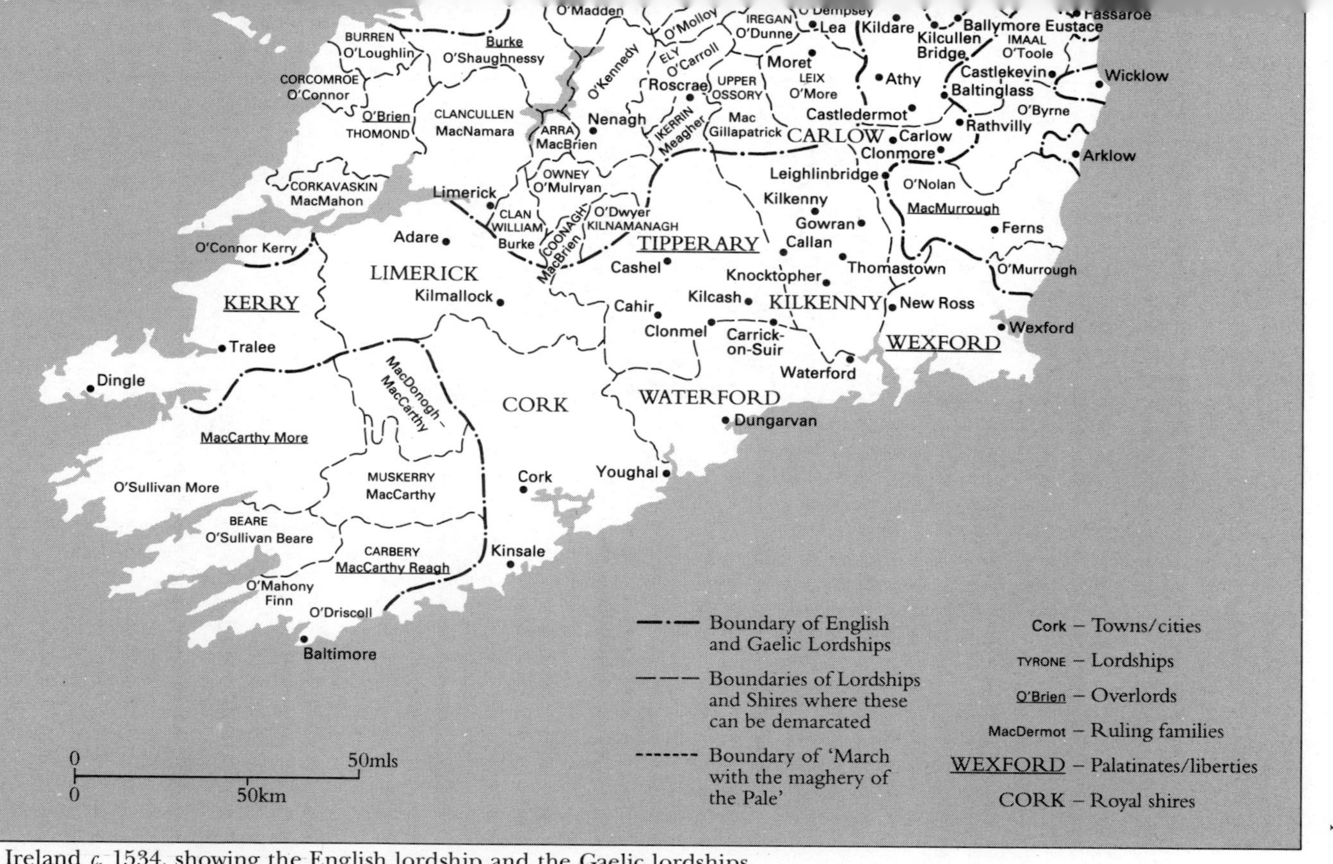

3. Ireland *c.* 1534, showing the English lordship and the Gaelic lordships.
(After: Steven G. Ellis, *Tudor Ireland: Crown, Community and the Conflict of Cultures 1470–1603*, London, 1985.)

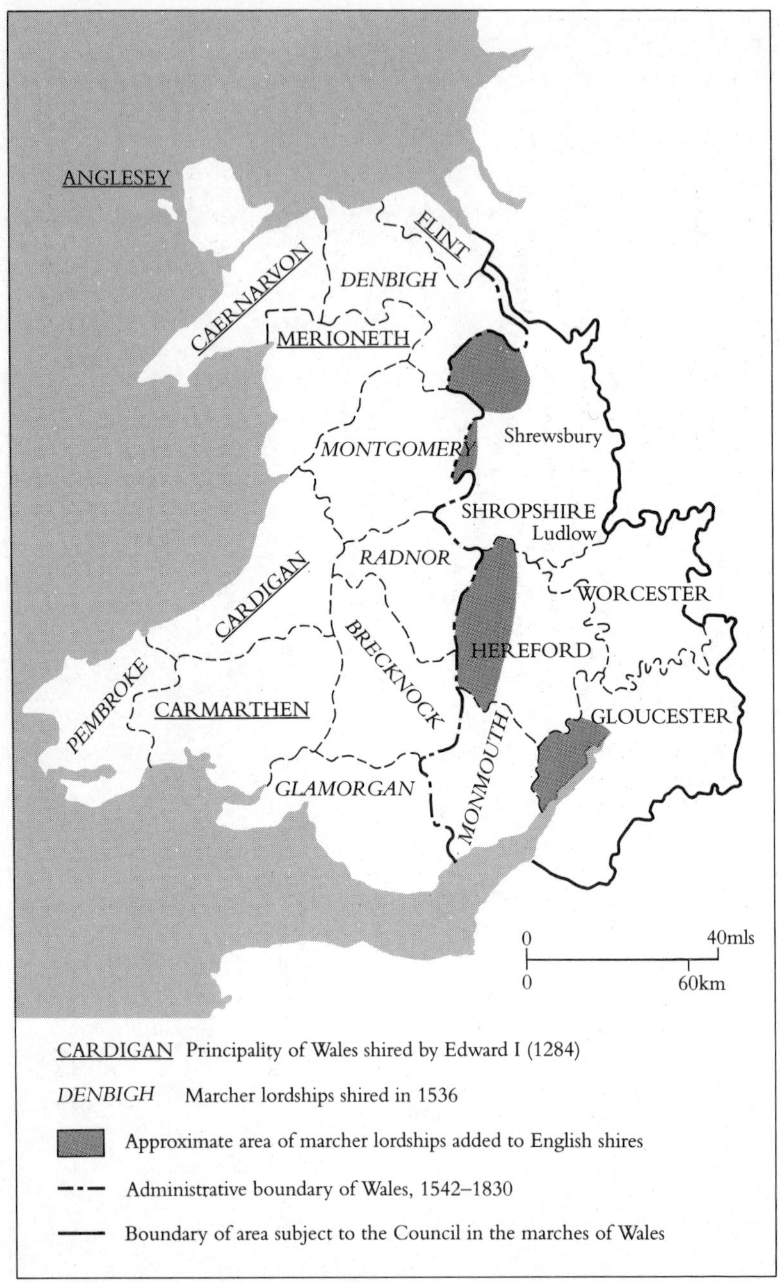

4. Wales and the union with England, 1536–43
(After: A.G.R. Smith, *The Emergence of a Nation State: The Commonwealth of England 1529–1660* London, 1984.)

NOTES

1. Tynedale was annexed to Northumberland in 1495
2. Redesdale was annexed to Northumberland in *c.* 1542
3. Hexham became part of Northumberland in 1572
4. Tynemouth became part of Northumberland in 1536
5. Norhamshire, Islandshire and Bedlington constituted North Durham in this period
6. The West March comprised Cumberland and the barony of Westmorland
7. The Middle March comprised all the territory between Durham and the border except for the north-east corner (the East March)

5. The Anglo-Scottish border region.
(After: Steven G. Ellis, *Tudor Frontiers and Noble Power: The Making of the British State* Oxford, 1995.)

Index

Where several members of the same family are listed, every attempt has been made to group these under the family name. This includes royal dynasties, such as Tudor and Stewart.